HARCOURT
Science

Harcourt School Publishers

Orlando • Boston • Dallas • Chicago • San Diego

www.harcourtschool.com

The **blue and yellow macaw** (*Ara ararauna*) lives in the trees of the rain forest in South America and Central America. It can grow to be about 33 in. (84 cm) in length. It is the largest member of the parrot family. Its favorite food is the seed of the fruit of one rain forest tree. Blue and yellow macaws often gather at "lick" areas to eat mineral- and salt-bearing clay. The inside covers of this book show a closeup of blue and yellow macaw feathers.

Copyright © by Harcourt, Inc.
2005 Edition

Printed in the United States of America

ISBN 0-15-322921-7

11 12 13 14 15 16 17 032 10 09 08 07 06 05 04

Authors

Marjorie Slavick Frank
Former Adjunct Faculty Member
Hunter, Brooklyn, and
    Manhattan Colleges
New York, New York

Robert M. Jones
Professor of Education
University of Houston–
    Clear Lake
Houston, Texas

Gerald H. Krockover
*Professor of Earth and Atmospheric
    Science Education*
School Mathematics and
    Science Center
Purdue University
West Lafayette, Indiana

Mozell P. Lang
Science Education Consultant
Michigan Department
    of Education
Lansing, Michigan

Joyce C. McLeod
Visiting Professor
Rollins College
Winter Park, Florida

Carol J. Valenta
*Vice President—Education, Exhibits,
    and Programs*
St. Louis Science Center
St. Louis, Missouri

Barry A. Van Deman
*Program Director, Informal Science
    Education*
Arlington, Virginia

UNIT A

LIFE SCIENCE

A World of Living Things

UNIT B

LIFE SCIENCE

Looking at Ecosystems

UNIT C

EARTH SCIENCE
Earth's Surface

UNIT D

EARTH SCIENCE

Patterns on Earth and in Space

UNIT E · PHYSICAL SCIENCE
Matter and Energy

UNIT F

PHYSICAL SCIENCE
Forces and Motion

Planning an Investigation

How do scientists answer a question or solve a problem they have identified? They use organized ways called **scientific methods** to plan and conduct a study. They use science process skills to help them gather, organize, analyze, and present their information.

Nathan is using this scientific method for experimenting to find an answer to his question. You can use these steps, too.

STEP 1 Observe, and ask questions.

- Use your senses to make observations.
- Record **one** question that you would like to answer.
- Write down what you already know about the topic of your question.
- Decide what other information you need.
- Do research to find more information about your topic.

What soil works best for planting marigold seeds?

I need to find out more about the different kinds of soils.

STEP 2 Form a hypothesis.

- Write a possible answer, or hypothesis, to your question. A **hypothesis** is a possible answer that can be tested.
- Write your hypothesis in a complete sentence.

My hypothesis is: Marigold seeds sprout best in potting soil.

STEP 3 Plan an experiment.

- Decide how to conduct a fair test of your hypothesis by controlling variables. **Variables** are factors that can affect the outcome of the investigation.
- Write down the steps you will follow to do your test.
- List the equipment you will need.
- Decide how you will gather and record your data.

I'll put identical seeds in three different kinds of soil. Each flowerpot will get the same amount of water and light. So, I'll be controlling the variables of water and light.

STEP 4 Conduct the experiment.

- Follow the steps you wrote.
- Observe and measure carefully.
- Record everything that happens.
- Organize your data so you can study it carefully.

I'll measure each plant every 3 days. I'll record the results in a table and then make a bar graph to show the height of each plant 21 days after I planted the seeds.

STEP 5 Draw conclusions and communicate results.

- Analyze the data you gathered.
- Make charts, tables, or graphs to show your data.
- Write a conclusion. Describe the evidence you used to determine whether your test supported your hypothesis.
- Decide whether your hypothesis was correct.

Hmmm. My hypothesis was not correct. The seeds sprouted equally well in potting soil and sandy soil. They did not sprout at all in clay soil.

INVESTIGATE FURTHER

If your hypothesis was correct . . .

You may want to pose another question about your topic that you can test.

If your hypothesis was incorrect . . .

You may want to form another hypothesis and do a test of a different variable.

I'll test this new hypothesis: Marigold seeds sprout best in a combination of clay, sandy, and potting soil. I will plan and conduct a test using potting soil, sandy soil, and a combination of clay, sandy, and potting soil.

Do you think Nathan's new hypothesis is correct? Plan and conduct a test to find out!

Using Science Process Skills

When scientists try to find an answer to a question or do an experiment, they use thinking tools called **process skills.** You use many of the process skills whenever you speak, listen, read, write, or think. Think about how these students use process skills to help them answer questions, do experiments, and investigate the world around them.

HOW SCIENTISTS WORK

What Sarah plans to investigate

Sarah collects seashells on her visit to the beach. She wants to make collections of shells that are alike in some way. She looks for shells of different sizes and shapes.

Process Skills

Observe—use the senses to learn about objects and events.

Compare—identify characteristics of things or events to find out how they are alike and different.

Classify—group or organize objects or events in categories based on specific characteristics.

How Sarah uses process skills

She **observes** the shells and **compares** their sizes, shapes, and colors. She **classifies** the shells first into groups based on their sizes and then into groups based on their shapes.

What Ling plans to investigate

Ling is interested in learning what makes the size and shape of a rock change. He plans an experiment to find out whether sand rubbing against a rock will cause pieces of the rock to flake off and change the size or shape of the rock.

How Ling uses process skills

He collects three rocks, **measures** their masses, and puts the rocks in a jar with sand and water. He shakes the rocks every day for a week. Then he measures and **records** the mass of the rocks, the sand, and the container. He interprets his data and concludes that rocks are broken down when sand rubs against them.

Use a Model—make a representation to help you understand an idea, an object, or an event, such as how something works.

Predict—form an idea of an expected outcome, based on observations or experience.

Infer—use logical reasoning to explain events and draw conclusions based on observations.

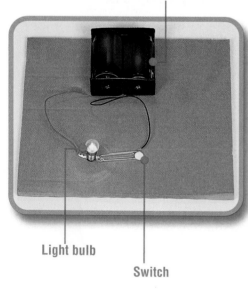

Batteries

Light bulb

Switch

What Justin plans to investigate

Justin wants to find out how the light switch in his bedroom works. He uses batteries, a flashlight bulb, a bulb holder, thumbtacks, and a paper clip to help him.

How Justin uses process skills

He decides to **use a model** of the switch and the wires in the wall. He **predicts** that the bulb, wires, and batteries have to be connected to make the bulb light. He **infers** that moving the paper clip interrupts the flow of electricity and turns off the light. Justin's model verifies his prediction and inference.

What Kendra plans to investigate

Kendra wants to know what brand of paper towel absorbs the most water. She plans a test to find out how much water different brands of paper towels absorb. She can then tell her father which brand is the best one to buy.

How Kendra uses process skills

She chooses three brands of paper towels. She **hypothesizes** that one brand will absorb more water than the others. She **plans and conducts an experiment** to test her hypothesis, using the following steps:

- Pour 1 liter of water into each of three beakers.
- Put a towel from each of the three brands into a different beaker for 10 seconds.
- Pull the towel out of the water, and let it drain back into the beaker for 5 seconds.
- Measure the amount of water left in each beaker.

Kendra **controls variables** by making sure each beaker contains exactly the same amount of water and by timing each step in her experiment exactly.

Process Skills

Hypothesize—make a statement about an expected outcome.

Plan and Conduct an Experiment—identify and perform the steps necessary to test a hypothesis, using appropriate tools and recording and analyzing the data collected.

Control Variables—identify and control factors that affect the outcome of an experiment so that only one variable is changed in a test.

Reading to Learn

Scientists use reading, writing, and numbers in their work. They read to find out everything they can about a topic they are investigating. So it is important that scientists know the meanings of science vocabulary and that they understand what they read. Use the following strategies to help you become a good science reader!

Before Reading

- Read the **Find Out** statement to help you know what to look for as you read.
- Think: I need to find out what the parts of an ecosystem are and how they are organized.

- Look at the **Vocabulary** words.
- Be sure that you can pronounce each word.
- Look up each word in the Glossary.
- Say the definition to yourself. Use the word in a sentence to show its meaning.

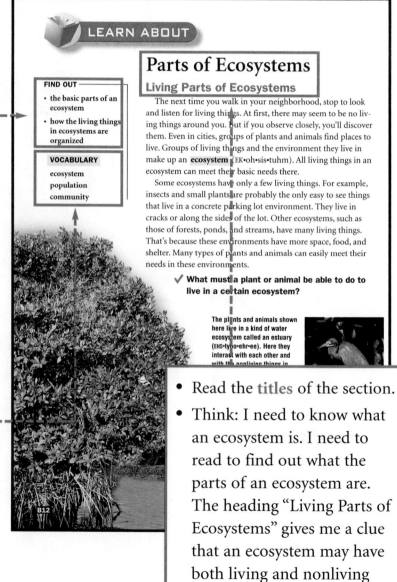

LEARN ABOUT

Parts of Ecosystems

Living Parts of Ecosystems

The next time you walk in your neighborhood, stop to look and listen for living things. At first, there may seem to be no living things around you. But if you observe closely, you'll discover them. Even in cities, groups of plants and animals find places to live. Groups of living things and the environment they live in make up an **ecosystem** (EK•oh•sis•tuhm). All living things in an ecosystem can meet their basic needs there.

Some ecosystems have only a few living things. For example, insects and small plants are probably the only easy to see things that live in a concrete parking lot environment. They live in cracks or along the sides of the lot. Other ecosystems, such as those of forests, ponds, and streams, have many living things. That's because these environments have more space, food, and shelter. Many types of plants and animals can easily meet their needs in these environments.

✔ **What must a plant or animal be able to do to live in a certain ecosystem?**

The plants and animals shown here live in a kind of water ecosystem called an estuary (EHS•tyoo•ehr•ee). Here they interact with each other and with the nonliving things in

FIND OUT
- the basic parts of an ecosystem
- how the living things in ecosystems are organized

VOCABULARY
ecosystem
population
community

B12

- Read the **titles** of the section.
- Think: I need to know what an ecosystem is. I need to read to find out what the parts of an ecosystem are. The heading "Living Parts of Ecosystems" gives me a clue that an ecosystem may have both living and nonliving parts.

During Reading

Find the **main idea** in the first paragraph.

- Groups of living things and their environment make up an ecosystem.

Find **details** in the next paragraph that support the main idea.

- Some ecosystems have only a few living things.
- Environments that have more space, food, and shelter have many living things.
- Plants and animals in an ecosystem can meet all their basic needs in their ecosystem.

Check your understanding of what you have read.

- Answer the question at the end of the section.
- If you're not sure of the answer, reread the section and look for the answer to the question.

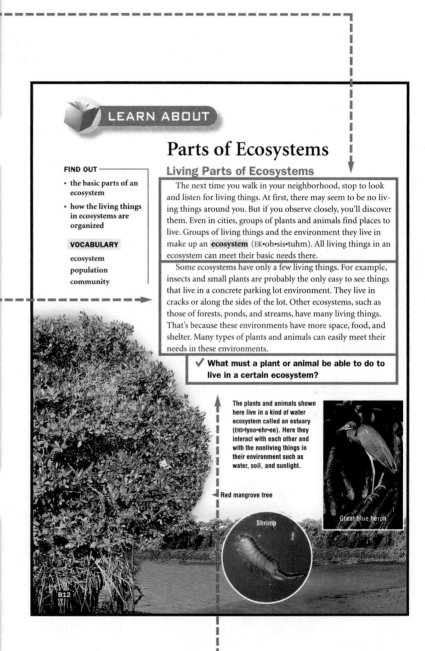

LEARN ABOUT

Parts of Ecosystems

Living Parts of Ecosystems

FIND OUT

- the basic parts of an ecosystem
- how the living things in ecosystems are organized

VOCABULARY

ecosystem
population
community

The next time you walk in your neighborhood, stop to look and listen for living things. At first, there may seem to be no living things around you. But if you observe closely, you'll discover them. Even in cities, groups of plants and animals find places to live. Groups of living things and the environment they live in make up an **ecosystem** (EK•oh•sis•tuhm). All living things in an ecosystem can meet their basic needs there.

Some ecosystems have only a few living things. For example, insects and small plants are probably the only easy to see things that live in a concrete parking lot environment. They live in cracks or along the sides of the lot. Other ecosystems, such as those of forests, ponds, and streams, have many living things. That's because these environments have more space, food, and shelter. Many types of plants and animals can easily meet their needs in these environments.

✓ What must a plant or animal be able to do to live in a certain ecosystem?

The plants and animals shown here live in a kind of water ecosystem called an estuary (EHS•tyoo•ehr•ee). Here they interact with each other and with the nonliving things in their environment such as water, soil, and sunlight.

◄ Red mangrove tree

Shrimp

Great blue heron

B12

After Reading

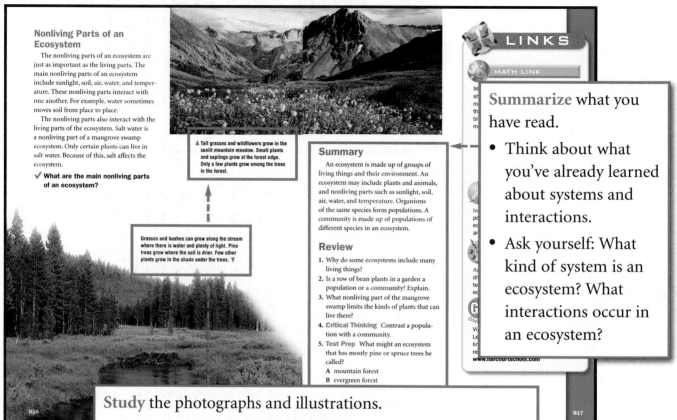

Nonliving Parts of an Ecosystem

The nonliving parts of an ecosystem are just as important as the living parts. The main nonliving parts of an ecosystem include sunlight, soil, air, water, and temperature. These nonliving parts interact with one another. For example, water sometimes moves soil from place to place.

The nonliving parts also interact with the living parts of the ecosystem. Salt water is a nonliving part of a mangrove swamp ecosystem. Only certain plants can live in salt water. Because of this, salt affects the ecosystem.

✔ **What are the main nonliving parts of an ecosystem?**

▲ Tall grasses and wildflowers grow in the sunlit mountain meadow. Small plants and saplings grow at the forest edge. Only a few plants grow among the trees in the forest.

Grasses and bushes can grow along the stream where there is water and plenty of light. Pine trees grow where the soil is drier. Few other plants grow in the shade under the trees. ▼

B16

Summary

An ecosystem is made up of groups of living things and their environment. An ecosystem may include plants and animals, and nonliving parts such as sunlight, soil, air, water, and temperature. Organisms of the same species form populations. A community is made up of populations of different species in an ecosystem.

Review

1. Why do some ecosystems include many living things?
2. Is a row of bean plants in a garden a population or a community? Explain.
3. What nonliving part of the mangrove swamp limits the kinds of plants that can live there?
4. **Critical Thinking** Contrast a population with a community.
5. **Test Prep** What might an ecosystem that has mostly pine or spruce trees be called?
   A mountain forest
   B evergreen forest

B17

LINKS

MATH LINK

www.harcourtschool.com

Summarize what you have read.

• Think about what you've already learned about systems and interactions.

• Ask yourself: What kind of system is an ecosystem? What interactions occur in an ecosystem?

Study the photographs and illustrations.

• Read the captions and any labels.

• Think: What kind of ecosystem is shown in the photographs? What are the nonliving parts of the ecosystem? What living parts of the ecosystem are shown?

For more reading strategies and tips, see pages R38–R49.

Reading about science helps you understand the conclusions you have made based on your investigations.

Writing to Communicate

Writing about what you are learning helps you connect the new ideas to what you already know. Scientists **write** about what they learn in their research and investigations to help others understand the work they have done. As you work like a scientist, you will use the following kinds of writing to describe what you are doing and learning.

In **informative writing,** you may

• describe your observations, inferences, and conclusions.

• tell how to do an experiment.

In **narrative writing,** you may

• describe something, give examples, or tell a story.

In **expressive writing,** you may

• write letters, poems, or songs.

In **persuasive writing,** you may

• write letters about important issues in science.

• write essays expressing your opinions about science issues.

Writing about what you have learned about science helps others understand your thinking.

Using Numbers

Scientists **use numbers** when they collect and display their data. Understanding numbers and using them to show the results of investigations are important skills that a scientist must have. As you work like a scientist, you will use numbers in the following ways:

Measuring

Scientists make accurate measurements as they gather data. They use many different measuring instruments, such as thermometers, clocks and timers, rulers, a spring scale, and a balance, and they use beakers and other containers to measure liquids.

For more information about using measuring tools, see pages R2–R6.

Interpreting Data

Scientists collect, organize, display, and interpret data as they do investigations. Scientists choose a way to display data that helps others understand what they have learned. Tables, charts, and graphs are good ways to display data so that it can be interpreted by others.

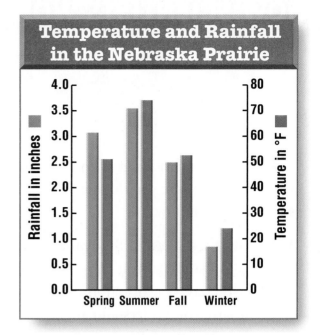

Temperature and Rainfall in the Nebraska Prairie

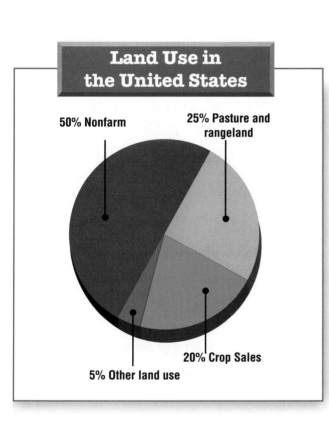

Land Use in the United States

50% Nonfarm

25% Pasture and rangeland

20% Crop Sales

5% Other land use

Using Number Sense

Scientists must understand what the numbers they use represent. They compare and order numbers, compute with numbers, read and understand the numbers shown on graphs, and read the scales on thermometers, measuring cups, beakers, and other tools.

Good scientists apply their math skills to help them display and interpret the data they collect.

In Harcourt Science you will have many opportunities to work like a scientist. An exciting year of discovery lies ahead!

Safety in Science

Doing investigations in science can be fun, but you need to be sure you do them safely. Here are some rules to follow.

 Think ahead. Study the steps of the investigation so you know what to expect. If you have any questions, ask your teacher. Be sure you understand any safety symbols that are shown.

Be neat. Keep your work area clean. If you have long hair, pull it back so it doesn't get in the way. Roll or push up long sleeves to keep them away from your experiment.

 Oops! If you should spill or break something or get cut, tell your teacher right away.

Watch your eyes. Wear safety goggles anytime you are directed to do so. If you get anything in your eyes, tell your teacher right away.

Yuck! Never eat or drink anything during a science activity unless you are told to do so by your teacher.

 Don't get shocked. Be especially careful if an electric appliance is used. Be sure that electric cords are in a safe place where you can't trip over them. Don't ever pull a plug out of an outlet by pulling on the cord.

Keep it clean. Always clean up when you have finished. Put everything away and wipe your work area. Wash your hands.

In some activities you will see these symbols. They are signs for what you need to act safely.

CAUTION
Be especially careful.

CAUTION
Wear safety goggles.

CAUTION
Be careful with sharp objects.

CAUTION
Don't get burned.

CAUTION
Protect your clothes.

CAUTION
Protect your hands with mitts.

CAUTION
Be careful with electricity.

A World of
Living Things

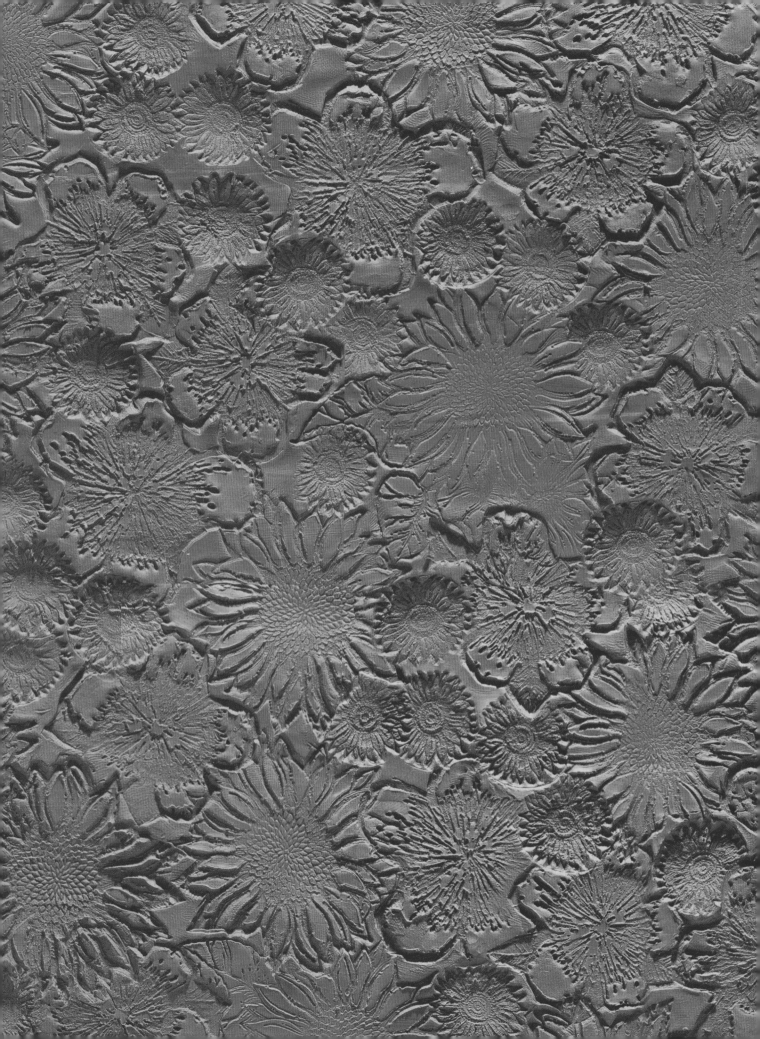

A World of Living Things

UNIT EXPERIMENT

Water Sources and Plant Growth

All living things have basic needs that are met in a variety of ways. While you study this unit, you can conduct a long-term experiment related to the basic needs of plants. Here are questions to think about. Does the type of water used affect how a plant grows? For example, will plants watered with pond water grow taller than plants watered with tap water or rainwater? Plan and conduct an experiment to find answers to these or other questions you have about water sources and plant growth. See pages x–xix for help in designing your experiment.

Living Things

The world is filled with all kinds of living things. In this chapter you'll explore the different types of living things and find that they all have at least one thing in common: they are all made up of cells.

Vocabulary Preview

cell
cell membrane
cytoplasm
nucleus
cell wall
chloroplast
microorganism
vertebrate
invertebrate
arthropod
embryo
flower
fruit
fungi
hyphae
spore
mold

Fast Fact

The top eight inches of soil covering one acre may contain as much as five and a half tons of fungi and bacteria.

Fast Fact

A honey mushroom growing in Michigan is one of Earth's largest and oldest living things. This single fungus stretches through 37 acres of the forest floor—an area as big as 33 football fields! It grows about 20 centimeters (8 in.) per year. Scientists have used the growth rate to calculate the fungus's age—more than 1,500 years.

Fast Fact

Animals come in all shapes and sizes. The largest fish on Earth are whale sharks. They can be more than 12.5 meters (41 feet) long and can weigh more than 20 metric tons (22 tons).

The Largest Animals

Type of Animal	Size	Weight
African bull elephant (land mammal)	3.2 m (10.5 ft)	5.8 metric tons (about 6.4 tons)
North African ostrich (bird)	2.5 m (8.2 ft)	156 kg (344 lb)
Blue whale (sea mammal)	30 m (98 ft)	136 metric tons (150 tons)
Saltwater crocodile (reptile)	4.7 m (15.4 ft)	113 kg (249 lb)

▲ Whale shark

What Are Cells?

In this lesson, you can . . .

INVESTIGATE the parts of cells.

LEARN ABOUT different types of cells.

LINK to math, writing, literature, and technology.

△ *Closteria* are green algae that grow in fresh water. They are known for their sickle-shaped cells.

INVESTIGATE

Make a Model Cell

Activity Purpose The freshwater algae in the photograph, the mold that grows on bread, a pine tree, and a house cat are all living things. As living things they share one feature in common—they are all made up of cells. *Cells* are the building blocks of living things. In this investigation you will **make a model** of a cell. You will then **observe** your model to **draw conclusions** about the makeup of cells.

Materials

- gelatin
- small plastic cup
- paper plate
- malted milk balls
- gelatin candies
- marker
- plastic knife
- plastic spoon
- raisins

Activity Procedure

1. Use the marker to write your group's name on a plastic cup. Then, pour the liquid gelatin your teacher provides into the plastic cup until it is two-thirds full. Allow the gelatin to chill until set.

2. Gently remove the gelatin from the cup. Use the knife to slice the gelatin mold in half. Place the gelatin halves on the paper plate. The gelatin is the cytoplasm of your cell. *Cytoplasm* is a jellylike material that fills the space in a cell.

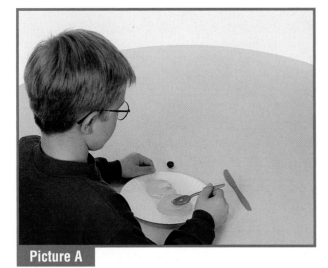

Picture A

Picture B

3 Using the spoon, make a small hole in the center of one of the gelatin halves. Place the malted milk ball in the hole. This is your cell's nucleus. The *nucleus* determines the cell's activities. (Picture A)

4 Scatter a few raisins and gelatin candies within the cytoplasm. The raisins represent the structures that release energy for the cell (mitochondria). The candies are storage areas for the cell (vacuoles). (Picture B)

5 Carefully place the plain half of the gelatin on top of the half that contains the cell parts. Your cell is now ready to observe.

Draw Conclusions

1. **Observe** your model. What cell part makes up the greatest part of your model? What can you conclude from this observation?

2. What cell part is at the center of your cell? Where in the cell are all the other cell parts located?

3. **Scientists at Work** Scientists often use **models** to better understand complex structures. How does your cell model help you **draw conclusions** about the structure of cells? What things about a cell does your model NOT tell you?

Investigate Further Make a drawing of your cell model, and label each part with the name of the cell part it represents. Then compare your model to the pictures of cells on pages A7 and A8. How are the drawings similar? How are they different?

Process Skill Tip

You cannot see most cells and the parts they contain without using a microscope. But by **using a model**, you can learn about what parts make up most cells and **draw conclusions** about how these parts are organized within a cell.

Cells

VOCABULARY

cell
cell membrane
cytoplasm
nucleus
cell wall
chloroplast
microorganism

Building Blocks

Imagine walking through a toy store. In the distance you see a castle that looks large enough to enter. As you get nearer to the castle, you observe it has been built using a number of smaller blocks. Like the castle, living things are also made up of smaller units. These building blocks of living things are cells. A **cell** is the basic unit of structure and function in a living thing.

All living things are made up of cells. Some, such as bacteria, are made of only one cell. Others, like you, are made up of many millions of cells. Most cells are too small to be seen without a microscope. But each cell is a tiny living unit. Most cells carry out all the activities needed to stay alive.

✔ **What is a cell?**

◀ The basic units of this gray elephant sculpture are small blocks that fit together.

▲ The basic units of this cork tree are cells. The cells shown are from its bark. The smooth parts of the tree trunks are where farmers have harvested the bark.

Animal Cells

MITOCHONDRIA (myt•oh•KAHN• dree•uh) The mitochondria break down materials to release energy for the cell.

CYTOPLASM The jellylike substance that fills most of the cell is cytoplasm (SY•toh•plaz•uhm). Most other cell parts float within the cytoplasm.

CELL MEMBRANE The cell membrane surrounds an animal cell and controls what materials go into and out of the cell.

VACUOLE (VAK• yoo•ohl) A vacuole is a space in the cytoplasm that acts like a storage area. Some vacuoles store things the cell needs, such as food and water. Other vacuoles store wastes until they can be moved out of the cell.

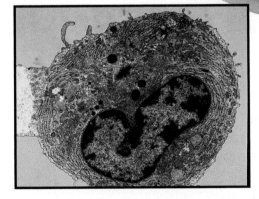

NUCLEUS The nucleus controls all cell activities, including how the cell grows, develops, and divides.

◀ This is what one type of animal cell looks like when viewed through a microscope. It has been dyed to make its parts easier to see.

As you saw in the investigation, cells are made up of many smaller parts. Some parts are common to *all* cells. For example, all cells have a cell membrane. The thin wall of the **cell membrane** encloses a cell and gives a cell its shape. It also is a sort of gatekeeper. It controls what enters and leaves a cell. All cells also have **cytoplasm**, a jellylike substance that fills most of the space in a cell. Other cell parts float in the cytoplasm. Cytoplasm is made up mostly of water.

Most cells have a nucleus, located near the center of a cell. The **nucleus** controls all cell activities. It is like the brain of a cell.

Other cell structures are scattered throughout the cell. Look at the animal cell to find out more about these cell parts and their roles in an animal cell.

✔ **What parts are common to all cells?**

Plant Cells

CELL WALL The cell wall is a stiff structure that surrounds the cell membrane of a plant cell. It keeps the cell rigid, helping the entire plant to keep its shape.

CELL MEMBRANE The cell membrane surrounds the cell and directs materials into and out of the cell.

This is what one type of plant cell looks like when viewed through a microscope. It has been dyed to make its parts easier to see. ▼

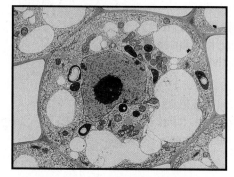

CHLOROPLASTS (KLOR•uh•plasts) are scattered throughout the cytoplasm of a plant cell. The chloroplasts give plants their green color and are used in making food.

NUCLEUS

VACUOLE A vacuole is a temporary storage area for either materials the cell needs or for waste materials. Plant cells usually have fewer and larger vacuoles than animal cells. Most plant cells have just one vacuole.

CYTOPLASM The cytoplasm is the jellylike substance that fills most of a cell between the nucleus and cell membrane.

MITOCHONDRIA The mitochondria carry out the activities that release energy for the cell.

All cells are not identical, just as all living things are not identical. Cells differ in size and shape. Different kinds of cells also have different parts.

The outermost part of an animal cell is the cell membrane. Plant cells have a cell membrane, but it is not the outermost part of the cell. Plant cells have a stiff wall surrounding the cell membrane. The **cell wall** is a structure that keeps the cell rigid and provides support to the entire plant.

Plant cells also have chloroplasts scattered throughout their cytoplasm. **Chloroplasts** contain chlorophyll—the green pigment plants need to make their food.

✔ **What cell parts are found in plant cells, but not in animal cells?**

One-Celled Microorganisms

All plants and animals are made up of many cells. Many other living things are made up of only one cell. These living things, often called **microorganisms**, are so small they can be seen only with a microscope. These tiny creatures live all around you—in air, water, soil, and even inside other living things.

Like plant cells and animal cells, the cell of a single-celled microorganism is made up of smaller parts. These cell parts carry out all the life processes that keep the cell alive.

✔ **What are microorganisms?**

▼ This pond provides a home to many different one-celled microorganisms.

◄ The cell of a paramecium (pair•uh•MEE•see•uhm) has structures that allow it to move about and catch food.

There are many kinds of algae such as these. They all have chloroplasts and make their own food. The cells of algae are surrounded by cell walls. ►

◄ This *Euglena* (yoo•GLEE•nuh) has parts that allow it to move and catch food as an animal does. It also has chloroplasts, so it can make its own food, as a plant does.

An amoeba (uh•MEE•buh) uses its cytoplasm to help it capture food and move about. This causes the amoeba to constantly change shape. ►

Many-Celled Microorganisms

Some microorganisms are made up of many cells. These cells work together to carry out the processes that keep the organism alive.

The cells of a many-celled microorganism are not all alike. Some cells are specialized, or have features to carry out a specific job. For example, some cells have structures to move and to get food. Other cells have features to digest food.

✔ **What are specialized cells?**

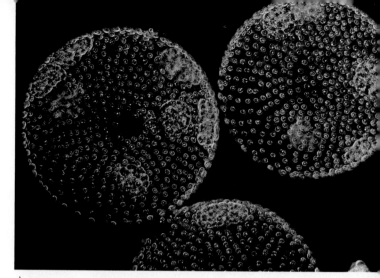

▲ *Volvox* are single-celled microorganisms that live in colonies. When they live in colonies, individual *Volvox* cells specialize to carry out the processes that keep the colony alive. Some cells work to move the colony. Others work to get food.

THE INSIDE STORY

Rotifers

Rotifers are microscopic wormlike animals that make their homes in pond water, oceans, and moist soil. Although they feed on one-celled life, they are many-celled.

1. A rotifer's cells are specialized to carry out different tasks. For example, cells surrounding the mouth of a rotifer have *cilia* (SIHL•ee•uh). These hairlike parts move back and forth, causing a current that draws food into the mouth of the rotifer.

2. Once food is taken into a rotifer, it is broken into smaller pieces by tiny jawlike structures. The food particles then move to the stomach and pass through the intestines.

Summary

All living things are made up of one or more cells. Each cell is made up of smaller parts that carry on all the processes needed to keep the cell alive. Plant cells have a cell wall and chloroplasts, parts that are not found in animal cells. Microorganisms are living things that are too small to be seen without a microscope. They are made up of only one or a few cells.

Review

1. Why are cells called the building blocks of living things?

2. What cell part controls all of a cell's activities?

3. How are chloroplasts important to plant cells?

4. **Critical Thinking** How is the single cell of a *Euglena* like a plant cell? How is it like an animal cell?

5. **Test Prep** One example of a microorganism is —

   A a cork tree

   B a dog

   C an amoeba

   D a snake

LINKS

MATH LINK

Use a Rule Two kinds of cells in your blood are red blood cells and white blood cells. Your blood contains only 1 white blood cell for every 1,000 red blood cells. If a sample of blood has 3,000 red blood cells, how many white blood cells would you expect to find in the sample?

WRITING LINK

Informative Writing—Description Suppose you've discovered a new kind of living thing. For your teacher, write a paragraph explaining how you could study the cells of this new living thing to identify it as a plant or an animal.

LITERATURE LINK

Exploring the Human Body Would you like to learn more about the different kinds of cells that make up your body? Read *The Magic School Bus: Inside the Human Body* by Joanna Cole.

GO ONLINE TECHNOLOGY LINK

Learn more about cells by using the activities and information provided on The Harcourt Learning Site.
www.harcourtschool.com

LESSON 2

What Are Animals?

In this lesson, you can . . .

INVESTIGATE sponges.

LEARN ABOUT features of animals.

LINK to math, writing, social studies, and technology.

Comparing Real and Artificial Sponges

Activity Purpose The sponges you use for cleaning are most likely made by people. But these sponges look like animals called sponges that live at the bottoms of oceans or lakes. In this investigation you will **observe** features of an artificial sponge and **compare** them with the skeleton of a real sponge.

Materials

- small, equal-sized pieces of a natural sponge and an artificial sponge
- hand lens
- 1 plastic cup
- water
- clock with second hand
- measuring cup
- paper towel

Activity Procedure

1 Make a chart like the one here.

Characteristic	Natural Sponge	Artificial Sponge
What it looks like		
What it feels like		
How heavy it feels		
How much water it holds		

◀ This blue-ringed octopus is one of millions of living things classified as animals. Although it is beautiful, its bite can kill.

A12

2 **Observe** each piece of sponge to see how it looks and feels. **Record** your observations in the chart.

3 Use a hand lens to **observe** each piece of sponge more closely. **Record** your observations in the chart. You may wish to use drawings to record some of your observations. (Picture A)

4 Half-fill the plastic cup with water. Put the natural sponge in the cup and push it down into the water. Allow the sponge to remain in the water for 30 seconds.

5 Remove the sponge from the cup. Hold the sponge over the measuring cup and squeeze out the water in the sponge. **Record** in your chart the amount of water held by the sponge. (Picture B)

6 Repeat Steps 4 and 5 for the artificial sponge.

Picture A

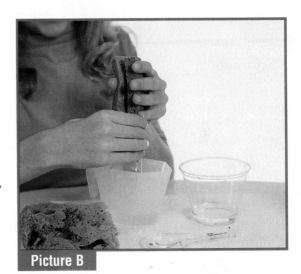

Picture B

Draw Conclusions

1. What features were similar for both the natural sponge and the artificial sponge?

2. What differences did you observe in the two sponges?

3. **Scientists at Work** Scientists **infer** what happens in nature by making careful observations. Natural sponges cannot move around to get food. They get food from water that passes through their bodies. Based on your observations, what can you **infer** about the ability of sponges to move water through their bodies?

Investigate Further At one time all the sponges used by people were the skeletons of sponge animals. Today people use artificial sponges for most tasks. Use reference sources to find out what artificial sponges are made of and why people use these sponges instead of natural sponges.

Process Skill Tip

When you **infer**, you use what you observe to explain something that happens. You make observations by using your senses (sight, touch, hearing, taste, smell) to gather information. An inference is a possible conclusion that is based on information you gather with your senses.

Features of Animals

Body Types

FIND OUT

- features of animals
- some examples of simple and complex animals

VOCABULARY

vertebrate
invertebrate
arthropod

Animals are many-celled living things that cannot make their own food. Some animals, called simple animals, have bodies made up of only a few types of cells.

The simplest animals are sponges. A sponge is an animal with a bag-shaped body that lives in water. The sides and bottom of this "bag" are made up of two layers of cells with a jellylike material between them. Like a bag, the top of a sponge is open. As you saw in the investigation, a sponge has many small openings, called pores. Water enters a sponge through these pores. The water has food and oxygen in it. As this water moves through the cells on the inside of the sponge, tiny "whips" on these cells remove food from the water. The water then leaves the sponge through the opening at the top.

▼ Tiny "whips" on the cells inside a sponge draw water in through the pores of the sponge. Food is then removed from the water before it leaves through the opening at the top of the sponge.

Red fire sponge

Earthworms live in soil. Food enters these tube-shaped animals through the mouth. Undigested food then passes out the other end of the earthworm. ▶

Worms are simple animals that have a tube-shaped body. Animals with a tube-type body have more body parts than bag-type animals. For example, an earthworm has several body parts that help it get and use food.

Most animals you know are complex animals. Complex animals have bodies made up of many parts. A snail, for example, has a shell that supports and protects its body. It also has a head that contains sense organs and a mouth. Food eaten by a snail is broken down by the parts that make up its digestive tract.

✔ **What are some examples of simple and complex animals?**

▼ Snails live on land, in fresh water, and in salt water. Many snails have heads with tentacles and eyes on stalks. They have a broad, flat foot that is used for creeping. Snails have a well-developed digestive system that includes a stomach and an intestine.

Body Support

Animals can be divided into two groups based on the structures that support their bodies. **Vertebrates**, or animals with a backbone, form one group. An internal skeleton made of bone and cartilage supports a vertebrate's body. Birds, snakes, bats, and humans are vertebrates.

Most animals are **invertebrates**, animals that do not have a backbone. An outer covering, such as a shell, usually supports the body of an invertebrate. **Arthropods** are the largest group of invertebrates. Arthropods are animals, such as ants, spiders, and crabs, that have legs with several joints.

✔ **What is one way of grouping animals?**

▲ Insects are one kind of arthropod. Like other arthropods, this beetle has jointed legs and an exoskeleton, or outer skeleton, that supports its body.

Spiders also are arthropods. They do not have a backbone but do have eight jointed legs and an exoskeleton. ▶

Centipedes are arthropods. They have one pair of jointed legs attached to each body segment. These animals are supported by an exoskeleton. ▼

Ants are insects. They have six jointed legs and are supported by an exoskeleton. ▼

▲ This is the skeleton of a bat, the only mammal that flies. Mammals are vertebrates. Like all vertebrates the bat has a backbone and an internal skeleton. Like other mammals it also has fur on the outside of its body and gives birth to live young that it nurses with milk from the mother.

Summary

Animals are many-celled living things that cannot make their own food. Sponges, the simplest animals, have bag-type bodies that are made up of only a few kinds of cells. Worms have tube-type bodies and a few body parts. Complex animals have many body parts. Animals that have a backbone and an internal skeleton are vertebrates. Animals that do not have a backbone and often are supported by an outer skeleton are invertebrates.

Review

1. What type of body does a sponge have?
2. What is the main difference between a simple animal and a complex animal?
3. What are arthropods?
4. **Critical Thinking** Are sponges, worms, and snails vertebrates or invertebrates? Explain.
5. **Test Prep** Which of the following is an arthropod?

   A human   **C** bat

   B crab   **D** snail

LINKS

MATH LINK

Identify Lines of Symmetry One way scientists classify body plans is by symmetry, the arrangement of body structures in relation to a line. The lines divide an animal's body into parts that are mirror images of each other. Some animals can be divided by one line. Others can be divided by many lines. Obtain pictures of ten animals from discarded magazines. Paste each picture onto a sheet of paper. Find and draw the lines of symmetry for each animal.

WRITING LINK

Narrative Writing—Story Suppose you discover a new simple animal. Write a story about a day in its life. In your story tell how the animal moves, gets food, and supports its body.

SOCIAL STUDIES LINK

Invertebrates and Disease Many invertebrates spread disease. Use reference sources to find out about three diseases spread by invertebrates. Make a chart that identifies the diseases, how each is spread, its symptoms, and where in the world each occurs.

GO ONLINE TECHNOLOGY LINK

Learn more about animal features by visiting the Smithsonian Institution Website: **www.si.edu/harcourt/science**

 Smithsonian Institution®

A17

LESSON 3

What Are Plants with Seeds?

In this lesson, you can . . .

INVESTIGATE ways to classify seeds.

LEARN ABOUT features of plants with seeds.

LINK to math, writing, health, and technology.

Cones and Fruits

Activity Purpose You read in Lesson 1 that cells often specialize to carry out certain tasks. Seeds are formed from plant cells that are specialized for reproduction. In this investigation you will **observe** two kinds of plant structures that contain seeds and **compare** them to infer how the roles of each structure differ.

Materials

- cone from pine, fir, or other cone-bearing plant
- hand lens
- grape
- tweezers
- plastic knife

Activity Procedure

1. **Observe** the cone and the grape. Describe how each looks, feels, and smells. Record your observations.

2. Now **observe** the cone and the grape more closely with a hand lens. Be sure to look closely at and between the scales of the cone. **Record** your observations.

3. The seeds in a cone are located between the cone's scales. Use your fingers to widen the space between several scales of the cone as much as possible. Then use the tweezers to remove the seeds from between the scales. (Picture A)

◀ The delicious fruit of this watermelon is actually a protective covering for the many seeds inside.

Picture A

Picture B

4 **Observe** the seeds with the hand lens and **record** your observations.

5 Use the plastic knife to cut the grape in half. Look for the seeds of the grape. **Record** your observations. (Picture B)

6 Use the tweezers to remove the seeds from the grape. **Observe** the seeds with the hand lens and **record** your observations. Be sure to wash your hands after handling the pine cone and grape.

Draw Conclusions

1. Both cones and fruits contain seeds. Compare the cone and fruit you observed in this activity.

2. **Compare** the shapes of the seeds from the cone and the grape.

3. **Scientists at Work** Scientists **compare** objects by using what they have **observed** about each object. Scientists have observed that when mature, the scales of a cone spread apart, allowing the seeds to fall from the cone. When a fruit matures, the entire fruit, along with its seeds, drops from a plant. Use this observation to **compare** the roles of cones and fruits.

Investigate Further Obtain several other types of fruit. Cut each fruit open to **observe** its seeds. Make a table in which to **classify** the seeds you observe according to their shapes.

> **Process Skill Tip**
>
> When you **observe**, you use your senses to gather information. You can use observations to **compare**, or see the similarities and differences between things.

Features of Plants with Seeds

Cone-Bearing Plants

Have you tried to grow a plant by placing a seed in soil? A seed is a plant part from which a new plant can grow. A seed is made up of a young plant, called an **embryo** (EHM•bree•oh), and stored food enclosed in an outer coating.

As you saw in the investigation, seeds may be found in cones or in fruits. Plants that form seeds are classified into two groups—cone-bearing plants such as pine trees, and flowering plants such as grape vines.

Most cone-bearing plants have both male and female cones. Male cones produce pollen, structures that are specialized for reproduction. Wind may carry this pollen to a female cone. There a cell from the pollen joins with an egg, a female reproductive cell. After the cells join, they form a single cell that divides many times and develops into a seed.

Seeds form inside the large cone that grows from the center of the cycad. ▼

The cycad (SY•kad) is a cone-bearing tree that grows in warm, wet climates. They are not palm trees, although their leaves look like palm leaves. ▼

Cycad

Cone-bearing plants include pines, firs, spruces, redwoods, junipers, hemlocks, and cycads. When cones first form, they are fleshy and tightly closed. In time the scales open to release pollen or to allow pollen to enter.

Seeds develop between the cone scales. These seeds do not have an outer covering. As the seeds develop, the cone dries out and becomes woody. The scales open more and the seeds are released.

✔ **Where do the seeds of a pine tree form?**

Pine trees produce many cones each year. These cones are smaller than those of cycads. ▶

Junipers are cone-bearing plants that grow well in rocky and sandy areas. ▼

White pine tree

The seeds of the white pine develop on the scales of the cone. ▼

The scales of a juniper cone grow together to form a blue-colored berry that holds one to four seeds.

Western juniper tree

A21

Fruit-Bearing Plants

Most plants you are familiar with form seeds in flowers. **Flowers** are reproductive structures. The male part of a flower forms pollen. The female part forms eggs.

As in cone-bearing plants, seeds form in a flower after a pollen cell and an egg join. As the seed forms, the part of the flower holding the seed changes and becomes a fruit. A **fruit** is the part of a flowering plant that contains and protects the seeds.

✔ **What is a fruit?**

Peach tree

As seeds develop in the American holly, the bottoms of its blossoms become bright, red berries. The berries are holly fruits. ▶

▲ The tiny blossoms of this peach tree produce the cells that join to form seeds. In time the blossoms are replaced by the tasty, juicy fruit you call a peach. The seed is inside the peach pit.

The seeds of this rose grow in a part of the plant called a rose hip. A rose hip is a rose fruit. ▼

American holly tree

▲ A single pumpkin fruit may provide a covering for hundreds of pumpkin seeds.

Summary

A seed is a plant part from which a new plant can grow. Plants with cones and plants with flowers reproduce by seeds. Cone-bearing plants produce uncovered seeds. Fruits cover and protect the seeds of flowering plants.

Review

1. What is a seed?

2. What kinds of plants form seeds?

3. What are three examples of cone-bearing plants?

4. **Critical Thinking** How are the seeds of cone-bearing plants and flowering plants different?

5. **Test Prep** The main job of a fruit is to —

    A protect the seeds inside

    B provide food for people

    C form pollen cells

    D grow into a new plant

LINKS

MATH LINK

Divide Whole Numbers The information on a seed packet states that each plant requires 4 square inches of space in which to grow. If you have 144 square inches of space available in a container, what is the greatest number of seeds you should plant?

WRITING LINK

Expressive Writing—Poem Imagine you are a sprouting seed. Write a poem to describe your life as you sprout and begin to grow up through the soil.

HEALTH LINK

Seeds as Food People eat many seeds. Survey your local supermarket to find examples of ten or more seeds that people eat. Make a list of what you find. Combine your list with those of other students. Use library resources to find out nutrition facts about the seeds. Then plan healthful menus for three meals or snacks that include different seeds.

GO ONLINE TECHNOLOGY LINK

Learn more about how plants grow from seeds by visiting this Internet site: **www.scilinks.org/harcourt**

SCI LINKS
THE WORLD'S A CLICK AWAY

LESSON 4

What Are Fungi?

In this lesson, you can . . .

INVESTIGATE
mushroom cap spore prints.

LEARN ABOUT
features of fungi.

LINK to math, writing, health, and technology.

INVESTIGATE

Observing Spore Prints

Activity Purpose

Mushrooms belong to the group of living things known as *fungi* (fuhn•JY). One feature of fungi is that they reproduce using spores. A spore is a specialized cell from which a living thing can form. In this investigation you will **observe** a mushroom and the spores it produces. You will then **infer** what part of the mushroom produces spores.

Materials

- white paper
- two kinds of mushrooms
- hand lens

Activity Procedure

1. Obtain two different kinds of mushrooms. **Observe** all parts of each mushroom and make a drawing of what you see.

2. Carefully separate the cap of each mushroom from the stalk.

3. Write your name at the bottom of a clean sheet of white paper. Then place the paper on a surface as directed by your teacher. Place each of your mushroom caps on the paper so the tops face up. (Picture A)

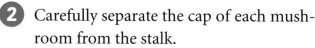

◄ This mushroom is very colorful, but it is also very poisonous.

Picture A

Picture B

④ Without moving the mushroom caps, trace around the outside edge of each cap with a pencil. Be sure to wash your hands after handling the mushrooms.

⑤ Allow the mushrooms to remain undisturbed overnight.

⑥ Gently lift and remove each mushroom cap from the paper. **Observe** the pattern left on the paper. Draw and **record** your observations.

⑦ The pattern beneath each mushroom cap is formed by spores. **Observe** the spores with a hand lens. Draw and describe what you observe. Be sure to wash your hands after handling the mushrooms. **CAUTION** Dispose of the caps and spores as your teacher tells you. (Picture B)

Draw Conclusions

1. **Compare** and **contrast** the mushrooms you observed.

2. Describe the patterns formed by the spores.

3. **Scientists at Work** Scientists infer what happens in nature by making careful observations. Based on what you **observed** in the investigation, what can you **infer** about where the spores of a mushroom are formed?

Investigate Further Do you think other mushrooms will make spore prints like the ones you just observed? **Form a hypothesis** about mushrooms and spore prints. Then **plan and conduct an experiment** to test your hypothesis.

Process Skill Tip

When you **observe**, you use your senses to gather information about everything around you. When you **infer**, you use observations to state a conclusion or explanation.

Features of Fungi

Fungal Structure

As you learned in the investigation, a mushroom is a kind of fungus. **Fungi** are single-celled or many-celled living things that cannot make their own food.

Like plants, the cells of this mushroom are surrounded by a cell wall. Unlike the cells of plants, the cells do not have chloroplasts and some have more than one nucleus. ▶

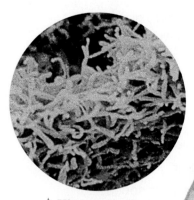

▲ Microscopic view of mushroom cells

Fungi were once classified as plants. Like plants, fungi often grow in soil and have cells with cell walls. But fungi differ from plants in important ways. For example, fungi cannot make their own food. Fungi must absorb food from other living things or from dead things. Cells of fungi may also have more than one nucleus. Today scientists classify fungi in their own group.

▲ The chanterelle is an edible mushroom found in the woods during summer and autumn. Never eat *any* wild mushroom unless a trusted adult says it is safe.

▲ People search forests in the early spring for the 15 types of edible morel fungi, which are related to mushrooms.

As you saw in the investigation, a mushroom has a cap and a stalk. It also has threadlike parts called **hyphae** (HY•fee) that anchor the fungus. The hyphae also break down and absorb food from the soil. Fungi grow by making new hyphae.

Many gills are under the cap of a mushroom. Some cells in the gills are specialized for reproduction. When nuclei in these cells join, they form a spore. A **spore** is a cell that can grow into a new fungus.

✔ **What are hyphae?**

Mushroom Life Cycle

❹ The two nuclei in the cells under the mushroom cap grow together. The new nucleus in each cell divides and makes spores. The spores fall from the cap. ▽

❶ A spore falls to the ground and hyphae grow into the soil.

❸ The mushroom matures, forming a cap with gills on the underside. ▶

❷ Hyphae from two fungi grow together to form cells that have two nuclei. A new mushroom grows out of the ground.

A27

Other Types of Fungi

Mushrooms are only one kind of fungi. Other kinds of fungi include bracket fungi, molds, yeasts, and mildews. **Molds** are very common fungi that look cottony or woolly. Some fungi also live together with algae, forming a type of living thing called a lichen (LYK•uhn).

✔ **Besides mushrooms, what other living things are fungi?**

Bread mold grows on bread and vegetables, which it uses as food. ▼

▲ Bracket fungi look like mushrooms without stalks. They often grow on tree limbs or logs, which they break down for food.

Penicillium (pen•ih•SIHL•ee•uhm) is a green-colored mold that grows and feeds on fruits. The antibiotic penicillin is made from some types of this mold. ▼

▲ Yeasts are single-celled fungi that often grow in flowers, where they feed on nectar. Some yeasts are used to make bread and other products. Other yeasts can make people sick.

British soldier lichen

▲ A lichen is a living thing formed by a fungus and an alga that live together and depend on each other to live. The alga makes food for the fungus. The fungus provides the alga with a moist, warm place to live.

Summary

Fungi are single-celled and many-celled living things that cannot make their own food. The cells of fungi have cell walls like plant cells but do not have chloroplasts. Cells of fungi may also have more than one nucleus. Examples of fungi include mushrooms, bracket fungi, molds, yeasts, and mildews. Some fungi live closely together with algae to form lichens.

Review

1. What is a fungal spore?
2. Where do the spores of a mushroom form?
3. How do most fungi get their food?
4. **Critical Thinking** How do fungi feeding on dead plants help a pond or a forest?
5. **Test Prep** Which of the following is **NOT** a type of fungus?

   A mold   C yeast

   B mildew   D alga

LINKS

MATH LINK

Make a Graph The mushrooms people eat as food are made up of about 90 percent water, 3 percent protein, 5 percent carbohydrates, 1 percent fat, and 1 percent vitamins and minerals. Make a bar graph or a circle graph to show what nutrients make up a mushroom.

WRITING LINK

Informative Writing—Description Find a recipe for a dish that uses mushrooms. Make an illustrated recipe card to explain how to make the dish.

HEALTH LINK

Uses of Fungi Find out ways in which fungi are used in cooking and food-making. You might investigate bread-making (yeasts), cheese-making (molds), or the use of different mushrooms in Asian cooking. Use library resources to find out the nutritional values of the foods. Then make a poster to illustrate what you learned.

TECHNOLOGY LINK

Learn more about fungi by viewing *Oak Wilt* on the **Harcourt Science Newsroom Video.**

Discovering CELLS

A white blood cell (stained blue) surrounds bacteria (stained orange) and destroys them.

The History of Cells

1665
Robert Hooke names the "cell."

1796
The first vaccine, which protected people from smallpox, is discovered.

1838, 1839
Schleiden and Schwann discover that all living things are made up of cells.

| A.D. 1600 | A.D. 1700 | A.D. 1800 | A.D. 1900 |

1677
An improved microscope enables scientists to view microorganisms.

1953
Scientists discover the structure of DNA.

In 1665, English scientist Robert Hooke peered through his homemade microscope. Studying cork tissue, he named the little boxes he saw "cells." Hooke didn't realize it at the time, but his discovery of cells would have a great impact on biology.

Plants and Animals

It was nearly 200 years before scientists began to realize that Hooke's cells were a part of all living things. In 1831 scientists observed the nucleus of a cell and named it "little nut." They had no idea how important it was to the cell. In 1838 Matthias Schleiden studied a variety of plant tissues and found that every type was made of many cells. A year later Theodor Schwann found that all animal tissues, too, were made of cells. Schleiden and Schwann are considered to have begun the cell theory. This states that cells are the building blocks of life and that cells come from other cells.

Cells and Germs

Development of the cell theory led to interest in single-celled organisms. In 1857, after researching single-celled organisms, Louis Pasteur (loo•EE pahs•TOOR) showed that some single-celled microorganisms, such as bacteria, can enter into and infect an organism, causing disease. Pasteur's germ theory changed medicine. Disease-causing organisms could now be identified, and methods could be developed to fight them.

Vaccines and Antibiotics

Pasteur's work also contributed to the development of vaccination. This is a process in which a killed or weakened microorganism is used to prevent infection by similar, but deadly, microorganisms. Pasteur developed the first vaccine against rabies. By the turn of the century, many other scientists were studying microorganisms and disease. By the 1940s, scientists had developed antibiotics, such as penicillin, to fight bacterial infections.

Mysteries of the Cell Unraveled

Cell research wasn't limited to medicine. Scientists were also researching cell parts and their functions. In 1953 scientists discovered the structure of DNA. This is the chemical inside the nucleus that contains all the information a cell needs to function and reproduce.

Today scientists research how certain molecules are used by and affect cells. Scientists are also working to alter or control chemical processes in cells that cause diseases or disorders.

THINK ABOUT IT

1. How did Pasteur's research with single-celled organisms improve people's lives?
2. In addition to Hooke's observations of cells, what other scientific evidence led to the development of the cell theory?

1997
Scientists clone a living organism—a sheep—by implanting the nucleus from a body cell of an adult sheep into a fertilized egg cell.

A.D. 2000

2000
Scientists finish a rough draft that describes about 3.5 billion chemical pieces that make up all of human DNA.

Because of the efforts of microbiologists in Tennessee, the Ocoee River, once so polluted that scientists couldn't find anything living in it, has become a haven for recreation and wildlife.

Gary Sayler
MICROBIOLOGIST

"The joy of working in this field is that microbes have been on the planet for billions of years and are responsible for the environment that now sustains human life."

Dr. Gary Sayler works with organisms too small to be seen with the unaided eye. Dr. Sayler, a microbiologist (my•kroh•by•AHL•uh•jihst) at the University of Tennessee, realizes that experiments with microbes—another name for microorganisms—could lead to important discoveries. Microbiologists study how microbes live and how they interact with other living things. Dr. Sayler's special interest is how microbes interact with the environment and the organisms within it.

In college Dr. Sayler first studied to be a dentist and then switched to studying bacteria. At about the same time, he became interested in the environment. Like many others in the late 1960s, Dr. Sayler became aware of the bad effects of pollution.

Besides working at the University of Tennessee, Dr. Sayler is director of the Center for Environmental Biotechnology (CEB) in Knoxville, Tennessee. Scientists at CEB have made light-producing microbes that can detect and destroy harmful pollutants.

If pollutants are present, the microbes light up. The microbes also degrade, or "eat," the pollutants. As they "eat," the microbes give off light. This tells scientists that the microbes are doing their job. The amount and location of the light show the amount and location of the pollutants.

THINK ABOUT IT

1. How do Dr. Sayler's light-producing microbes help reduce pollutants in soils and water?

2. What is Dr. Sayler's special area of interest?

CLASSIFYING FLOWERING PLANTS

How can you classify flowering plants?

Materials

- 3 zip-top bags, each containing a flower and a leaf from a different type of flowering plant
- paper
- colored pencils

Procedure

1. Observe and sketch the contents of each bag.
2. Count and record the number of petals on each flower.

3. Observe and record how the veins are arranged in the leaves. Note whether the veins look like lines that never cross (parallel lines) or cross many times like a fishing net (intersecting lines).

Draw Conclusions

Flowering plants are classified as monocots or dicots. The petals of monocot flowers are usually arranged in threes and their leaves have parallel veins. The petals of dicot flowers are usually arranged in fours or fives and the veins in their leaves are like nets. Classify each flower and leaf you observed. Record this information on your sketch.

MAKE A MODEL SPONGE

How are the cell layers arranged in a sponge?

Materials

- 4 paper strips labeled inner cell layer, jellylike layer, outer cell layer, pores
- modeling clay in three colors
- 4 map pins

Procedure

1. Mold one color of clay into the shape of an open paper bag.

Sponge cross section ▶

2. Mold a second color of clay around the first.
3. Mold a third layer of clay around the second.
4. Make tiny holes through your sponge layers.
5. Decide what each layer and the holes represent. Attach the labels to your model, using pins.

Draw Conclusions

How could you use your model to explain to a younger student how water moves through a sponge? How could you improve your model?

Review and Test Preparation

Vocabulary Review

Use the terms below to complete the sentences. The page numbers in ( ) tell you where to look in the chapter if you need help.

cell (A6)

cell membrane (A7)

cytoplasm (A7)

nucleus (A7)

cell wall (A8)

chloroplast (A8)

microorganism (A9)

vertebrate (A16)

invertebrate (A16)

arthropod (A16)

embryo (A20)

flower (A22)

fruit (A22)

fungi (A26)

hyphae (A27)

spore (A27)

molds (A28)

1. A common type of fungi that look cottony or woolly are called ____.

2. The long threadlike parts that make up the body of a fungus are ____.

3. The part of a plant cell that provides support to a plant is the ____.

4. An animal with a backbone is a ____.

5. The young plant inside a seed is called an ____.

6. The basic unit of structure of all living things is the ____.

7. A snail is an example of an ____, or an animal without a backbone.

8. Most of the inside of a cell is taken up by ____.

9. A yeast is an example of a ____ because it is made of only one cell.

10. An insect is an example of an invertebrate that is also an ____.

11. The ____ is the control center of a cell.

12. Flowering plants produce seeds that are protected by a ____.

13. The outermost part of an animal cell is the ____.

14. The green plant-cell part used in food-making is the ____.

15. Like those of plants, the cells of ____ are enclosed by a cell wall.

16. A ____ contains reproductive parts of a fruit-bearing plant.

17. The cell part that allows material into and out of a cell is the ____.

18. A small cell that can grow into a new fungus is called a ____.

Connect Concepts

Fill in the blanks in the chart with the right words.

bag-type   **worm**   **snail**

Three Body Types of Animals Are:		
19. ____, which is shown by the sponge	20. tube-type, which is shown by the ____ and	21. complex type, which is shown by the ____

Check Understanding

Write the letter of the best choice.

22. Fungi cannot make their own food because —
    A their cells have cell walls
    B their cells have more than one nucleus
    C their cells have no chloroplasts
    D they are not made of cells

23. An example of a microorganism is the —
    F paramecium
    G sponge
    H mushroom
    J snail

24. Examples of cone-bearing plants include —
    A pines, peach trees, and roses
    B pines, cycads, and firs
    C peach trees, watermelons, and pumpkins
    D pumpkins, cycads, and ginkgoes

25. All fruit-bearing plants make seeds in —
    F spores   H mitochondria
    G cones   J flowers

26. The part of a cell that stores waste or materials that the cell needs is the —
    A nucleus   C vacuole
    B cytoplasm   D mitochondria

27. An example of a microorganism with many cells is a —
    F amoeba   H paramecium
    G rotifer   J spore

28. One reason that water is important to life is that the _____ is made mostly of water.
    A vacuole   C cytoplasm
    B nucleus   D shell

Critical Thinking

29. If you were looking at cells from an onion stem and from a mushroom under a microscope, how could you tell which cells came from which living thing?

30. What are three characteristics that fungi share with animals?

31. Both bats and insects have legs with joints. Why is a bat not classified as an arthropod?

Process Skills Review

32. How can you **use a model** of cells to help someone **draw conclusions** about the differences between plant cells and animal cells?

33. What observation would help you **infer** whether a plant forms covered seeds or uncovered seeds?

34. Observe the plant cell shown on page A8 and the cells of the mushroom shown on page A26. How do the cells **compare**?

35. You **observe** several new mushrooms in a yard the day after a rainstorm. What are two things you might **infer** based on this observation?

Performance Assessment

Make Model Cells

With a partner, make models of a plant cell, an animal cell, and the cell of a fungus. Label the parts of each cell. Be sure your cell shows the following parts, as appropriate: cell membrane, cell wall, cytoplasm, nucleus, chloroplasts.

Animal Growth and Adaptations

Vocabulary Preview

environment
climate
oxygen
shelter
metamorphosis
adaptation
camouflage
mimicry
instinct
migration
hibernation

Try to think of as many kinds of animals as you can. You can probably think of a lot, and there are thousands more—all different from one another. But all animals have something in common. They all have adaptations that help them live and grow.

Fast Fact

Ostriches are the largest birds in the world. Their strong legs help them run up to 64 km/hr (40 mi/hr). They can also use their legs to kick animals that may threaten them.

Fast Animals

Animal	Speed in km/hr (mi/hr)	
Peregrine falcon	320	(200)
Cheetah	103	(64)
Hummingbird	97	(60)
Jack rabbit	71	(44)
Dolphin	26	(16)

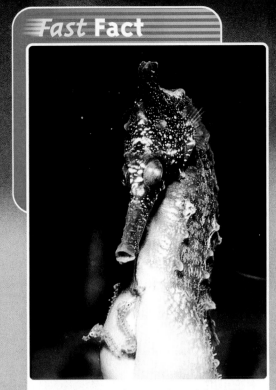

The male seahorse gives birth! The female seahorse lays eggs in the male's pouch. He then carries them until they hatch.

Scientists think that Aldabra tortoises live longer than any other animals. It's hard to know for sure, though, because the tortoises have outlived many of the people studying them. Scientists estimate that these tortoises may live longer than 100 years!

What Are the Basic Needs of Animals?

In this lesson, you can . . .

INVESTIGATE animal needs.

LEARN ABOUT how animals meet their needs.

LINK to math, writing, social studies, and technology.

◄ This tiger hunts for food in tall grasses and tropical wetlands. Food is a basic need of animals.

INVESTIGATE

Basic Needs of Mealworms

Activity Purpose Have you ever had a pet or watched animals in a zoo? Then you know that an animal has needs. Animals meet their needs in different ways. In this investigation you will make observations to help you **infer** what those needs are.

Materials

- bran meal
- spoon
- 2 shallow dishes
- plastic shoe box
- flake cereal
- water
- 10 cm square of poster board
- mealworms
- paper towel

Activity Procedure

1 Make a chart like the one on the next page to **record** your observations and measurements.

2 **Measure** two spoonfuls of bran meal. Put them into a shallow dish. Put it at one end of the shoe box. Count 20 flakes of cereal. Put them into another shallow dish. Put this dish at the other end of the shoe box. Fold the paper towel into a square. Moisten it and put it in the center of the shoe box.

3 Fold about 1 cm down on opposite sides of the poster board. It should stand up like a small table. (Picture A) Put it over the paper towel. (Picture B)

Mealworm Observations

Condition	Location	Size and Appearance	Food Measurements	Other
One hour in dark				
Overnight in dark				
Bright sunlight				

4 Put the mealworms in the shoe box next to, but NOT on, the towel. Put the lid on the box. Then put the shoe box in a dark place for an hour. Be careful not to spill anything.

5 Take the box to a dimly lit area. Open the lid, and **observe** the contents. Try to find the mealworms. **Record** your observations. Put the lid back on.

6 Put the box in a dark place overnight. Again, take the box to a dimly lit area. **Observe** the contents of the box. **Record** your observations. **Measure** the bran meal and count the cereal flakes. Record your measurements.

7 Put the box into bright sunshine for a few minutes. Does anything change? What can you **infer** from the location of the mealworms?

Picture A

Picture B

Draw Conclusions

1. What happened to the mealworms?

2. What happened to the food? Why?

3. **Scientists at Work** Scientists learn by **observing.** What can you **infer** about animal needs by observing the mealworms?

Investigate Further How could you find out which food the mealworms liked best? **Plan an investigation.** Decide what **hypothesis** you would like to test and what procedure you will follow.

Process Skill Tip

Observations and inferences are different. When you **observe**, you use your senses and then record information from your senses. When you **infer**, you use what you have observed to form an opinion called an inference.

How Animals Meet Their Needs

Where Animals Meet Their Needs

FIND OUT

- **five basic needs all animals have**
- **how some animals meet each need**

VOCABULARY

environment
climate
oxygen
shelter
metamorphosis

You learned in the investigation that animals have some basic needs in common. These include the need for food, water, and a place to live. As you read on, you will find that animals have other needs, too.

Animals meet their needs in the environment in which they live. An **environment** (en•VY•ruhn•muhnt) is everything that surrounds and affects an animal. It includes the plants and other animals in the area, as well as the rocks, soil, air, and water. Everything, both living and nonliving, is part of an environment.

In the pages that follow, you will read about several different environments and the many ways animals meet their needs in each one.

✔ **What makes up an animal's environment?**

A vulture finds its food in the desert. ▼

This desert area in Arizona is dry and has little vegetation.

When the sun is too hot, this tortoise lies in the shade or under the sand.

Kangaroo rat ▶

The Need for the Right Climate

The climate of an area is part of the area's environment. **Climate** is the average temperature and rainfall of an area over many years. Animals are adapted to live in almost every climate on the earth, including those with very little rainfall.

Deserts are natural land environments where the climate is dry all year round. The plants and animals that live in a desert must be able to survive with very little water.

Vultures, foxes, snakes, tortoises, kangaroo rats, and other small animals all live in desert environments. Vultures live in nests in cacti, bushes, or small trees. Kangaroo rats and foxes live in burrows in the ground.

Tortoises and kangaroo rats feed on leaves, fruits, and seeds of desert plants. Vultures, snakes, and foxes feed on other animals. Because there is little rainfall, there are few streams or lakes from which to drink. Desert animals get much of their water from the food they eat.

Different animals meet their needs in a tropical rain forest. There, the climate is wet and warm year-round. Monkeys and hummingbirds live in the trees. Jaguars, a type of large cat, hunt along the forest floor.

✔ **How are the climates of a desert and a tropical rain forest alike? How are they different?**

▲ Ocean mammals, such as this whale, come to the water's surface to breathe.

The Need for Oxygen

Animals need **oxygen**, one of the many gases in air. Many land animals get oxygen by breathing air into their lungs. Ocean mammals, such as whales and dolphins, come to the water's surface to breathe air into their lungs.

Most fish get oxygen from the water around them. Fish and many other ocean animals have body parts called gills. As water moves over the gills, the oxygen in the water passes into the fish's blood.

✔ **Where do fish get the oxygen they need?**

▲ Brown bears eat both plants and animals. This bear is trying to catch a salmon.

The Need for Food

In any environment, an animal needs energy and materials to live and grow. For example, a hummingbird needs energy to beat its wings 70 times per second so it can fly near a flower and drink the nectar. A cheetah needs energy to run fast so it can catch its prey. Like all animals, humming-birds and cheetahs get the energy and mate-rials they need from the food they eat.

All animals need food, but different animals eat different kinds of food. If you visit the plains of Africa, you may see zebras grazing on grasses, rhinos feeding on low shrubs, and giraffes nibbling leaves on the high branches of trees. Like most animals in the world, these African animals are plant eaters. Some animals, however, are meat eaters. Living among the zebras and rhinos are meat-eating lions, wild dogs, and leopards. Still other animals eat both plants and animals.

✔ **Why do animals need food?**

◀ Giraffes feed mostly on leaves high on acacia (uh•KAY•shuh) trees.

This chameleon (kuh•MEEL•yuhn) eats insects. ▶

The Need for Water

Animals also need water. They lose water by sweating, panting, or other means. That water must be replaced. Most animals replace the lost water by drinking from ponds, lakes, streams, and puddles.

Deserts, however, usually don't have bodies of water or even damp soil. Desert animals must get water in other ways. Kangaroo rats eat seeds that provide them with some water. Also, their bodies produce water as their food is digested and used. Kangaroo rats hardly ever need to drink.

✓ **Where do animals get the water they need?**

Desert fox

Gray fox

Arctic fox

▲ Each type of fox finds shelter in its environment.

▲ These African elephants drink at watering holes to get the water they need.

The Need for Shelter

Most animals need shelter in their environment. A **shelter** is a place where an animal is protected from other animals or from the weather.

Foxes find or dig shelters in their environment. A gray fox may climb a tree to find a hollow place to hide in. An arctic fox may dig into the snow for shelter during a blizzard. Desert foxes dig connecting tunnels under the sand to protect themselves from the desert heat.

Rocks, logs, leaves—almost anything in an environment—can be a shelter for an animal. A rock may shelter a snake from the desert heat. A woodpile may shelter a field mouse from a summer storm. A rotting log on the forest floor may shelter dozens of different insects.

✓ **How does weather affect animals' needs for shelter?**

Animals and Their Young

Animals of all species need to have young. Without having young, all of a species would soon die and disappear. The young grow, become adults resembling their parents, and produce young of their own. Animals grow and develop in many different ways.

Insects such as butterflies lay hundreds of eggs. The eggs hatch into wormlike larvae called caterpillars. As a caterpillar grows, it *molts,* or sheds its outer skin, several times. The last time a caterpillar molts, it seals itself inside a tough shell, or *chrysalis* (KRIS•uh•lis). Inside the chrysalis the caterpillar's body slowly changes. Finally an adult butterfly breaks out of the chrysalis. This process of change from an egg to an adult butterfly is called **metamorphosis** (met•uh•MAWR•fuh•sis). Almost all insects, many invertebrates that live in water, and amphibians go through some kind of metamorphosis.

Animals such as birds, fish, reptiles, and mammals do not go through metamorphosis. Instead, the young are born or hatched looking much like their parents.

Mammals care for their young until the young are old enough to meet their needs on their own. For example, a koala gives birth before the young koala is fully developed. The newborn koala crawls into its mother's pouch, where it is fed and protected for six months. It then spends another six months riding on its mother's back before it is able to meet its needs on its own. Only then does it leave its mother.

✔ **Why would an animal that has only a few young take care of them for months after birth?**

This young penguin is asking for food from its mother. ▼

◀ **Butterfly metamorphosis**

4. Adult

3. Chrysalis (pupa)

2. Caterpillar (larva)

1. Egg

A young koala spends six months in its mother's pouch and six months holding on to its mother's back before it can live on its own.

Summary

Animals have some basic needs in common. These include the need for the right climate and for oxygen, food, water, and shelter. Animals of a species must reproduce in order for the species to survive. Animal young grow to resemble their parents. Each type of animal meets its needs in its own way.

Review

1. What is an environment?
2. What five basic needs do animals have?
3. Why do animals produce young?
4. **Critical Thinking** Choose an animal and describe the shelter it needs.
5. **Test Prep** Which of the following is **NOT** a need of animals?
   A food
   B oxygen
   C clothing
   D shelter

LINKS

MATH LINK

Add Whole Numbers Suppose you are to report on how many animals you can find in a wooded area near your home. You count 12 snakes, 8 chipmunks, 15 squirrels, and 20 birds. Find the total number of mammals and nonmammals.

WRITING LINK

Informative Writing—Report Choose an animal, and investigate its environment and how it meets its needs. List some questions you want to answer about your animal. Use library resources, encyclopedias, or the Internet to find your answers. Then write an article for your school newspaper to report your findings.

SOCIAL STUDIES LINK

Human Shelters People build many kinds of homes. The building materials and shapes of the homes are different in different environments. Investigate one kind of home in a certain climate of the world. Explain how the climate affects the building materials and the shape of the home.

GO ONLINE TECHNOLOGY LINK

Learn more about young animals by visiting the Smithsonian Institution Internet site.
www.si.edu/harcourt/science

 Smithsonian Institution®

How Do Animals' Body Parts Help Them Meet Their Needs?

In this lesson, you can . . .

INVESTIGATE how the shape of a bird's beak is related to the food it eats.

LEARN ABOUT animal adaptations, including different body parts.

LINK to math, writing, and technology.

INVESTIGATE

Bird Beaks and Food

Activity Purpose Different birds have different types of beaks. A hummingbird's beak is long and straight. A hawk's beak is short and hooked. The tools in this investigation stand for beaks of different sizes and shapes. You will **use a model** to find what kind of "beak" works best for picking up and "eating" different foods.

Materials

- chopsticks or 2 blunt pencils
- pliers
- clothespin
- spoon
- forceps
- plastic worms
- cooked spaghetti
- cooked rice
- raisins
- birdseed
- peanuts in shells
- water in a cup
- small paper plates

▼ In what ways are this picture of chopsticks and this bird's beak alike?

Activity Procedure

Bird Food and Beak Observations		
Food	Best Tool (Beak)	Observations

1 Make a chart like the one above.

2 Put the tools on one side of the desk. Think of the tools as bird beaks. For example, the pliers might be a short, thick beak.

3 Put the rest of the materials on the other side of the desk. They stand for bird foods.

4 Put one type of food at a time in the middle of the desk. Try picking up the food with each beak. (Picture A)

5 Test all of the beaks with all of the foods. See which beak works best for which food. **Record** your observations in your chart.

Picture A

Draw Conclusions

1. Which kind of beak is best for picking up each food? Which is best for crushing seeds?

2. By **observing** the shape of a bird's beak, what can you **infer** about the food the bird eats?

3. **Scientists at Work** Scientists often **use models** to help them test ideas. How did using models help you test ideas about bird beaks?

Investigate Further Find a book about birds. Identify real birds that have beaks like the tools you used in this investigation. Make a booklet describing each beak type and how birds use it to gather and eat food. Include your own pictures of the beaks and of the matching foods each beak can best gather and eat.

Process Skill Tip

Observing many kinds of real birds would be difficult to do in your classroom. **Using models** of birds' beaks makes it easier to infer how real beaks work.

Animal Adaptations: Body Parts

FIND OUT

- ways birds are adapted to meet their needs
- other types of animal adaptations

VOCABULARY

adaptation
camouflage
mimicry

A Closer Look at Bird Beaks

Finches on the Galápagos Islands in the Pacific Ocean look very much alike. However, their beaks are different in size and shape. Scientists observed and recorded information about where the finches lived, the shapes of their beaks, and their food sources. Scientists noted that some finches eat seeds, others eat fruit, and still others eat insects.

Scientists used the evidence they gathered just as you did in the investigation. They inferred that the differences in the finches' beaks are adaptations to the kinds of foods the finches eat. An **adaptation** is a body part or behavior that helps an animal meet its needs in its environment. The scientists saw that the seed eaters have thick, heavy beaks. The fruit eaters have short, stubby beaks. The insect eaters have sharp, pointed beaks.

✔ **How does having a thick, heavy beak help a bird eat seeds?**

The house finch uses its short, stubby beak to eat fruit. ▼

A Darwin's finch uses its thick, heavy beak to crack open large seeds. ▼

▲ The European goldfinch eats insects with its sharp, pointed beak.

▲ An osprey's talons (TAL•uhnz), or claws, are adapted for catching and carrying its prey.

Other Bird Adaptations

Like finches, all other birds have beaks that help them get food from their environment. Birds also have many other adaptations that help them live. These include the size of an owl's eyes and the shape of a hawk's claws. Although birds have the same basic needs, they have different adaptations that help them meet their needs in different ways.

Feathers keep birds warm and dry and help them fly. Feathers are very light, and they give a bird's body a smooth surface over which air flows easily. Another adaptation for flying is hollow bones. A bird's bones are filled with air pockets. These make a bird especially light.

But not all birds fly. Some flightless birds have adaptations for running. The ostrich's long legs and two-toed feet allow it to run at speeds up to 64 kilometers (about 40 mi) per hour. Some water birds don't fly or run. Penguins are the largest group of flightless water birds. As you can see in the picture, their bodies have adaptations for moving in water. Almost everything about a bird's body, from its beak to its feet, is an adaptation that helps it meet its needs.

✔ **How do strong claws help a hawk meet its need for food?**

Penguins use their wings as flippers and their feet for steering. They can swim underwater as fast as 35 kilometers (about 22 mi) per hour. That's about the fastest you can pedal a bicycle. ▶

Body Coverings

Every animal's body covering is an adaptation that helps the animal survive. You have learned that feathers protect birds and help them fly. The fur or hair that covers most mammals helps keep them warm. Some mammals have sharp hairs that are adaptations for protection. Others have whiskers—stiff hairs that function as sense organs. Many fish are covered with scales. The scales help protect the fish from disease and from other animals that live in the water. A reptile's scales protect it from injury and from drying out. The scales on a snake overlap to form a smooth covering that helps the snake move.

✔ **What are three different kinds of body coverings?**

▲ Both pictures show the same porcupine fish. Which shows the fish using an adaptation to scare away predators?

◀ The hairs of a polar bear's thick fur are actually clear, not white. They allow light to get to the bear's dark skin, helping the bear stay warm in the cold Arctic climate.

◄ The scales of an iguana are an adaptation that protects it from enemies and helps keep it from losing body moisture.

In the summer the American bison sheds its heavy winter fur. ►

Dolphins and other marine mammals have little hair on their bodies. This helps them glide through the water easily. Under their skin, these animals have layers of fat that help keep them warm. ▼

The hedgehog rolls into a ball when it is in danger. Its spines are hairs that form a prickly protection. ▼

Color and Shape

The snowshoe hare is white in winter and brown in summer. Its changing fur color is an adaptation that makes the hare difficult for other animals to hunt because the hare blends in with its environment. The hare's seasonal color changes are an example of camouflage. **Camouflage** (KAM•uh•flahzh) is an animal's color or pattern that helps it blend in with its surroundings. Camouflage is an adaptation that helps an animal hide.

Many animals have body coverings and shapes that are camouflage. For example, a tiger's fur is striped. The stripes help the tiger blend in with the light and shadows of the tall grass in its environment. Toads—with their bumpy, brownish skin—look like pebbles on the forest floor. A chameleon's color changes to match its surroundings. The dark skin on an alligator's back makes it blend into the swamps where it lives.

▲ A chameleon's skin can change color in minutes. This form of camouflage enables the chameleon to blend in with the tree in which it waits for food.

Mimicry (MIM•ik•ree) is an adaptation in which an animal looks very much like another animal. The viceroy butterfly is a good example of mimicry. It looks like the monarch butterfly, which tastes bad to birds. Birds often mistake the viceroy for a monarch and leave it alone.

✔ **How is a viceroy butterfly a mimic?**

▲ The body covering of a snowshoe hare is brown during the summer. In winter a thick coat of white fur covers the hare's body.

A52

Summary

Animals have adaptations, which enable them to meet their needs. Adaptations include body coverings and the shapes, sizes, and colors of body parts.

Review

1. List three bird adaptations.

2. Choose an animal. What needs of the animal can be met by its body covering?

3. Choose an animal you know about. Give three examples of how its adaptations help it meet its needs.

4. **Critical Thinking** How are mimicry and camouflage different? How are they alike?

5. **Test Prep** Which adaptation would best help a hawk catch a mouse?

   A talons
   B camouflage
   C hollow bones
   D feathers

Can you find the differences between these two butterflies? The one on the right is a viceroy. Unlike the monarch, it has an extra black stripe across its back wings. Because the viceroy mimics the monarch, it avoids being eaten by hungry birds. ▼

LINKS

MATH LINK

Measure and Compare Length Choose a bird to research. Draw a life-size picture of the bird viewed from the side. Use a ruler to help you make accurate measurements. Paint or color the bird to show what it looks like. Cut out the bird, and compare it to the birds your classmates drew. Decide how to order the birds by size.

WRITING LINK

Informative Writing—Explanation Choose an animal to "interview." Write a list of questions you could ask the animal. Include questions about how it meets its basic needs and which of its adaptations are especially helpful. Research the animal to find answers to your questions. Using your interview notes, write an article for your school newspaper explaining how the animal meets its needs.

GO ONLINE TECHNOLOGY LINK

Learn more about reptile body adaptations by visiting the Smithsonian Institution Internet site.
www.si.edu/harcourt/science

 Smithsonian Institution®

How Do Animals' Behaviors Help Them Meet Their Needs?

In this lesson, you can . . .

INVESTIGATE a behavior of some butterflies that helps them survive.

LEARN ABOUT other animal behaviors that are adaptations.

LINK to math, writing, social studies, and technology.

Monarch Butterfly Travel

Activity Purpose Monarch butterflies cannot live through cold winters. From observations, scientists know that the butterflies travel south for the winter. To discover where the butterflies go and the paths they take to get there, scientists have tagged some of the butterflies. The tags let the scientists track the butterflies as they fly between their summer and winter homes. In this investigation you will learn where the butterflies go during the cold winter months.

Materials

- outline map of North America
- 2 pencils of different colors

Activity Procedure

1 Label the directions north, south, east, and west on your map.

2 During the summer many monarch butterflies live in two general areas. Some live in the north-eastern United States and around the shores of the Great Lakes. Others live along the south-western coast of Canada and in the states of Washington and Oregon. Locate these two large general areas on your map. Shade each area a different color. (Picture A)

◄ Monarch butterfly

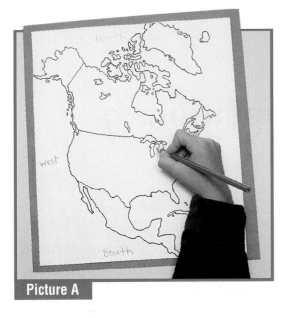

Picture A

Picture B

3 At summer's end large groups of monarchs gather and travel south for the winter. Most of those east of the Rocky Mountains fly to the mountains of central Mexico. But some of these butterflies make their way to Florida. Butterflies west of the Rocky Mountains fly to sites along the California coast. All these areas have trees where the butterflies can rest, temperatures that are cool yet above freezing, and water to drink. Find these areas on your map. Shade each winter area the same color as the matching summer area. Then use the right color to draw the most direct route from north to south over land. (Picture B)

Draw Conclusions

1. **Compare** the climate where the monarch butterflies spend the summer with the climate where they spend the winter.

2. What can you **infer** about how the behavior of the butterflies helps them meet their needs?

3. **Scientists at Work** Scientists use maps and graphs to **communicate** data and ideas visually. How does making a map of butterfly movements help you understand where monarchs travel?

Investigate Further Many kinds of birds, fish, and mammals travel to different places when the seasons change. Research the travel route of one of these animals. Use a map to show the route.

Process Skill Tip

Sometimes the best way to **communicate** what you have learned is to use a graphic, a visual display such as a map, rather than words.

Animal Adaptations: Behaviors

Instincts

In the investigation, you learned that monarch butterflies fly south for the winter. They go to places where they have the food and climate they need to survive. The *behavior*, or action, of flying south is not something monarchs have learned. It is an instinct. An **instinct** (IN•stingkt) is a behavior that an animal begins life with. Instincts are adaptations that help animals meet their needs.

✔ **What instinct do monarch butterflies have?**

Migration

Like the monarch butterfly, some other animals travel long distances to meet their needs. For example, female Atlantic green turtles go to Ascension Island in the South Atlantic Ocean to lay their eggs. They bury the eggs in the sand on the beach. After hatching, the young turtles move toward the ocean. Then they swim toward feeding areas along the coast of Brazil, more than 1000 kilometers (about 620 mi) away. When the female turtles become adults, they return to Ascension Island to lay their eggs. The turtles do not learn from other turtles where the feeding areas are or how to get to Ascension Island. They know by instinct where to go. Scientists hypothesize that the turtles are able to use Earth's magnetic field to guide them as they swim.

The Atlantic green turtle's instinct for travel to Ascension Island is an example of migration. **Migration** (my•GRAY•shuhn) is the movement of a group of one type of animal from one region to another and back again. It is a behavioral adaptation.

Many birds migrate to environments where there is food and a good climate. For instance, the pectoral sandpiper travels from northern Canada to southern South America each fall. These birds return to Canada in the spring when the weather in Canada warms up.

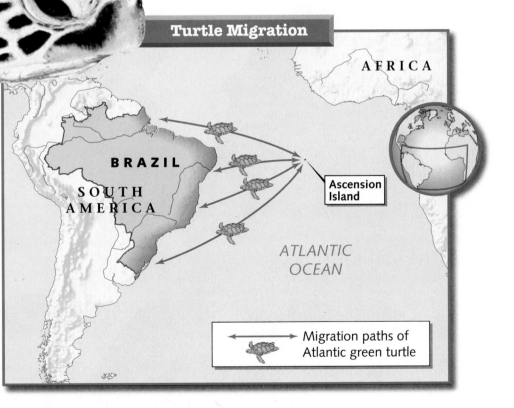

Turtle Migration

AFRICA

BRAZIL

SOUTH AMERICA

Ascension Island

ATLANTIC OCEAN

Migration paths of Atlantic green turtle

◄ Instinct guides this Atlantic green turtle to and from nesting grounds on Ascension Island.

Some animals have an instinct to migrate to places where their young can survive. Gray whales spend the summer in areas where they can find food easily—near the North Pole. In the winter they migrate to the warm waters off Mexico, where they give birth to their young.

Pacific salmon also migrate before producing their young. Salmon hatch from eggs in rivers and streams. Then they swim to the ocean, where they spend most of their lives. When these salmon are ready to produce young of their own, they migrate to the same stream where they hatched.

✔ **Name some animals that migrate.**

▲ These birds migrate each year. In the fall, they fly south. In the spring, they return to the north to lay their eggs and raise their young.

▼ Pacific salmon attempt to leap over whatever is in their way as they travel upstream to the place where they were hatched.

Hibernation

Not all animals have the instinct to migrate as winter brings colder temperatures and a lack of food. Instead, some animals adapt to these changes by hibernating. **Hibernation** (hy•ber•NAY•shuhn) is a period when an animal goes into a long, deep "sleep." An animal prepares to hibernate by eating extra food and finding shelter. During hibernation the animal's body temperature drops and its breathing rate and heartbeat rate fall. As a result, the animal needs little or no food. The energy it does need comes from fat stored in its body.

The ground squirrel is an animal that hibernates. As winter approaches, the squirrel goes into an underground nest. Within a

▲ Many North American bats hibernate in caves or rocky places.

few hours, its body temperature drops to 15°C (about 59°F), and its heartbeat rate and breathing rate fall. Before long, the squirrel is taking only about four breaths per minute.

✓ **How does an animal's body change during hibernation?**

THE INSIDE STORY

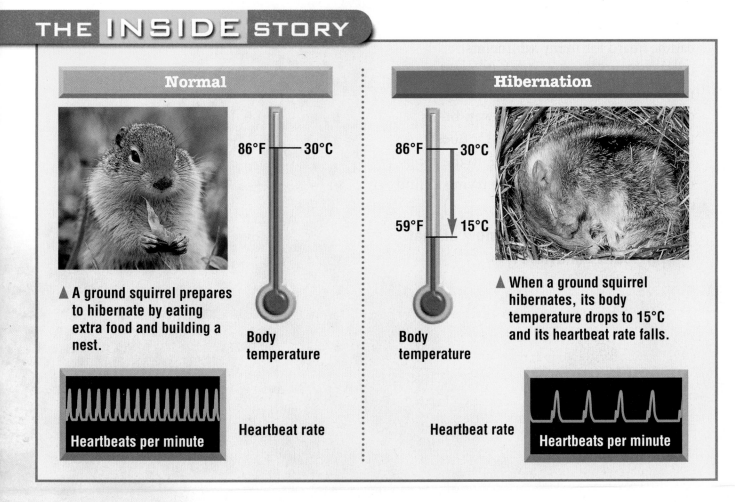

Normal

86°F — 30°C

Body temperature

▲ A ground squirrel prepares to hibernate by eating extra food and building a nest.

Heartbeats per minute

Heartbeat rate

Hibernation

86°F — 30°C

59°F — 15°C

Body temperature

▲ When a ground squirrel hibernates, its body temperature drops to 15°C and its heartbeat rate falls.

Heartbeat rate

Heartbeats per minute

Learned Behaviors

Some animal behaviors are not instincts. They are learned. For instance, adult tigers are excellent hunters, but tigers aren't born knowing how to hunt. Tiger cubs learn to hunt by watching their mothers hunt and by playing with other tiger cubs.

Chimpanzees, too, learn many behaviors that help them survive. Chimps use sounds to communicate with one another. A loud call is a warning. A soft grunt is a happy sound. Young chimps learn the meanings of the sounds by observing the adults in their environment. Observation also helps a young chimp learn how to build a leafy nest for sleeping and how to use a stone to crack open a nut.

Some animals are difficult to study, so we know less about them. For example, the humpback whale makes sounds that can be heard for many kilometers under water. Scientists think that males might use these "songs" to attract females or to tell other males to stay away. But is the act of singing an instinct? Or does a whale learn a song by listening to the songs of other whales? Scientists are trying to find out.

✔ **What animals do you know of that can learn behaviors?**

The chimpanzee's loud cry warns other chimps of possible dangers. ▼

This mother cheetah will teach her cubs to hunt. ▶

▲ Humpback whales make sounds that can be heard many kilometers away under water.

Summary

Animals behave in ways that enable them to meet their needs. The behaviors are adaptations to their environments. Some of the behaviors are instincts. Others are learned.

Review

1. How is an instinct different from a learned behavior? Give an example of each.

2. What is migration? How does migration help an animal meet its needs? Give an example.

3. What is hibernation? How does hibernation help an animal meet its needs? Give an example.

4. **Critical Thinking** Suppose a dog barks when a stranger comes close to its home. Suppose it also barks when asked to speak. Which behavior is probably learned? Which is instinct? Explain your answers.

5. **Test Prep** An animal's body temperature drops for a long period when it is —
   A migrating
   B sleeping
   C hibernating
   D hunting

LINKS

MATH LINK

Measure Length Use a globe and a map to measure the migration path of monarch butterflies from Minneapolis, Minnesota, to Mexico City. How is measuring different on the globe and on the map?

WRITING LINK

Narrative Writing—Personal Story Suppose you are an animal that migrates in the spring and fall. Tell what kind of animal you are, where you live in the summer, and where you spend the winter. For your teacher, make a log of the things you might do and see as you travel.

SOCIAL STUDIES LINK

Migration Barriers Study the needs and migration behaviors of deer. Think of ways that people might make it difficult for deer to migrate. Make a large drawing showing the deer's migration routes and any barriers that may be built or caused by people living nearby. Explain your drawing in writing.

TECHNOLOGY LINK

To learn more about instincts, watch the video *Monarch Migration* on the **Harcourt Science Newsroom Video.**

Robot Roaches and Ants

Scientists are finding new uses for insects— both real insects and mechanical ones.

Roaches for Research

Most people think of roaches as pests, and they want to get rid of them. But scientists in Japan are raising these insects. Hundreds of roaches are grown in plastic bins in a laboratory at Tokyo University. Because the American cockroach is harder to kill and bigger than other species, the scientists have chosen it for their experiments.

For some of the roaches, surgery is done to take off their wings and antennae.

Cockroach wearing a control backpack

Then the roaches are fitted with tiny backpacks, weighing about 3 grams ($\frac{1}{10}$ oz). Cockroaches can carry up to 20 times their own weight, and the backpacks are only about twice a roach's weight. Each backpack has tiny wires that guide the roach. Electricity from the wires makes the roach jump forward or backward or turn left or right.

Small Is Beautiful

Japanese scientists hope to use these specially equipped insects as tiny explorers. For example, with a microcamera added to the pack, a roach might crawl through rubble. It could be guided to search for people trapped during a fire or an earthquake. The roaches also could go into other places that are too small or dangerous for people.

There are still problems for scientists to solve. Although the roaches may live for several months, they may stop responding to the electricity. Also, scientists are still studying the nervous systems of roaches to decide on the best places to attach the wires.

Ant Attack!

If you don't like the idea of a living robot roach, what about artificial ants? At the Massachusetts Institute of Technology, scientists are building microrobots. Each tiny robot is only about the size of a walnut. But it has 17 different *sensors*, devices for observing its environment.

The robot ants are being programmed to mimic, or act like, real members of an ant colony. They can hunt for food, pass messages to one another, and play games such as tag and follow the leader. The designers of the ants hope that the robots someday will help doctors. They might also just help with simple tasks around the home.

In England, another group of researchers is also trying to make robots that mimic ants. They hope to use the robots to inspect bundles of wire inside telephone cables. The ants could find which sections of cable are used least. Then system managers could route calls to those sections. This would avoid overuse of some phone lines.

With this kind of microtechnology, we may someday think of roaches and ants as friends, not pests!

THINK ABOUT IT

1. What insects or insect behaviors do you know about that might be useful for technology?
2. How would it be useful for robot roaches to look for survivors of earthquakes or fires?

CAREERS
ENTOMOLOGIST

What They Do
Entomologists study the ecology, life cycles, and behavior of the more than $1\frac{1}{2}$ million species of insects. Most entomologists work for state agriculture departments, universities, or industry. Some study how to protect crops and other materials from insect damage. Others study how to protect helpful insect species.

Education and Training
Most entomologists have a college degree in entomology or biology. Many have a Ph.D. in entomology.

WEB LINK
For Science and Technology updates, visit the Harcourt Internet site.
www.harcourtschool.com

Jane Goodall
ANIMAL BEHAVIORIST

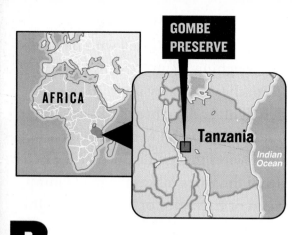

GOMBE PRESERVE

AFRICA

Tanzania

Indian Ocean

"Chimpanzees have given me so much. The long hours spent with them in the forest have enriched my life beyond measure. What I have learned from them has shaped my understanding of human behavior, of our place in nature."

Probably the most famous animal behaviorist of all time, Jane Goodall has spent most of her life studying wild chimpanzees. She set up her camp in the Gombe Stream Game Preserve in Tanzania in 1960. Over the next 35 years, Dr. Goodall and her team of researchers made important observations of chimpanzee behavior and ecology. One of her most important discoveries was that chimpanzees can make and use tools. Before this discovery, people believed that only humans could make tools.

At first Dr. Goodall had trouble finding wild chimpanzees to study. The animals were very shy and tended to avoid people.

When she did spot a family group, she had to observe them from a distance, with binoculars. After more than a year, the chimps got used to her presence. Then she could observe them up close. In time, Dr. Goodall was able to distinguish individual chimpanzee personalities and gave each chimp a name. She gave chimps within each family group names that started with the same letter.

Today Dr. Goodall travels around the world giving lectures about her experiences at Gombe. She also speaks to school groups about "Roots and Shoots," an environmental education program for young people.

THINK ABOUT IT

1. Why was finding out that chimpanzees can make tools an important discovery?
2. Why do you think it took Dr. Goodall so long to get close to the chimps?

BUILDING A BIRD'S NEST

How do birds construct their nests?

Materials

- large paper plate
- small branches, twigs, leaves
- string or yarn
- purchased feathers (optional)
- mud

Procedure

❶ Build a bird's nest on a plate. Place your branches, twigs, leaves, string, and feathers in a way that makes the nest a sturdy shelter. Use the mud like glue.

❷ Share your building methods with a classmate.

Draw Conclusions

Was it easy or hard to build a sturdy nest? What body parts and behaviors do you think help birds build their nests?

EARTHWORM INSTINCTS

What is an earthworm instinct for keeping safe?

Materials

- black paper
- white paper
- scissors
- tape
- baking pan, 9 in. × 13 in.
- water
- earthworm

Procedure

❶ Cut black paper to fit the bottom of one half of the baking pan. Cut white paper to fit the other half. Line the bottom of the pan with the pieces of paper.

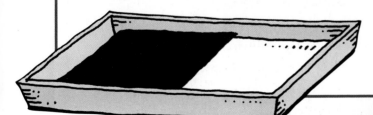

❷ Tape a black paper lid over the black-paper half of the pan to make a "cave."

❸ Moisten the paper in the bottom of the pan. Put the pan in a well-lighted place. Put an earthworm on the white side of the pan.

❹ Observe the earthworm for 5 minutes. Record your observations.

❺ Repeat Steps 3 and 4 two more times.

Draw Conclusions

Why do you think the earthworm moved as it did? How do you think its movement is related to instinct?

Vocabulary Review

Use the terms below to complete the sentences. The page numbers in ( ) tell you where to look in the chapter if you need help.

environment (A40)   **camouflage** (A52)

climate (A41)   **mimicry** (A52)

oxygen (A41)   **instinct** (A56)

shelter (A43)   **migration** (A57)

metamorphosis (A44)   **hibernation** (A59)

adaptation (A48)

1. The body changes that a butterfly goes through as it grows from an egg into an adult are called ____.

2. An adaptation in which an animal looks like another animal is ____.

3. A place such as a burrow where an animal can protect itself is a ____.

4. A body part or behavior that enables an animal to meet its needs is called an ____.

5. The average temperature and rainfall of an area over a long time make up its ____.

6. ____ enables an animal to blend in with its surroundings.

7. A period when an animal goes into a long, deep sleep is called ____.

8. A behavior such as migration that an animal does not have to learn is an ____.

9. The movement of a group of one type of animal from one region to another is ____.

10. Everything that surrounds and affects an animal is its ____.

11. Some animals meet their need for ____ by breathing.

Connect Concepts

Use the Word Bank to complete the graphic organizer below.

camouflage
food
instincts
learned
needs
oxygen
shelter
water

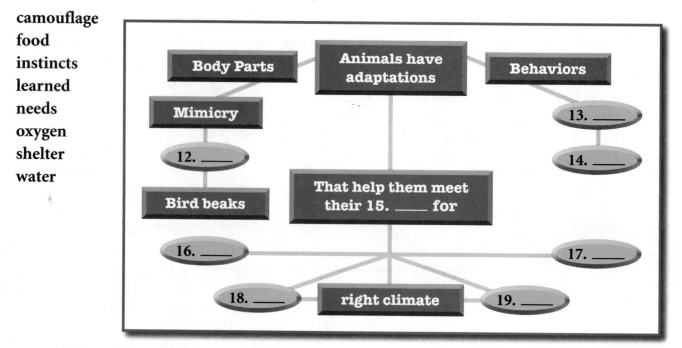

Body Parts

Animals have adaptations

Behaviors

Mimicry

13. ____

12. ____

14. ____

Bird beaks

That help them meet their 15. ____ for

16. ____

17. ____

18. ____

right climate

19. ____

Check Understanding

Write the letter of the best choice.

20. When a winter storm is coming, animals often look for —
    A drinking water
    B a partner
    C shelter
    D an open area

21. A bird's hollow bones help the bird _____ more easily.
    F fly   H hop
    G heal   J eat

22. When preparing to hibernate, animals must —
    A grow a thinner coat
    B lose weight
    C eat extra food
    D breathe faster

Use the photos below to answer Questions 23–24.

23. What process is shown here?

24. Explain the changes going on.

Critical Thinking

25. Rabbits have large ears. Infer how this adaptation helps rabbits meet their needs.

26. Because humans can think, they can adapt to new environments by making things or changing behaviors. Describe how your life would change if you moved to a place where the climate was very different from where you live now.

Process Skills Review

27. How did you use your observations of the mealworms in Lesson 1 to **infer** about animals' needs?

28. **Compare** tools and birds' beaks.

29. Which is more useful for **communicating** information about migration routes—a data table or a map? Explain your answer.

Performance Assessment

Animal Plan

Work with a partner. Design and make a model of an animal that has adaptations for living in a desert. Explain how these adaptations would help the animal meet its needs.

Plant Growth and Adaptations

Vocabulary Preview

carbon dioxide
nutrient
photosynthesis
dormancy
transpiration
taproot
fibrous root
germinate
stamen
pistil
pollination
spore
tuber

If you went into your school-yard, how many different plants could you find? Even if your schoolyard is paved, there are probably plants growing in the cracks in the cement or along the edges of the yard. There are many different kinds of plants. But all plants need the same basic things to live and grow.

Fast Fact

Some living things work together. Ants defend the bullhorn acacia from other insects, mammals, and even other plants. In return, the plant provides food for the ants!

Some of the oldest known living things are trees. Plants that live for a long time have adaptations that help protect them from dangers in the environment. The thick, spongy bark of the giant sequoia protects it from being damaged by insects. The insects eat the bark instead of the inner wood.

How Long Some Plants Live

Plant	Oldest Individual Known
Bristlecone pine	5,000 years
Giant sequoia	2,500 years
Saguaro cactus	200 years

Fast **Fact**

The dodder doesn't make its own food, but scientists still classify it as a plant because it produces flowers and seeds. The dodder meets its needs by getting food, water, and nutrients from other plants.

LESSON 1

What Do Plants Need to Live?

In this lesson, you can . . .

INVESTIGATE the effect of light on plants.

LEARN ABOUT what plants need to live.

LINK to math, writing, social studies, and technology.

How Light Affects Plants

Activity Purpose Did you know that as plants make food for themselves, they also make the oxygen that keeps you alive? In this investigation, you will **control variables** to see how sunlight affects this process.

Materials

- 2 large plastic containers
- water
- 2 pieces of elodea
- 2 clear funnels
- 2 test tubes
- sunlight or desk lamp

Activity Procedure

1 Fill one container about $\frac{2}{3}$ full of water. Place one piece of elodea in the water.

2 Turn a funnel wide side down, and place it in the water over the elodea. There should be enough water in the container so that the small end of the funnel is just below the water. (Picture A)

◀ All plants need water. This cactus has adaptations that allow it to live in areas that have little water.

Picture A

Picture B

3 Fill a test tube with water. Cover the end with your thumb and turn the tube upside down. Place the test tube over the end of the funnel. Allow as little water as possible to escape from the tube. (Picture B)

4 Repeat Steps 1–3 using the second container, funnel, piece of elodea, and test tube.

5 Set one container of elodea in sunlight or under a desk lamp. Set the other in a dark place such as a closet.

6 After several hours, **observe** the contents of each container.

Draw Conclusions

1. **Compare** the two test tubes. What do you **observe**?

2. One test tube is now filled partly with a gas. What can you **infer** about where the gas came from?

3. **Scientists at Work** Scientists **control variables** to learn what effect each condition has on the outcome of an experiment. What one variable did you change in this investigation? Which variables were the same in both containers?

Investigate Further How fast can a plant make oxygen? Repeat the procedure for the plant placed in light, but use a graduate instead of a test tube. **Measure** the amount of oxygen in the graduate every 15 minutes for 2 hours. **Record** your findings. Make a line graph to show how fast the plant produced oxygen.

Process Skill Tip

A variable is a condition that can be changed. When you **control variables** in an experiment, you change only one condition. You keep all other conditions the same.

Life Support for Plants

Basic Needs

Plants are living things. They have many of the same needs as animals. They use energy from food to grow. They use gases from the air. They need water and the right climate. But there is one big difference between plants and animals—plants can make their own food.

To live, a plant needs four things from its environment—air, nutrients, water, and light. Air contains the carbon dioxide a plant needs. **Carbon dioxide** (KAR•buhn dy•AHKS•yd) is a gas breathed out by animals. There is plenty of this gas in the air. Soil provides most plants with needed nutrients. **Nutrients** (NOO•tree•uhnts) are substances, such as minerals, that all living things need to grow. A plant gets water from rain. Some of the water is taken in by the plant's leaves, but most of it is taken in by roots. Though some plants do well in shade, no plant can live in total darkness.

In the investigation, you saw that light affects how a plant gives off oxygen. Oxygen is given off as plants make food. Light provides the energy for the food-making process.

✔ **What four things do plants need to live?**

FIND OUT

- **four basic needs of plants**

- **how plants make food**

VOCABULARY

carbon dioxide
nutrient
photosynthesis

▼ These flowers are healthy. They are growing in clean air. They also are receiving plenty of water, nutrients from the soil, and sunlight.

Making Food

A plant makes its own food by a process that is called **photosynthesis** (foht•oh•SIN•thuh•sis). *Photo* means "light" and *synthesis* means "putting together." Photosynthesis takes place in a plant's leaves. Light is trapped by chlorophyll, the material that makes a leaf green. The energy from the light starts the food-making process. Without light, plants could not make the food they need to live and grow.

Carbon dioxide and water are the two main materials that the plant uses to make food. The food made is sugar. The leaves take in carbon dioxide, and the roots take in water. The water travels through tubes in the stem to the leaves. The leaves then use the energy from light to make sugar from the carbon dioxide and water. Oxygen is a waste product of photosynthesis. It is given off by the leaves.

✔ **What does a plant need to carry out photosynthesis?**

Photosynthesis

This is a close-up view of the bottom of a leaf. Tiny holes like this take in carbon dioxide and give off oxygen and water vapor. ▼

The roots take in water from the soil, and tubes in the stem carry water to the leaves.

Chlorophyll in leaves traps the energy from light. The energy helps the plant use carbon dioxide and water to make sugar as food.

Tubes in leaves get water from the roots. Different tubes carry food to the rest of the plant.

The leaves take in carbon dioxide gas from the air.

The leaves give off oxygen and water vapor.

Photo

Diagram

The waterlily's leaves float on the water's surface to take in sunlight. Its roots are in the soil at the bottom of the pond. ▶

Adaptations for Different Environments

Plants live all over Earth's surface. Like animals, plants have adaptations that help them live in different climates and conditions.

Most of the plants that you've seen live on land. Some plants, however, have adaptations that allow them to live in water. For example, waterlilies live in some ponds and lakes. They grow from soil below the water. Sunlight filters through the water to reach the young waterlily. The plant's stems grow toward the surface, taking along the leaves, which are rolled up like tubes. At the surface

◀ Vines can cling to almost anything to reach sunlight.

the leaves unroll to form flat pads. They are then ready to take in sunlight and carbon dioxide. The roots take in water and nutrients from the muddy bottom. The long stems move the materials back and forth between the leaves and the roots. In this way, all the waterlily's needs are met.

Vines have a different type of stem adaptation that helps them meet their needs. Vines often grow on forest floors, where the light is dim. To reach sunlight, vines have long stems with adaptations for clinging to other objects for support. These adaptations help vines climb fences, walls, rocks, and even other plants.

Cacti and other desert plants have adaptations for living with very little water. In some deserts, it may be months or even years between rain showers. Cacti can survive these dry spells because they have thick stems that store water. The plant uses this water when no groundwater is available. When it finally does rain, the roots of the cactus plant can collect water quickly because they grow just below the surface of the ground.

✔ **How do stems that are adapted for climbing help vines meet their needs?**

▲ This barrel cactus has a
thick stem that stores water.

Summary

Plants need air, nutrients, water, and light to live. Their leaves make food through photosynthesis. Plants have adaptations to help them meet their needs in different settings.

Review

1. What are the four things that plants need to live?

2. What provides the energy for photosynthesis to take place?

3. What adaptations do cacti have for life in the desert?

4. **Critical Thinking** What would happen if there were no carbon dioxide in the air?

5. **Test Prep** Which of the following provides most plants with nutrients?

   A air

   B water

   C soil

   D sunlight

LINKS

MATH LINK

Make Bar Graphs Keep track of the heights of two plants that are given different amounts of water for several weeks. Use *Graph Links* or another computer graphing program to make a bar graph to show how water amounts affected the plants.

WRITING LINK

Informative Writing—Compare and Contrast For a younger child, compare ways that plants live in the wild and in homes. Describe how plants in both places meet their needs. In what ways do they meet their needs differently?

SOCIAL STUDIES LINK

History A plant conservatory (kuhn•SER•vuh•tawr•ee) is a building where unusual plants are grown and displayed. Use library reference materials to find out more about conservatories. Choose a conservatory, and write a short report about when and why it was built. Include in your report pictures of plants found in the conservatory.

TECHNOLOGY LINK

Learn more about growing conditions for plants by viewing *Bloomin' Business* on the **Harcourt Science Newsroom Video.**

How Do Leaves, Stems, and Roots Help Plants Live?

In this lesson, you can . . .

INVESTIGATE how plants "breathe."

LEARN ABOUT different parts of plants.

LINK to math, writing, art, and technology.

◄ Wild orchids grow in many parts of the world. Where are the roots, stems, and leaves on this orchid?

INVESTIGATE

How Plants "Breathe"

Activity Purpose It sounds strange to say that plants "breathe." But they do. They need to exchange gases as animals do. In this investigation you will look for evidence that a plant breathes through its leaves.

Materials
- leafy potted plant
- petroleum jelly
- 2 clear plastic bags
- twist ties

Activity Procedure

1. Make a chart like the one below.

2. Put a thin layer of petroleum jelly on both the top and bottom surfaces of a leaf on the plant. (Picture A)

3. Put a plastic bag over the leaf. Gently tie the bag closed. Do this just below the place where the leaf attaches to the stem. (Picture B)

Plant Leaf	Observations
Leaf with petroleum jelly	
Leaf with no petroleum jelly	

Picture A

Picture B

4. Put a plastic bag over a second leaf and seal it. Do not put any petroleum jelly on this leaf.

5. Put the plant in a place that gets plenty of light, and water it normally.

6. After two days, **observe** the two leaves. **Record** your observations on your chart.

Draw Conclusions

1. **Compare** the two plastic bags. What do you **observe**?

2. What can you **infer** from what you **observed** in this investigation?

3. **Scientists at Work** Scientists often **compare** objects or events. Comparing allows the scientists to see the effects of the variables they control. Compare the leaves you used in this investigation. What can you **infer** about the effect of the petroleum jelly?

Investigate Further Find out where gases are exchanged in a leaf. This time, coat the top side of one leaf and the bottom side of another leaf. Tie a plastic bag over each leaf. What do you **observe**? What can you **infer**?

> **Process Skill Tip**
>
> When you **compare** objects or events, you look for ways they are alike. You also look for ways they are different.

The Functions of Plant Parts

FIND OUT

- **how leaves, stems, and roots help plants live**
- **unusual adaptations plants have**

VOCABULARY

dormancy
transpiration
taproot
fibrous root

Leaves

The leaves of different plants can be very different in shape and size. All leaves, however, work to help plants live. There are two main types of leaves—needles and broad leaves. Most conifers, trees such as pine and spruce, and many cacti have needles. Needle-shaped leaves help prevent water loss. Most other plants have broad leaves. Broad leaves are wide and flat. Beech, oak, and maple trees have broad leaves. So do rosebushes and English ivy.

In colder climates, broad-leafed trees shed their leaves each fall. They do this to save energy. Winter days are shorter and colder. There is less daylight for photosynthesis. So, the trees enter a state of **dormancy**, or lower activity, until spring.

You already know that leaves carry on photosynthesis. In the investigation, you saw that moisture forms as a leaf "breathes." The water drops that formed inside the uncoated leaf's bag were caused by transpiration. **Transpiration** (tran•spuh•RAY•shuhn) is the giving off of water by plant parts. As the sun heats a leaf, it causes water to become a gas called water vapor. The waxy surface of most leaves keeps water from escaping, but water vapor can escape from tiny holes in the leaves. These are the same holes where gases are exchanged during breathing.

✔ **What is transpiration?**

— Lemon

— Eastern hemlock

— White mulberry

◄ The leaves of lemon and white mulberry trees are broad. Eastern hemlock trees have leaves shaped like flat needles.

Stems

Stems support plants and give them shape. They also contain tubes that carry water and minerals from the roots and food from the leaves to all parts of the plant. Stems also store water and food.

Many plant stems, such as those of garden flowers, are soft and flexible, or easy to bend. They have a thin, waxy covering that protects them. Most plants with this kind of stem are small and live for only one growing season. When the next season starts, they must grow again from seeds or from the plant's roots.

Other plants have stiff, woody stems. Woody stems are hard and thick. They have a layer of bark that protects them. Each year, woody stems grow thicker and sometimes taller. Plants with these tough stems can live many years. Trees and shrubs have woody stems.

✓ **Which type of plant usually grows for only one season?**

▲ This mountain laurel has a woody stem.

◄ This blue phlox has a flexible stem.

▲ A long, thick taproot firmly holds a dandelion in the ground. The taproot reaches deep into the ground.

Shallow-growing fibrous roots hold this marigold in the soil. ►

Roots

Roots form the third main part of vascular (VAS•kyuh•ler) plants—plants that have tubes. Most roots are underground and hold plants in the soil. Roots also take in water and nutrients that plants need for photosynthesis. Some roots store food made by leaves.

Roots have adaptations to help plants meet their needs. Some plants have taproots. A **taproot** is one main root that grows deep into the soil. If you have ever tried to pull up a dandelion, you know how well taproots hold plants in place.

Smaller roots branch off from the taproot. Tiny root hairs that take in water and nutrients grow from the taproot.

A plant with **fibrous** (FY•bruhs) **roots** has many roots of the same size. Fibrous roots grow long but not deep. The fibrous roots also have root hairs that take in water and nutrients from the soil. Grass has fibrous roots.

✓ **Cacti have roots that are close to the surface of the soil. Which type of roots are they?**

Unusual Adaptations

You may have read science-fiction stories about human-eating plants. Plants don't really eat humans, but some of them do eat meat. Some plants that grow in poor soils have leaf adaptations that let them trap and eat insects. Such plants still make their own food. Insects just provide needed nutrients that may be missing in the soil.

THE INSIDE STORY

The Venus' Flytrap

Each living thing can sense and respond to some stimulus (STIM•yoo•luhs), or condition, in its environment. For example, when you sense cold, you put on a jacket. The Venus' flytrap is an unusual plant because it has a quick response to a certain stimulus.

1. An insect sees the leaf of a Venus' flytrap as a safe place to land and a possible source of food.

2. When it lands, the insect touches special hairs. Touching any two hairs is the trigger stimulus. The plant responds by snapping the leaf shut. The points on the edges of the leaf halves lace together, trapping the insect inside.

3. Once the leaf is fully closed, digestive juices dissolve the soft parts of the insect. It may take weeks for the plant to fully digest the insect. When the leaf reopens, the insect's skeleton and wings are blown away by the wind. The leaf is then ready for another insect.

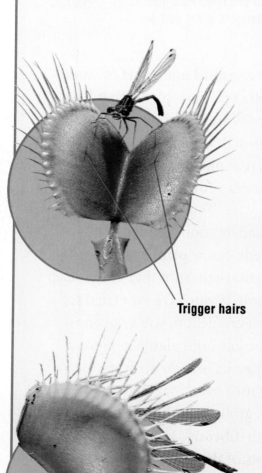

Trigger hairs

Some meat-eating plants have a smell that attracts their prey. Insects that land on them become trapped by a sticky surface or fall into a pool of liquid and drown. Then the plant's digestive juices dissolve the insect. Sundews and cobra lilies catch their prey in these ways. Other meat-eating plants have active traps with parts that move. The pictures on the facing page show how a Venus' flytrap works.

✔ **How do adaptations for trapping insects help some plants meet their needs?**

Summary

Plants have leaf, stem, and root adaptations that help them meet their needs. Some plants have parts that trap and digest insects to get needed nutrients.

Review

1. What are the two types of leaves? What is one unusual leaf adaptation?

2. What is the main difference between the two types of stems?

3. Which parts of roots take in nutrients for a plant?

4. **Critical Thinking** Moisture from leaves is produced by transpiration. Why can you use the presence of moisture as evidence that a plant is exchanging gases, or "breathing"?

5. **Test Prep** An insect is to a meat-eating plant as a _____ is to a human.

   A helper
   B drink of water
   C candy bar
   D vitamin pill

LINKS

MATH LINK

Classify Shapes Collect leaves of different shapes and sizes. Make a Venn diagram by overlapping two circles made of yarn. Place leaves in your diagram by ways they are alike and ways they are different.

WRITING LINK

Narrative Writing—Story Science-fiction writers often take an ordinary fact of nature and exaggerate it. Making a Venus' flytrap into a human-eating plant is an example. Think of a plant adaptation that interests you. Exaggerate the facts, and write a short story for a classmate.

ART LINK

Symmetry Get a broad leaf from a tree. Cut the leaf in half along the large vein that runs down the middle. Stand a mirror on edge along the cut side of a leaf half. When you look in the mirror, does the leaf appear whole? Tape your leaf part down on white paper. Carefully draw an identical but opposite side to make the leaf look whole.

GO ONLINE TECHNOLOGY LINK

Learn more about garden plants from all over the world by visiting the National Museum of Natural History Internet site. **www.si.edu/harcourt/science**

 Smithsonian Institution®

LESSON 3

How Do Plants Reproduce?

In this lesson, you can . . .

INVESTIGATE how plants grow from seeds.

LEARN ABOUT plant life cycles.

LINK to math, writing, social studies, and technology.

INVESTIGATE

Seedling Growth

Activity Purpose It's not often that you can see a seed start to grow into a plant. This process is usually hidden by soil until the tiny stem grows above the ground. In this investigation, you will **observe, measure,** and **compare** the growth of two types of seeds.

Materials

- 2 paper towels
- small, clear jar or cup
- alfalfa seed
- bean seed
- water
- hand lens
- yarn
- ruler

Activity Procedure

1. Fold a paper towel, and place it around the inside of the jar.

2. Make the second paper towel into a ball, and place it inside the jar to fill the space.

3. Place the alfalfa seed about 3 cm from the top of the jar, between the paper-towel lining and the jar's side. You should be able to see the seed through the jar.

4. Place the bean seed in a similar position on the other side of the jar. (Picture A)

5. Pour water into the jar to soak the towels completely.

6. Set the jar in a warm place, and leave it there for five days. Be sure to keep the paper towels moist.

◀ New raspberry bushes can grow from seeds. The seeds are inside the berries.

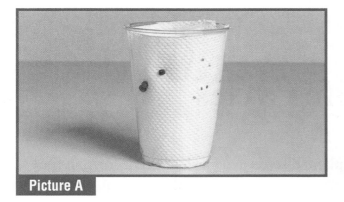

Picture A

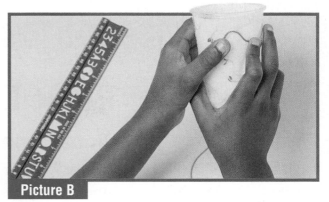

Picture B

Seed Growth

	Alfalfa		Bean	
	Size	Other Observations	Size	Other Observations
Day 1				
Day 2				

7 Make a chart like the one above.

8 Use the hand lens to **observe** the seeds daily for five days. **Measure** the growth of the roots and shoots with the yarn. Use the ruler to measure the yarn. **Record** your observations on your chart. (Picture B)

Draw Conclusions

1. What plant parts grew from each seed?

2. **Compare** the growth of the roots and shoots from the two seeds. Did they grow to be the same size? Did they grow at the same rate?

3. **Scientists at Work** Scientists take a lot of care to **measure** objects the same way each time. Think about how you measured the plants. How do you know your measurements were accurate?

Investigate Further The bean and alfalfa seedlings will continue to grow after the first five days. Plant each of the seedlings in soil. Then **plan and conduct an experiment** to find out whether alfalfa or beans grow better in dry conditions. You will probably need to use three or more seedlings of each type.

Process Skill Tip

One way to compare objects accurately is to **measure** them. An instrument such as a ruler or a balance is used to measure. A scientist often repeats measurements to make sure that they are as accurate as possible.

A83

Plant Life Cycles

Plants from Seeds

FIND OUT

- ways plants reproduce
- how seeds are spread

VOCABULARY

germinate
stamen
pistil
pollination
spore
tuber

Have you ever planted seeds in a garden? Seeds form in the cones of conifers. Seeds also form in the flowers of flowering plants. When a flower dries up and falls away, fruit forms around the young seeds. The fruit protects the seeds. Inside each seed is a tiny plant and the food it needs to start growing.

Seeds are the first part in a flowering plant's life cycle. To begin to grow, seeds need warmth, water, and air. Most seeds don't get what they need, so they don't grow. However, when a seed has its needs met, it **germinates** (JER•muh•nayts), or sprouts. Seedlings that sprout in soil may keep growing. They grow to become adult, or mature, plants. The mature plants form flowers.

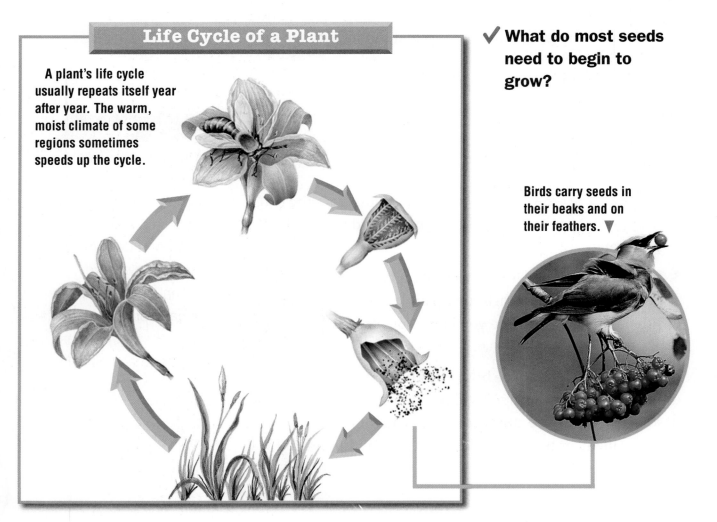

Life Cycle of a Plant

A plant's life cycle usually repeats itself year after year. The warm, moist climate of some regions sometimes speeds up the cycle.

✓ **What do most seeds need to begin to grow?**

Birds carry seeds in their beaks and on their feathers. ▼

Flower Parts and Seeds

Flowers have parts that work together to make seeds. The **stamen** (STAY•muhn) makes pollen, a kind of powder. The top of the **pistil** (PIHS•tuhl) collects pollen. The bottom of the pistil is the ovary where seeds form. An apple core is an apple tree ovary.

Seeds form after a flower is pollinated. **Pollination** (pahl•uh•NAY•shuhn) happens when pollen is carried from a stamen to a pistil by wind or animals. For example, bees, birds, and bats feed on nectar, a sweet liquid in some flowers. Pollen sticks to the animals' bodies. When they leave or visit another flower, the pollen is transfered to the pistil.

✔ **Where do seeds form in a flower?**

STAMEN
stigma
stile
ovary
PISTIL
sepal
ovule

Plants from Spores

Not all plants have flowers that form fruits and seeds. Some plants grow from spores. **Spores** (SPOHRZ) are tiny—in fact, most spores are made of only one cell and can be seen only with a microscope.

Spores are like seeds in some ways. Like seeds, spores contain food. Some spores have thick walls that allow them to stay in-active for months. They can be carried by wind, water, and animals.

Spores germinate if they land where conditions are good. But the tiny plants that begin to grow are not complete. Adult plants form only after two different parts of these tiny plants join. Mature spore-making plants grow from the joined parts.

✔ **How are spores spread?**

Ferns reproduce by tiny spores. The yellow spots on the back of this fern leaf are capsules where spores form. ▶

New Plants from Old

Growing plants from seeds and spores can take a long time. Some plants have adaptations that let them make new plants in other ways.

A spider plant sends out buds on a type of stem called a runner. Buds are immature, or young, plant shoots. When these buds touch the ground, they form roots and begin to grow.

Tulips grow from bulbs. A bulb is a kind of bud that grows underground. Bulbs can be split into pieces. Each piece can grow into a new plant. You may have helped someone plant bulbs in the fall to have flowers the next spring.

Some plants grow from a piece of stem put in water. Many people who grow plants indoors start new ones by cutting off a branch of the stem. Then they trim off lower leaves and put that piece in water. New roots grow from it. The new stem with roots is planted in soil.

People have come up with ways to join two or more different plants to make a new plant. The process is called *grafting*. To graft plants, people attach a cut stem of one plant to a slice in the stem of another plant. The joined stem uses the roots of the other plant to get water and nutrients.

Grafting is used to make a new plant with the good characteristics of each plant. For example, branches of different apple trees can be joined to the trunk of another tree. The tree then grows apples that may have more desirable flavors and sizes.

The spider plant sends out runners with buds attached. ▼

Three different branches were grafted to one trunk. That is why this small tree has three different colors of flowers. ▶

Potato tubers develop "eyes," each of which can make a new plant. ▶

Potatoes are **tubers** (TOO•berz), or swollen underground stems. Tubers are often dug up to eat. They also can be cut into pieces and planted. Each piece of a potato that has a bud, or "eye," can make a new plant.

✔ **What process ends with a "new and improved" plant?**

Summary

Plants reproduce by seeds and spores. A flower begins to form seeds when pollen from a stamen is collected by a pistil. Many plants can also grow from buds, bulbs, tubers, and stem pieces.

Review

1. What must both seeds and spores do before they begin to grow in soil?

2. How do animals help pollinate plants?

3. Spider plants, tulips, and potatoes can grow from seeds. How are their other ways of reproducing alike?

4. **Critical Thinking** If you had a leafy plant with damaged roots, how might you start a new plant?

5. **Test Prep** Which part of a flowering plant protects seeds?

 A flowers

 B fruit

 C capsules

 D birds

LINKS

MATH LINK

Use Fractions Wrap 10 bean seeds and 10 corn seeds in a moist paper towel. Seal them in a plastic bag for a week. What fraction of each seed group sprouts? Why might this information be important to a gardener?

WRITING LINK

Expressive Writing—Poem Haiku is a form of Japanese poetry. Haiku are often written about a season, such as fall. Write a haiku for a family member about what plants are like during your favorite season.

SOCIAL STUDIES LINK

Grains Around the World All grains are seeds. Many grains are important food sources. Find out which grains are eaten in different parts of the world. Use a world map to show which grains are grown in different areas of the world.

TECHNOLOGY LINK

Learn more about growing plants under different conditions—on a computer screen! Try *Do You Have a Green Thumb?* on **Harcourt Science Explorations CD-ROM.**

SUPER-VEGGIES

Researchers have found ways to make eating your vegetables more appealing.

BetaSweet carrots

Why Improve Vegetables?

"No dessert until you've finished your vegetables!" If you've ever heard those words, at last there's good news for you! Researchers at Texas A&M University are working on superveggies. These vegetables are better-tasting than many well-known vegetables. They also have more of some nutrients. So people who eat only a few vegetables will still get plenty of nutrients. Superveggies also may prevent or fight diseases such as cancer and heart disease. Many different vegetables are being tested. They include onions, potatoes, peppers, corn, broccoli, cabbage, tomatoes, leeks, and Brussels sprouts.

A Sweet Success

A big success story is the BetaSweet carrot. It is sweeter and crisper than regular carrots are, and its color is maroon! It has extra beta carotene (BAYT•uh KAIR•uh•teen), which your body changes to vitamin A. Eating just one-third of a BetaSweet carrot would meet your daily need for beta carotene.

Dr. Leonard M. Pike is the scientist who is heading research at the Vegetable Improvement Center at Texas A&M. He first got the idea for a maroon carrot in 1989. He saw carrots grown from Brazilian seeds. These carrots had maroon patches mixed in with the carrots' normal orange color. He began trying to design a carrot that had more flavor and nutrition.

New Veggies on the Horizon

Another new veggie to watch for is a cucumber that's orange inside! This special cucumber tastes like other cucumbers. But like BetaSweets, it also gives you a higher level of vitamin A.

How would you like a rose-colored onion with a mild flavor? These onions are meant to be eaten raw. Cooking destroys some of the important nutrients that make them look and taste different.

Researchers are also working on types of peppers that will have more vitamin C than an orange. Specially marked bell peppers and chili peppers may be in grocery stores soon. So be sure to "eat your superveggies"!

THINK ABOUT IT

1. If you could ask scientists to improve the nutrition, flavor, or color of certain fruits or vegetables, which ones would you choose?

2. One third of a BetaSweet carrot gives you all of one nutrient you need for a day. In the future, people might need less of all foods to get all needed nutrients. Do you think people will eat less food?

CAREERS
GENETIC ENGINEER

What They Do A genetic engineer in agriculture works with plants to make them stronger or more healthful. For example, a genetic engineer might find a gene that helps a plant live for a while without water. That gene might be put into other plants to make them stronger, too. Genetic engineers also work with animals.

Education and Training

People who want to be genetic engineers study biology in college. They must learn about cell division and DNA. Most get advanced college degrees in genetics and plant or animal sciences.

WEB LINK
For Science and Technology updates, visit the Harcourt Internet site.
www.harcourtschool.com

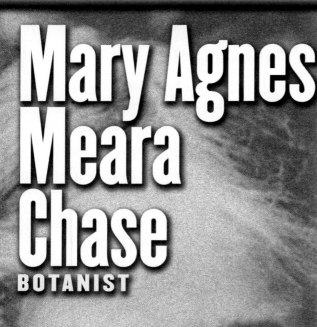

Mary Agnes Meara Chase

BOTANIST

"If it were not for grasses, the world would never have been civilized."

MEXICO

PUERTO RICO

VENEZUELA

Agnes Chase devoted her life to the study of grasses. She worked as a botanist (BAH•tuhn•ist), a scientist who studies plants, for the United States Department of Agriculture (USDA). She collected and described over 10,000 species of grasses. Early in her career, Chase made sketches of plants. She also helped write a book called *The Manual of Grasses.*

To a botanist, grasses include more than what grows in a front yard or at a park. Grasses also include grains such as rice, wheat, oats, rye, hay, and corn. Sorghum, bamboo, and sugar cane are also grasses. All these grasses are food for animals and for people. They provide building material and sugar. They also build up the land and prevent soil erosion. At the USDA, Chase helped scientists experiment with crops. The scientists wanted to develop nutritious plants that also resisted disease.

Chase often traveled to collect plants. She visited Europe twice and traveled to Mexico and Puerto Rico to study grasses and get samples. After she retired, Chase went to Venezuela because its government asked for her help in collecting and studying grasses. While there, she encouraged students from South America to come to the United States to study. Some of the students who did come lived at her home in Washington, D.C.

Chase wrote over 70 different books and magazine articles. She kept on working, without pay, after she retired. She was in charge of the National Herbarium at the Smithsonian Institution. She eventually donated her personal collection to the Smithsonian Institution.

THINK ABOUT IT

1. What grasses do you eat regularly?
2. What features of grasses make them useful to people?

PLANT COLORS

What dyes do plants contain?

Materials

- dry yellow onion skins
- dry red onion skins
- pot
- water
- hot plate
- white cotton cloth
- string
- oven mitt

Procedure

1. An adult will boil each color of onion skins in water for about 20 minutes.

2. Tightly tie the cotton cloth into bunches with the string. Leave a length of string that you can use to hold the cloth.

3. Using an oven mitt, hold the string and put the cloth into one of the pots of hot onion water for about 5 minutes. Let the cloth cool. Then unwrap it and let it dry.

Draw Conclusions

What color did the cloth turn? Compare your cloth to one that was dyed with different colored onion skins. Why are the cloths different?

IDENTIFYING TREES

How can you identify trees?

Materials

- 3 zip-top bags, each containing leaves, bark, and seeds from a different type of tree
- paper
- colored pencils

Procedure

1. Observe the contents of each plastic bag.

2. For each bag, make a page that someone else could use to identify the tree without seeing the bag. Include any sketches or descriptions you think are important.

Draw Conclusions

What plant parts are in the bags? What other tree parts could be used to identify a tree? Compare your pages to the key or guidebook your teacher gives you. Try to name each tree.

Vocabulary Review

Use the terms below to complete the sentences. The page numbers in ( ) tell you where to look in the chapter if you need help.

carbon dioxide (A72)   **germinate** (A84)

nutrient (A72)   **stamen** (A85)

photosynthesis (A73)   **pistil** (A85)

dormancy (A78)   **pollination** (A85)

transpiration (A78)   **spores** (A85)

taproot (A79)   **tuber** (A87)

fibrous roots (A79)

1. Water loss from a plant due to evaporation is _____.

2. Carrots have a _____, a single main root that grows deep into the soil.

3. *Sprout* is another word for _____.

4. Animals breathe out a gas called _____.

5. A substance a plant needs in order to grow is a _____.

6. The way a plant makes food is _____.

7. A root system that has many roots of the same size is made up of _____.

8. Potatoes have a swollen underground stem called a _____.

9. Tiny reproductive cells of ferns are _____.

10. The part of a flower where seeds form is the _____.

11. Pollen is made by the _____ of a flower.

12. When broad-leafed trees shed all their leaves in the fall, they are entering a period of _____.

13. The movement of pollen to the pistil of a flower is called _____.

Connect Concepts

Use the terms in the Word Bank to complete the concept map.

carbon dioxide   **fibrous roots**

nutrients   **photosynthesis**

taproots

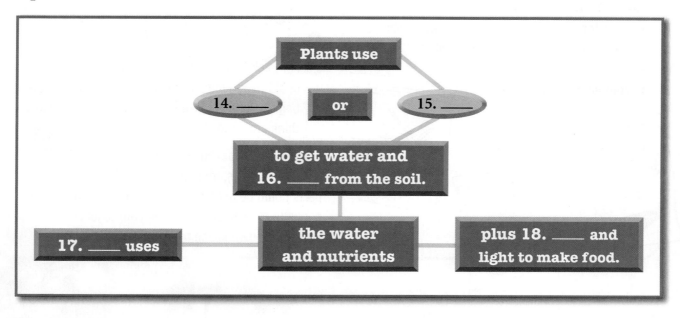

Plants use

14. _____   or   15. _____

to get water and 16. _____ from the soil.

17. _____ uses   the water and nutrients   plus 18. _____ and light to make food.

Check Understanding

Write the letter of the best choice.

19. A plant with a thick stem for storing water would probably grow in the —
    A ocean   C forest
    B mountains   D desert

20. Transpiration by plants could help form —
    F carbon dioxide
    G symmetry
    H rain clouds
    J oxygen

21. A seed eaten by a bird —
    A cannot grow
    B will probably make the bird sick
    C may become several seeds
    D may germinate far from where it was eaten

22. Which process can end with a "new and improved" plant?
    F grafting
    G cutting up tubers
    H placing cuttings in water
    J splitting apart bulbs

23. Which of the following terms does **NOT** belong with the others?
    A seed   C spore
    B flower   D fruit

Critical Thinking

24. Why do you think photosynthesis is one of the most important processes on Earth?

25. The fact that plants have many ways to spread seeds can cause problems for gardeners. Why is this?

Process Skills Review

26. You want to find out if a certain plant grows best in a hot, warm, or cool climate. What **variables** should you **control**? What variable will you **test**?

27. You want to buy a new pair of shoes. What are three shoe features you could **compare**?

28. You need to **measure** how fast a friend can run 25 meters. What two measuring instruments would you need?

Performance Assessment

Arctic Plant

The Arctic is very cold. The water and soil there are frozen most of the year, and the growing season is very short. Design and draw a plant that could live in the Arctic. Label the adaptations your plant has that help it live in this harsh climate. How would it reproduce?

Human Body Systems

Your body is made up of many different parts that work together. Think about all the parts you are using right now. Your eyes are sending messages to your brain. Your lungs are moving gases, your heart is pumping blood, and your muscles are keeping you sitting straight in your chair. You may also be digesting your breakfast or lunch! You probably didn't realize you were so busy!

Fast Fact

You don't have the same body you had a few weeks ago. Each day, your body replaces millions of cells that have worn out. Some cells are replaced every couple of days. Other cells must last your entire lifetime.

When Cells Are Replaced	
Stomach cells	2–3 days
Skin cells	19–34 days
Red blood cells	120 days
Brain cells	Never

These red blood cells are shown magnified about 25,000 times.

How Do the Skeletal and Muscular Systems Work?

In this lesson, you can . . .

INVESTIGATE types of muscle tissue.

LEARN ABOUT the skeletal and muscular systems.

LINK to math, writing, technology, and other areas.

INVESTIGATE

Muscle Tissues

Activity Purpose The muscles you probably know most about are the ones you use to play or do work. There are also muscle types that you may not know you use, such as those in the digestive system and the heart. In this investigation you will **observe** and **compare** three types of muscles.

Materials

- Microslide Viewer
- Slide A—skeletal muscle tissue
- Slide B—smooth muscle tissue
- Slide C—heart muscle tissue

Skeletal muscle

▲ Slide A

Smooth muscle

▲ Slide B

◀ This boy uses the muscles in his leg to kick the soccer ball.

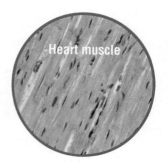

Heart muscle

▲ Slide C

Activity Procedure

Type of Muscle	Observations	Ways Like Other Types of Muscle	Ways Different from Other Types of Muscle
Slide A			
Slide B			
Slide C			

 Make a chart like the one shown.

2 Use the Microslide Viewer to carefully **observe** the muscle tissue on microslide 1 or the picture of Slide A on page A96. (Picture A)

3 Take notes to describe the way the tissue looks. What shapes do you see? Are there any colors or patterns?

4 **Record** your observations on your chart as notes or sketches.

5 Repeat Steps 2–4 for microslides 2 and 3, or Slides B and C on page A96.

Picture A

Draw Conclusions

1. Describe each type of muscle tissue.

2. How do the tissues look the same? How do they look different?

3. **Scientists at Work** Many scientists use microscopes in their work. What does a microscope do that makes it possible to **observe** and **compare** muscle tissues?

Investigate Further If you have access to a microscope, use one to **observe** prepared slides of different kinds of tissue. See page R3 for help in using a microscope. Cells from different kinds of tissue in your body look different. Find pictures of other kinds of tissue, such as nerve tissue, bone tissue, and blood tissue. **Compare** these tissues to the muscle tissues you looked at.

Process Skill Tip

Observing and comparing are two skills you often use together. To **observe**, you may need to use a tool, such as a microscope. Comparing uses information gained from observations. When you **compare**, you look for ways things are alike and ways things are different.

The Skeletal and Muscular Systems

Structures of the Body

The body is like a wonderful machine that needs very little help to keep running smoothly. When it does go wrong, it often can repair itself. The more the body is used, the stronger it gets. Have you ever wondered how this "machine" is put together?

Your body is made up of the basic building blocks of life—cells. There are many types of cells, including bone cells, muscle cells, blood cells, and nerve cells. Every cell in your body has a specific job.

Cells of the same type work together to form **tissue**. Bone cells make up bone tissue. Muscle cells make up muscle tissue.

Tissues of different kinds work together in **organs**. Organs are body parts that do particular jobs. Bone tissue and other tissues form organs called bones. Muscle tissue and other tissues form organs called muscles.

Groups of organs that work together form *systems*. Your body has many systems. Bones working together make up the skeletal system. Muscles working together make up the muscular system.

✔ **What are organs made up of?**

FIND OUT

- the basic parts that make up the whole body
- how the skeletal and muscular systems work

VOCABULARY

tissue

organ

cardiac muscle

smooth muscle

striated muscle

Bone cells form bone tissue. ▼

Bone cells

Bone tissues form bones, one of the organs in the body. ▶

Tissue

Bone

Bones form the skeletal system, or the skeleton. Each body system is built in a similar way—cells, tissues, organs, systems. ▼

The Muscular System

Your body has three types of muscles—skeletal muscles, cardiac muscles, and smooth muscles. All these muscles move parts of your body. They do this by becoming shorter and then by getting longer.

Skeletal muscles move your head, arms, legs, fingers, and toes. Skeletal muscles can't push. They can only pull. For this reason, skeletal muscles must work in pairs to move bones back and forth. You can control your skeletal muscles.

✔ **Which type of muscles can you control by thinking?**

Upper arm—biceps

Triceps

The bones in the hands and feet are short.

Lower arm—radius and ulna

Upper arm—humerus

Collarbone

Breastbone

Ribs

Backbone—spinal column

Pelvis

Shoulder—deltoid

Inside your ribcage is your heart. It is made of cardiac muscle. This type of muscle works automatically—without your thinking about it.

Smooth muscle helps organs inside your body do their jobs. Like cardiac muscles, they work automatically.

The Skeletal System

Your skeleton is made up of many bones. They support your body and give it shape. They also help you move and protect the organs inside your body.

Your bones meet at joints. Some joints open and close as the hinge of a door does. Your knees work this way. Other joints let a bone move in many directions. Your shoulder works this way.

✔ **What do bones do for organs inside your body?**

Upper leg—quadriceps

Hamstring

Upper leg—femur

Lower leg—calf muscle

Lower leg—tibia and fibula

A Closer Look at Muscles

As you saw in the investigation, skeletal muscles have light and dark stripes. They are called **striated** (STRY•ayt•uhd) **muscles**. The stripes are patterns made by the working parts of the muscle cells. The fibers in a skeletal muscle can be up to 30 centimeters (12 in.) long. Some muscles have more than 2000 fibers packed tightly together.

Smooth muscle does not have stripes. It is found in the walls of organs such as the stomach, intestines, blood vessels, and bladder. Smooth muscle works by squeezing and relaxing slowly and smoothly. Its fibers are shorter than the fibers in skeletal muscle.

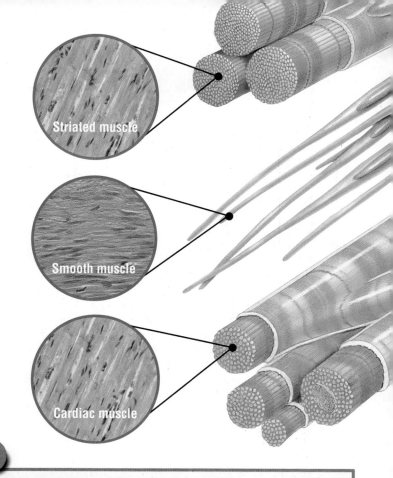

Striated muscle

Smooth muscle

Cardiac muscle

THE INSIDE STORY

Arm Movement

The biceps (BY•seps) and triceps (TRY•seps) muscles work together to move the lower arm. They both attach to the bones of the lower arm on one end and the bones of the upper arm on the other. The biceps is on the front of the arm, and the triceps is on the back.

1 When the biceps becomes shorter, it pulls up on the bones of the lower arm. For the bones to move, the triceps must relax and become longer. As the biceps gets shorter and the triceps gets longer, the arm bends.

2 To straighten the arm, the triceps becomes shorter while the biceps relaxes and becomes longer. This pulls the arm straight.

1 Biceps

Triceps

2

◀ Muscles are made up of muscle fibers bundled together.

Cardiac muscle has stripes, but not as many as skeletal muscle. Cardiac muscle makes up the walls of the heart. Although cardiac muscle squeezes and relaxes without stopping, it never gets tired.

✓ **Which type of muscle doesn't have stripes?**

Summary

The body is made up of basic parts called cells. Cells make up tissues, tissues make up organs, and organs make up body systems. The skeletal and muscular systems work together to help the body move.

Review

1. What are the basic building blocks of life?
2. How do the skeletal and muscular systems work to move the body?
3. Which type of muscle works without ever stopping?
4. **Critical Thinking** Why is it good that people don't have to think about smooth muscles doing their jobs?
5. **Test Prep** _____ move bones in different directions.
   A Muscle pairs
   B Smooth muscles
   C Cardiac muscles
   D Cells

LINKS

MATH LINK

Multiply Whole Numbers Count the number of times your heart beats in one minute. This is your heart rate. Use this number to figure about how many times your heart beats in an hour and in a day.

WRITING LINK

Narrative Writing—Story Suppose you take a long hike. Write a story from the point of view of the muscles you would use. Describe for another classmate what it is like to walk and climb.

LITERATURE LINK

Let's Exercise Exercise is important for muscles and bones. Learn about exercise by reading *Staying Healthy: Let's Exercise* by Alice B. McGinty.

HEALTH LINK

Nutrition Find out what kinds of foods are important for building strong bones and muscles. Which ones would you like to try? Prepare a menu of meals and snacks for a day. Include foods that help build strong bones.

TECHNOLOGY LINK

Learn more about ways to keep your bones healthy by viewing *Bone Health* on the **Harcourt Science Newsroom Video.**

How Do the Respiratory and Circulatory Systems Work?

In this lesson, you can . . .

INVESTIGATE
breathing rates.

LEARN ABOUT
the respiratory and
circulatory systems.

LINK to math,
writing, and
technology.

INVESTIGATE

Breathing Rates

Activity Purpose Your breathing rate when you are active is different from the rate when you are sitting quietly. It may change even as you walk across the classroom or down the street. In this investigation you will **measure** your breathing rate after you do three different activities.

Materials

- stopwatch, timer, or
  clock with second hand

Activity Procedure

1 Make a chart like the one on the next page.

2 While you are sitting, count the number of times you breathe out in one minute. **Record** the number on your chart.

◀ Swimming is healthful exercise for both the respiratory and circulatory systems.

3 Stand up and march in place for one minute. Raise your knees as high as you can. As soon as you stop marching, begin to count the number of times you breathe out. Count your breaths for one minute. **Record** the number of breaths on your chart.

4 Rest for a few minutes, and then run in place for one minute. As soon as you stop running, begin to count the number of times you breathe out. Count your breaths for one minute. **Record** the number on your chart. (Picture A)

5 Make a bar graph to show how your breathing changed for each activity.

Picture A

Activity	Number of Breaths
Sitting	
After marching for 1 minute	
After running for 1 minute	

Draw Conclusions

1. Which activity needed the fewest breaths? Which needed the most breaths?

2. What can you **infer** about breathing from what happened in this investigation?

3. **Scientists at Work** Scientists don't usually **measure** something just once. What could you do to be sure your breathing rate measurements were correct?

Investigate Further Does your breathing rate increase if you exercise longer? **Form a hypothesis** about breathing and length of exercise. Then **plan and conduct an experiment** to test your hypothesis. You may want to build on what you have done already in this investigate. For example, march in place for two minutes, and then count your breaths. Run in place for two minutes, and then count your breaths.

Process Skill Tip

Measuring should be repeated. Scientists often measure more than once to be sure their measurements are correct. They compare the sets of measurements to look for patterns and possible mistakes.

The Respiratory and Circulatory Systems

FIND OUT

- what breathing does for the body
- why blood is important to the body's cells

VOCABULARY

lungs
capillary
heart
artery
vein

The Respiratory System

Your body's cells need oxygen to work. When you breathe in, you take in oxygen your cells need. As your cells do work, they give off carbon dioxide. When you breathe out, you get rid of carbon dioxide that cells give off.

You saw in the investigation that your breathing rate goes up as your body works harder. That's because as muscles do more work, they need more oxygen. They also give off more carbon dioxide. You breathe in and out faster to bring in more oxygen and to get rid of more carbon dioxide.

The main organs of the respiratory system are the **lungs**. Air enters your body through your nose and mouth. It goes down your *trachea* (TRAY•kee•uh) to your lungs. As you breathe in, your chest gets bigger and your lungs fill with air.

Your trachea divides to form a system of tubes in your lungs. These tubes look like the branches of a tree. The branches get smaller and smaller until they end in air sacs. All around the air sacs are tiny blood vessels called **capillaries** (KAP•uh•lair•ees). The walls of the air sacs and the capillaries are very thin. Oxygen passes easily through these walls, moving from the air sacs into blood in the capillaries. Carbon dioxide passes the other way, from blood in capillaries into the air in the air sacs.

✔ **What are the main organs of the respiratory system?**

The Circulatory System

The capillaries around the air sacs in your lungs are part of your circulatory system. Your circulatory system includes your heart and all of your blood vessels, the tubes blood flows through. The job of the circulatory system is to take blood to all of your body's cells.

The **heart** is the muscle that pumps blood through your blood vessels to all parts of your body. It is only as big as your fist. It is very strong and works all the time, resting only between beats.

Blood leaves the heart through blood vessels called **arteries**. Arteries branch out to all parts of your body. They become smaller and smaller until they become tiny capillaries.

The capillaries carry blood to every cell in your body. There, oxygen passes from the blood into the cells. Carbon dioxide passes from cells into the blood. After the blood flows through the capillaries, it

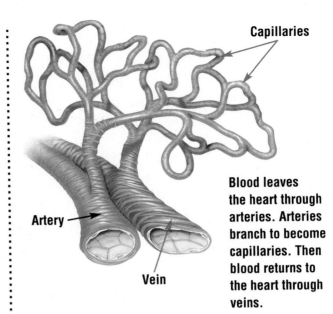

Capillaries

Artery

Vein

Blood leaves the heart through arteries. Arteries branch to become capillaries. Then blood returns to the heart through veins.

enters the veins. **Veins** are the large blood vessels that return the blood to your heart.

✔ **Which part of the circulatory system pumps blood to all body parts?**

Vein

Trachea

Artery

Lungs

▼ The respiratory system brings oxygen into the body.

Heart

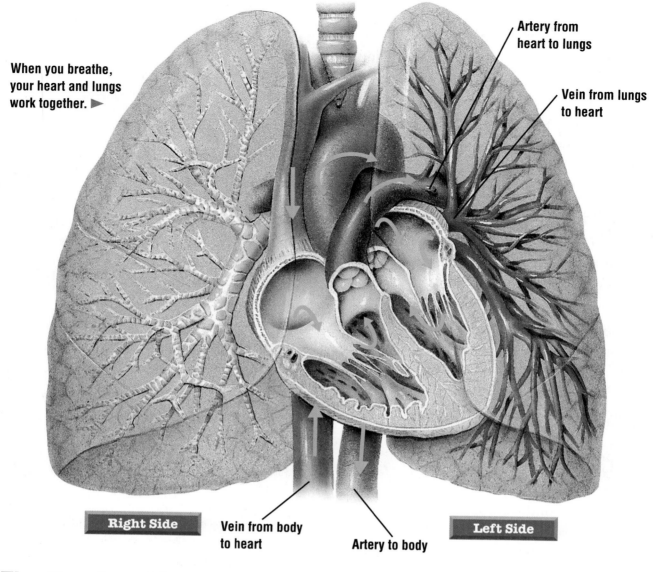

When you breathe, your heart and lungs work together. ▶

Artery from heart to lungs

Vein from lungs to heart

Right Side

Vein from body to heart

Artery to body

Left Side

The Heart and Lungs Work Together

The heart and lungs work together to bring oxygen into your body and to take away carbon dioxide. Each time you breathe in, the blood in your lungs gets fresh oxygen. This blood then travels to the heart, which pumps it to other parts of the body.

The heart has four sections called *chambers.* Each chamber acts as a pump. The chambers keep blood that enters the heart from mixing with blood that leaves the heart. The chambers are connected by openings. Each opening is covered by a valve that opens in only one direction. Each valve closes when its chamber is full.

Blood follows a one-way path through the heart. Blood from the lungs enters the top left chamber. The muscles of the chamber then shorten. This makes the space smaller, forcing the blood out. The only place it can go is into the lower left chamber.

This chamber is the main pump. It pushes blood through the whole body. When this chamber is full, it pushes the blood out of the heart and into the body's largest artery. The blood goes to all of the body, carrying oxygen to cells and picking up carbon dioxide. Then it returns to the heart.

Blood returning to the heart goes into the top right chamber. The muscles of this chamber force the blood into the chamber below.

The lower right chamber pumps the blood to the lungs. Here carbon dioxide leaves the blood and more oxygen enters. The blood is ready for another trip to the heart. It will be pumped around the body once again.

✔ **What makes blood follow a one-way path through the heart?**

Summary

Lungs are the organs the body uses to breathe. Breathing trades carbon dioxide, a waste cells give off, for oxygen, which cells need. Blood carries gases to and from cells through blood vessels. The heart pumps blood through the body.

Review

1. Why is it easy for gases to pass between air sacs and blood?

2. Which blood vessels take blood away from the heart?

3. Which blood vessels in the lungs help your body take in and give off gases?

4. **Critical Thinking** What do you think would happen if blood entering the heart mixed with blood leaving the heart?

5. **Test Prep** Which is a waste product of cells?
   A blood
   B water
   C oxygen
   D carbon dioxide

LINKS

MATH LINK

Interpret Data Knowing your target heart rate helps you exercise at a safe and healthful level. When you exercise, keep your heart rate between the maximum and minimum rates.

Exercise Heart Rate

Age	Minimum	Maximum
8	127	180
9	$126\frac{1}{2}$	179
10	126	$178\frac{1}{2}$
11	125	178

Do you think a 13-year-old would have a higher or lower maximum exercise heart rate than an 11-year-old? Why?

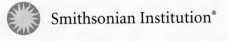

WRITING LINK

Expressive Writing—Song Lyrics Write a funny song for a younger student. Tell about a molecule of oxygen that enters the lungs. Explain what happens when it refuses to go to just any cell because it wants only to visit the big toe.

TECHNOLOGY LINK

ONLINE

Learn more about keeping heart beats regular by visiting the Smithsonian Institution Internet site.
www.si.edu/harcourt/science

✷ Smithsonian Institution®

How Do the Nervous and Digestive Systems Work?

In this lesson, you can . . .

INVESTIGATE
the sense of touch.

LEARN ABOUT
the nervous and digestive systems.

LINK to math, writing, health, and technology.

 **INVESTIGATE**

The Sense of Touch

Activity Purpose To protect itself, the body must notice things that touch it. Some parts of the body have a better sense of touch than others. In this investigation you will first **predict** which of three areas of your body is the most sensitive to touch. Then you will **compare** how sensitive the areas are.

Materials

- index card
- ruler
- 8 toothpicks
- tape
- blindfold (optional)

Activity Procedure

1 Make a copy of the chart on the next page.

2 Look at the areas of the body listed on the chart. **Predict** which one has the best sense of touch. Write your prediction on the chart. Explain your choice.

3 Measure a space 1 cm wide on one edge of the index card. Mark each end of the space, and write the distance between the marks. Tape a toothpick to each mark so that one end of each toothpick sticks out about 1 cm past the edge of the card. Make sure the toothpicks point straight out from the edge of the card.

◄ This baseball catcher needs alert senses to catch the ball.

	Prediction: Distance Between Toothpicks When Two Toothpicks First Felt		
	Palm	Lower Arm	Upper Arm
Prediction			
Actual			

Picture A

4 Repeat Step 3 for the other three sides of the index card. However, use spaces 2 cm, 5 cm, and 8 cm wide, one for each side.

5 Have a partner test your sense of touch. Ask him or her to lightly touch one body area listed on the chart with the toothpicks on each edge of the index card. Begin with the 1-cm side, and then use each side in turn with 2 cm apart, 5 cm apart, and 8 cm apart. Don't watch as your partner does this. (Picture A)

6 For each area, tell your partner when you first feel two separate toothpicks touching your skin. Have your partner write the distance between these toothpicks on the chart.

7 Switch roles and test your partner.

Draw Conclusions

1. Which of the body parts felt the two toothpicks the shortest distance apart?

2. Based on this test, which of these body parts would you **infer** has the best sense of touch? Explain.

3. **Scientists at Work** Using what you observed in this investigation, which part of your body do you **predict** to be more sensitive, your fingertip or the back of your neck?

Investigate Further Have your partner use the toothpicks to test your fingertip and the back of your neck to check the **prediction** you just made.

The Nervous and Digestive Systems

The Nervous System

None of your body systems could work without the help of your nervous system. It controls all parts of your body. Your nervous system is always receiving messages from your body and sending out responses.

Your **brain** is the control center of your nervous system. It and all other parts of the system are made up of nerve cells, or **neurons** (NOO•rahns). The brain uses information it gets from your body to direct how each body system works.

Your brain gets a lot of information from the sense organs in your head—your eyes, ears, tongue, and nose. Your brain also gets information from other parts of your body. In the investigation, you tested the sense of touch in different parts of your arm. Your brain told you what you felt.

Your body has **nerves**, or groups of neurons, that pass along information. The sense organs in your head have nerves that connect directly to your brain. Your spinal cord connects the nerves in the rest of your body to your brain. Your **spinal** (SPY•nuhl) **cord** is a tube of nerves that runs through your spine, or backbone.

FIND OUT

- how the nervous system controls all the body's systems
- what the digestive system does for the body

VOCABULARY

brain
neuron
nerve
spinal cord
esophagus
stomach
small intestine
large intestine

▲ Information going to and from the brain travels along nerve cells.

This is how neurons look when viewed through a microscope. ▶

Information from your body travels to your brain. Your brain acts on the information and sends a message back. For example, if you are at bat in a baseball game, your eyes watch the ball. They send information to your brain about the speed and direction of the ball. In less than a second, your brain decides whether or not to swing at the pitch.

If you decide to swing, your brain will send information down your spinal cord to nerves in your arms. The message will tell your arm muscles when and how hard to swing. If you hit the ball, your brain will tell your leg muscles to run. The more you practice, the better your brain will get at telling your muscles just how to hit the ball.

✔ **Which body part tells a batter whether or not to swing at a ball?**

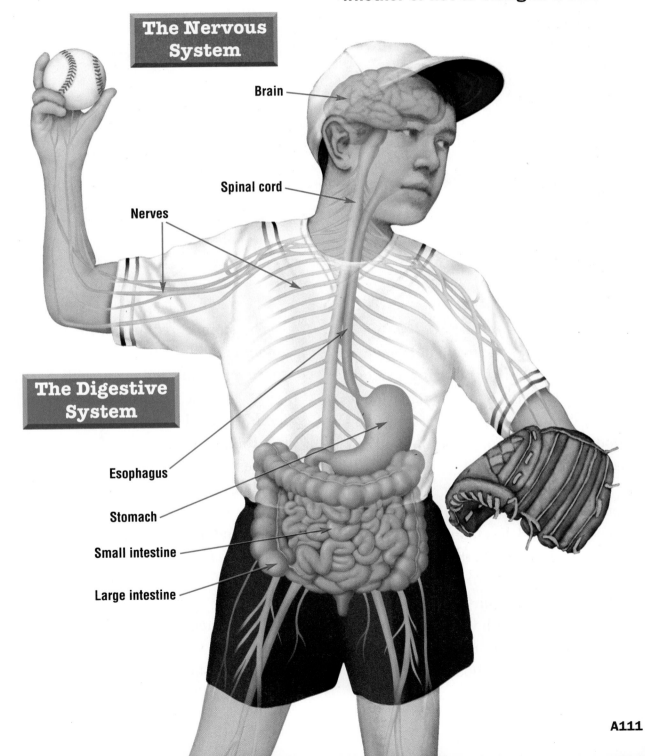

The Nervous System

Brain

Spinal cord

Nerves

The Digestive System

Esophagus

Stomach

Small intestine

Large intestine

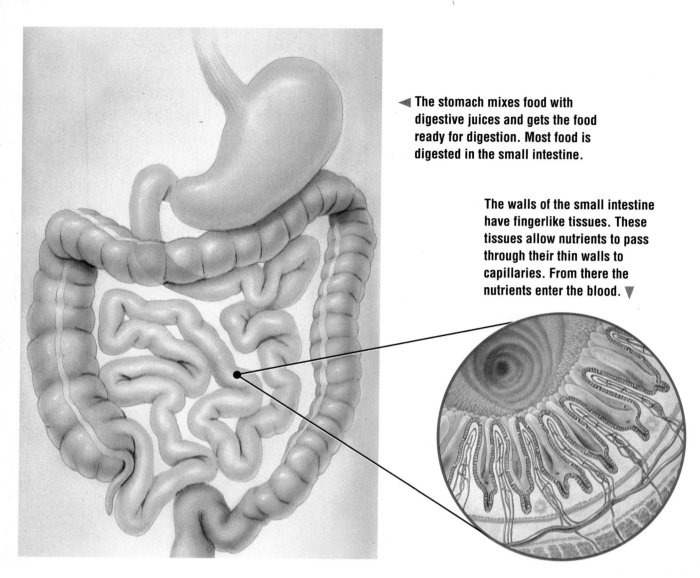

The stomach mixes food with digestive juices and gets the food ready for digestion. Most food is digested in the small intestine.

The walls of the small intestine have fingerlike tissues. These tissues allow nutrients to pass through their thin walls to capillaries. From there the nutrients enter the blood. ▼

The Digestive System

The digestive system also does an important job for the whole body. It provides nutrients to all the body's systems. It does this by breaking down, or digesting, the food you eat into nutrients your body's cells can use.

Digestion begins in your mouth. When you chew, your teeth grind up food into smaller pieces. Saliva (suh•LY•vuh) softens the food and begins to digest it.

After you swallow, the food enters your **esophagus** (ih•SOF•uh•guhs), a tube that connects your mouth with your stomach. The actions of smooth muscles in your esophagus move the food down to your stomach.

The **stomach** is a bag made up of smooth muscles. The stomach muscles squeeze the food and mix it with digestive juices. The juices digest some parts of the food. The food is mixed and squeezed until it becomes mostly liquid.

The liquid food then passes into the **small intestine** (ihn•TES•tuhn), a long tube of muscle. Different digestive juices are added, and other parts of the food are digested. The small intestine does more than any part of the digestive system to digest food.

The nutrients from the digested food pass through the walls of the small intestine into capillaries. Blood carries these nutrients to the body's cells.

The last part of the digestive system is the **large intestine**. Most food that reaches the large intestine can't be broken down any more. The large intestine removes water from this food. What is left of the food travels through the large intestine until it passes out of the body.

✔ **What part of the digestive system does the most to digest food?**

Summary

The brain sends messages to and from all parts of the body through the spinal cord and nerves. It controls the way all other body systems work. The digestive system breaks down food to provide nutrients for all the body's cells. The blood carries these nutrients to every cell in the body.

Review

1. How does the brain connect with other parts of the body?
2. What gives information to the brain?
3. Where does digestion begin?
4. **Critical Thinking** Why would not chewing food enough make it harder for the digestive system to do its job?
5. **Test Prep** Which part of the digestive system makes food mostly liquid?
   A stomach
   B esophagus
   C small intestine
   D large intestine

LINKS

MATH LINK

Make a Bar Graph Nerves can send messages back and forth at the amazing speed of 430 kilometers per hour. Find two things that travel faster than nerve messages and two that travel more slowly. Make a bar graph to show and compare all five speeds.

WRITING LINK

Informative Writing—Explanation You have seen how the nervous system controls your muscles. Write a paragraph for your school newspaper. Explain what your nervous system does when you score a point in your favorite sport.

HEALTH LINK

Nutrition Read about the Food Guide Pyramid on pages R8–R9 of the Health Handbook. Make your own model of the pyramid. Draw or cut out pictures of foods for each food group. Glue them to your model.

GO ONLINE TECHNOLOGY LINK

Visit The Harcourt Learning Site for related links, activities, and resources.
www.harcourtschool.com

SKIN ADHESIVE

Almost everyone is badly cut at some time and has to get the cut stitched closed in an emergency room. Now, researchers are trying to make such stitches a thing of the past!

This cut is being glued closed with skin adhesive.

Super Surgical Glue

Stitches are used 86 million times a year all over the world. Doctors predict that half of the cuts will soon be repaired by skin adhesive (ad•HEE•siv), or artificial glue. It is like other "super" glues. But it is made to stick together living layers of skin!

Now, This Won't Hurt!

There are lots of good reasons to use this product. It takes less time than stitches. Doctors simply squeeze it out of a tube, much like rolling on lip gloss. Stitching a cut takes an average of $12\frac{1}{2}$ minutes. Using adhesive takes only about $3\frac{1}{2}$ minutes.

Stitched wounds are three times as likely to become infected as are wounds closed by adhesive. And adhesive stretches with the skin, so cuts don't break open when the patient stretches or moves. The skin adhesive comes off with dead skin cells. As a result, no visit to the doctor is needed to remove it, unlike stitches. Best of all, applying skin adhesive doesn't hurt, so skin doesn't have to be "numbed" first. For these reasons, the adhesive is comfortable for the patient and easier for the doctor. An added bonus is that it usually costs less than stitches.

Still to Come

Other companies are working to make adhesives for other medical work. One company has made an adhesive that also kills germs. Scientists are working to find adhesives to glue bone grafts, to close spinal fluid leaks, and to seal holes in the digestive tract. A spray adhesive may be used for burns. The adhesive would protect tender new skin as the new skin grows.

Don't Try This at Home!

CAUTION If you have a cut or wound, do *not* try to glue it closed. Get help from an adult. Surgical adhesives are **NOT** just like the glues at school or home. Only surgical adhesives are for use on skin.

THINK ABOUT IT

1. Why would a spray type of skin adhesive be helpful for burn patients?
2. What other medical uses can you think of for skin adhesives? Are there nonmedical ways they might be used?

CAREERS
SURGICAL NURSE

What They Do Surgical nurses help patients before, during, and after surgery. They may help the surgeon during an operation. They also may stay with a patient in the recovery room after surgery.

Education and Training Many nurses have college degrees in nursing. Some learn in programs offered through hospitals. Some take two-year community college programs. Surgical nurses must take courses in surgical nursing. They must also study and train during their career. All nursing programs require practice on the job. All states require nurses to pass a national exam.

 WEB LINK
For Science and Technology updates, visit the Harcourt Internet site.
www.harcourtschool.com

Rosalyn Sussman Yalow
MEDICAL PHYSICIST

"You won't all win Nobel Prizes, but the important thing is that you set goals for yourself and then live up to them."

RIA test equipment

Dr. Rosalyn Yalow knows about setting goals. By the time she was a teenager, she knew she wanted to have a career in science, marry, and raise a family. At that time, it was unusual for a woman to plan to have both a career and a family.

Yalow valued education and was especially good at math. She attended Hunter College and the University of Illinois at Urbana-Champaign.

While at the University of Illinois, Yalow became interested in radioactive particles. These are given off when atoms break apart. Yalow later set up a laboratory in what had been a janitor's closet at the Veteran's Administration Hospital in the Bronx. Dr. Solomon Berson became her research partner. They worked together for over 20 years.

Berson and Yalow found that radioactive particles could help measure antibodies in the blood. They could also detect the level of certain hormones. Their method is called radioimmuno-assay (ray•dee•oh•im•yoo•noh•AS•ay), or RIA. It takes only a small amount of blood. This was important because earlier methods required almost a cup of blood! RIA measures very precisely. It can detect amounts as small as one billionth of a gram. This precision helps doctors diagnose and treat many different diseases.

Dr. Berson died in 1972, and Yalow continued her work with a new research partner. Yalow was the first woman to receive the Albert Lasker Basic Medical Research Award. In 1977 she received the Nobel Prize for Medicine and Physiology.

THINK ABOUT IT

1. How are science and detective work alike?
2. Why is it sometimes helpful for scientists to work together on a large project?

MUSCLE MODEL

How does the biceps muscle work?

Materials
- 2 boards (about 5 cm × 25 cm)
- duct tape
- scissors
- long balloon
- string

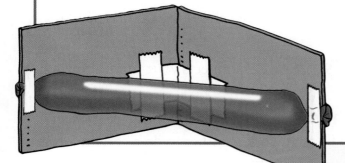

Procedure
1. Place the boards end to end. Use duct tape to make a hinge connecting the boards.
2. Blow up the balloon about one-fourth full.
3. Using the string, tie the two ends of the balloon to the outside ends of the boards.
4. Open and close the model you made.
5. Record your observations.

Draw Conclusions
Explain how this model is like the biceps muscle and the upper and lower bones of the arm.

REACTION TIME

How does practice affect the nervous system?

Materials
- meterstick

Procedure
1. Work with a partner. Put your forearm flat on your desktop with your hand extending over the edge.
2. Have your partner hold the meterstick above your hand so that the zero mark is between your index finger and your thumb.
3. Have your partner drop the meterstick without giving you any warning. Catch the meterstick as quickly as you can.
4. Record the number that was between your fingers when you caught the stick. This is the distance the meterstick fell before you caught it.
5. Repeat the test ten times. Record the distance the stick fell each time.

Draw Conclusions
Make a line graph of your results. Did your reaction times change? In what way?

Vocabulary Review

Use the terms below to complete the sentences. The page numbers in ( ) tell you where to look in the chapter if you need help.

veins (A105)   **spinal cord** (A110)
tissue (A98)   **striated muscle** (A100)
brain (A110)   **esophagus** (A112)
organ (A98)   **lungs** (A104)
neurons (A110)   **stomach** (A112)
cardiac muscle (A99) **capillaries** (A104)
nerves (A110)   **small intestine** (A112)
smooth muscle (A99) **heart** (A105)
arteries (A105)   **large intestine** (A113)

1. Two long tubes of muscle that lead from the stomach and help absorb food are the ____ and the ____.

2. Your ____ is a bag made up of muscles that churns food.

3. Three main parts of your nervous system are the ____, ____, and ____.

4. From your heart, blood first flows away through ____ to the body, then through ____, and back to the heart through ____.

5. Your ____ is the organ that pumps blood.

6. The ____ are the main organs of the respiratory system.

7. The cells that form nerves are ____.

8. A group of cells of the same type is a ____.

9. The ____ connects your mouth to your stomach.

10. An ____ is made up of different tissues that work together to do a certain job in the body.

11. The three types of muscles in your body are ____, or heart muscle; ____; and ____.

Connect Concepts

Use concepts from the chapter to complete the concept map.

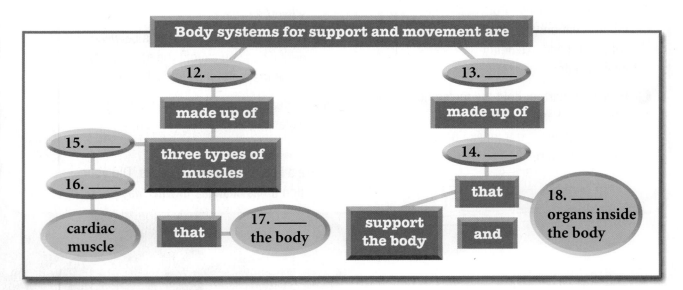

Check Understanding

Write the letter of the best choice.

19. Leg muscles that you use when you lift a box are —

   A smooth muscles

   B striated muscles

   C cardiac muscles

   D heart muscles

20. The brain is ____ that is part of your nervous system.

   F an organ

   G a leg

   H a cell

   J a system

21. When you exercise, your body needs more ____, so you breathe faster.

   A oxygen

   B water

   C carbon dioxide

   D speed

22. When blood passes through ____, it exchanges oxygen and carbon dioxide.

   F arteries

   G veins

   H the heart

   J capillaries

23. Which body system tells you when to reach for and catch a falling book?

   A muscular

   B skeletal

   C nervous

   D respiratory

Critical Thinking

24. Why isn't the heart made up of smooth muscles like other organs inside your body?

25. Which body system would smoking cigarettes affect most directly? Explain.

26. How might a serious injury to your spinal cord affect the rest of your body?

Process Skills Review

27. What features would you look for if you wanted to **compare** bones in the human body?

28. How would you **measure** the number of times students dropped pencils during class?

29. To **predict** who would win a race, what would you want to know?

Performance Assessment

Digestion Model

With a partner, make a small model or a poster showing how your digestive system would digest an apple.

UNIT A EXPEDITIONS

There are many places where you can discover a world of living things. By visiting the places below, you can study the diversity of living things and find out about the needs of many different plants and animals. You'll also have fun while you learn.

Zoo Atlanta

WHAT A collection of habitats with animals from different places around the world

WHERE Atlanta, Georgia

WHAT CAN YOU DO THERE? See gorillas, chimpanzees, and other primates from Africa; tigers from Sumatra; flamingos from Chile; and giant pandas from China.

The Missouri Botanical Garden

WHAT A collection of gardens highlighting different species of plants from around the world

WHERE St. Louis, Missouri

WHAT CAN YOU DO THERE? Tour artificial deserts, rain forests, and other environments. See flowers blooming all year in climate-controlled buildings.

GO ONLINE Plan Your Own Expeditions

If you can't visit Zoo Atlanta or the Missouri Botanical Garden, visit a zoo or a garden near you. Or log on to The Learning Site at **www.harcourtschool.com** to visit these and other science sites to study plants and animals from around the world.

Looking at Ecosystems

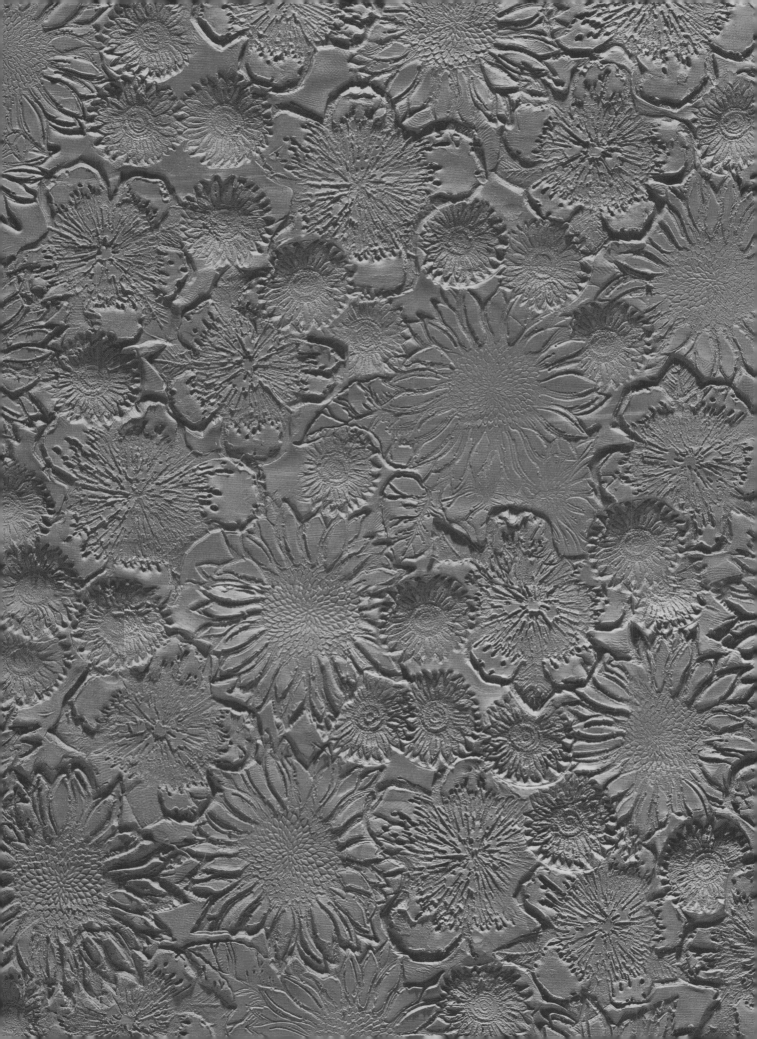

UNIT B — LIFE SCIENCE

Looking at Ecosystems

UNIT EXPERIMENT

Environmental Changes and Plant Growth

An organism's environment is all the living and nonliving things that surround it. Environments are always changing, sometimes quickly and sometimes very slowly. While you study this unit, you can conduct a long-term experiment about how plants respond to changes in their environment. Here are some questions to think about. How does polluted soil affect the growth of plants? How do other types of pollution affect plants? Plan and conduct an experiment to find answers to these or other questions you have about ecosystems. See pages x–xix for help in designing your experiment.

Ecosystems

Did you ever stop to think why living things live where they do? A maple tree wouldn't grow well in a desert. An elephant probably wouldn't survive in the Arctic. All living things have adaptations to meet their needs in areas where they are found. If the areas change, some living things may find it hard to survive.

Vocabulary Preview

system
stability
ecosystem
population
community
habitat
niche
producer
consumer
decomposer
energy pyramid
food web
climate
diversity
salinity
intertidal zone
near-shore zone
open-ocean zone

Fast Fact

Some living things stay in a small area. A pine tree doesn't move at all during its lifetime. A mouse stays close to its nest. Wolves and caribou (KAIR•uh•boo) may travel hundreds of kilometers to find food and shelter.

How Far Living Things Travel		
Living Thing	**Distance Traveled**	
Pine tree	0 m	(0 ft)
Mouse	60 m	(200 ft)
Wolf	520 km	(320 mi)
Caribou	1600 km	(1000 mi)

Bridges disturb living things in the areas where they are built. But they also can help. These cliff swallows have turned a bridge into a home. The bridge shelters their mud nests from rain. And like a cliff, the bridge is high in the air.

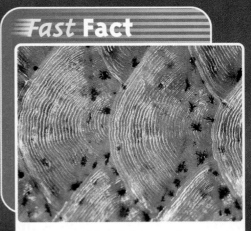

You can tell a fish's age by looking at its scales. The process is much like counting rings to figure out how old a tree is!

Caribou travel great distances to find lichens (LY•kuhnz) to eat.

What Are Systems?

In this lesson, you can . . .

 INVESTIGATE how parts of a system interact.

 LEARN ABOUT characteristics of systems.

LINK to math, writing, technology, and other areas.

 **INVESTIGATE**

How Parts of a System Interact

Activity Purpose The plants, soil, air, light, and water in nature are parts of a system. In this investigation you will **make a model** that includes all these parts. You will see how the parts interact, or affect each other.

Materials

- 2 empty 2-L soda bottles
- scissors
- gravel
- sand
- soil
- 6 small plants
- spray bottle containing water
- clear plastic wrap
- rubber bands

Activity Procedure

1. **CAUTION** **Be careful when using scissors.** Cut the tops off the 2-L bottles.

2. Pour a layer of gravel in the bottom of each bottle. Cover this with a layer of sand.

3. Add a layer of soil to each bottle, and plant three plants in each bottle. (Picture A)

◄ The fish, plant, and water in this fishbowl form a small system.

Picture A

Picture B

4 Spray the plants and the soil with water. Cover the tops of the bottles with plastic wrap. You may need to use the rubber bands to hold the plastic wrap in place. You have now made two examples of a system called a *terrarium* (tuh•RAIR•ee•uhm). (Picture B)

5 Put one terrarium in a sunny spot. Put the other in a dark closet or cabinet.

6 After three days, **observe** each terrarium and **record** what you see.

Draw Conclusions

1. Which part of the system was missing from one of the terrariums?

2. What did you **observe** about the two systems?

3. **Scientists at Work** Scientists learn how different things interact by putting them together to form a system. What did your **model** show you about the interactions among plants, soil, air, light, and water?

Investigate Further **Hypothesize** what would happen if a terrarium had no water. Make another terrarium, but this time don't add any water. Put the terrarium in a sunny spot, and **observe** it after three days. What has happened?

Characteristics of Systems

FIND OUT

- what makes up a system
- how a system gains stability

VOCABULARY

system
stability

System Parts

You and your friends have probably run through a sprinkler on a hot summer day. The cold water splashed on your skin and cooled you off. You may have slipped and slid on wet grass. Although you may not think of it in this way, you, the grass, and the sprinkler were part of a system. A **system** is a group of parts that work together as a unit. You made a simple system when you built your terrariums. A system also has cycles and processes that interact, or affect each other.

Everything in a yard, including the house, plants, people, animals, hose, sprinkler, and water, is part of a system. The people, plants, and animals are the living parts of the system. The rest of what makes up a yard are the nonliving parts of the system. Both the living and nonliving things play important roles in keeping the yard system working right.

The edges of the yard system are easy to see. It is easy to say what is inside and what is outside the system. The edges of many natural systems aren't as easy to see. Often, scientists must decide where the edges of a natural system will be for the purposes of their studies. For example, a scientist might choose to study one tree, a group of trees, or a whole forest.

✔ **What are the living parts of a yard system?**

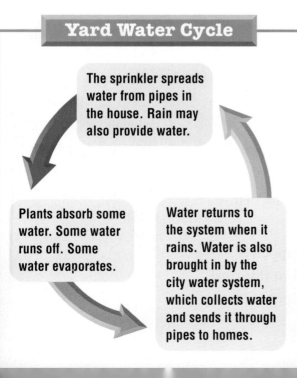

Yard Water Cycle

The sprinkler spreads water from pipes in the house. Rain may also provide water.

Plants absorb some water. Some water runs off. Some water evaporates.

Water returns to the system when it rains. Water is also brought in by the city water system, which collects water and sends it through pipes to homes.

Interactions

The parts of a system interact with other parts of the system. You turn on a faucet to get water. The hose carries the water to a sprinkler that sprays the water. You use the water to cool your body. The grass uses the water to grow. You walk on the grass.

Most systems also interact with the outside. The yard system is an open system because it takes in things called *inputs* from outside the system. Energy from the sun is one input. Water is also an important input. The water may come in the form of rain or from the city's water supply.

Open systems also let things out. *Outputs* are things that leave a system. One output from the yard system is water. Some of the water in the yard runs off into the street. Some evaporates into the air.

The opposite of an open system is a closed system. A closed system has no inputs

▲ This diagram shows some parts of a typical yard system.

or outputs. Very few systems are really closed. Most have some connection to the outside.

✔ **What two features do open systems have?**

A yard forms a simple system that has many parts. ▼

Stability and Change

All systems follow patterns of changes. You sometimes must look carefully to see these patterns because they occur over time. In a yard the cycle of periods of sunshine and periods of shade each day is a pattern. The cycle of being wet and being dry is another pattern. Patterns show a kind of stability. **Stability** (stuh•BIL•uh•tee) means that over time the changes in a system cancel each other out. For example, if something is added, it is later taken out. The system stays in balance.

▲ The yard changes as the seasons change. In fall and winter, the plants stop growing or die. In spring and summer, they grow.

Stability is important because almost all natural systems have it. The yard system has stability. The sun shines in part of the yard each morning. In the afternoon that part is shady. The grass may dry out after a few days without rain, but eventually it gets water from rain or from a sprinkler.

✔ **What is stability?**

◀ Grass grows as it gets water and sunlight. This change is canceled out by the person who cuts the grass. The length of the grass is stable. It is always about the same.

▲ Because the pattern of change is repeated every year, you know that every spring plants will again begin to grow.

Summary

A system is made up of parts that interact. Open systems take in inputs and give off outputs. Patterns and cycles in systems show stability. A system has stability when the changes in it cancel each other out.

Review

1. Describe two ways in which the parts of a yard system interact.

2. How are inputs and outputs of a system alike?

3. What patterns show that a yard system is stable?

4. **Critical Thinking** How do areas of sunshine follow a pattern in a yard that has trees?

5. **Test Prep** A system that is in balance is said to have —
   A openness
   B stability
   C input
   D output

LINKS

MATH LINK

Make a Graph Use library resources to find your area's average temperature for each month. Make a bar graph to show what you found. Will the pattern repeat? Explain your answer.

WRITING LINK

Narrative Writing—Story The sun is the source of energy for almost all systems that include living things. Write a story called "What If the Sun Suddenly Got Dimmer?" for your friends to read. Tell what would happen to systems of living things on Earth.

HEALTH LINK

Body Systems Make a chart of a body system. Label the parts of the system. Describe what they do and how they interact.

LITERATURE LINK

Disappearing Lake Read *Disappearing Lake—Nature's Magic in Denali National Park* by Debbie S. Miller. Write a paragraph telling about one of the cycles described in the book.

GO ONLINE — TECHNOLOGY LINK

Learn more about natural systems and stability by visiting this Internet site.
www.scilinks.org/harcourt

SCi LINKS™
THE WORLD'S A CLICK AWAY

What Makes Up an Ecosystem?

In this lesson, you can . . .

INVESTIGATE an ecosystem.

LEARN ABOUT living and nonliving parts of ecosystems.

LINK to math, writing, art, and technology.

Frogs are often seen near water ecosystems.

An Ecosystem

Activity Purpose Ecosystems are all around you. A back yard is an ecosystem. Ecosystems are in your school's playground and walkways. A vacant lot is an ecosystem. An ecosystem can be found anywhere plants and animals interact with the world around them. In this investigation you will **observe** an ecosystem at your school to discover what lives there.

Materials

- meterstick
- chalk
- stakes
- string
- hand lens
- hand trowel

Activity Procedure

1 Use the meterstick to **measure** a square area that is 1 m long and 1 m wide. It can be on grass, bare dirt, or the cracked concrete of a wall or sidewalk. Mark the edges of the square with the chalk or with the stakes and string. (Picture A)

2 **Observe** your study area. Look for plants and animals that live there. Use the hand lens. **Record** all the living things you see. Describe any signs that other living things have been there.

3 *In soil or grass,* use the trowel to turn over a small area of soil. Look for insects or other living things. (Picture B) **Count** and **record** any living things you find. Then **classify** them. Be sure to fill in the holes you dig in your area.

Picture A

Picture B

4. *In concrete or brick areas,* **observe** areas along the sides of the concrete or bricks that may contain soil and places for plants to grow. **Count** and **record** the number of each type of living thing you find. Then **classify** each.

5. **Communicate** your results to your class. Describe your study area. Identify the living things you found.

Draw Conclusions

1. What living things did you find in your study area? Which kind of living thing was most common in your area?

2. How was your study area different from those of other student groups?

3. **Scientists at Work** Scientists often **observe** an ecosystem at different times of the day and in different seasons. This is because different animals can be seen at different times. **Predict** the different animals you might see if you observed your study area at different times of the day or at different times of the year.

Investigate Further Choose an area that is like the area you **observed**. Repeat the investigation. What was the same? What was different? Why were there differences?

Process Skill Tip

When you **observe** an area that includes living things, you need to be aware at all times. Some living things appear only for a short time. Others may never appear when you are there but may leave signs that they were there.

Parts of Ecosystems

Living Parts of Ecosystems

FIND OUT

- **the basic parts of an ecosystem**

- **how the living things in ecosystems are organized**

VOCABULARY

ecosystem
population
community

The next time you walk in your neighborhood, stop to look and listen for living things. At first, there may seem to be no living things around you. But if you observe closely, you'll discover them. Even in cities, groups of plants and animals find places to live. Groups of living things and the environment they live in make up an **ecosystem** (EK•oh•sis•tuhm). All living things in an ecosystem can meet their basic needs there.

Some ecosystems have only a few living things. For example, insects and small plants are probably the only easy to see things that live in a concrete parking lot environment. They live in cracks or along the sides of the lot. Other ecosystems, such as those of forests, ponds, and streams, have many living things. That's because these environments have more space, food, and shelter. Many types of plants and animals can easily meet their needs in these environments.

✔ **What must a plant or animal be able to do to live in a certain ecosystem?**

The plants and animals shown here live in a kind of water ecosystem called an estuary (EHS•tyoo•ehr•ee). Here they interact with each other and with the nonliving things in their environment such as water, soil, and sunlight.

◄ Red mangrove tree

Shrimp

Great blue heron

Populations

A group of the same species living in the same place at the same time is a **population** (pahp•yoo•LAY•shuhn). A forest may have several populations of different kinds of trees. Trout may be one of several populations of fish in a stream. Deer may form a population among other animals in a meadow.

Populations live in environments to which they are adapted. Some environments are difficult to live in. The organisms that live there must have unusual adaptations to survive. For example, an estuary forms where fresh water from a river flows into salt water of an ocean. Sometimes estuary water has a lot of salt. Sometimes it has only a little. Most trees and plants cannot live in water that changes in this way. Mangrove (MAN•grohv) trees, however, have roots and leaves that get rid of salt. This adaptation allows them to grow in salt water or in fresh water.

Scientists usually name ecosystems such as estuaries after the main population of plants that live there. Estuaries that have mostly mangrove trees are called mangrove swamps. A *swamp* is an area that is sometimes or always covered in shallow water.

✔ **How is the mangrove tree different from most other trees?**

A population of mangrove trees gives populations of gray snapper fish and egrets a place to live. ▶

Egrets

Gray snapper

Communities

In most ecosystems, plants of the main population are where other organisms interact. Mangrove tree branches hang over the water and attract insects looking for food and shelter. Schools, or groups, of archerfish may live among the roots of mangrove trees. Archerfish can shoot a jet of water up to $1\frac{1}{2}$ meters (about 5 ft) above the water, knocking insects off branches. The fish then eat the insects that fall into the water. A flock of lesser blue herons may feed in or near the shallow water at the roots of the trees. There they find fish, frogs, and other small animals to eat.

All these animals and plants live together and interact with one another in many ways. A **community** (kuh•MYOO•nuh•tee) is made up of all the populations that live in the same area. The plants and animals that live together depend on one another to survive. The animals in a community eat plants and other animals in the community.

THE INSIDE STORY

The Formation of a Mangrove Swamp

Each spring hundreds of mangrove flowers blossom and form fruit. Inside each fruit is a seed.

About two months after the fruit forms, the seed inside grows roots and stems. It becomes a seedling. While it is still attached to the tree, the seedling becomes able to live in salt water. This gets it ready to safely fall from the tree into the soil or salt water below.

One seedling may float thousands of miles. When its base touches ground, it begins to put out roots. If the temperature and soil are right, the seedling takes root. Over time, it grows into a mature tree.

A mangrove's spear-shaped seedling is 15 to 30 centimeters (about 6 to 12 in.) long. The seed stores nutrients to keep it alive after it falls from the parent tree. Some seedlings fall like darts and land directly in soil. Others land in water and float to a new place to grow. ▼

The plants need animals to carry away seeds and to add nutrients to the soil. Sometimes communities provide shelter. The tangled mangrove roots shelter many small fish. The fish swim and reproduce among the roots.

✓ **In what ways are the living things in a community important to one another?**

▲ Underwater mangrove roots provide a place for fish and other animals such as sponges, oysters, and shrimp to find food and shelter.

This mangrove sapling, or young tree, will grow several centimeters a year. The branching roots above the ground grow in the sapling's third or fourth year. The tree will grow to be 15 to 30 meters (about 50 to 100 ft) tall. ▼

In about 25 years, this sapling and others from the parent tree will form a small population of mangrove trees. The roots trap soil and dead plants and animals. They shelter fish and other animals. ▼

Nonliving Parts of an Ecosystem

The nonliving parts of an ecosystem are just as important as the living parts. The main nonliving parts of an ecosystem include sunlight, soil, air, water, and temperature. These nonliving parts interact with one another. For example, water sometimes moves soil from place to place.

The nonliving parts also interact with the living parts of the ecosystem. Salt water is a nonliving part of a mangrove swamp ecosystem. Only certain plants can live in salt water. Because of this, salt affects the ecosystem.

✔ **What are the main nonliving parts of an ecosystem?**

▲ Tall grasses and wildflowers grow in the sunlit mountain meadow. Small plants and saplings grow at the edge of the trees. Only a few small plants grow among the trees.

Grasses and bushes can grow along the stream where there is water and plenty of light. Pine trees grow where the soil is drier. Few other plants grow in the shade under the trees. ▼

Summary

An ecosystem is made up of groups of living things and their environment. An ecosystem may include plants and animals, and nonliving parts such as sunlight, soil, air, water, and temperature. Organisms of the same species form populations. A community is made up of populations of different species in an ecosystem.

Review

1. Why do some ecosystems include many living things?
2. Is a row of bean plants in a garden a population or a community? Explain.
3. What nonliving part of the mangrove swamp limits the kinds of plants that can live there?
4. **Critical Thinking** Contrast a population with a community.
5. **Test Prep** What might an ecosystem that has mostly pine or spruce trees be called?
   - **A** mountain forest
   - **B** evergreen forest
   - **C** deep woods
   - **D** green woods

LINKS

MATH LINK

Make a Line Graph Make a line graph showing population changes in a small meadow ecosystem over a period of three years. How are the numbers of birds and grasshoppers related? Why might this happen?

	1996	1997	1998
grasshoppers	500	280	350
birds	80	120	100
mice	120	100	125
snakes	18	10	12
hawks	1	2	1

WRITING LINK

Informative Writing—Description Suppose you are a scout ant in a backyard ecosystem. Describe the populations and community you find during one day.

ART LINK

Art in Nature Make a collage of three different ecosystems. Label the ecosystems and the main living things in each ecosystem.

GO ONLINE TECHNOLOGY LINK

Visit the Harcourt Learning Site for related links, activities, and resources.
www.harcourtschool.com

LESSON 3

What Are Habitats and Niches?

In this lesson, you can . . .

INVESTIGATE the homes and roles of living things.

LEARN ABOUT living things in ecosystems.

LINK to math, writing, social studies, and technology.

INVESTIGATE

The Homes and Roles of Living Things

Activity Purpose You have learned what some animals eat, how they act, and where they live. In this investigation you will use what you know. You'll also find out more about animals' homes and their roles, or the things they do in their communities. For example, the role of some animals is to eat other animals. The role of other animals is to eat only plants.

Materials

- index cards
- crayons or markers
- reference books about animals

Activity Procedure

1 Each member of your group should choose five different animals.

2 Draw a picture of each of your animals on a separate index card. (Picture A)

 A spider's web is its home. The spider also uses the web to trap insects for food.

Picture A

Picture B

3 Using five more cards, draw the homes of your animals or show them in their roles. (Picture B) Look up information about your animals in reference books if you need help.

4 Gather all the cards. Mix up the cards, and place them face down. Take turns playing Concentration®. Turn over two cards at a time until you find a pair that shows an animal and its home or role. Explain how the two cards match. Play until all the matches have been made.

Draw Conclusions

1. What new animals did you learn about as you played the game?

2. Which was easier to identify, an animal's home or its role? Explain your answer.

3. **Scientists at Work** Scientists often make **inferences** based on things they have **observed** and their past experiences. What inferences did you make as you tried to explain how two cards matched?

Investigate Further Choose an animal card, and think of another animal that may have the same home or role. Suppose the new animal meets its needs in the same community. **Form a hypothesis** about how it will interact with the other animals. Will they try to eat the same food or use the same places for shelter? Will the new animal keep the animal on the card from meeting its needs? Use library resources to test your hypothesis.

Process Skill Tip

When you **infer**, you try to explain what has happened based on things you have **observed** or that you already know. An inference is a possible explanation for an observation.

Living Things in Ecosystems

Homes for Living Things

In the investigation, you saw places that are homes to animals. Plants and fungi have homes, too. These homes meet the needs of the organisms living there. An environment that meets the needs of an organism is called its **habitat** (HAB•ih•tat). The habitats of some organisms are whole ecosystems. This is often true for birds that can fly from place to place. The habitats of other organisms may be just small parts of ecosystems. For example, fungi may grow only in certain areas of a forest floor.

Some habitats overlap, or take up some of the same space. When they do, similar organisms may compete, or try to get the same food or space. For example, two species of fish living in the same pond may compete for the same insects as food. Organisms that are very different may not need to compete. Even though birds and caterpillars live in the same habitat, they meet their needs in different ways.

✔ **When might living things have to compete?**

FIND OUT

- examples of habitats and niches in ecosystems

- how plants and animals interact and change their environments

VOCABULARY

habitat   niche

producer   food web

decomposer

energy pyramid

consumer

Many organisms live in the pine forest. Each meets its needs by living in a different part of the forest. ▼

Roles

Although caterpillars don't often compete with birds, they must avoid the birds around them. That's because some birds eat caterpillars. Part of the birds' **niche** (NICH), or role, in their habitat is to eat insects.

An organism's niche includes all the ways it meets its basic needs—how it gets shelter, how it produces young, and how it gets food and water. What an organism eats is an important part of its niche. What a living thing eats affects the populations around it.

The sun is the main source of energy for *all* living things. Animals don't get energy directly from the sun. Many eat plants, however, which use sunlight to make food. Animals that don't eat plants still depend on the energy of sunlight. They eat animals that eat plants.

When scientists describe the way energy moves through ecosystems, they use the term *food chains*. Food chains have three levels. Green plants and some protists and monerans are **producers** (proh•DOOS•erz) in food chains, because they make their own food. Consumers make up the next level of a food chain. **Consumers** (kuhn•SOOM•erz) eat other living things for energy. The last level is made up of decomposers. **Decomposers** (dee•kuhm•POHZ•erz) feed on the wastes of plants and animals or on their remains after they die. They return nutrients to the soil for plants to use as the cycle begins again.

✔ **What are the three levels of every food chain?**

Two Food Chains

These diagrams show two food chains. One is in a freshwater ecosystem, and one is in a forest edge ecosystem. Identify the producers, consumers, and decomposers in each food chain.

Algae are protists that use the energy of the sun to make food.

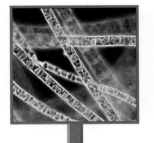

Blueberry bushes grow in sunny areas at the edge of a forest.

Snails eat the algae, using the energy from the algae to live and grow.

To get the energy they need, bears eat berries, insects, and many other plants and animals.

When a snail dies, fungi and other organisms break down the snail's body.

Bacteria in soil decompose the wastes produced by the bear. When broken down, the wastes add nutrients to the soil.

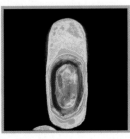

B21

Moving Energy

All organisms in an ecosystem need energy from food to live. A diagram called an **energy pyramid** shows how much food energy is passed from one organism to another along a food chain. The base of an energy pyramid represents producers. These organisms use energy from the sun to make food through photosynthesis. Some of this food is stored in the plant. The rest is used for life processes.

The other levels of an energy pyramid represent consumers. Just above the producers are plant-eating consumers. Plant eaters use most of the energy from plants for life processes. Only a small amount is stored in their bodies. The same is true for the transfer of food energy to each higher level of the pyramid. Only about ten percent of the food energy of each level is passed up to organisms in the next level.

✔ **Why is a diagram of energy levels in an ecosystem in the shape of a pyramid?**

Only about ten percent of the energy in a plant is passed on to the organism that eats it. ▼

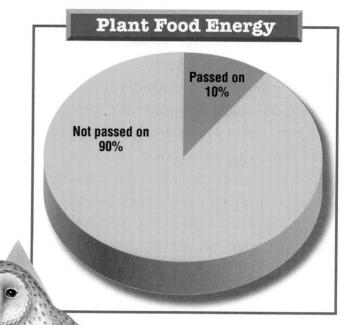

Plant Food Energy

Passed on
10%

Not passed on
90%

◄ There is less food energy available at each higher level of an energy pyramid. This is why there are fewer barn owls than snakes and fewer snakes than squirrels.

Food Webs

A food chain shows one pathway for food energy from organism to organism in an ecosystem. But most organisms get energy from more than one source. For example, squirrels and deer eat both acorns and blueberries. A red wolf might eat a deer one day and a squirrel three days later. A diagram that shows how these food chains connect and overlap is called a **food web**.

✔ **What does a food web show?**

A Forest Food Web

See how many paths you can trace up along the arrows from the bottom of this forest food web to the top.

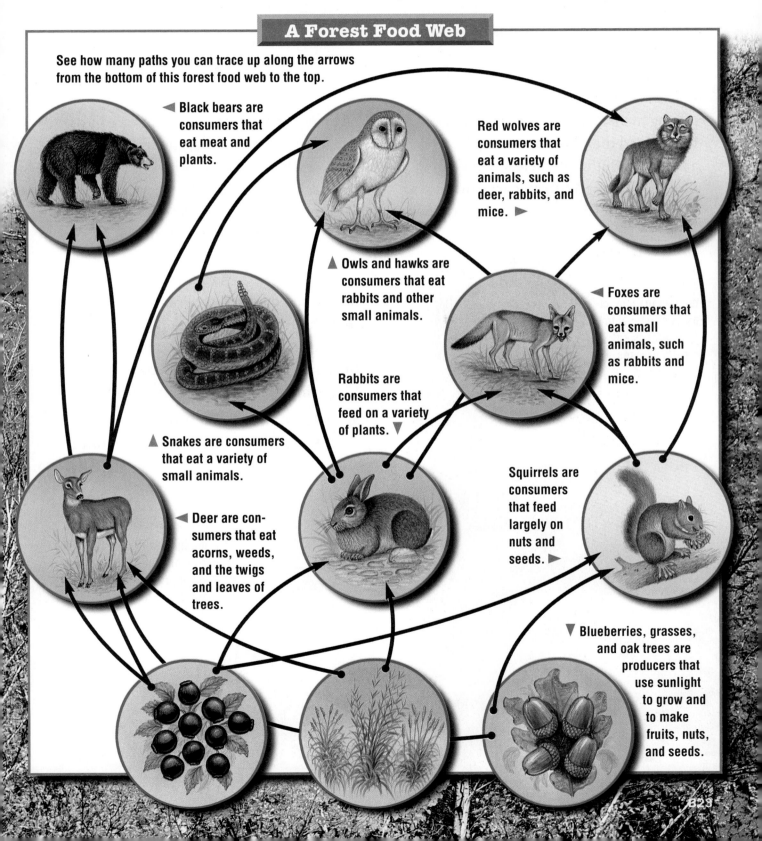

◄ Black bears are consumers that eat meat and plants.

Red wolves are consumers that eat a variety of animals, such as deer, rabbits, and mice. ►

▲ Owls and hawks are consumers that eat rabbits and other small animals.

◄ Foxes are consumers that eat small animals, such as rabbits and mice.

▲ Snakes are consumers that eat a variety of small animals.

Rabbits are consumers that feed on a variety of plants. ▼

◄ Deer are consumers that eat acorns, weeds, and the twigs and leaves of trees.

Squirrels are consumers that feed largely on nuts and seeds. ►

▼ Blueberries, grasses, and oak trees are producers that use sunlight to grow and to make fruits, nuts, and seeds.

B23

Causes of Change

As organisms meet their needs, they affect their environments. Usually the changes they cause are small and help keep an ecosystem stable.

Some changes affect other organisms. As animals eat plants or other animals, they reduce the number of organisms in their habitat. For example, there are many insects in a bird's habitat. When a bird eats insects, it helps keep the number of insects from getting too large. This helps keep the bird's habitat and the whole ecosystem healthy and stable. But when there are too many birds eating insects, they reduce the insect population quickly. In time, there will not

▲ Lichens slowly break down rock. Rain washes minerals from the rock into the soil. These added nutrients help improve the soil in a habitat.

be enough for the birds to eat. Some birds will leave the area or die, and fewer young birds will be born. This brings the ecosystem back into balance.

Some changes caused by organisms affect the nonliving parts of an ecosystem. Worms and lichens make the soil of their habitats better. Some natural changes, however, can be unwanted by people. Prairie dogs are thought to harm rangeland. Their holes are dangerous for grazing cattle and sheep. Over time, most changes in nature balance out. No harm is done and stability is kept.

✔ **What can happen if too many insect-eating birds live in a habitat?**

Prairie dogs live underground in colonies. They dig tunnels to connect parts of the colony. Prairie dogs eat mostly grasses. ▶

◀ Although prairie dog holes are dangerous for cattle, prairie dogs improve a habitat by digging and mixing soil.

▲ Gypsy moth caterpillars eat the leaves of trees. They sometimes eat so many leaves that the trees die. This not only damages the caterpillars' habitat, but also affects other animals in a forest ecosystem.

Summary

An environment that meets the needs of an organism is called its habitat. An organism's niche is its role within the habitat. As organisms in an ecosystem carry out their roles, they can affect both living and non-living parts of the ecosystem.

Review

1. What happens when two similar animals share a habitat?

2. What type of organism breaks down the remains of dead plants and animals?

3. How can one organism help control the population of another organism?

4. **Critical Thinking** What could happen to an ecosystem that had mice if cats were added to it?

5. **Test Prep** Which of the following is a producer?

   A fox   C fungus

   B chicken   D grass

LINKS

MATH LINK

Collect Data and Estimate Suppose that in 5 minutes you counted 5 grasshoppers on a square meter of your yard. Assume that these insects are spread out evenly in your yard. Estimate the number of grasshoppers on the whole yard if its area is 40 square meters.

WRITING LINK

Informative Writing—Report Your city plans to cut down a forest to make room for a new shopping mall. The city wants you to find out what organisms would be affected by cutting down the forest. Find out which organisms make up a forest ecosystem. Then classify the organisms by their habitats and niches, and prepare a report for the mayor.

SOCIAL STUDIES LINK

State Symbols Each of the 50 states has different environments for wildlife. Each state government chooses a bird, a flower, and a tree to represent the state. Make simple maps of your state and of two neighboring states. Find out the wildlife symbols of the states. On the maps, draw and label the symbols.

TECHNOLOGY LINK

Learn more about animals in a marine ecosystem by viewing *Tide Pool* on the **Harcourt Science Newsroom Video.**

What Are Tropical Rain Forests and Coral Reefs?

In this lesson, you can . . .

INVESTIGATE a coral reef.

LEARN ABOUT tropical ecosystems.

LINK to math, writing, literature, and technology.

INVESTIGATE

A Coral Reef

Activity Purpose One of the most interesting ecosystems is a coral reef. With its many different plants and animals, it looks like a colorful underwater garden. In this investigation you will make a diorama of a coral reef and identify its parts.

Materials

- box
- blue paint or blue construction paper
- paintbrushes
- glue or tape
- scissors
- modeling clay
- fishing line
- thumbtacks
- chenille stems
- construction paper
- plastic wrap

Activity Procedure

1. Look through the lesson, and use library resources to find pictures of reef organisms and their habitats.

2. Plan a diorama that uses the materials your teacher provides. Try to find the best material for each living and nonliving thing you will show.

◄ This moray eel hides in the reef, looking for a small fish for its next meal.

Picture A

Picture B

3 Follow your plan. Keep in mind colors, sizes, and the best use of space. (Picture A)

4 Label the organisms in your diorama. (Picture B)

Draw Conclusions

1. What organisms did you include in your diorama?

2. Tell three things you learned while building your diorama.

3. **Scientists at Work** When scientists build a **model** of an organism that is very small, they may make it hundreds of times bigger. If you tried to build your diorama to scale, you may have found it hard to show the very smallest organisms. How could you show large models of the tiniest organisms and still build your diorama to scale?

Investigate Further A diorama can show only part of the picture. Write a paragraph or two describing other organisms that could live near your reef scene.

Process Skill Tip

A diorama is a three-dimensional (3-D) **model**. To be realistic, its parts should be built to scale. For example, some models are 10 times smaller than the real organisms they stand for. An animal that is actually 10 cm long would be 1 cm long in such a model. An animal that is really 1 cm long would be shown as 1 mm long.

Tropical Ecosystems

Tropical Rain Forests

Tropical rain forests grow along the equator, an area that has a lot of rainfall and high temperatures all year. The **climate** (KLY•muht), or average weather over a long time, allows many plants to grow well.

Rain-forest trees grow tall and form a canopy (KAN•uh•pee), or roof. Their leaves shelter the area below, blocking most of the sunlight. Vines grow up the trunks of trees to reach the light. Many plants and animals live high in the canopy. There they can use the sunlight and open space.

The forest floor is home to plants that grow well in shade. Plants that need lots of light make a thick ground cover only where a tree has fallen. The fallen tree makes an opening in the canopy.

Rotting plant material covers much of the rain-forest floor. Decomposers are always at work there. When you think of the many organisms living among the trees, the floor seems unimportant. The rain forest, however, depends on decomposing and

FIND OUT

• how tropical rain forests and coral reefs are alike

• what the resources of reefs and rain forests are and why they are important

VOCABULARY

climate
diversity
salinity

Located near the equator, tropical rain forests are some of the wettest land ecosystems on Earth. Daily temperatures can range from 20°C (68°F) to 34°C (about 93°F). ▼

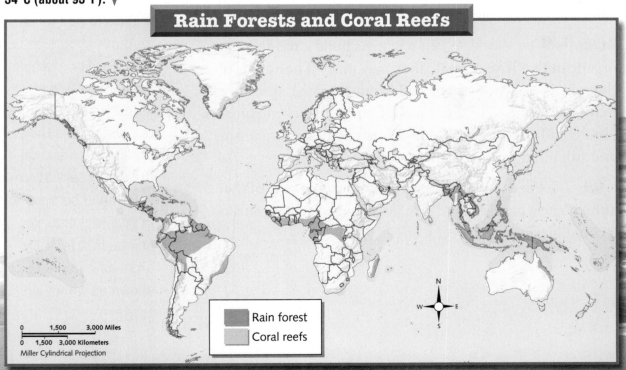

Rain Forests and Coral Reefs

0   1,500   3,000 Miles
0 1,500 3,000 Kilometers
Miller Cylindrical Projection

■ Rain forest
■ Coral reefs

Morpho butterfly

Capuchin

Toucan

recycling of nutrients. Most of this recycling takes place in the forest floor.

A rain forest has a great **diversity** (duh•VER•suh•tee), or variety, of plants and animals. In fact, a rain forest has more species of plants and animals than any other ecosystem on Earth.

Near the tops of trees, there are habitats for thousands of species. Mammals such as spider monkeys and lemurs (LEE•merz) play on sturdy tree limbs. Toucans, macaws (muh•KAWZ), and other colorful birds nest in the branches. Butterflies fly around, drinking nectar from orchids that grow on tree branches. Mosses and ferns cling to tree branches.

Anaconda

Rain-forest orchid

✔ **What makes a tropical rain forest different from any other ecosystem?**

Capybara

River turtle

Giant river otter

Tiger centipede

Caiman

Piranha

Coral Reefs

Coral reefs are a lot like rain forests, only under water. These ecosystems are also located in tropical climates near the equator. Such areas have plenty of sunlight. The sea water is clean and warm all year long. The water's **salinity** (suh•LIN•uh•tee), or the amount of salt in it, is constant. All these conditions are needed for a coral reef to grow.

Coral reefs look like colorful landscapes of cliffs and canyons. They are made up of the rocky skeletons of many tiny animals called *corals*. Corals live in colonies. One colony may look like a big, fan-shaped leaf. Another may look more like a giant brain.

Coral colonies are made up of tiny soft-bodied animals called polyps (PAHL•ips), which are no bigger than your thumb. A young colony of them may have only a few polyps. Older colonies may have millions of polyps.

Coral polyps build limestone skeletons around their bodies by taking calcium out of sea water. Flower-like tentacles, or arms, reach out from the skeletons. The tentacles trap small plants and animals. Prey is stung and then pulled into the coral's mouth. Coral polyps also can get nutrients from algae that live inside their skeletons.

When a polyp dies, its skeleton is left. Another polyp then moves in and adds more limestone. A coral reef can grow like this for many years. Some old reefs cover many square kilometers.

Coral Reef Water Temperatures

When the water temperature is 32°C (90°F) or warmer, it is too warm. Coral polyps may die.

— 32°C

— 30°C

When the water temperature is between 18° and 30°C (about 64° and 86°F), corals live and grow well.

— 18°C

— 16°C

When the water temperature falls to 16°C (about 61°F) or below, coral polyps can't live.

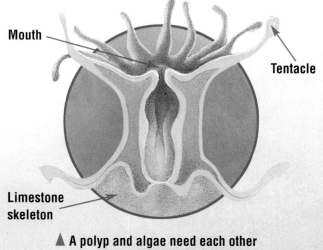

Mouth

Tentacle

Limestone skeleton

▲ A polyp and algae need each other to survive. The polyp gets food and oxygen from the algae. The polyp gives the algae carbon dioxide.

Parrotfish

Sea urchin

Giant clam

The many branches, holes, and layers of the reef offer places for animals to rest. Cracks provide places to hide. Thousands of species are known to live among coral reefs.

Many of the creatures of coral reefs are easy to see. Brightly colored angelfish and striped butterfly fish guard their home areas. Sea horses hold on to the reef by their tails. Other creatures are harder to see. Flat flounders lay hidden on the sandy ocean floor around the reef. Hungry scorpion fish blend in with the colorful coral. Each animal has its habitat and niche in the coral reef ecosystem.

✔ **How does a coral polyp build its skeleton?**

▼ Diatoms (DY•uh•tomz) are plantlike protists that have hard outer body coverings.

Sea fan

Clownfish

Octopus

Cleaner wrasse

Grouper

Decorator crab

Crinoid

Staghorn coral

Anemone

Brain coral

Resources from the Tropics

Both tropical rain forests and coral reefs are treasure chests of life. Each is home to thousands of species of organisms, many of which are found nowhere else on Earth. From these organisms come hundreds of different products that people need and use.

Wood is one important rain-forest resource. Rain forests provide about 20 percent of the wood used in industry around the world. They also are an important source of foods, including fruits, nuts, and spices. As much as 80 percent of the world's food comes from plants found in tropical rain forests. Raw materials to make furniture, cooking oils, waxes, and dyes also come from rain forests. No rain-forest products are more important than medicines being made from rain-forest plants. And new medicines are still being discovered.

Resources from coral reefs are not as widely used. Some coral is used to make jewelry and other ornaments. Some sponges that grow in the reefs have many uses. Stores that sell tropical fish are full of animals that came from coral reefs. Some people keep these animals in tanks as a hobby.

✔ **How are tropical rain forests and coral reefs alike?**

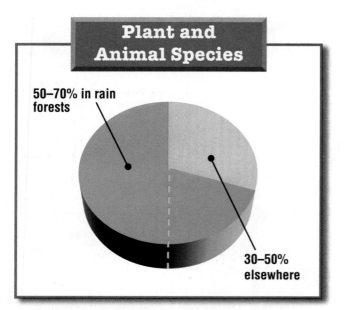

Plant and Animal Species

50–70% in rain forests

30–50% elsewhere

▲ Of all the world's plant and animal species, 50 to 70 percent can be found in tropical rain forests.

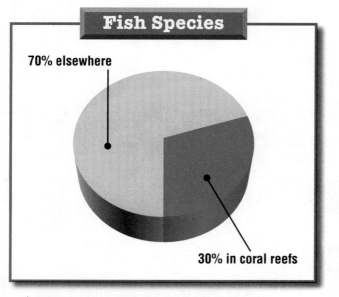

Fish Species

70% elsewhere

30% in coral reefs

▲ Coral reefs provide habitats for 30 percent of all fish species.

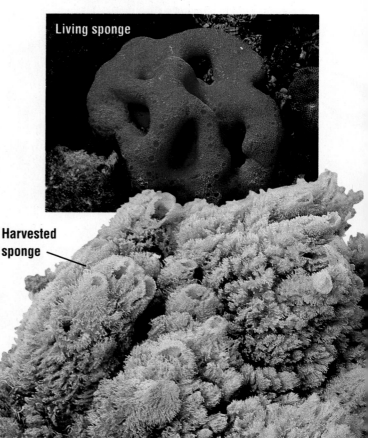

Sponges are sea animals that live attached to rocks, plants, and other objects beneath the water's surface. Some sponges are harvested and sold. ▼

Living sponge

Harvested sponge

▲ Liana vines are used to make curare ▶ (kyoo•RAH•ray), a drug. Resources from rain forests are used to produce about one out of every four medicines made today.

TUBOCURARINE
Chloride for injection (USP)
Multiple dose
3 mg (20 Units/mL)
Sterile for intravenous use

Summary

Tropical rain forests and coral reefs are ecosystems that provide habitats for a large variety of plants and animals. They both provide resources found nowhere else on Earth.

Review

1. Where do most plants and animals live in a tropical rain forest?

2. Why is the salinity of salt water important for a living coral reef?

3. What are three resources from tropical rain forests?

4. **Critical Thinking** Why is it important to protect tropical rain forests and coral reefs?

5. **Test Prep** The floor of a tropical rain forest is covered with —

   A grasses
   B dead plant material
   C blooming flowers
   D animals

LINKS

MATH LINK

Make a Graph Use a computer program such as *Graph Links* to make a bar graph that compares the amount of rainfall each year in a rain forest, a desert, and your hometown.

WRITING LINK

Informative Writing—Compare and Contrast Suppose that you have just returned from exploring a tropical rain forest and a coral reef. For a school newspaper, write a story called "A Day in the Life of a Coral Reef and a Rain Forest." Make an outline of your story. List which features you will compare and contrast. The outline also should tell which creatures you will show, photos you will need, and so on.

LITERATURE LINK

At Home in the Rain Forest Read *At Home in the Rain Forest* by Diane Willow. Take an exciting journey through the layers of a rain forest, from its treetops to the forest floor.

TECHNOLOGY LINK

Learn more about the parts of a coral reef ecosystem by exploring *Coral Reefs— A Visit to the Deep* on the **Harcourt Science Explorations CD-ROM.**

What Are Some Saltwater Communities?

In this lesson, you can . . .

INVESTIGATE how salt water and fresh water mix.

LEARN ABOUT some saltwater communities.

LINK to math, writing, health, and technology.

Salt Water and Fresh Water

Activity Purpose   Ocean water is salty. The water that flows in rivers and streams is fresh. At the edges of continents, fresh water in rivers and streams flows into salty ocean water. In this investigation you will **observe** what happens when salty water flows into fresh water. Then you will use your observations to **infer** what happens when rivers and streams flow into the ocean and what happens when the tides change.

Materials

- blue food coloring
- plastic shoe box
- plastic cup
- water
- salt
- spoon
- ruler

Activity Procedure

1 Put a tablespoon of salt in a cup of water and stir.

2 Add a couple of drops of blue food coloring to the salt water and stir again.

◀ Humpback whales sometimes do high backward leaps out of the water. The whales eat krill, small fish, and plantlike microorganisms that they strain from the water by using comblike teeth called baleen (buh•LEEN).

B34

Picture A

Picture B

3 Half-fill a plastic shoe box with fresh water.

4 Slowly and carefully pour the salt water into one end of the shoe box. Pour the salt water along the side of the shoe box so that you disturb the fresh water as little as possible. **Observe** what happens. (Picture A)

5 Blow on the water's surface to simulate wind. **Observe** what happens.

6 Dip the ruler into the water at one end of the shoe box. Slowly move the ruler up and down to simulate waves. **Observe** what happens. (Picture B)

Draw Conclusions

1. What did you **observe** when the salt water was added to the fresh water? Which is heavier, salt water or fresh water?

2. What did you **observe** when you made waves by blowing and by moving the ruler?

3. **Scientists at Work** What can you **infer** would happen when the tide rises and brings salty water into the mouth of a river? What can you infer would happen when the tide falls?

Investigate Further The area where fresh water and salt water meet and mix is called an estuary. In addition to tidal changes, the position of sea level affects where estuaries are located. Based on what you learned in this activity, **hypothesize** how rising sea level would affect estuaries.

Process Skill Tip

Scientists sometimes build models to show events that occur in the natural world. Then they **observe** their models and use their observations to **infer** what happens when these events occur in the natural world.

Saltwater Communities

Saltwater Environments

FIND OUT

- examples of saltwater communities

- how saltwater organisms interact

VOCABULARY

intertidal zone
near-shore zone
open-ocean zone

In this chapter you have learned about some communities that exist on land. Yearly temperature and rainfall are factors that determine the kinds of living things in land communities. In the ocean, water depth and availability of light are important factors that determine what lives in a community.

The ocean can be divided into three life zones. The **intertidal zone** is a narrow strip along the shore that is covered with water during high tides and exposed during low tides. Plants and animals in this zone must be able to live through the daily changes caused by tides. The **near-shore zone** starts at the low-tide mark and goes out into the ocean. The water is shallow here, so light can shine through the water all the way to the bottom. With plenty of light for photosynthesis, this zone has many kinds of life. The **open-ocean zone** is the deepest part of the ocean. Sunlight cannot reach the bottom, so very few organisms are found deep under water. However, living things are found near the ocean surface in the open-ocean zone.

✓ **Where are the three life zones in the ocean?**

The intertidal zone is a narrow band that hugs the shore, the area where the land meets the ocean. It is located between the high- and low-tide marks.

The near-shore zone lies outside the intertidal zone. Here the water is shallow, so light can reach the ocean floor.

The open-ocean zone extends from the near-shore zone out to the deepest parts of the ocean. Light cannot reach the bottom because the water is too deep.

Salt Marsh

Salt marshes are in the intertidal zone near the mouths of rivers. As tides rise and fall, parts of the marsh are flooded with salt water and then left exposed to the drying wind and sun. As you learned in the investigation, the salt content of the water also changes with the tides. As the tide comes in, the water gets saltier; as it goes out, the water gets fresher. Plants and animals in a salt marsh must have adaptations to live through these constant changes.

✔ **For what environmental conditions must salt marsh organisms have adaptations?**

Salt marshes are some of the most productive ecosystems on Earth. Nutrients deposited by rivers and washed in by the tides help many marsh plants to grow. The plants, in turn, provide food and shelter for animals.

Mammals such as this nutria and birds such as herons and egrets live in the salt marsh and eat the many small animals living there.

Spartina (spahr•TYN•uh) is a grass that grows well in salt marshes. It lives where few other plants can survive. It has narrow, tough blades and glands that get rid of excess salt. Few animals eat this plant when it is alive, but many eat dead and decaying spartina plants.

Many animals, such as fish, crabs, and shrimps, live among spartina. The stems, leaves, and roots provide shelter. The young of many species use the salt marsh as a nursery. Without the food and shelter given by marsh plants, few of these animals would live and grow into adults.

Fish such as mullet dig in the mud around the roots of plants as they hunt for the microscopic organisms they eat.

Animals in a salt marsh must have adaptations to live with the rising and falling of the tides. Some have hard shells that protect them when the tide is out. Some, like crabs, bury themselves in the soupy mud.

Nutria

Mullet

Brown shrimp

Spartina

Crab

Kelp Forest

Kelp forests are like forests on land, except they are full of seaweed instead of trees. These underwater forests grow in the near-shore zone, in cold, shallow water along rocky coastlines. The shallow water allows the kelp to get the sunshine it needs to grow. The rocky bottom provides a place for the rootlike holdfasts, or anchors, to attach. From these holdfasts long streamers of kelp grow up toward the surface. Each leaf has bladders, or bags, full of a gas to keep the plant floating upright. Like forests on land, kelp forests have different layers, and each layer is full of life. Different kinds of animals live in each layer.

✓ **Where do kelp forests grow?**

Sea otters are predators that swim among all the layers of the kelp forest. They dive all the way to the bottom to catch their favorite food—sea urchins. Then they bring their catch up to the surface and float on their backs while they eat. ▼

◄ Some kelp streamers can grow as high as a 20-story building.

Small animals such as shrimps and snails inch along the kelp streamers and eat plant and animal matter. Predators such as garibaldi, a bright orange fish, live among the kelp streamers. They feed on the smaller animals that cling to the kelp.

Wolf eel

Sea urchins live on the rocky bottom and eat kelp and bottom-dwelling animals. Other animals, such as wolf eels, hunt and eat the sea urchins.

Open-Ocean Zone

The open-ocean zone is very deep, so sunlight cannot filter all the way to the bottom. Plantlike organisms can live only near the surface, where sunlight is available for photosynthesis. Food chains begin with plantlike microorganisms, such as diatoms (DY•uh•tahmz), that float near the surface. Microscopic animal-like organisms feed on the plantlike organisms. In turn, the animal-like organisms are eaten by animals, and so on up the food chain. Many different food chains, with fish and other sea creatures of all sizes, exist in the open-ocean zone.

✓ **Why aren't plantlike organisms found throughout the open-ocean zone?**

Krill are small animals that swim in the open ocean, feeding on tiny plantlike microorganisms, such as diatoms. They are very important in the open-ocean food web because many animals eat them, including fish, squids, sea birds, and whales.

Diatoms are plantlike microorganisms that float near the surface of the open ocean. They are covered by two shells of glasslike material that fit together like a box and lid.

Jellyfish float in the upper layers of the open ocean. They capture food with their long, thin tentacles.

Many of the fish in the open ocean, like these tuna, are streamlined so they can hunt their food or swim quickly away from predators.

Squids swim in the open ocean and hunt small fish. They have a slender body with fins on one end. The other end is a large head surrounded by ten long, flexible arms called tentacles. ▶

Deep-Sea Vent Communities

Most areas of the deep ocean have hardly any life. But areas near hot spots on the ocean floor along undersea mountain ranges have many living things. The organisms there are very different from those found anywhere else on Earth. Everywhere else, food chains begin with organisms that use the energy from the sun to make food. The food chains that exist at the mid-ocean ridges work without sunlight.

Tall, chimneylike vents, called hydrothermal (hy•droh•THUHR•muhl) vents, spew out clouds of sulfides, a kind of chemical, and hot water. Food chains begin with huge colonies of bacteria that use the sulfides for energy. The bacteria, in turn, become food for other living things, such as giant tube worms, dinner-plate-sized clams, blind crabs and shrimps, and strange-looking fish.

✔ **How do the food chains that exist around the deep-sea hydrothermal vents differ from food chains found anywhere else on Earth?**

Thick plumes of what looks like black smoke come out of tall, chimneylike hydrothermal vents at the mid-ocean ridges. The thick black smoke is actually sulfide-rich water that is very hot—about 350°C (662°F). ▽

This map shows the locations of some of the deep-sea hydrothermal vents that scientists have found. ▷

ATLANTIC OCEAN

PACIFIC OCEAN

Blind crabs are among the residents of the deep-sea vent community. These crabs have no need to see, because there is no light so far beneath the ocean's surface. ▽

Giant tube worms three meters (about 10 ft) long live near vents. They have red, gill-like organs that they pull in when disturbed. They get food from bacteria that live within their organs. ▽

Summary

The ocean can be divided into three life zones. Salt marshes are part of the intertidal zone. Plants and animals that live there must have adaptations for the changes caused by tides. Kelp forests are part of the near-shore zone. Because the water is shallow, sunlight can reach the bottom and support the growth of kelp and many animals. The open-ocean zone is the deepest part of the ocean. The deep-sea floor has hardly any life, except near hydrothermal vents.

Review

1. How are plants that live in a salt marsh different from other plants?

2. What is at the base of a food chain at the deep-sea hydrothermal vents?

3. What is at the base of a food chain in the open ocean?

4. **Critical Thinking** How is a kelp forest the same as a forest on land? How is it different?

5. **Test Prep** An example of a saltwater community in the intertidal zone is —

    A a kelp forest

    B a salt marsh

    C a deep-sea hydrothermal vent

    D the open ocean

LINKS

MATH LINK

Estimate Surface Area The oceans cover about 71 percent of Earth's surface. The total surface area of Earth is about 317,000,000 square kilometers. Calculate the surface area of all the oceans. Then find a map of the Great Lakes, the largest group of freshwater lakes in the world. Estimate their total surface area.

WRITING LINK

Informative Writing—Reporting from the *ALVIN* *ALVIN* is a deep-sea submersible that has been used to explore deep-sea hydrothermal vent communities. Imagine that you are on board *ALVIN* as it approaches a deep-sea hydrothermal vent. Write a report about what you see and hear.

HEALTH LINK

Iodine in Your Diet If you eat seafood and seaweed, then you are probably getting enough iodine, a very important element in your diet. Find out why iodine is important for your health and how to get enough in your diet.

GO ONLINE TECHNOLOGY LINK

Learn more about kelp forests by visiting the sciLINKS site:
www.scilinks.org/harcourt

Computer Models of ECOSYSTEMS

What would happen to a marsh ecosystem if 24 alligators were released in it? What would happen to a pond ecosystem if all the lily pads died? Scientists are using computers to help answer questions like these.

Virtual Reality

Have you ever played a video game with scenes in it that looked almost real? That kind of game is a kind of computer model. It helps you understand what a real place might be like. Currently, scientists are using computers to make models of ecosystems. To make an ecosystem model, scientists first collect a lot of data about the ecosystem. For example, they measure animal populations, plant populations, growthrates, fire, rain, disease, and climate. Then they put the data into a computer program.

When the program runs, "life" in the ecosystem happens in fast-forward motion. Watching a wetland age in a model is much faster than waiting for real-life changes. The computer predicts how the ecosystem will change over time. It tells scientists how many plants and animals will grow and how populations will affect each other.

Predicting the Future

Suppose a scientist wants to know what a certain wetland ecosystem will look like after 100 years. When the model is complete, the computer could predict how the wetland will look 10, 20, 50, or 100 years from now. For example, it could show the population of each kind of animal and plant. It could tell how much water is in the wetland. It might even tell how many herons are eating the fish.

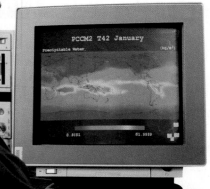

◄ Scientist using a computer model

Changing the Future

Once scientists have a good model of an ecosystem, they can experiment using just the model. They might add 24 alligators or remove all the lily pads. The computer will tell them whether the alligators take over or whether the frogs leave.

The better the data that scientists use, the more they can learn from computer models. Scientists might even make a good model of something as big and complicated as a forest during a fire.

THINK ABOUT IT

1. How could computer models help scientists during a drought?
2. How could computer models help city planners decide where to place a shopping mall?

CAREERS
COMPUTER PROGRAMMER

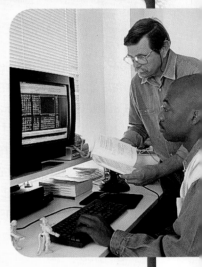

What They Do Computer programmers write step-by-step instructions for computers. The instructions tell computers what to do with the information that is given to them. Computers are used in almost all areas of life today, including science, medicine, business, and communication. Programmers work in all these areas and others.

Education and Training Most programmers are college graduates. They have taken courses in math, computer science, and business. Data processing and classes in modeling are also good choices for study.

GO ONLINE

WEB LINK
For Science and Technology updates, visit the Harcourt Internet site.
www.harcourtschool.com

Henry Chandler Cowles
ECOLOGIST

"By burying the past, the dune offers to plant life a world for conquest . . . . The advance of a dune makes all things new."

View from Indiana Dunes

Dr. Henry Chandler Cowles loved the Indiana Dunes on the southern shore of Lake Michigan. He studied and wrote about them while studying botany (the science of plants) at the University of Chicago. The papers he wrote helped create a new field of study, *ecology* (ee•KAHL•uh•jee). Cowles said the job of an ecologist was to discover the relationships between plants and their environment.

Cowles looked for such relationships at the Indiana Dunes. He studied the dunes' distance from the lake, their types of soil, and when seeds and spores germinated on the dunes. He compared the Indiana Dunes to the dunes at Cape Cod and to other dunes. Between 1897 and 1931, he took thousands of photographs of the dunes and of the Midwestern plains.

Cowles's photographs show that plant communities are always changing as the environment changes. He hypothesized that ecosystems were never twice alike. For example, a 1910 photo shows a cottonwood tree on top of a dune. One year later, sand had buried the tree.

The University of Chicago has kept Cowles's photographs for a long time. Many of them have been made into slides.

After Cowles stopped teaching, the photographs were stored in the university's library. The National Park Service sometimes studies them before restoring sections of a park. The slides were recently cleaned and repaired as part of a Library of Congress project.

THINK ABOUT IT

1. Henry Chandler Cowles took photographs as part of his research. How might a scientist record his or her research today?

2. Why do you think scientists would want to restore Cowles's old photographs?

DOWN AT THE ROOTS

What roles does grass play in an ecosystem?

Materials

- trowel or small shovel
- hand lens
- white paper

Procedure

❶ Dig out a small plug of grass, about the size of your palm. Include all the roots. **CAUTION** **Get permission from an adult before you dig.**

❷ Put the grass sample on a clean piece of white paper. Observe the grass and roots with a hand lens. Record your observations.

❸ Choose three blades of grass. Measure the lengths of each root and blade. Record your measurements.

Draw Conclusions

How do the lengths of the blades and roots compare? What roles can you infer grass roots and blades play in an ecosystem? How do you know?

PERSONAL FOOD CHAIN

What is the original energy source for the foods you eat?

Materials

- 2 large sheets of paper
- pencil

Procedure

❶ On one sheet of paper, list foods a person might eat during three meals. Draw a picture of a person at the top of the other sheet of paper.

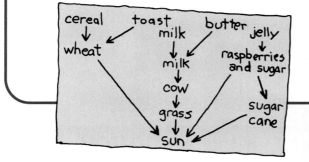

❷ Draw three arrows beneath your picture, and list the foods eaten at each meal. Leave plenty of space below each food item.

❸ Draw an arrow beneath each food item, and identify where each got its energy when it was living.

Draw Conclusions

What is the original source of energy for all the foods the person ate?

Vocabulary Review

Use the terms below to complete the sentences. The page numbers in ( ) tell you where to look in the chapter if you need help.

system (B6)	**decomposer** (B21)
stability (B8)	**energy pyramid** (B22)
ecosystem (B12)	**food web** (B23)
population (B13)	**climate** (B28)
community (B14)	**diversity** (B29)
habitat (B20)	**salinity** (B30)
niche (B21)	**intertidal zone** (B36)
producer (B21)	**near-shore zone** (B36)
consumer (B21)	**open-ocean zone** (B36)

1. All the populations that live in the same place make up a ____.

2. An organism's role in its ____, or home, is called its ____.

3. A group of parts that work as a unit is called a ____.

4. The three levels that are part of any food chain are ____, ____, and ____.

5. Coral reefs are affected by the ____, or saltiness, of ocean water.

6. ____ is reached when the changes in a system are balanced.

7. A ____ shows how several food chains connect and overlap.

8. Populations and the environment in which they interact form an ____.

9. All the coral polyps living in a reef form a ____ of polyps.

10. Rain forests and coral reefs are important because they have great variety, or ____, of living things.

11. An ____ is a diagram that shows the amount of energy passed from one organism to another along a food chain.

12. ____ is the average weather over a long time.

13. From deepest to shallowest, the three ocean zones are ____, ____, and ____.

Connect Concepts

Use the terms in the Word Bank to complete the graphic organizer.

ecosystems
producers
population
consumers
community
decomposers

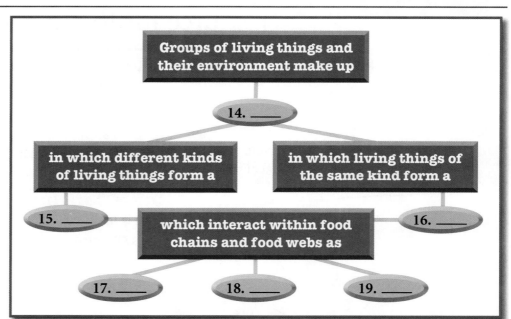

Groups of living things and their environment make up

14. ____

in which different kinds of living things form a

in which living things of the same kind form a

15. ____

16. ____

which interact within food chains and food webs as

17. ____   18. ____   19. ____

Check Understanding

Write the letter of the best choice.

20. Which of these is **NOT** a system?
    A grass, soil, water sprinkler
    B sun, algae, snails, fungi
    C grass, shrubs, trees
    D coral, clown fish, salt water, bacteria

21. Which of these are consumers in a coral reef ecosystem?
    F algae   H monkeys
    G clownfish   J bacteria

22. For an insect, the space under a rock is likely its —
    A population   C food source
    B niche   D habitat

23. A rain forest and all the organisms that live there are —
    F a population H a community
    G an ecosystem J a habitat

24. Robins, earthworms, and grass live in a yard. These three groups make up a —
    A species   C community
    B habitat   D population

Critical Thinking

25. Explain how rain and water that runs off help maintain the stability of a yard.

26. In a meadow ecosystem, rabbits eat only plants. They eat plants faster than the plants can grow back. What must happen to bring the ecosystem into balance?

Process Skills Review

27. Suppose you put all your favorite plants in a terrarium. You include a cactus, a violet, and a grass plant. **Predict** what will happen. Explain your answer.

28. Suppose that last night during a rainstorm you heard something turn over a trash can. When you turned on the light, you saw an animal run through the mud and briefly get caught in your fence. What experiences and clues could you use to **infer** the identity of the animal?

29. Suppose you knew that an animal lived only in trees and was very slow-moving. **Infer** which of the following it might feed on. Explain how you made your choice.

    mice   grass   caterpillars
    snakes   leaves   birds

30. If you wanted to show the colors and markings of two animals, would it be better to draw pictures of them or **model** them in clay? What if you needed to show their body shapes as well?

31. Suppose you **observe** many jellyfish floating on the surface in an area of the ocean. What can you **infer** about other organisms in the area?

Performance Assessment

Model an Ecosystem

Make a poster or diagram that illustrates an ecosystem of a lost land somewhere on Earth. The poster should show living and nonliving things. Add labels to identify the parts of the ecosystem you drew. Then write about a population living there, its habitat and niche, and how the climate affects its food sources.

Protecting Ecosystems

Vocabulary Preview

succession
reclamation
conservation
redesign
preservation

What would you do if you were living in a cold climate and your furnace didn't work? You might put on more clothes or find another way to heat your home. Or you might just move! Living things in nature face similar problems if their environments change. In this chapter you'll find out how people help protect ecosystems from harmful changes.

Fast Fact

Black-footed ferrets are the only type of ferret still living in the wild. Changes in the environment have reduced the population of ferrets to the point that they have been placed on the endangered species list. The ferret shown on page B49 is being released to help increase the number of wild ferrets. Because ferrets can get the flu from people, the man is wearing a surgical face mask.

Fast Fact

Causes of Species Endangerment

Cause	Percent of Endangered Species Affected
Habitat loss	88 %
Competition with other species	46 %
Pollution	20 %
Hunting	14 %
Disease	2 %

Earth's Surface

UNIT EXPERIMENT

Earthquake-Resistant Structures

Earth's surface is always changing. Volcanoes and earthquakes are major causes of those changes. Fossils can provide a record of changes that happened long ago. While you study this unit, you can conduct a long-term experiment about how buildings are affected by earthquakes. Here are some questions to think about. How can you build a structure for earthquake conditions? What building shapes resist earthquake damage? Plan and conduct an experiment to find answers to these or other questions you have about Earth's surface. See pages x–xix for help in designing your experiment.

Earthquakes and Volcanoes

Earth is a planet that is always changing. When Earth's crust moves, earthquakes occur and volcanoes erupt. While both can be dangerous and scary, they are also natural Earth processes that have shaped the surface of our world.

Fast Fact

One day in 1943 the volcano Paricutín appeared in a farmer's field in Mexico. Six days later it was 150 meters (500 ft) high and still growing! Eventually it covered an entire town including this building!

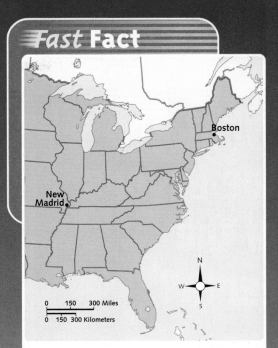

One of the most powerful earth-quakes in United States history happened in 1812 in New Madrid, Missouri. The shaking was felt over 5 million square kilometers (2 million sq mi). It rang church bells in Boston 1600 kilometers (1000 mi) away!

Fast Fact

Iceland is a nation built on volca-noes. In fact, most houses in Ice-land are heated with water from volcanic hot springs like this one!

Sources of Heat in Iceland's Homes

Source	Percent
Volcanic hot springs	85%
Electricity	12%
Oil	3%

What Are the Layers of the Earth?

In this lesson, you can . . .

INVESTIGATE the layers of the Earth.

LEARN ABOUT how huge pieces of Earth's crust and mantle act on each other.

LINK to math, writing, literature, and technology.

The Layers of the Earth

Activity Purpose Have you ever wondered what the inside of Earth looks like? It is not possible to cut Earth in half, but scientists know that our planet is made up of several layers. In this investigation you will **measure** how thick the parts of an apple are. Then you will compare them with Earth's layers.

Materials
- half of an apple
- metric ruler

Activity Procedure

1. **Observe** the apple half carefully. Draw a picture of this piece of the apple. Show its layers. (Picture A)

2. A thin peel covers the outside of the apple. Use the ruler to **measure** the thickness of the peel. **Record** your measurement on your drawing.

3. The thick, white part that you eat is the middle of the apple. **Measure** the thickness of this layer. **Record** your measurement on your drawing. (Picture B)

◄ Giant slabs, or pieces, of Earth's crust and mantle collided, or hit each other, to produce the spectacular Himalayas (him•uh•LAY•uhz).

Picture A

Picture B

4 Deep inside the apple is the core. **Measure** the core, starting at the center of the apple. **Record** your measurement on your drawing.

5 Like the apple, Earth has three main layers. The crust is Earth's outside layer. The mantle is the thick, middle layer of Earth. Deep inside Earth is the core. Work with a partner to explain which parts of the apple are like the core, mantle, and crust of Earth.

Draw Conclusions

1. **Use numbers** to **compare** the layers of the apple. Which layer is the thinnest?

2. Which of Earth's layers is most like the apple peel? Explain your answer.

3. **Scientists at Work** Scientists use many kinds of tools to **measure** objects and their characteristics. How did using a ruler help you describe the apple's layers?

Investigate Further Use a small gum ball, modeling clay, and colored plastic wrap to make a cut-away model of Earth's layers. Which material will you use to stand for the core? Which material should you use to stand for the crust? For the mantle? Tell how you could **use numbers** to make your model more accurate.

Process Skill Tip

Scientists use tools such as rulers, scales, and balances to make measurements. You can **measure** using standard units. The numbers you get from measuring can be more useful than words for talking about an object.

Earth's Structure

Earth's Layers

FIND OUT

- about Earth's layers
- how slabs of Earth's crust and upper mantle move

VOCABULARY

crust
mantle
core
plate

Earth is made up of three layers. As you learned in the investigation, these layers are the crust, the mantle, and the core.

Earth's **crust** is the layer we can walk on. The crust includes the rock of the ocean floor and large areas of land called continents (KAHN•tuh•nuhnts). Asia is the largest continent, followed by Africa, North America, South America, Antarctica, Europe, and Australia. The United States is on the continent of North America.

Below the crust is the **mantle** (MAN•tuhl). It is the thickest layer of the planet. Most of the mantle is solid rock. Some of this layer, though, is partly melted. This partly melted rock flows slowly like a very thick liquid.

Deep inside Earth is the **core** (KOHR). The core is a dense ball made mostly of two metals, iron and nickel.

✔ **What are Earth's three main layers?**

We live on Earth's crust. The crust under the continents is much thicker than the crust under the oceans. ▼

Deep Inside Earth

Earth's core can be divided into two layers. The *inner core* is a solid ball made mostly of iron and nickel. It is the hottest layer of Earth. It may be as hot as the surface of the sun. Earth's *outer core* is a pool of hot, liquid metal.

✔ **Which of Earth's layers is the hottest?**

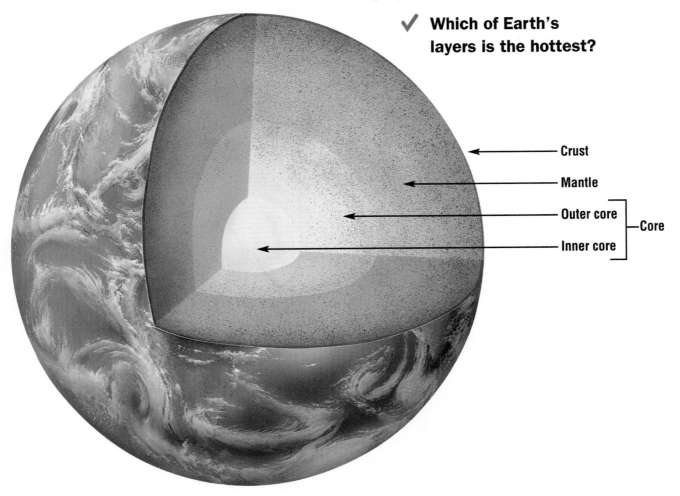

Crust

Mantle

Outer core ⎤

Inner core ⎦ Core

Thickness of Earth's Layers

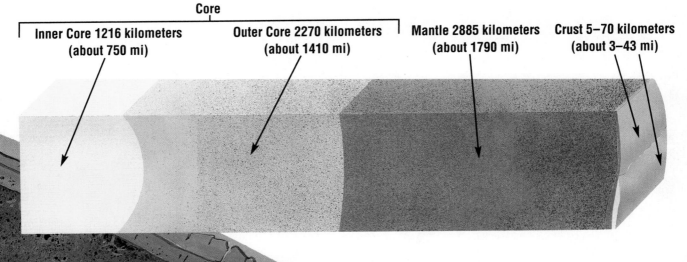

Core

Inner Core 1216 kilometers (about 750 mi)

Outer Core 2270 kilometers (about 1410 mi)

Mantle 2885 kilometers (about 1790 mi)

Crust 5–70 kilometers (about 3–43 mi)

How Plates Move

Earth's crust and upper mantle are broken into continent-sized slabs called **plates**. Plates move very slowly across Earth's surface on a thin layer of partly melted mantle. Most plates move only a few centimeters a year, or about the same length your fingernails grow each year. Plates can move away from each other, toward each other, or past each other.

Look at the diagram below. It shows two plates moving away from each other. This type of plate motion usually happens on ocean floors. New ocean-floor crust forms where the plates move apart. A long chain of mountains called the Mid-Atlantic Ridge runs along the ocean floor in the middle of the Atlantic Ocean. It formed where two plates of Earth's crust are moving apart.

✔ **How fast do Earth's plates move?**

ICELAND

▼ Iceland is slowly being split into two pieces. A large crack, or rift, is forming as two of Earth's plates move away from each other.

▼ These two plates are moving away from each other.

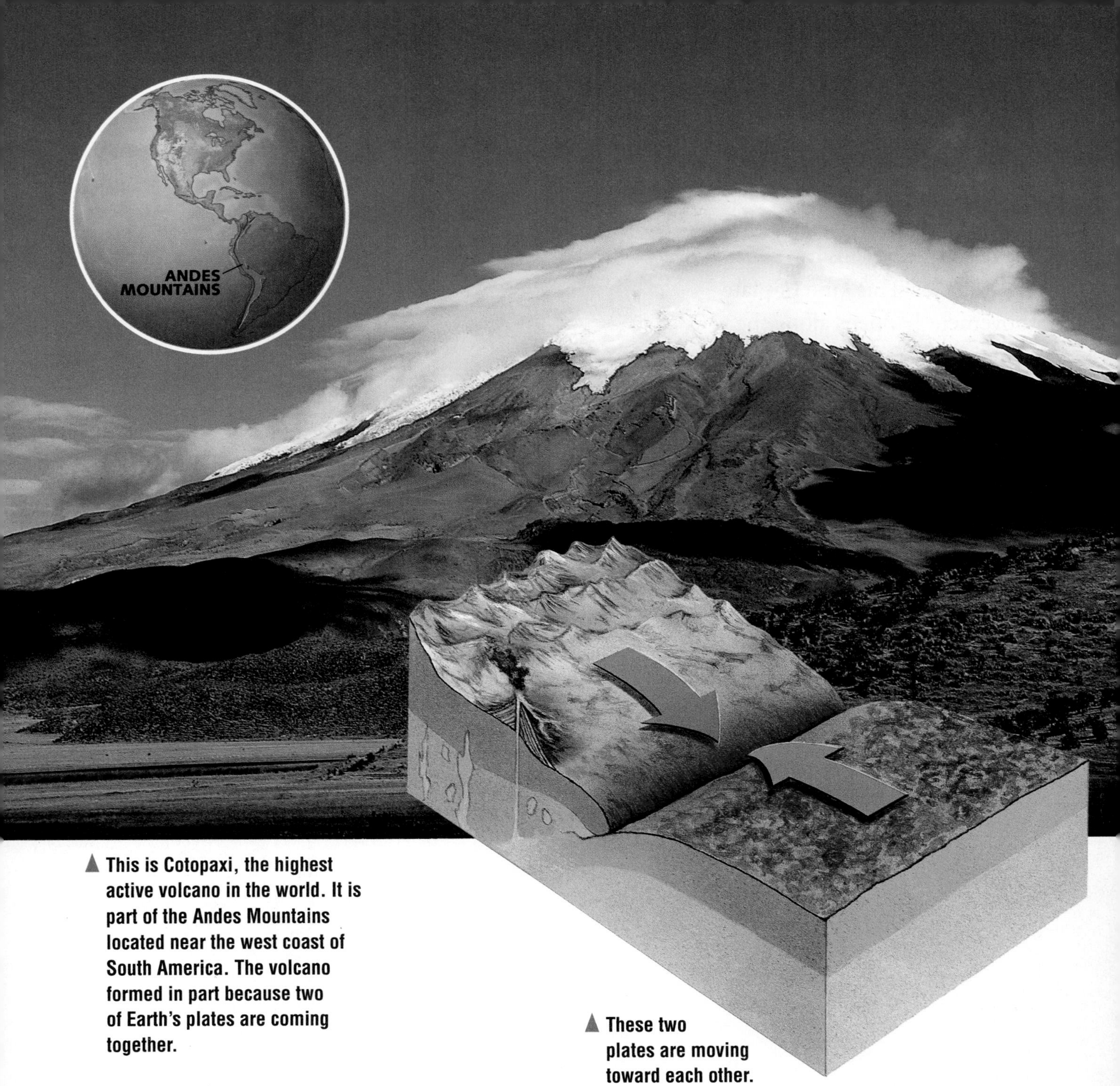

▲ This is Cotopaxi, the highest active volcano in the world. It is part of the Andes Mountains located near the west coast of South America. The volcano formed in part because two of Earth's plates are coming together.

▲ These two plates are moving toward each other.

Plates Move Together

The diagram above shows plates moving toward each other. Mountains form when plates come together. Sometimes one plate is pushed below the other plate. This can form volcanoes. At other times the plates meet like cars in a slow-motion, head-on crash. The material on the plates wrinkles and forms high mountains. The Himalaya Mountains of Asia formed in this way. Because the plates are still moving, the mountains continue to grow a little taller each year.

✓ **What usually happens when plates come together?**

Plates Move Past Each Other

The diagram to the right shows plates moving past each other. The rocks along the crack between the plates stick and then move suddenly. This can cause earthquakes. This kind of plate movement happens along the San Andreas fault in California.

✓ **What often happens as plates slide past each other?**

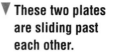

▼ These two plates are sliding past each other.

The San Andreas fault runs through many miles of desert and mountains in southern California. The frequent earthquakes in southern California are caused by quick, large movements of the two pieces of Earth's crust that form the fault. ▼

Summary

Earth is made up of three layers. The crust is the outer layer of Earth. The mantle is the middle layer. The inner layer of Earth is the core. Earth's crust and upper mantle are broken into giant plates that move very slowly.

Review

1. What are the three layers of Earth?
2. Which layers of Earth make up plates?
3. Describe the three ways plates can move.
4. **Critical Thinking** Why do you think volcanoes may form when one plate is pushed under another?
5. **Test Prep** Which of Earth's layers forms the continents?

    A crust   C outer core
    B mantle   D ocean floor

Fault

LINKS

MATH LINK

Rate of Plate Movement If two of Earth's plates that are touching one another are moving apart at a rate of 3 cm per year, how long will it take for the plates to be 12 cm apart?

WRITING LINK

Expressive Writing—Poem Write a poem for a younger child using the letters in the word *Earth*. Begin the first line of the poem with a word that starts with *E*. Start the second line of the poem using the letter *A*, and so on. Include facts about Earth's layers in your poem.

LITERATURE LINK

The Magic School Bus Inside the Earth What if you were taking a trip to the center of the Earth? Compare and contrast each layer of the planet. Now read *The Magic School Bus Inside the Earth* by Joanna Cole. How does Ms. Frizzle's trip compare to yours?

TECHNOLOGY LINK

Learn more about Earth's plates by visiting the Smithsonian National Air and Space Museum Internet site.
www.si.edu/harcourt/science

 Smithsonian Institution®

LESSON 2

What Causes Earthquakes?

In this lesson, you can . . .

INVESTIGATE the shaking of Earth caused by moving plates.

LEARN ABOUT why earthquakes occur.

LINK to math, writing, technology, and other areas.

Earthquakes

Activity Purpose What happens when you snap your fingers? First, you put your middle finger against your thumb. As you press your finger and thumb together and try to move one past the other, they stick for a moment. When the fingers come apart, your middle finger hits your palm. This causes the air to vibrate, or shake. You hear a snap. In this investigation you will **make a model** of something like a finger snap. You'll show how Earth's plates sometimes stick and then move past each other, making Earth's crust vibrate.

Materials

- 3-in. × 5-in. self-stick note
- small plastic cup
- water

Activity Procedure

1. Stick the self-stick note to a table. Be sure that about 1 in. of the short side of the self-stick note is hanging over the edge of the table. (Picture A) Also make sure the self-stick note is firmly stuck in place.

◄ An earthquake can destroy a city in seconds.

Picture A

Picture B

2 Fill the cup ¼ full with water. Place the cup on the center part of the self-stick note that is on the table.

3 Carefully and firmly pull the self-stick note straight out from under the cup. (Picture B) The sticky part of the note will stop you from easily pulling it all the way out. **Observe** what happens to the water.

Draw Conclusions

1. How is snapping your fingers like the movement of the self-stick note?

2. What did you **observe** about the water in the cup when you pulled on the self-stick note?

3. **Scientists at Work** Scientists often **infer** things based on their observations. What can you infer might happen when plates are moving past one another if the pressure between the plates is suddenly changed?

Investigate Further Use two 3-in. × 5-in. self-stick notes to model two plates sticking. Bend the notes so that the sticky parts face each other. Touch the sticky parts together and slide one note past the other. How does the shape of the note papers change? How do they move?

Process Skill Tip

Observations and inferences are different. **Observations** are made with your senses. **Inferences** are opinions you form based on your observations.

Earthquakes and How They Are Measured

How Earthquakes Occur

FIND OUT

- what causes earthquakes
- how earthquakes are measured

VOCABULARY

earthquake
fault
focus
epicenter
seismograph

In the investigation, you made a model of an earthquake. An **earthquake** (ERTH•kwayk) is a vibration, or shaking, of Earth's crust. Most earthquakes occur along faults. A **fault** is a break in the crust along which rock moves. Rock on either side of a fault can move up and down, side to side, or both.

Many earthquakes happen where plates are moving past each other. Sometimes the rocks along a fault get stuck and don't move for a while. But the plates are still moving and causing pressure on the rocks. When the pressure builds up enough, the rocks break and the plates move suddenly. This releases, or sets free, the energy that has built up. The energy takes the form of vibrations that move through Earth's crust. You made a model of this sticking and slipping in the investigation. When the self-stick note that stood for the rocks moved, you saw the released energy cause vibrations in the water in the cup.

◄ Scientists record more than 30,000 earthquakes each year in California.

▲ The San Andreas fault is two plates sliding past each other. This fault runs through most of California and is about 1000 kilometers (about 610 mi) long.

C14

Damage is usually worst near an earthquake's epicenter. ▶

▲ Energy in the form of vibrations moves out in all directions from the focus of an earthquake.

The picture above shows two plates sliding past each other. These two plates had been stuck, but they recently moved, and an earthquake occurred. The point underground where the movement first took place is called the **focus** (FOH•kuhs). When rocks slip at the focus, energy moves out in all directions through the rock around it. Damage from the vibrations caused by this release of energy is usually centered around the epicenter. The **epicenter** (EP•ih•sent•er) is the point on the surface that is right above the focus.

Earthquakes such as the one in the picture happen often along the San Andreas

fault. Dozens of major earthquakes have occurred along this well-known fault. In 1906 an earthquake caused fires that burned down most of the city of San Francisco. The 1989 Loma Prieta (LOH•muh pree•AY•tuh) earthquake postponed the third game of the World Series. That earthquake caused about $6 billion in damage. In 1994 the Northridge earthquake caused parts of the crust in Los Angeles to move 20 centimeters (about 8 in.). More than 3000 homes were destroyed. Ten highway bridges and seven concrete parking garages fell down. The total damage was more than $20 billion.

✔ **What causes an earthquake?**

How Earthquakes Are Measured

You saw in the investigation how the water rippled as the self-stick note was pulled from under the cup. The ripples, or waves, traveled through the water. In the same way, the energy from an earthquake travels as waves through the Earth. Scientists can measure this energy in different ways.

A **seismograph** (SYZ•muh•graf) is an instrument that records earthquake waves. A seismograph has two main parts: a pen and a paper-covered rotating drum. As the drum turns, the pen marks a line. When an earthquake happens, the line gets jagged. The more jagged the line, the stronger the earthquake is.

Scientists also use numbers to measure earthquakes. The Mercalli (muhr•KAH•lee) scale measures the movement and damage that an earthquake causes. The scale uses Roman numerals from I to XII. An earthquake measuring III on this scale makes

▲ Earthquake watching stations usually have many seismographs like this one.

hanging objects swing back and forth. An earthquake measuring X on this scale causes brick buildings to crumble.

You are probably more familiar with the Richter (RIK•tuhr) scale. This scale uses the numbers 1 through 9 to measure the energy an earthquake releases. An earthquake measuring 3.0 on the Richter scale releases about 30 times the amount of energy as an earthquake measuring 2.0. It releases 900 times the energy of an earthquake measuring 1.0.

✔ **What are two scales that scientists use to measure earthquakes?**

Mercalli Scale

The stronger the earthquake, the bigger the waves recorded on a seismograph.

Mercalli scale III: A hanging lamp swings. (about Richter scale 2.0 at the epicenter)

Mercalli scale V: Bricks or plaster may fall. (about Richter scale 4.0 to 5.0 at the epicenter)

Mercalli scale VII: Brick structures are damaged. (about Richter scale 6.0 at the epicenter)

Summary

A fault in Earth's crust is a break along which rocks move. An earthquake is the vibrations produced when energy builds up and is quickly released along a fault. Scientists use the Mercalli scale and the Richter scale to measure earthquake intensity.

Review

1. What causes an earthquake?
2. What is a fault?
3. How do scientists measure the damage caused by an earthquake?
4. **Critical Thinking** Why are there so many earthquakes in California?
5. **Test Prep** What is the point below Earth's surface where an earthquake begins?

   A epicenter
   B focus
   C fault
   D core

Mercalli scale X: Buildings are severely damaged. (about Richter scale 7.0 at the epicenter)

LINKS

MATH LINK

Collect, Organize, and Display Data Research some of the most damaging earthquakes in history. Make a time line showing the order in which they occurred. Include the Richter scale value if it is available.

WRITING LINK

Expressive Writing — Friendly Letter Suppose you have survived an earthquake. For a younger student, write a letter that describes what causes an earthquake or how an earthquake affects buildings. Use at least three of the terms from this lesson.

HEALTH LINK

Earthquake Safety Use library references to find out how to stay safe during an earthquake. Make a poster that shows what you found.

DRAMA LINK

Earthquakes in Movies Find a movie or play about an earthquake or a prediction of an earthquake. Describe how such events affect the characters.

TECHNOLOGY LINK

To learn more about predicting earthquake damage, watch *Quake Liquid Soils* on the **Harcourt Science Newsroom Video.**

Turner Le@rning®

How Do Volcanoes Form?

In this lesson, you can . . .

INVESTIGATE how a volcano erupts.

LEARN ABOUT how volcanoes form.

LINK to math, writing, social studies, and technology.

◄ Some volcanoes look like fountains when they shoot molten rock into the air.

INVESTIGATE

Volcanic Eruptions

Activity Purpose Have you ever had a balloon pop because you filled it with too much air? If so, you now know that balloons can stand only a certain amount of pressure before they pop. In some ways a volcano is like a balloon. In this investigation you will **make a model** that shows what happens when pressure builds up in a volcano.

Materials

- 1-L plastic bottle
- small piece of modeling clay
- aluminum pie plate
- puffed rice cereal or tiny pieces of plastic foam
- funnel
- air pump

Activity Procedure

1 Ask your teacher to make a hole near the bottom of the bottle. Use the clay to stick the bottom of the bottle to the pie plate. (Picture A)

2 Use the funnel to fill the bottle $\frac{1}{4}$ full with the rice cereal or foam.

Picture A

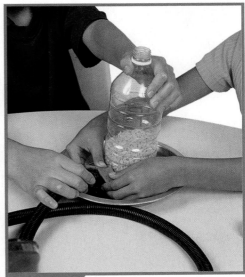

Picture B

3 Attach the air pump to the hole in the bottle. Put a piece of clay around the hole to seal it. (Picture B)

4 Pump air into the bottle. **Observe** what happens.

Draw Conclusions

1. What happened to the cereal when you pumped air into the bottle?

2. How could you make more cereal shoot out of the bottle?

3. **Scientists at Work** Scientists often **make a model** to help them understand things that happen in nature. How is the bottle used to model an erupting volcano?

Investigate Further Some volcanoes have steep sides. Others have gently sloping sides. Make models using some fine sand and gravel to test this **hypothesis:** A volcano is steeper if it forms from thicker lava. What property of lava is modeled by the size of the pieces of sand and gravel? What are some other materials you could use to model lava?

Volcanoes

How Volcanoes Form

VOCABULARY

volcano
magma
lava
vent
magma chamber
crater

A **volcano** is a mountain that forms when red-hot melted rock flows through a crack onto the earth's surface. Melted rock inside Earth is called **magma** (MAG•muh). Melted rock that reaches Earth's surface is called **lava** (LAH•vuh).

Some volcanoes form in the ocean where plates are moving away from each other. As the plates move apart, magma slowly rises toward the surface from deep in the mantle. When the magma gets to the surface, it cools and hardens to form new ocean floor.

Other volcanoes form where plates are moving toward each other. When a plate made of ocean crust collides with, or hits, one made of continental crust, the plate made of ocean crust is forced down into the mantle. There it partly melts, forming magma. The magma flows onto the surface through a rocky opening called a **vent** to form volcanic mountains. The volcanic mountains in the Andes in South America and in the Cascade Range in the northwestern United States formed this way.

Some volcanoes form when a plate moves over a hot spot in the mantle. Fountains of hot rock punch through the crust to form volcanoes. The volcanic islands of Hawai'i formed this way.

✔ **What are three ways volcanoes form?**

When plates collide, one plate may be forced down into the mantle. Deep inside Earth, the plate material melts to form magma. ▼

Magma rises to Earth's surface through volcanoes. ▶

Types of Volcanoes

Not every volcano erupts in the same way. Some shoot runny lava high in the air. Others ooze lava like soft-serve ice cream coming out of a machine. Part of what erupts from some other volcanoes is lava chunks that have already hardened into rock. Each type of eruption forms a different type of mountain.

Shield volcanoes are large mountains with gentle slopes. They form from runny lava. Many of the volcanoes in Hawai'i are shield volcanoes. One of the largest is Mauna Loa on the main island of Hawai'i. Mauna Loa rises 9000 meters (about 30,000 ft) from the ocean floor.

Cinder cone volcanoes are small volcanoes made of hardened lava chunks called cinders. Cinder cones have steep sides. They are usually less than 300 meters (about 1000 ft) tall.

Composite (kahm•PAHZ•it) *volcanoes* are medium-sized mountains. They are made up of layers of lava that alternate with layers of cinders. These mountains have steep peaks and gently sloping sides. Mount Fuji (FOO•jee) in Japan, Mount Pelée (PEH•lay) on the island of Martinque (mahr•tuh•NEEK), and Mount Vesuvius (veh•SOO•vee•uhs) in Italy are composite volcanoes.

✔ **Why don't all volcanic mountains look the same?**

Magma flows onto the surface from a vent and becomes lava.

Magma rises toward the surface through a rocky tube called a conduit.

Lava and other kinds of volcanic materials can build up to form a mountain like the one shown here.

A magma chamber is an underground pool that holds hot magma.

Volcanoes Build

Some volcanoes form under the ocean where slabs of Earth's crust and upper mantle are moving away from each other. Where this happens, magma flows from the magma chamber toward the crust. When it reaches the crust, the magma flows through a large crack in the ocean floor. As it cools and hardens, new ocean floor forms.

Volcanic eruptions also form new crust on continents. The mountains discussed on page C21 are examples of land added to the continents.

Crater Lake, which is shown on this page, is also an example of how volcanoes add to Earth's landscape. This landform is what is left of an eruption in southern Oregon about 7000 years ago.

Although volcanic eruptions are often harmful, they can have good effects on the land around them. The soil around an active volcano often has minerals that help crops

THE INSIDE STORY

The Formation of Crater Lake

A large basin, or crater (KRAY•ter), formed at the top of the volcano when it fell in on itself after the eruption. Over time, this basin filled with rainwater to form a lake. Crater Lake is about 10 kilometers (about 6 mi) in diameter and nearly 600 meters (almost 2000 ft) deep.

2. The eruption was so powerful that it left the magma chamber below the volcano almost empty.

1. Seven thousand years ago, Mount Mazama, the volcano that became Crater Lake, exploded with violent force.

grow. The minerals are carried to the soil by rainwater that flows over hardened lava. For example, many types of plants grow in the soils surrounding the slopes of Mount Vesuvius in Italy. Fruits and vegetables grow well in the soils near the bottom of the mountain. Hardwood trees grow well in soils on the slopes that formed from the lava.

✓ **Name two ways volcanoes build the land.**

In 1707 Mount Fuji on Honshu, Japan, erupted. The eruption sent out about a cubic kilometer of dust, ash, and rock. ▼

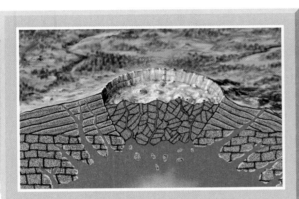

3. The top of the mountain fell into the empty magma chamber, leaving a crater. Later, a much smaller eruption formed an island called Wizard Island.

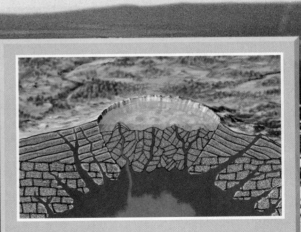

4. Long after the volcano erupted, rainwater filled the crater to form a large lake. Today, Crater Lake is one of Oregon's most popular places. It is the United States's fifth oldest national park.

▲ The volcanoes in Hawai'i erupt quietly but often blanket the ground with lava.

Volcanoes Destroy

The lava and gases that erupt from volcanoes are very hot and often destroy everything in their path. When Mount St. Helens in Washington State erupted in 1980, the temperature of the ash and gases reached about 800°C (1470°F)! The blast blew down trees as far as 25 kilometers (about 15 mi) from the volcano. At least 60 people died because of this volcanic explosion. The clouds of ash and gases were so thick that some of these people died because they couldn't breathe.

In 1983 Colo volcano on the Indonesian island of Una Una erupted. Scientists there had warned people of the possible danger. All of the 7000 people who lived in the area left their homes and went to safe places.

▲ Volcanoes have destroyed property by spraying ash over houses and other buildings.

Deadly Volcanic Eruptions

Year	Volcano	Fatalities
1792	Unzen, Japan	About 14,500 people lost their lives, mainly from the tsunami (wave) caused by the eruption.
1815	Tambora, Indonesia	About 92,000 people died, mainly from starvation.
1902	Mount Pelée, Martinique	About 28,000 people lost their lives, mainly because of the ash cloud.
1980	Mount St. Helens, Washington	About 60 people were killed. Scientists had predicted the eruption and warned people to leave.
1991	Mount Pinatubo, Philippines	More than 700 people lost their lives, mainly from the heavy fall of ash.

◀ An explosion of ash, rock, and gases from a volcano often kills everything in its path. These trees were flattened by the eruption of Mount St. Helens in 1980.

When the volcano erupted, houses, crops, livestock, and nearly everything else in the area were destroyed. But no people died.

✔ **What are some harmful effects of volcanoes?**

Summary

A volcano is a mountain that forms when melted rock called lava flows out onto Earth's surface. Most volcanoes form along plate edges. Volcanic eruptions add crust to the Earth and can be harmful. Lava flows can make soils rich in minerals that help crops grow.

Review

1. What are the three kinds of volcanoes?
2. What is a magma chamber?
3. How can volcanic eruptions be harmful?
4. **Critical Thinking** Compare magma and lava.
5. **Test Prep** What is the name of the rocky tube in a volcano through which magma travels?
   A magma chamber
   B conduit
   C crater
   D lava

LINKS

MATH LINK

Organize Data Look at the chart on page C24. It lists eruptions in the order in which they happened. List the volcanoes in another type of order. Use library reference materials to find other volcanic eruptions to add to your chart.

WRITING LINK

Informative Writing — Description Write an article that describes the journey of the rock that erupts to form a volcano. Begin with the colliding of plates. End with lava erupting from the volcano. Be sure to include the effects of the volcano on the land and its people.

SOCIAL STUDIES LINK

Locate on a Map Use library reference materials to find out the ten most recent major volcano eruptions. Highlight the location of each on a copy of a world map. Write the name of the continent on which each volcano is located.

TECHNOLOGY LINK

Learn more about volcano eruptions by visiting this Internet site.
www.scilinks.org/harcourt

Dante
Robot Volcano Explorer

Suppose you're a scientist who wants to explore a volcano. You want to know about the air and gases inside the volcano and about the kinds of rock and ash. You think the harsh environment is similar to what people might experience on another planet. There's only one problem—real danger. In 1993, eight scientists died trying to get samples. You don't want to risk your life.

Dante II climbing down into Mt. Spurr

Robot Explorers

Luckily, there's a solution to your problem. It's *Dante* (DAHN•tay), a walking robot designed to explore volcanoes. *Dante* was named for an Italian writer who wrote about an imaginary trip to the Underworld. In January 1993 *Dante* tried to explore an Antarctic volcano. But wires that sent information from the robot to the scientists broke. *Dante* had to be hauled out.

Dante II

The designers of *Dante* returned to the Field Robotics Center at Carnegie Mellon University in Pittsburgh. Using what they learned from *Dante*, they built a new robot, *Dante II*. In August 1994 *Dante II* entered the crater of Mount Spurr, a volcano in Alaska. *Dante II* sent images to scientists about 130 kilometers (80 mi) away. Using a laser to scan the surroundings, *Dante II* made 3-D maps. It also had a video camera. For a week the robot explored the crater and analyzed the gases.

Dante II had a snowshoe on each of its eight legs. It was designed to move on its own, following preset directions. But it could also be controlled by the scientists far away.

A Near Disaster

A week of warm weather melted about 2 meters (6 ft) of snow. This caused problems when *Dante II* tried to climb out of the volcano crater. The snowshoes on its legs were no longer useful, and the robot fell. Engineers tried to lift *Dante II* using a helicopter, but a cable broke. Finally, two people had to hike into the crater. They put the robot into a sling, hanging from a helicopter.

Dante's Future

Dante II now travels around the country as part of a science exhibit. Its designers are working on improved robots. Their goal is to use similar robots to explore distant planets.

THINK ABOUT IT

1. How might an Antarctic volcano be like a planet other than Earth?
2. Why do you think *Dante II* had eight legs?

CAREERS
FIELD GEOLOGY TECHNICIAN

What They Do Field geology technicians set up, use, and repair geology equipment. The equipment is used for measuring rocks, minerals, volcanoes, and other parts of Earth's surface. The technicians work both in the laboratory and outdoors. They measure, calculate, and record results. They also communicate conclusions. They work with scientists and help them, often using computers, robots, and other machines.

Education and Training To be a field geology technician, you need at least two years of training. You might go to a community college or a technical institute. Some field geology technicians have a college degree in geology.

WEB LINK
For Science and Technology updates, visit the Harcourt Internet site.
www.harcourtschool.com

GO ONLINE

Hiroo Kanamori
SEISMOLOGIST

"I have many fond memories of pondering over some curious problems, coming up with some rough ideas, and finally solving them to my satisfaction."

1923 earthquake damage in Tokyo

Dr. Hiroo Kanamori (hee•roh•oh kahn•ah•moh•ree) studies earthquakes and teaches at the California Institute of Technology, or Caltech. He began studying earthquakes in Japan at Tokyo University. Later, he came to this country to study and decided to stay.

Kanamori tries to find out what causes earthquakes and how to reduce their effect on society. He has developed ways to analyze data from earthquakes that happened long ago. The data is from before modern earthquake science tools were made or used. For example, he studied the 1923 earthquake in Tokyo.

The motion, forces, and energy of California earthquakes are of special interest to Kanamori. His work has helped reduce earthquake hazards.

For example, people can better prepare for an earthquake if they understand earthquakes better. They can also design stronger buildings that can survive earthquakes. Kanamori is pleased to see his work used to make people safer.

Kanamori has published several articles on earthquakes and on Earth's structure. He says he has been lucky to work with many good people, both in Japan and in the United States.

THINK ABOUT IT

1. In what way does Dr. Kanamori share credit for his work?

2. What kinds of things would a person have to know to study earthquakes?

MOVING MAGMA

How does toothpaste in a tube move like magma in a volcano?

Materials

- paper towel
- half-full tube of toothpaste, with cap

Procedure

1 Place the paper towel on the table. Be sure the cap to the toothpaste is on the tube loosely. Do <u>not</u> screw it on tight.

2 Squeeze the tube of toothpaste from the bottom. Continue squeezing until the toothpaste has risen to the top of the tube.

3 Continue squeezing the tube as the toothpaste spills onto the sides of the tube.

4 Observe the toothpaste as it hardens after rising out of the tube.

Draw Conclusions

How is the movement of the toothpaste similar to the movement of magma? How is the hardened toothpaste outside the tube like lava?

MAKING SEISMIC WAVES

How does movement of Earth's plates make waves in Earth?

Materials

- 9 in. × 13 in. cake pan
- apron
- safety goggles
- water
- food coloring
- spoon
- foam blocks
- sandpaper
- masking tape

Procedure

1 **CAUTION** **Put on your apron and safety goggles.** Fill the pan with about $\frac{1}{2}$ in. of water. Color the water with a few drops of food coloring. Use the spoon to mix the color.

2 Tape sandpaper to the long, thin side of each of the foam blocks. Place the blocks in the water. Push them together so that the sandpaper sides are touching.

3 Quickly slide the two blocks along each other in opposite directions.

4 Observe what happens to the water around the two blocks.

Draw Conclusions

What happens if you move the blocks more slowly? Describe how this model is similar to moving plates in an earthquake.

Vocabulary Review

Use the terms below to complete the sentences. The page numbers in ( ) tell you where to look in the chapter if you need help.

crust (C6)   seismograph (C16)
mantle (C6)   volcano (C20)
core (C6)   lava (C20)
plates (C8)   magma (C20)
earthquake (C14)   vent (C20)
fault (C14)   magma chamber (C21)
focus (C15)   crater (C22)
epicenter (C15)

1. An underground holding pool for hot magma is called a ____.

2. Scientists use a ____ to measure earthquake waves.

3. A vibration of Earth's crust is an ____.

4. A large basin that can form at the top of a volcano is a ____.

5. Most of the magma from a volcano comes up through a rocky opening called a ____.

6. ____ is melted rock that flows out onto Earth's surface.

7. If you somehow dug down to Earth's center, the first two layers you would pass through are the ____ and ____.

8. Hot, melted rock that is underground is called ____.

9. The deepest layer of Earth is the ____.

10. The point on Earth's surface that is directly above an earthquake's focus is the ____.

11. Earth's crust and upper mantle are broken into several ____.

12. A mountain that forms from lava is a ____.

13. The ____ of an earthquake is the point underground where the movement of the earthquake first takes place.

14. A break in the crust along which rocks move is a ____.

Connect Concepts

Use the terms in the Word Bank to complete the concept map.

crust
earthquakes
core
mantle
volcanoes
plates

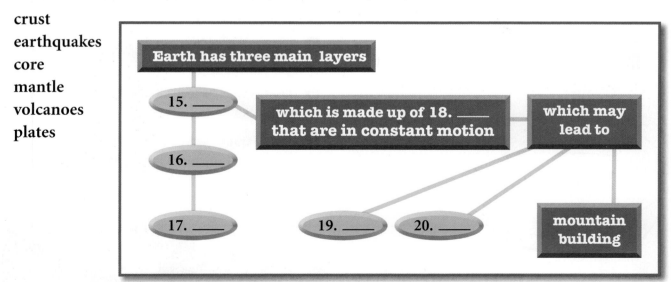

Check Understanding

Write the letter of the best choice.

21. When a volcano collapses into itself at its top, it forms a —
    A crater
    B magma chamber
    C plate
    D vent

22. The plates of Earth's crust and mantle can **NOT** usually move —
    F toward each other
    G away from each other
    H very slowly
    J very quickly

23. The layer of Earth that is the hottest is the —
    A mantle
    B inner core
    C outer core
    D crust

24. _____ are mountains made of lava layers that alternate with layers of cinders.
    F Cinder cones
    G Shield volcanoes
    H Composite volcanoes
    J Crater volcanoes

25. Volcanoes can be useful to people because volcanoes —
    A add minerals to the soil
    B spread ash
    C send out lava and gases that are very hot
    D cause huge waves

Critical Thinking

26. What happens to Earth's crust and mantle during an earthquake? How is this reaction of Earth's crust similar to what happens when a volcano erupts?

27. Scientists sometimes put seismographs on a volcano to help them predict when the volcano will erupt. Why do you think a seismograph might be useful in this situation?

Process Skills Review

28. Why is **making models** a useful way to study volcanic eruptions?

29. Suppose you are pumping up a bicycle tire. What would you observe happening to the tire as you pumped air into it? **Infer** what would happen if you pumped too much air into the tire.

30. How could **measuring** be useful as you pump up the bicycle tire?

Performance Assessment

Plate Model

Use clay to make models of two of Earth's plates. Move the clay to show how plates might behave during an earthquake. Now use the clay to show two ways plates can form volcanoes.

Fossils

The history of life on Earth is buried under your feet. You might find clues left behind in a back yard by someone who lived in the house years ago. If you know where to look, you might even find clues left behind millions of years ago by dinosaurs.

Vocabulary Preview

fossil
trace fossil
mold
cast
fossil fuel
petroleum
natural gas
peat
lignite
bituminous coal
anthracite

Fast Fact

The first fossil now known to be a dinosaur bone was found in England in 1685. Because no one knew about dinosaurs in those days, people thought it was a giant human leg bone. The bone was 6 meters (about 20 ft) long! This exhibit at the Tyrrell Museum shows a large lambeosaur and smaller dromaeosaurs. Notice how big the lambeosaur leg bones are compared with the girl.

Ammonoids (AM•uh•noydz) are a type of shellfish that lived long ago. The largest found so far was dug up in the Westphalia region of Germany. Its spiral shell is almost 2 meters (about $6\frac{1}{2}$ ft) across.

Footprints like these were the first dinosaur footprints discovered in North America. They were found in the Connecticut Valley by Pliny Moody, a 12-year-old farm boy!

How Do Fossils Form?

In this lesson, you can . . .

 INVESTIGATE how animal parts can be preserved as a fossil.

 LEARN ABOUT ways in which some fossils form.

LINK to math, writing, art, and technology.

This is a fossil ammonoid (AM•uhn•oyd). Ammonoids had hard shells and lived in ancient oceans.

INVESTIGATE

Making a Fossil

Activity Purpose When a living thing dies, its soft parts quickly rot away. The hard parts, such as bones or woody stems, take much longer to decay, or rot away. Long ago some of these hard parts were buried and became fossils. In this activity you will **make a model** of the hard and soft parts of an "animal." Then you will **observe** how parts of your model "decay."

Materials
- 8 sugar cubes
- glue gun, low temperature
- strainer
- sink or large bowl
- warm water

 CAUTION

Activity Procedure

1 Glue together four sugar cubes to make one 2 × 2 layer. **CAUTION** **The tip of the glue gun is hot.** Make a second 2 × 2 layer with the other four cubes. (Picture A) Let the layers dry for five minutes.

2 Spread glue on top of one layer, and place the second layer on top of it. Let the glue dry overnight.

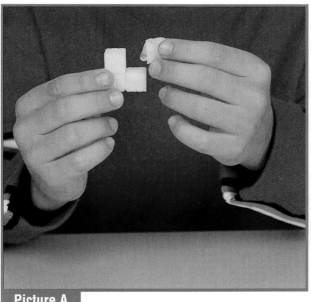

Picture A

Picture B

3 Put the two-layered structure in the strainer. Put the strainer in the sink or over a bowl. (Picture B) Pour warm water over the structure and **observe** what happens.

4 What happens to the sugar? Does anything happen to the dried glue?

Draw Conclusions

1. In your model what parts of a plant or an animal did the sugar cubes stand for? What parts of a plant or an animal did the dried glue stand for?

2. In your model, what process did the warm water stand for?

3. **Scientists at Work** Scientists often **make inferences** based on their observations. What can you infer about how fossils form, based on what you learned in the investigation?

Investigate Further Do you think fossils are still being made? **Form a hypothesis** about how the soft and hard parts of a piece of cooked chicken will change if it is buried and left alone for a couple of weeks. **Plan and conduct an experiment** to test your hypothesis. Be sure to wear goggles and rubber gloves when you handle the meat after it has been buried. What else do you think must happen for a piece of chicken to become a fossil?

Process Skill Tip

When you don't know enough to be sure why something happens, you may infer an explanation. When you **infer**, you use what you already know to explain your observations. When more information is available, you might find out whether your inference is right or wrong.

Fossil Formation

How Fossils Form

FIND OUT

• where most fossils are found

• how some fossils form

VOCABULARY

fossil
trace fossil
mold
cast

Some rocks hold clues to life on Earth long ago. These clues, called **fossils**, are found most often in sedimentary rocks such as sandstone, shale, and limestone. This is because most fossils formed when a dead plant or animal was buried quickly by sediments such as sand or mud. As with your model in the investigation, the soft parts of the plant or animal decayed, or rotted away. The hard parts took longer to decay. They were preserved, or saved, by being buried. Unburied parts would have been eaten or destroyed by weather. As the sediments hardened, the remains became trapped in rock and formed a fossil.

Fossils also can form in other ways. Not all fossils are parts of once-living things. Some fossils are traces, such as footprints, left by living things. Sometimes the shape of a plant or an animal is left as a hollow in a rock. The hollow left behind is a fossil. If minerals fill the hollow, the new rock they form is also a fossil.

✔ **How do most fossils form?**

▲ The bones of this dinosaur skull were buried in a layer of sedimentary rock.

◀ This fossil shell, buried deep beneath the desert, gives scientists clues about Earth's past. What might scientists be able to infer about this particular place on Earth?

Trace Fossils

Wood, bones, teeth, and shells aren't the only things that become fossils. **Trace fossils** show changes long-dead animals made in their surroundings. Tracks, burrows, droppings, and worm holes are some examples of trace fossils. They give scientists clues about animals. They tell how an animal might have moved. They show how big or small it might have been. They also show what it might have eaten. The photographs on this page show different types of trace fossils.

✔ **What is a trace fossil?**

▲ Fossilized tracks give clues about an animal's size and how it moved. The dinosaur track above is found in limestone near Glen Rose, Texas. It is many years old. The tracks above left were made recently in sand by a living bird. How might they become a fossil?

Scientists can learn a lot about what an animal ate by looking at coprolites (KAHP•roh•lyts). Coprolites are animal droppings that have become fossils. ▶

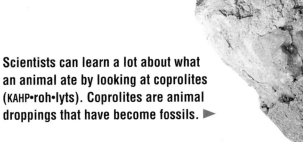

◀ A worm made this burrow, or tunnel, as it hunted for food in soft sediment. When the sediment was buried and hardened into rock, the burrow was preserved.

C37

Other Types of Fossils

Usually, the parts of living things that make up fossils are changed as rock forms. For example, fossil molds and casts form after the parts are destroyed. A **mold** is an imprint made by the outside of a dead plant or animal. A mold forms when water slowly washes animal or plant remains out of rock. The space left in the rock layer matches the shape of the once-living thing. Sometimes sediments or minerals fill a mold and form a **cast**. The cast has the same outside shape as the original living thing.

Sometimes chemical and physical changes take place as remains become fossils. Heat and pressure may destroy most of the buried remains. Only a thin film, or sheet, of black carbon is left. This type of fossil is called a carbon film.

Some fossils form when minerals slowly take the place of original, once-living material. Fossils that form in this way are called *petrified* (PET•trih•fyd) fossils. *Petri-* means "stone." The trees in Petrified Forest National Park became fossils in this way. Their wood was replaced by the mineral quartz.

A whole plant or animal, including soft parts, can become a fossil. Sometimes insects were trapped in the sticky sap of trees. When the sap hardened, the whole insect was preserved. Large animals such as woolly mammoths have also been trapped and preserved in glacier ice.

Tar pits have also preserved once-living things. Animals got stuck when they tried to walk through the sticky tar. Plants and plant parts were blown or fell into the tar and got stuck. Many animal fossils have been found in the La Brea (luh BRAY•uh) tar pits in Los Angeles, California. They include deer, elephants, horses, birds, and saber-toothed tigers.

✓ **How were whole plants or animals preserved as fossils?**

◄ Fossil molds and casts give clues about the outside of the once-living thing.

◄ A carbon film forms when heat and pressure force out most of the materials that made up a once-living thing. Only a thin sheet of carbon is left. What kind of organism is this a fossil of?

Millions of years ago, this dragonfly got stuck in sap from a pine tree. Later the sap hardened to form a clear yellow material called *amber.* ►

▲ Petrified Forest National Park in Arizona has many petrified logs like this one. The fossils began forming when water containing minerals soaked into fallen trees. As the wood slowly rotted away, minerals took its place.

Summary

Fossils are the remains of living things that lived on Earth long ago. Fossils are usually made of the hard parts of plants and animals. But they can form in several other ways. For example, trace fossils, such as tracks, burrows, and droppings, give clues about what animals did.

Review

1. What are fossils?
2. How does a carbon film form?
3. How does a petrified fossil form?
4. **Critical Thinking** Compare and contrast trace fossils and mold fossils.
5. **Test Prep** Which of the following forms when a fossil mold is filled?
   A fossil cast
   B petrified fossil
   C carbon film
   D tar pit

LINKS

MATH LINK

Construct a Graph Many cities bury their trash in big holes called landfills. The trash often forms layers like those in sedimentary rock. If you dig a hole in a city landfill and find a newspaper dated 1900, what do you think is the age of that layer of the landfill? Design a graph that you could use to show the age of several landfill layers.

WRITING LINK

Narrative Writing—Story Find out how the Badlands of South Dakota formed. Then write a story for a classmate. Tell about a fourth grader hunting fossils in the Badlands. Be sure to give a detailed description of the setting of the story.

ART LINK

Lost-Wax Casting Ask an art teacher or use library resources to find out about the lost-wax casting method. With the help of an adult, try it. How is it like what happens when fossil casts and molds form?

TECHNOLOGY LINK

Learn more about finding fossils by investigating *Digging Up Dinosaurs* on **Harcourt Science Explorations CD-ROM.**

What Can We Learn from Fossils?

In this lesson, you can . . .

INVESTIGATE how scientists decide which events happened first.

LEARN ABOUT when certain living things appeared on Earth.

LINK to math, writing, physical education, and technology.

Sets of Animal Tracks

Activity Purpose Have you and your friends ever made footprints in snow or mud? If you then looked at the crisscrossing tracks, could you tell which were made first? In this investigation your group will **make a model** of several sets of tracks. You'll then share the model with another group of students. They will try to figure out the order in which the tracks were made.

Materials

- poster board
- markers, crayons, and colored pencils
- animal footprint stamps
- ink pad

Activity Procedure

1 On the poster board, draw a picture of an area where animal tracks are found. The picture might show a riverbank or a sandy beach. (Picture A)

2 Each person in your group should choose a different animal. Mark these animals' tracks on the poster board. Use the ink pad and stamps, or any of the other items. Make sure that some sets of tracks go over other sets. Keep a record of which animal made tracks first, second, third, and so on. (Picture B)

◀ This fossil is the skull of a protoceratops. Some pieces were missing, so scientists had to infer the shape of part of the skull.

Picture A

Picture B

3 When your group has finished making tracks, trade poster boards with another group. Try to figure out the order in which the other group's tracks were made. **Record** your conclusions in an ordered list. Give reasons for the order you chose. **Compare** your conclusions with the written record of the other group's track order.

Draw Conclusions

1. Did all the animals move in the same way? If not, how could you tell the kind of animal from the tracks it made?

2. How did your group decide which tracks were made first?

3. **Scientists at Work** Scientists can **infer** relationships among rock layers and the fossils they contain. They do this after carefully **observing** the rocks and fossils. What observations led you to infer the order in which the footprints were made?

Investigate Further Get a potato. Using a plastic knife, carefully carve the potato into an animal track stamp. Use an ink pad and the stamp to make some tracks on a sheet of paper. Have a classmate **infer** from the tracks how the "animal" moves. Does it slither? Does it walk on two legs or four legs? Or does the animal jump or fly to get from place to place?

Process Skill Tip

Observations and inferences are not the same. When you **observe**, you use your senses to see, touch, hear, smell, or taste an object. When you **infer**, you form an opinion. To do this, you use what you know about the object or situation.

Fossil Clues to the Past

How Living Things Have Changed

FIND OUT

- how life on Earth may have changed over time
- how scientists learn the ages of rocks and fossils

Fossils are like snapshots of the past. They are preserved evidence of how long-dead living things may have looked. Fossil evidence also can suggest how living things may have changed over time. Look at the pictures on this page. As you can see, some living things, like the ginkgo tree, have changed very little over time. Other living things have changed a lot during Earth's history. For example, *Archaeopteryx* (ar•kee•AHP•ter•iks) was a chicken-sized animal that lived on Earth millions of years ago. It was probably related to birds that live today. It had feathers and was shaped like a bird. Some scientists hypothesize that it could fly because its wings were like those of birds alive today. But like reptiles, it had claws, a long tail, and teeth.

The *Archaeopteryx* was a reptile that had some of a bird's features. ▼

Scientists think today's African elephants are related to *Gomphotherium*. ▶

▲ This chicken skeleton and the *Archaeopteryx* skeleton are alike in some ways and different in others.

Elephants, too, have changed over time as their environments changed. Some animal types that were like elephants died out. Other types changed slowly over a long time. Woolly mammoths lived during the long, cold Ice Age. Glaciers (GLAY•shurz), or huge sheets of ice, covered large parts of North America, Europe, and Asia during the Ice Age. Mammoths died out soon after it ended. Another elephant-like animal, *Gomphotherium* (gahm•foh•THEER•ee•uhm), was able to live. Scientists think today's African elephant is related to it.

✔ **How do scientists know that living things have changed over time?**

▲ Ginkgoes belong to a family of trees that lived about 175 to 200 million years ago. Does the ginkgo leaf of today look different from the ginkgo fossil?

Gomphotherium's tusks and long curling trunk were like those of elephants alive today. ▼

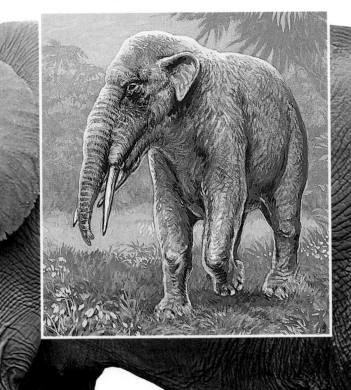

Thick hair and big curling tusks helped woolly mammoths live during the Ice Age. Even though mammoths looked much like elephants today, for some reason they died out when the climate changed. ▼

C43

Most fossils are found in sedimentary rocks. Getting fossils out of rocks can take a long time. People have to be careful not to break the fossils.

The Importance of Fossils

Fossils are important for many reasons. They tell us what living things were like in the past and how they have changed over a very long time. They also tell us what Earth was like long ago. For example, if we find rocks that have fossil shells, we know the rocks formed in or near water. Probably long ago the area where the rocks were found was under water. If rocks have fossil ferns, then the rocks probably formed in a swampy area.

Scientists can infer from fossils how an animal moved. As you saw in the investigation, fossil footprints can show how an animal walked. Bones also can show this. For example, the dinosaur in the pictures at the right had four legs. The front legs were much shorter, so the animal probably walked on only two legs.

The bones of this dinosaur were found at a place like the one above. Scientists put the bones together like a jigsaw puzzle. The skeleton stands the way the animal probably stood when it was alive.

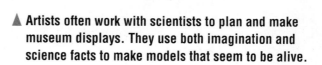

Artists often work with scientists to plan and make museum displays. They use both imagination and science facts to make models that seem to be alive.

If a fossil mold shows the animal's soft parts, scientists can tell more about how the animal looked. They can tell if it had skin, fur, feathers, or scales. More often, though, scientists infer how animals looked. To do this, they look at similar animals that are alive now.

✔ **Why are fossils important?**

Animatronic Dinosaur

1. Engineers designed and built this dinosaur robot. They used information from scientists who study dinosaurs. The engineers spent a long time testing the robot's movements. They made sure its movements matched the way scientists think real dinosaurs moved.

2. After the inside of the dinosaur was done, artists made the outside of the dinosaur. They carved blocks of plastic foam to make the skin. They burned scales into the foam to make the skin look like a reptile's scales. Then they painted the skin.

3. A team can make a life-sized robot like this in only two months. These dinosaur robots are often part of museum displays.

Uncovering Fossils

After a fossil bone is discovered, scientists record observations of it. They take photographs of the fossil in its original position and make a map of the area. Then scientists carefully remove the fossil from its rocky home. Hammers and chisels break away large pieces of rock. Small hand tools chip away the rock closest to the fossil. The fossil is painted with a special hardener to prevent crumbling. Then it is packed in foam or plaster for protection and taken to a laboratory for further study.

✓ **Why are fossils packed in foam or plaster?**

▲ Sometimes fossils are uncovered by accident as bulldozers carve a roadway in sedimentary rock.

◄ These fossil dinosaur eggs were found in Montana. They became fossils after they were covered with mud during a flood.

These glasslike fossils are brachiopods (BRAY•kee•oh•pahdz), sea animals with a hinged shell. The fossils formed inside limestone rock. The animals' parts were slowly replaced by silica, a mineral that makes up most sand. The fossils were uncovered when the limestone was eaten away with acid. ►

CANADA

Choteau

Missouri River

Helena **MONTANA**

Yellowstone River

IDAHO

Boise

WYOMING

Preserving Fossils

In the laboratory, scientists remove the foam or plaster jacket. Fine tools are used to carefully chip away any rock still on the fossil. Sometimes scientists use dental drills and picks to remove tiny pieces of rock. The fossil can also be placed in a solution of strong chemicals that eat away the rock without damaging the fossil. A plaster mold is made from the cleaned fossil. Plastic is poured into the mold. When the plastic dries, the mold is removed to reveal a perfect model of the fossil.

✔ **How does making a mold of a fossil help preserve it?**

▲ On the banks of the Ohio River lie rock layers containing fossils that are 386 million years old. The beds are preserved as part of a state park. From August to October the river is usually low and the fossil beds are easily seen. The fossils shown here are the remains of organisms that lived in an ancient coral reef.

Scientists make plastic casts from fossil molds so that they can observe traits of the fossil without handling it. They also use these casts to determine how different fossil bones fit together to form a skeleton. ▶

◀ Magnolia pod

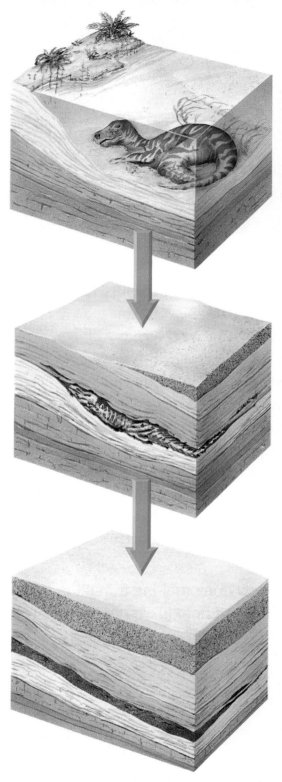

Scientists uncover many fossils as they examine and find the age of rock layers. The fossils on these pages show the diversity of living things during Earth's past.

The Ages of Rocks and Fossils

Scientists study rocks and fossils to find out how old the fossils are. Recall that some rocks form in layers. Each layer is newer than the one below it. Scientists study the order of these layers and compare the layers in different places. They can't tell exactly how old a layer is this way. However, they can tell whether a rock or fossil is older or younger than the layers above and below it.

Scientists find the age of rocks in another way. Some rocks have particles that decay, or break down over time, to form different particles. Many igneous rocks are like this. Scientists can compare the amounts of the original particles and the new particles that form to find out the age of the rock.

✔ **What are two ways scientists can find out the age of a rock?**

Fern in limestone ▼

▲ The oldest rocks are usually at the bottom of the "stack." The rock beds, or layers, at the top are younger. Sometimes, however, movement in Earth's crust can twist stacks of layers or turn them over.

▲ This fish was covered in hard, bony plates that acted like armor.

Summary

Fossils tell us about living things of the past, how living things have changed over time, and how Earth has changed. Fossils are evidence of the diversity of life that existed on Earth in the past.

Review

1. What is an example of a living thing that has changed little over time?

2. How was *Gomphotherium* like an African elephant?

3. How are layers of sedimentary rocks useful in finding out the age of fossils?

4. **Critical Thinking** Suppose scientists find a fossil like *Archaeopteryx*, but it does not have teeth or a tail. Would this support the hypothesis that *Archaeopteryx* is related to birds that are alive now? Explain.

5. **Test Prep** Suppose you observe several layers of rock that have been exposed by road work. The oldest rock is probably —

   A in the top layer
   B in the middle layer
   C in the bottom layer
   D just below the top layer

LINKS

MATH LINK

Compare Lengths Ammonoids, such as the one shown on page C33, were like squid except ammonoids had shells. Use reference materials to find the sizes of squid living now. Compare them with the ammonoid. Which animal is larger? What is the difference in size?

WRITING LINK

Informative Writing—Description Suppose you are hiking near a cliff. Suddenly you see something that looks like a large bone trapped in the rock. Describe for your teacher the animal whose fossil you found. Tell how you think it lived and how the fossil formed.

PHYSICAL EDUCATION LINK

Animal Movements With a partner, make a list of 10 different animals. Make sure that some of your choices move in different ways. Take the list outside and find an area of dry sand or dirt that will show tracks. Choose an animal from the list. Have your partner look away while you move the way the animal moves. Then have your partner guess the animal just by looking at the tracks.

TECHNOLOGY LINK

Learn more about recent fossil discoveries by viewing *Dinosaur Egg* on the **Harcourt Science Newsroom Video**.

How Do Fossil Fuels Form?

In this lesson, you can . . .

INVESTIGATE storage rocks.

LEARN ABOUT how fossil fuels form.

LINK to math, writing, technology, and other areas.

This tower separates petroleum into products such as asphalt, heating oil, and gasoline. ▽

INVESTIGATE

What Kinds of Rocks Store Petroleum

Activity Purpose The processes that formed plant and animal fossils also led to the formation of important energy resources. These resources include coal and oil, which also formed from the remains of living things. Oil forms in layers of sedimentary rock called *source rock*. Over time, that oil is squeezed from the source rock into other rock layers, called *storage rock*. In this investigation, you will **use numbers** to **compare** rocks and determine which rock stores oil best.

Materials

- limestone
- sandstone
- shale
- paper plates
- dropper
- mineral oil
- clock

Activity Procedure

1 Place the rock samples on separate paper plates. **Observe** each rock. **Predict** which will be the best storage rock.

2 Fill the dropper with mineral oil. Put 5 drops of oil on the limestone sample. (Picture A)

3 **Observe** and **record** the time it takes for the 5 drops of oil to soak into the limestone.

Picture A

Picture B

4 Continue adding oil, counting the drops, until the limestone will hold no more oil. **Record** the number of drops it takes. (Picture B)

5 Repeat Steps 2–4 with the other rock samples.

Draw Conclusions

1. Which rock soaked up the oil the fastest? What was the time?

2. Which rock soaked up the most oil? What was the number of drops?

3. Which rock is the best storage rock? Explain.

4. **Scientists at Work** Scientists often **use numbers** to **compare** things. How did you use numbers to compare the oil-storing ability of the rocks?

Investigate Further How could you determine which of the rocks is a source rock for petroleum? **Plan a simple investigation** to answer this question. Then decide what equipment you would need to carry out this investigation.

Process Skill Tip

You can **use numbers** to do many things. You can solve math problems, count objects, put things in order, or **compare** one thing with another. In this activity you compared the oil-storing ability of certain rocks.

How Fossil Fuels Form

Fossil Fuels

Dinosaurs and woolly mammoths are an important part of Earth's past. We learned about them by uncovering their fossils. But fossils are important for another reason. Coal, natural gas, and oil are valuable resources known as **fossil fuels**. They are called *fossil* fuels because they formed from the remains of once-living organisms.

Burning a fossil fuel releases large amounts of energy. That's one reason why people use fossil fuels more than any other energy source on Earth. Another reason is that fossil fuels are found in many places. In the last hundred years, the technology for finding fossil fuels has improved. This has increased the use of fossil fuels.

Fossil fuels are also important resources for making other products. For example, coal is used to make steel. And many chemicals, called petrochemicals (peht•roh•KEM•ih•kuhlz), are made from oil. Petrochemicals are used to make products such as medicines, makeup, paints, and plastics.

✔ **What are fossil fuels?**

Many energy stations burn coal to generate electricity. ▼

A lot of the items you use every day are made of chemicals that come from petroleum. ▼

Almost all cars run on gasoline, a fuel made from petroleum. ▼

C52

Energy from the Sun

Burning fossil fuels releases energy that originally came from the sun. The energy was stored in the bodies of ancient organisms that were buried in sediments millions of years ago. So coal, natural gas, and oil are found in layers of sedimentary rock.

Petroleum (peh•TROH•lee•uhm) or crude oil, is the world's most widely used fossil fuel. It produces a lot of heat when it is burned. Petroleum is used mainly for transportation, because it is easier to store and transport than coal and natural gas.

The petroleum used today formed when microorganisms died and fell to the bottoms of ancient seas. Over many years, layer upon layer of sediment covered them. Deep within the Earth, where there is a lot of heat and pressure, the organic matter of their decayed bodies slowly turned into petroleum and natural gas.

Natural gas is mostly a gas called *methane*. It is usually found with petroleum. Natural gas is used mostly for heating and cooking.

Coal seam

Miners travel deep into the Earth to dig coal from underground layers, or seams. ▶

The United States has large deposits of fossil fuels, especially coal and natural gas. But the United States uses so much petroleum that some is imported from places such as Saudi Arabia and Nigeria.

Electric energy stations use most of the coal mined in the United States. Years ago, burning coal produced clouds of black smoke. Today, stations that burn coal have ways to control pollution.

The world is slowly running out of fossil fuels. To conserve fuel resources, many nations are trying to cut down on their use of these fuels. They are beginning to use other energy sources such as wind, solar, and hydroelectric energy.

✔ **Where did the energy in fossil fuels come from originally?**

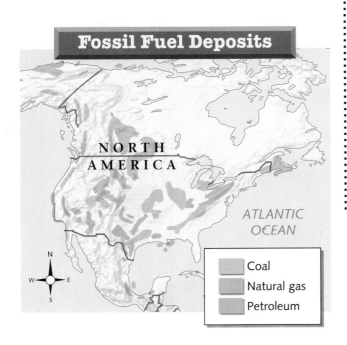

Fossil Fuel Deposits

NORTH AMERICA

ATLANTIC OCEAN

N W E S

Coal
Natural gas
Petroleum

Formation of Coal

Much of the coal used today comes from plants that lived in swamps millions of years ago. As the plants died, they sank to the bottom of the swamps. Mud and other sediments slowly covered the remains. Over many years the dead plants were buried deeper and deeper. Slowly, great pressure and microorganisms changed the remains into coal.

✔ **What changed plant remains into coal?**

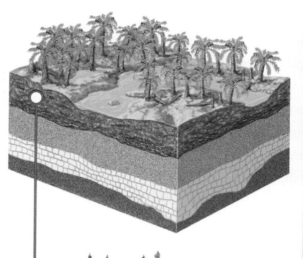

Millions of years ago, plants died and fell to the bottom of swamps. Because remains were buried quickly, little oxygen was available to help decay.

With time the dead plants were buried deeper. As with formation of carbon film fossils, the pressure changed the remains. Water and other substances were forced out, leaving mostly carbon behind.

As more time passed, the coal was buried deeper. The greater pressure changed the coal more.

If the coal was exposed to heat and great pressure, it became almost all carbon. This hard, black form of coal is a valuable fuel.

Time

Types of Coal

Coal is classified into four different types. The types are based on texture and the amount of carbon in the coal. These depend on how long and how deep the coal was buried. From least carbon to most carbon, the four types are peat, lignite (LIG•nyt), bituminous (by•TOO•muh•nuhs) coal, and anthracite (AN•thruh•syt).

✓ **How is coal classified?**

Less Carbon

More Carbon

Peat

Lignite

Bituminous coal

Anthracite

Peat is a dark yellow or brown crumbly material. It is made up of dead swamp plants that have been buried and squeezed for hundreds of years. It is mined by digging at Earth's surface. It still contains much water and must be dried before it is burned.

Lignite is sometimes called brown coal. It is a light brown, crumbly rock that contains more carbon than peat does. Because it burns at a cooler temperature than bituminous coal and anthracite, it is not as good a fuel.

Bituminous coal is the most useful type of coal. Because it burns at high temperatures, it is used as a fuel in factories and electric power stations. It contains more carbon and much less water than lignite or peat contains. Unfortunately, it also contains sulfur, which can cause air pollution.

Anthracite is a hard, black form of coal. It is almost entirely carbon. It burns very hot with little smoke or ash. Because of this, and because it is rare, it is a valuable energy resource.

Petroleum and Natural Gas

Petroleum and natural gas are found only in sedimentary rock. Almost 60 percent of the world's supply is in sandstone. The rest is in limestone and other porous rocks. Geologists can identify rock structures that are likely to hold petroleum and natural gas, so they know where to look for these resources.

Since the microorganisms that formed them lived in seas, many petroleum and natural gas deposits are found under water. Underwater drilling takes place from huge platforms built over the water. In the United States these platforms are located in the Gulf of Mexico and off the California coast.

Some deposits of petroleum and natural gas are under land, in places that were once shallow seas. Drilling for these deposits occurs in California, Texas, Alaska, and other states.

When a drill locates a deposit of petroleum or natural gas, the petroleum has to be pumped from the ground. Natural gas comes out by itself. If there is not enough petroleum in one area to be pumped out directly, hot water or steam is forced into the deposit through a nearby well. This forces the petroleum, which is less dense than water, to the surface.

Sometimes the petroleum is under such great pressure that it gushes to the surface. Gushers, as they are called, waste a lot of valuable petroleum. Modern wells are capped to keep this from happening.

✔ **How are petroleum and natural gas taken from the ground?**

◀ Drills sink deep into a pocket of petroleum. The petroleum is then pumped to the surface.

Summary

Coal, oil, and natural gas are fossil fuels. Fossil fuels formed over millions of years from the decayed remains of organisms. Coal formation can produce peat, lignite, bituminous coal, and anthracite. Petroleum and natural gas formed from microorganisms buried under ancient seas.

Review

1. List two products that contain petrochemicals made from petroleum.
2. What is most coal used for in the United States?
3. How did Earth's deposits of coal form?
4. **Critical Thinking** As coal forms, how does its carbon content change? How might this change affect its ability to heat?
5. **Test Prep** Which of these is **NOT** a stage in the formation of petroleum?

    A Microorganisms sink to the bottom of shallow seas.

    B Layers of mud pile on top of the remains.

    C Organisms in mud produce new microorganisms.

    D The remains slowly turn into petroleum.

LINKS

MATH LINK

Make a Bar Graph Use a computer and a graphing program such as *Graph Links* to make a graph showing the petroleum collected by the world's top five producers. How does the amount of petroleum the United States collects compare to that of other nations?

WRITING LINK

Informative Writing—Report As you watch TV commercials, look for those that show fossil fuels being used. Then write a report that can be used for a commercial that shows ways fossil fuels could be conserved. Present your commercial to your class.

SOCIAL STUDIES LINK

History of Petroleum When was petroleum first discovered? How was it first used? Write a short report on the early history of petroleum.

TECHNOLOGY LINK

GO ONLINE

Learn more about the formation of fossil fuels by visiting this Internet site.
www.scilinks.org/harcourt

SCI LINKS
THE WORLD'S A CLICK AWAY

Buried in Time

Duckbill dinosaur

Have you ever collected fossils? If you have, you are following a very old tradition. One of the Roman emperors had a fossil collection in his home. Some ancient Greek scientists found fossils of sea animals on mountains. The scientists reasoned that the mountains must have been under water at some time in the past. One of these scientists, Theophrastus (thee•uh•FRAS•tuhs), wrote a book about fossils.

Early Fossil Discoveries

The word *fossil* was first used in the 1500s. Georgius Agricola (JAWR•jee•uhs uh•GRIK•uh•luh) used it to refer to anything that was dug up. He thought fossils were just oddly shaped stones. He didn't realize that fossils were parts of things that once were alive.

Soon after Agricola, a German scientist, Konrad von Gesner, classified fossils into 15 different types. In the late 1500s a teacher

The History of Fossils

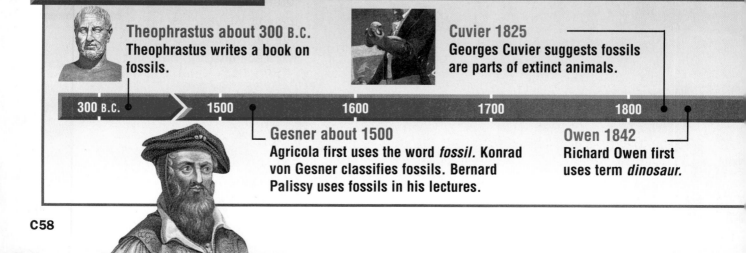

Theophrastus about 300 B.C.
Theophrastus writes a book on fossils.

Cuvier 1825
Georges Cuvier suggests fossils are parts of extinct animals.

300 B.C.   1500   1600   1700   1800

Gesner about 1500
Agricola first uses the word *fossil*. Konrad von Gesner classifies fossils. Bernard Palissy uses fossils in his lectures.

Owen 1842
Richard Owen first uses term *dinosaur*.

named Bernard Palissy (pah•lee•SEE) showed fossils to his students as part of his science lectures. He was the first person to understand that fossils are remains of once-living organisms.

The first major discovery of dinosaur bones happened in England during the early 1800s. Around this time Georges Cuvier (ZHAWRZH koo•VYAY) began studying fossils. He identified some fossil remains as those of a giant salamander. Cuvier thought that fossils were remains of long-dead plants and animals. He also thought that sudden, violent natural events, such as volcanic eruptions and earthquakes, had destroyed the organisms that became the fossils. Other scientists disagreed with this idea. They thought fossils were remains of animal types that still lived in unknown places on Earth.

Fossils—Ages Old

During the 1940s scientists began using radioactive materials to judge the age of rocks in which fossils were found. One

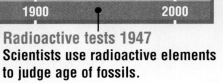

1900   2000

Radioactive tests 1947
Scientists use radioactive elements to judge age of fossils.

element that is naturally radioactive is called potassium-40, or K-40. It is found in many rocks. K-40 decays very slowly. As it decays, it changes into different elements. By comparing the amount of K-40 left with the amounts of those different elements, scientists can judge the age of the rock.

What Fossils Tell Us

When scientists first collected fossils, they tried to figure out what the ancient animals looked like. After putting together animal skeletons, they inferred what their body coverings looked like and how the animals lived. Sometimes scientists made mistakes. For example, they thought that *Tyrannosaurus rex* stood up straight and dragged its tail. Scientists now think it stood as shown on page C44. Scientists are still doing this kind of study today.

New discoveries are also being made as the same bones are examined again with new tools. For example, scientists in New Mexico hypothesize that one type of duckbill dinosaur made sounds like those of a musical instrument called a bassoon. Their hypothesis is based on computer models of the dinosaur's skull and CT scans, a special kind of X-ray picture. All these discoveries help us better understand what fossils can tell us.

THINK ABOUT IT

1. How did scientists who studied fossils build on what was already known?

2. Suppose you found a bone buried in your backyard and thought it might be a fossil. What would you do to find out?

Lisa D. White

MICROPALEONTOLOGIST

When she was young, Lisa White visited the California Academy of Sciences, near where she lived. She was most interested in the geology exhibits. In college, White was again drawn toward geology. During summers, she worked for the U.S. Geological Survey. The people there encouraged her fascination with climate change and geologic time. As a result, she became a paleontologist (pay•lee•uhn•TAHL•uh•jist), a scientist who studies fossils and Earth's past.

Dr. White became part of the Ocean Drilling Program, an international team of scientists, engineers, and technicians. The program makes six ocean cruises a year. Each cruise lasts about two months. The specially equipped ship is the only ship of its kind in the world.

The goal of the program is to find out about Earth's history. A special drill on the ship brings up core samples, or narrow tubes, of rock and sediment from the ocean floor. Each $9\frac{1}{2}$-meter (about 30-ft) long core is cut in half lengthwise. One-half of the core is preserved, much as books are stored in a library. The other half of the core is analyzed on the ship.

Dr. White studies the tiny fossils, or microfossils, of diatoms in the core samples. She tries to find the age of the fossils in each sample.

Dr. Lisa White now teaches at San Francisco State University. She grew up in that city, and is glad to be teaching at the school she once attended. She enjoys sharing her research experiences with students in her geology and oceanography classes.

THINK ABOUT IT

1. Why would collecting samples from the ocean floor be a good way to study fossils?
2. Why do you think Dr. White studies microfossils in core samples, and not fossils of large animals?

Ocean Drilling Program's ship

ACTIVITIES FOR HOME OR SCHOOL

CAST AND MOLD

How can you make a mold and a cast of a seashell?

Materials

- seashell
- plastic bowl
- petroleum jelly
- white glue
- clay

Procedure

1. Coat the ridges of the seashell with a thin layer of petroleum jelly. Press the seashell into the clay. Remove the seashell carefully from the clay. Place the clay with the imprint of the seashell in the plastic bowl.

2. Drizzle white glue in the shell imprint. Fill it completely.

3. Let the glue harden. When it has hardened completely, separate it from the clay.

Draw Conclusions

Which is the cast of your seashell? The mold?

RECONSTRUCTING THE PAST

How can you reconstruct past events using a "word fossil"?

Materials

- unlined paper
- ruler
- pencil
- scissors

Procedure

1. Write a paragraph that tells about a past event. The paragraph should be at least three sentences long. Leave a blank space between each line you write.

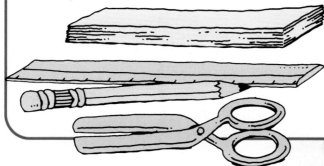

2. Cut the paragraph into square-edged pieces. Each piece should have one or two words written on it. The pieces are the "bones" of this "fossil."

3. Remove two or three bones, and put them in a safe place.

4. Mix up the rest of the bones, and exchange them with a partner.

5. Try to figure out what your partner's paragraph says. Check your guess with your partner.

Draw Conclusions

How did the missing bones affect Step 5? How is this puzzle like what scientists do with fossils?

Vocabulary Review

Use the terms below to complete the sentences. The page numbers in ( ) tell you where to look in the chapter if you need help.

fossil (C36) **natural gas** (C53)

trace fossil (C37) **peat** (C54)

mold (C38) **lignite** (C54)

cast (C38) **bituminous coal** (C54)

fossil fuel (C52) **anthracite** (C54)

petroleum (C53)

1. A ____ is a clue to the activity of an animal that lived long ago.

2. A ____ is a clue, preserved in rock, about life in the distant past.

3. A fossil imprint left by a plant or animal is called a ____.

4. If minerals fill a mold fossil and then harden, a ____ forms.

5. ____ is a gas made up mostly of methane.

6. A soft brown form of coal is ____.

7. ____ is another name for crude oil.

8. A hard black form of coal is ____.

9. A soft brown material made up of partly decayed plants is ____.

10. ____ is a fairly hard dark brown or black form of coal.

11. A ____ is a fuel such as coal, petroleum, or natural gas that formed in Earth from decayed organisms.

Connect Concepts

Use the terms in the Word Bank to complete the concept map.

buried	carbon film	cast	rock layers
fossils	mold	petrified	

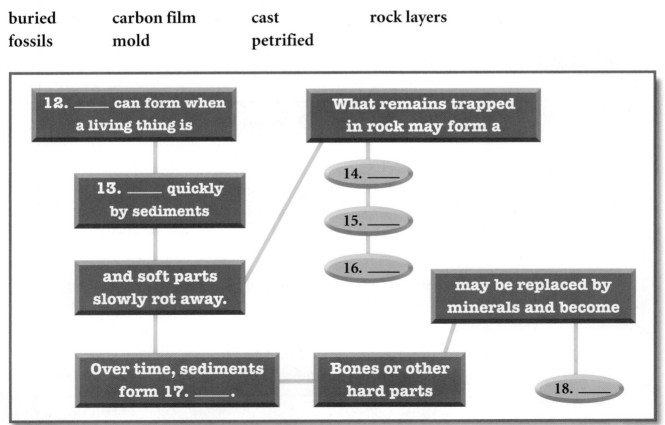

12. ____ can form when a living thing is

What remains trapped in rock may form a

13. ____ quickly by sediments

14. ____

15. ____

16. ____

and soft parts slowly rot away.

may be replaced by minerals and become

Over time, sediments form 17. ____.

Bones or other hard parts

18. ____

Check Understanding

Write the letter of the best choice.

19. The most likely place to find a fossil is ____ rock.

  A sedimentary

  B volcanic

  C igneous

  D metamorphic

20. A fossilized dinosaur footprint is an example of —

  F a cast

  G a trace fossil

  H a mold

  J index fossils

21. When woody material in a tree is replaced with minerals, the tree becomes —

  A petrified

  B a trace fossil

  C carbon film

  D amber

22. Fossil fuels include —

  F jet fuel, graphite, and lead

  G bauxite, oil, and coal

  H natural gas, oil, and coal

  J coal, oil, and peat

Critical Thinking

23. What could you infer about an animal from a fossil of its jawbone?

24. Would you be likely to find a fossil in igneous rock? Explain.

25. Explain why some animals and plants became fossils and others did not.

26. How does recycling plastic conserve fossil fuels?

Process Skills Review

27. Can you **infer** from the picture which rock layer is the oldest? Explain.

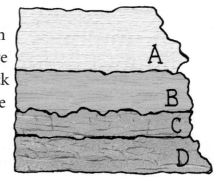

28. You find a fossil trilobite in a rock layer. You know when trilobites lived. What can you **infer** about other fossils in the same rock layer? Explain.

29. Your class's average height is 136 centimeters. A class from the next grade averages 141 centimeters in height. **Use numbers** to **infer** a yearly growth rate.

Performance Assessment

Fossil Search

You and a partner should each find five small objects in the classroom. Without your partner watching, make an imprint of part or all of each object in its own ball of soft clay. Return the objects. Then ask your partner to find the object that matches each imprint. How is this like a fossil mold? How could it model a fossil cast?

There are many places where you can learn about Earth's surface. By visiting the places below, you can observe some fossils and see what Earth's crust is like. You'll also have fun while you learn.

Falls of the Ohio State Park

WHAT A park on the Ohio River where fossils of animals and plants can easily be observed

WHERE Clarksville, Indiana

WHAT CAN YOU DO THERE? Visit the museum, see the exhibits, and explore the river bank for fossils.

The Museum of Science and Industry

WHAT A museum with many exhibits and science displays

WHERE Chicago, Illinois

WHAT CAN YOU DO THERE? Visit the museum, see the exhibits, and take the tour of Old Ben No. 17 coal mine.

GO ONLINE Plan Your Own Expeditions

If you can't visit the Falls of the Ohio State Park or the Museum of Science and Industry, visit a fossil site or a museum near you. Or log on to The Learning Site at **www.harcourtschool.com** to visit these science sites and learn more about Earth's surface.

Patterns on Earth and in Space

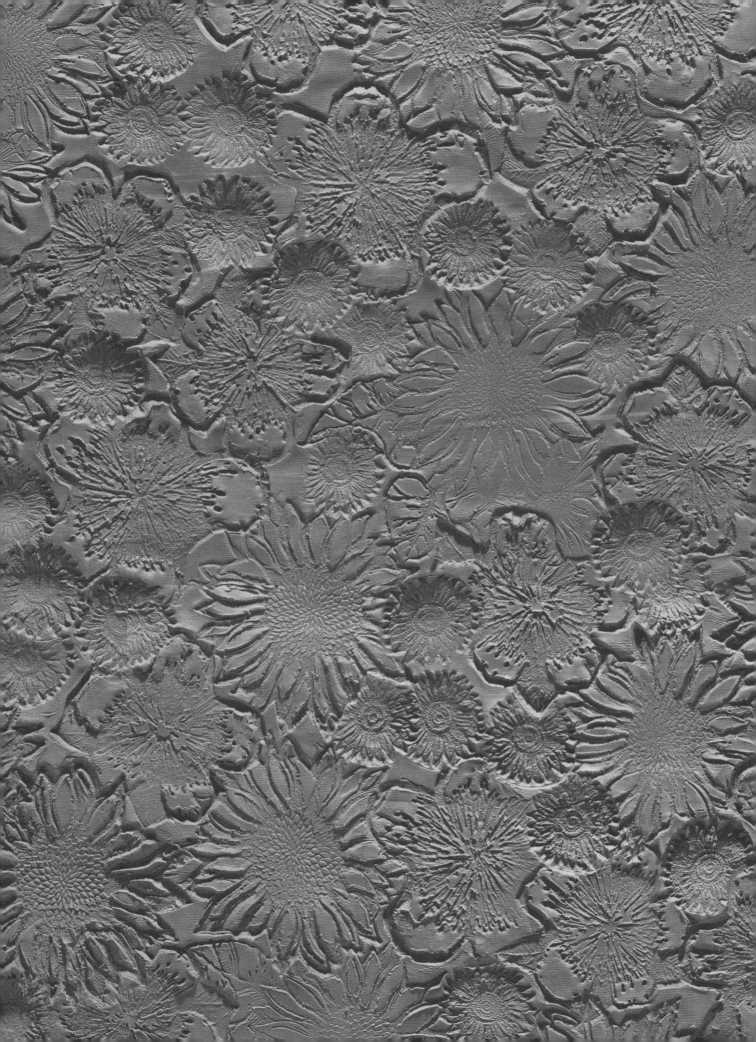

Patterns on Earth and in Space

UNIT EXPERIMENT

Clouds and Weather Prediction

Earth's atmosphere affects you every day. You want to know how hot or cold it is and if it will rain or snow. While you study this unit, you can conduct a long-term experiment about predicting weather. Here are some questions to think about. How can you use clouds to predict the weather? Is there a pattern of changes that goes with certain clouds? What weather conditions are associated with each cloud type? Plan and conduct an experiment to find answers to these or other questions you have about patterns on Earth and in space. See pages x–xix for help in designing your experiment.

Weather Conditions

Everyone talks about the weather, but weather forecasters get paid to talk about it. Many people depend on weather forecasts to plan their day. Sometimes forecasts of severe weather can even save lives.

Fast Fact

Right now, 2000 thunderstorms are happening around the Earth. While you are reading this sentence, lightning will strike the Earth about 500 times!

What Makes Up Earth's Atmosphere?

In this lesson, you can . . .

INVESTIGATE a property of air.

LEARN ABOUT Earth's atmosphere.

LINK to math, writing, art, and technology.

INVESTIGATE

A Property of Air

Activity Purpose Everything around you is matter. Matter is anything that takes up space and has weight. In this investigation you will **observe** a property of air. Then you will **infer** whether air is matter.

Materials
- metric ruler
- piece of string about 80 cm long
- scissors
- 2 round balloons (same size)
- safety goggles
- straight pin

Activity Procedure

1 Work with a partner. Use the scissors to carefully cut the string into three equal pieces.
 CAUTION **Be careful when using scissors.**

2 Tie one piece of the string to the middle of the ruler.

◀ Oxygen is part of the air you breathe. High on a mountain the particles of air are far apart. The climber can't get enough oxygen from the air. He needs extra oxygen from a tank to keep his body working properly.

3 Blow up the balloons so they are about the same size. Seal the balloons. Then tie a piece of string around the neck of each balloon.

4 Tie a balloon to each end of the ruler. Hold the middle string up so that the ruler hangs from it. Move the strings so that the ruler is balanced. (Picture A)

5 **CAUTION** **Put on your safety goggles.** Use the straight pin to pop one of the balloons. **Observe** what happens to the ruler.

Picture A

Draw Conclusions

1. Explain how this investigation shows that air takes up space.

2. Describe what happened when one balloon was popped. What property of air caused what you **observed?**

3. **Scientists at Work** Scientists often **infer** conclusions when the answer to a question is not clear or can't be **observed** directly. Your breath is invisible, but you observed how it made the balloons and the ruler behave. Even though you can't see air, what can you infer about whether or not air is matter? Explain.

Investigate Further The air around you presses on you and everything else on Earth. This property of air, called air pressure, is a result of air's weight. When more air is packed into a small space, air pressure increases. You can feel air pressure for your-self. Hold your hands around a partly filled balloon while your partner blows it up. Describe what happens. Then **infer** which property of air helps keep the tires of a car inflated.

Process Skill Tip

Observations and inferences are different things. An **observation** is made with your senses. An **inference** is an opinion based on what you have observed and what you know about a situation.

Earth's Atmosphere

The Air You Breathe

FIND OUT

- **some properties of air**
- **the layers of the atmosphere**

VOCABULARY

atmosphere
air pressure
troposphere
stratosphere

You can live for a few days without water and for many days without food. But you can live only a few minutes without air. Nearly all living things need air to carry out their life processes. The layer of air that surrounds our planet is called the **atmosphere** (AT•muhs•feer). When compared to the size of Earth, the atmosphere looks like a very thin blanket surrounding the entire planet.

The atmosphere wasn't always as it is today. It formed millions of years ago as gases from erupting volcanoes collected around the planet. This mixture of gases would have poisoned you if you had breathed it. But bacteria and other living things used gases in this early atmosphere. They released new gases as they carried out their life processes. Over time, the gas mixture changed slowly to become the atmosphere Earth has now.

The atmosphere now is made up of billions and billions of gas particles. Almost four-fifths of these gas particles are nitrogen. Oxygen, a gas that your body uses in its life processes, makes up about one-fifth of the atmosphere. Other gases, including carbon dioxide and water vapor, make up the rest of the atmosphere.

Although you can't see all of it, a thin blanket of air called the atmosphere surrounds Earth. ▼

Plants use carbon dioxide during the process of photosynthesis. Plants give off oxygen as photosynthesis occurs. Carbon dioxide also absorbs heat energy from the sun and from Earth's surface. This helps keep the planet warm.

Like carbon dioxide, water vapor can absorb heat energy. The amount of water vapor in the air varies from place to place. Air over bodies of water usually contains more water vapor than air over land. High in the air, water vapor condenses to form clouds.

Air has certain properties. As you saw in the investigation, air takes up space and has weight. All the particles of air pressing down on the surface cause **air pressure** (PRESH•er). Air pressure changes as you go higher in the atmosphere. The picture shows what a column of air might look like. At the surface of Earth, air particles are close together. The higher you go in the atmosphere, the farther apart the air particles are. So the air pressure is less as you go higher in the atmosphere.

✓ What is the atmosphere?

1 Air particles in the upper atmosphere have the least weight pressing on them. The particles are far apart. Air in this part of the atmosphere is much less dense than air lower in Earth's atmosphere.

2 Air near the middle of the atmosphere has more weight pressing down on it. So it is denser than air higher above Earth.

3 The weight of the entire column of air presses down on the air particles closest to Earth, forcing them close together. This makes air densest at Earth's surface. Air pressure is greatest where air is densest.

The mass of a 1-m × 1-m column of the Earth's atmosphere is about 10,000 kg. ▶

1 meter   1 meter

1

2

3

10000 kg

Atmosphere Layers

Earth's atmosphere is divided into four layers. The layer closest to Earth is the **troposphere** (TROH•poh•sfeer). We live in the troposphere and breathe its air. Almost all weather happens in this layer. In the troposphere, air temperature decreases as you go higher.

Some airplanes that travel long distances fly in the **stratosphere** (STRAT•uh•sfeer) to be above most bad weather. The stratosphere contains most of the atmosphere's ozone, a kind of oxygen. The ozone protects living things from the sun's harmful rays. Temperatures in the stratosphere increase with height.

In the mesosphere (MES•oh•sfeer), air temperature decreases with height. In fact, the mesosphere is the coldest layer of the atmosphere. The thermosphere (THER•moh•sfeer) is the hot, outermost layer of air. In the thermosphere, temperature increases quickly with height. Temperatures high in the thermosphere can reach thousands of degrees Celsius.

✔ **What are the four layers of the atmosphere?**

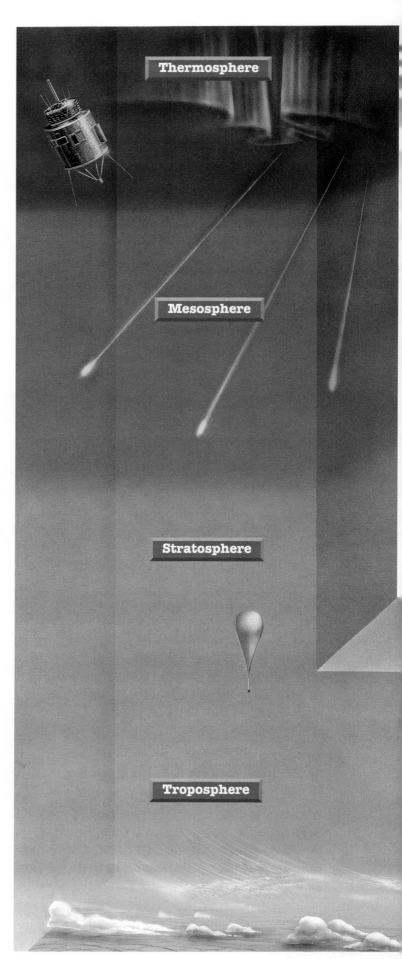

Earth's atmosphere is divided into four layers based on changes in air temperature. Each layer blends into the next. The thermosphere fades into outer space, where there is no air at all. ▶

Summary

The thin blanket of air that surrounds Earth is called the atmosphere. Earth's atmosphere is divided into four layers based on changes in temperature. The layers, starting with the one closest to Earth, are the troposphere, stratosphere, mesosphere, and thermosphere.

Review

1. What is the atmosphere?
2. How does air pressure change with height?
3. How is the atmosphere divided?
4. **Critical Thinking** Compare and contrast the stratosphere and the mesosphere.
5. **Test Prep** In which layer of the atmosphere does most weather occur?

   A troposphere
   B stratosphere
   C mesosphere
   D thermosphere

LINKS

MATH LINK

Solve a Two-Step Problem In the troposphere the air temperature drops about $6\frac{1}{2}$°C for every 1 kilometer increase in height. If the troposphere is about 10 kilometers thick and the air temperature at the ground is 30°C, what is the temperature at a height of 2 kilometers?

WRITING LINK

Informative Writing—Description Suppose that you are falling from space toward Earth. For your teacher, write a story describing what you see and feel as you go through each layer of the atmosphere.

ART LINK

Atmosphere Layers Paint a picture showing the atmosphere as you would see it from space. Label the layers.

GO ONLINE TECHNOLOGY LINK

Learn more about Earth's atmosphere and weather by visiting this Internet site.
www.scilinks.org/harcourt

SCI LINKS
THE WORLD'S A CLICK AWAY

2

How Do Air Masses Affect Weather?

In this lesson, you can . . .

INVESTIGATE wind speed.

LEARN ABOUT what causes weather.

LINK to math, writing, health, and technology.

Wind, which is air in motion, keeps these kites fluttering in the sky. ▽

Wind Speed

Activity Purpose Have you ever flown a kite? A strong wind makes the kite flutter and soar through the air. A gentle breeze is usually not enough to keep the kite flying. What is wind? Wind is air in motion. In this investigation you will make an instrument to **measure** wind speed.

Materials

- sheet of construction paper
- tape
- hole punch
- 4 gummed reinforcements
- glue
- piece of yarn about 20 cm long
- strips of tissue paper, about 1 cm wide and 20 cm long

Activity Procedure

1 Form a cylinder with the sheet of construction paper. Tape the edge of the paper to keep the cylinder from opening.

2 Use the hole punch to make two holes at one end of the cylinder. Punch them on opposite sides of the cylinder and about 3 cm from the end. Put two gummed reinforcements on each hole, one on the inside and one on the outside. (Picture A)

3 Thread the yarn through the holes, and tie it tightly to form a handle loop.

Wind Scale

Speed (km/h)	Description	Objects Affected	Windsock Position
0	no breeze	no movement of wind	
6–19	light breeze	leaves rustle, wind vanes move, wind felt on face	
20–38	moderate breeze	dust and paper blow, small branches sway	
39–49	strong breeze	umbrellas hard to open, large branches sway	

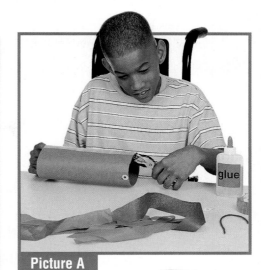

Picture A

4. Glue strips of tissue paper to the other end of the cylinder. Put tape over the glued strips to hold them better. Your completed windsock should look like the one shown in Picture B.

5. Hang your windsock outside. Use the chart above to **measure** wind speed each day for several days. **Record** your measurements in a chart. Include the date, time of day, observations of objects affected by the wind, and approximate wind speed.

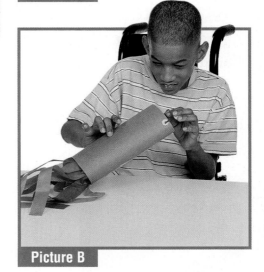

Picture B

Draw Conclusions

1. How fast was the weakest wind you **measured**? How fast was the strongest wind?

2. How did you determine the speed of the wind?

3. **Scientists at Work** *Light*, *moderate*, and *strong* are adjectives describing wind speed. Scientists often **use numbers** to describe things because, in science, numbers are more exact than words. What is the wind speed measurement in kilometers per hour if the wind is making large tree branches sway?

Investigate Further Use a magnetic compass to determine which way is north from your windsock. **Measure** both wind speed and direction each day for a week. **Record** your data in a chart.

Process Skill Tip

The **use of numbers** allows people to communicate precisely. Telling someone there is a gentle breeze is not as exact as saying the wind is blowing at 8 km/h.

Air and Weather

Air and the Sun

Have you ever watched a weather report on television? If so, you know that temperature, air pressure, and wind are some of the things reported. You also know that these weather conditions change every day. But do you know why?

Weather begins with the sun, which provides energy for making weather. But the amount of the sun's energy reaching Earth is not the same everywhere. More energy reaches the equator than the poles. This uneven heating is part of what causes air to move and what makes weather.

Most of the sun's energy never reaches Earth. It is lost in space. Of the tiny fraction of the sun's energy that does reach Earth, about three-tenths is reflected out into space. Another three-tenths warms the air. The other four-tenths warms the land and oceans. The atmosphere traps this heat much like the glass of a greenhouse. Without this **greenhouse effect**, Earth would reflect most of the sun's energy back into space and Earth's surface would be too cold to support life.

✔ **How does the atmosphere work like a greenhouse?**

FIND OUT

- how the sun affects weather
- what makes an air mass

VOCABULARY

greenhouse effect
air mass
front
cirrus
cumulus
cumulonimbus
stratus

▲ Have you ever seen ripples like these above a paved road on a hot day? The air just above the hot pavement is also hot. Light travels differently through hot air. That's why the view is blurry.

Sunlight passes through the atmosphere and warms Earth's surface. The greenhouse effect keeps most of the heat from escaping back into space. ▼

Not to scale

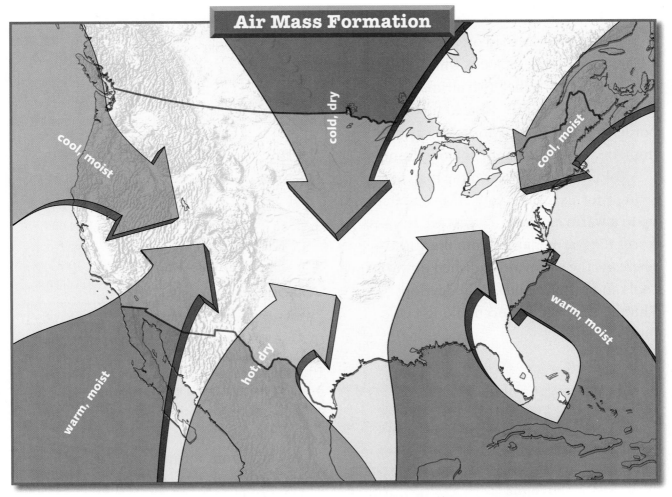

Air Mass Formation

▲ Air masses form over both land and water. The map shows where the air masses that affect North America form. Cool air masses are in blue colors. Warm air masses are in red colors.

Air Masses

If you could see the air around Earth from outer space, you would see large clumps of it forming, moving over Earth's surface, and slowly changing. These huge bodies of air, which can cover thousands of kilometers, are called air masses.

Like air heated by a hot road, an **air mass** has the same general properties as the land or water over which it forms. Two properties—moisture content and temperature—are used to describe air masses. Moist air masses form

over water. Air masses that form over land are generally dry. Air masses that form near Earth's poles are cold. Air masses that form in the tropics, or areas near the equator, are warm.

The map shows air masses forming and moving over the North American continent. You can see a polar air mass bringing cold, dry air from the north into the United States. You can also see warm, moist air coming in from the south as part of tropical air masses.

✔ **What is an air mass?**

D13

Air Masses Meet

Look again at the map on page D13. What do you think happens when different air masses meet? When two air masses meet, they usually don't mix. Instead they form a border called a **front**. Most of what you think of as weather happens along fronts.

A cold front is shown on the map to the right. It forms when a cold air mass catches up to a warm air mass. The colder air mass forces the warmer air up into the atmosphere. As the warm air is pushed upward, it cools and forms clouds. Rain develops. Thunderstorms often occur along a cold front.

▲ A line with triangles is the symbol for a cold front. The air is colder behind a cold front than ahead of it. The triangles point in the direction of movement. In which direction is this front moving?

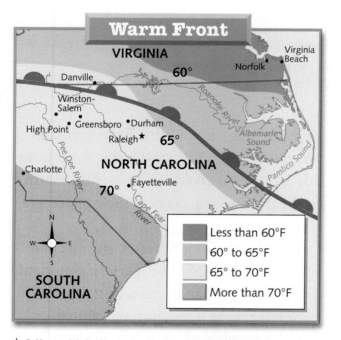

▲ A line with half-circles is the symbol for a warm front. The half-circles point in the direction the front is moving. The air is warmer behind this front than ahead of it.

A warm front forms when a warm air mass catches up to a cold air mass. The warm air slides up over the colder, denser air. Clouds form, sometimes many miles ahead of where the front is moving along the ground. Steady rain or snow may fall as the front approaches and passes. Then the sky becomes clear of clouds and the temperature becomes higher.

Sometimes a front stops moving. Such a front is called a stationary front. A stationary front can stay in one place for several days. The constant fall of snow or rain along a stationary front can leave behind many inches of snow or cause a flood.

✔ What is a front?

Clouds and the Weather

If you look up in the sky right now, you will probably see clouds with different shapes. Weather scientists classify a cloud based on its shape, its color, and where it forms in the atmosphere. The clouds you see are likely to be all the same type.

Because clouds form along a front, they can help predict weather. You know that big, dark storm clouds mean rain. But did you know that cirrus, or "horsetail," clouds can mean cooler, fair weather? Read the Inside Story to learn more about clouds and weather prediction.

✔ **How do weather scientists classify clouds?**

THE INSIDE STORY

Clouds

Learning about clouds and how they form can help you predict the weather. Read the captions below to learn more.

1. **Cirrus** These high-altitude clouds are made up of ice crystals. Winds stretch them into long, wispy horsetail or feather shapes. They usually go with cooler, fair weather.

2. **Cumulonimbus** If a cold front moves past, you'll probably see these clouds. They are towering and dark with a nimbus, or halo, of gray-white. If you see them, it's probably going to rain soon.

3. **Cumulus** These puffy cotton-ball clouds begin to form when water droplets condense at middle altitudes. Look for them on clear, warm days. They can become cumulonimbus, or thunderstorm, clouds.

4. **Stratus** You see these clouds on a gray, cloudy day. Stratus clouds form a low layer of dark gray. They can occur along warm fronts. Sometimes they bring light rain or snow showers.

This photo is the funnel cloud of a tornado, a destructive storm that forms in some severe thunderstorms. Winds in the funnel cloud can reach speeds of 480 kilometers (about 300 miles) per hour.

Air Masses Move

You can see air masses moving from place to place by watching how weather forms and changes. In the investigation you built a device to measure wind speed. Wind speed often increases as a front approaches. Wind direction also changes.

Air pressure also changes as air masses move over an area. As a cold front moves closer, air pressure often drops. Air pressure usually rises as the cold front moves over the area.

Temperature, too, changes as a front moves over an area. Warmer air is brought into a region by a warm front. Likewise, the temperature goes down when a cold front moves through an area.

✓ **How does air pressure change as a front moves toward and then over an area?**

▲ The wind direction on each side of this cold front is shown by the arrows.

◄ The arrow of a weather vane points to the direction from which the wind is blowing.

▲ The same cold front has moved and changed shape. The wind direction changes with the shape of the front.

Summary

The sun provides the energy to make weather. The atmosphere traps heat near Earth's surface much as a greenhouse does. Air masses form over continents and oceans. When two air masses meet, they form a front. Fronts are the areas where most weather happens.

Review

1. What is the greenhouse effect?
2. What is a weather front?
3. How does a cold front form?
4. **Critical Thinking** Why are weather forecasts sometimes incorrect?
5. **Test Prep** What kind of front forms when a warm air mass catches up to a cold air mass?

   A a warm front   **C** a rain front

   B a cold front   **D** a hot front

LINKS

MATH LINK

Subtract Decimals You're using a rain gauge to measure rainfall in your area. You recorded a rainfall of 0.3 inch but forgot to empty the gauge. The next time you checked, the gauge read 1.5 inches. How much new rain fell?

WRITING LINK

Expressive Writing—Poem Use what you've learned in this chapter so far. For a third-grade student, write a short poem about weather. Use these words in your poem: *air mass, cold front, warm front, rain,* and *clouds.*

HEALTH LINK

Severe-Weather Safety Find out what types of severe weather most often affect your area. Find out how to be prepared for severe weather. Also find out what to do to stay safe during severe weather. Write a safety checklist, and share it with your family.

TECHNOLOGY LINK

Learn more about forecasting severe weather by viewing *Tornado Tracking* on the **Harcourt Science Newsroom Video.**

How Is Weather Predicted?

In this lesson, you can . . .

INVESTIGATE how to measure air pressure.

LEARN ABOUT weather prediction.

LINK to math, writing, drama, and technology.

◀ Rain falls from clouds when water droplets in the clouds become big and heavy.

INVESTIGATE

Air Pressure

Activity Purpose You've learned that air pressure is the force with which the atmosphere presses down on Earth. You've also learned that air pressure changes as weather changes. In this investigation you will make a barometer, an instrument to **measure** air pressure.

Materials

- safety goggles
- scissors
- large, round balloon
- plastic jar
- large rubber band
- tape
- wooden craft stick
- small index card
- ruler

Activity Procedure

1. **CAUTION** Put on your safety goggles. Be careful when using scissors. Use the scissors to carefully cut the neck off the balloon.

2. Have your partner hold the jar while you stretch the balloon over the open end. Make sure the balloon fits snugly over the jar. Secure the balloon with the rubber band.

3. Tape the craft stick to the top of the balloon as shown. Make sure that more than half of the craft stick stretches out from the edge of the jar. (Picture A)

Picture A

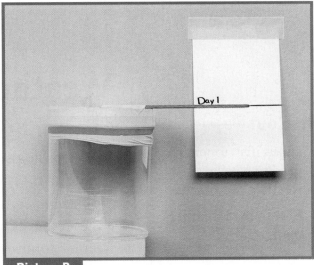

Picture B

4 On the blank side of the index card, use a pencil and a ruler to make a thin line. Label the line *Day 1*. Tape the card to a wall. Make sure the line is at the same height as the wooden stick on your barometer. (Picture B)

5 At the same time each day for a week, **measure** relative air pressure by marking the position of the wooden stick on the index card. Write the correct day next to each reading.

Draw Conclusions

1. Describe how air pressure changed during the time that you were **measuring** it.

2. What might have caused your barometer to show little or no change during the time you were taking **measurements?**

3. **Scientists at Work** Meteorologists are scientists who use instruments to **measure** weather data. How did your barometer measure air pressure?

Investigate Further Use your air pressure **measurements** and information from daily weather reports to **predict** the weather in your area for the next few days.

Weather Prediction

Measuring Weather

FIND OUT

- about instruments used to measure weather conditions

- how to read weather maps

VOCABULARY

barometer
humidity
hygrometer

Meteorologists (mee•tee•uhr•AHL•uh•jihsts) are scientists who study and measure weather conditions. Some of these conditions are air temperature, air pressure, and wind speed and direction. Meteorologists have developed tools for measuring each of these weather conditions.

When you want to know if it's hot or cold outside, you look at a thermometer or listen to a weather report. Thermometers measure the temperature of air. In the investigation, you measured another property of the atmosphere, air pressure. Air pressure is measured with an instrument called a **barometer** (buh•RAHM•uht•er). In one type of barometer, air presses down on the instrument, causing a needle to move. The needle points to a number that tells how much the air is pressing down. In other words, the instrument measures the weight of the air above it. You learned in Lesson 2 that the particles of air are closer together in a cold air mass than in a warm air mass. Most cold air masses are denser and so have higher air pressure than warm air masses.

This weather instrument is a rotating-drum barometer. It continuously records changes in air pressure. ▼

Earth's land surfaces heat faster than its bodies of water. So the air above land is usually warmer. That means it is also less dense. ▼

▲ Evaporating water adds more humidity to the air. Air masses that form over water have more moisture than those that form over land.

▲ This type of hygrometer (hy•GRAHM•uht•uhr) measures moisture in the air. The bulb of one thermometer is covered with a wet cloth. Then both thermometers are whirled in the air. The drier the air, the faster the water on the cloth evaporates (ee•VAP•uh•raytz), or dries up. This evaporation cools the cloth-covered thermometer. The temperatures of the wet and dry thermometers are compared to find the humidity.

Another characteristic of weather you can measure is **humidity** (hyoo•MID•uh•tee), or the amount of water vapor in the air. Humidity depends on several things. The area over which an air mass forms affects its humidity. For example, air masses that form over bodies of water have more moisture than air masses that form over land.

Temperature also affects how much moisture can be in the air. Warm air can have more water vapor than cool air. This is why water drops form on the outside of a glass of cold water during a warm day. Air near the glass cools. The air can no longer have as much water. The water vapor comes out of the air, forming drops.

In the investigation in Lesson 2, you made a windsock. With it you estimated the speed and direction of the wind. Meteorologists measure wind speed by using an instrument called an anemometer (an•uh•MAHM•uht•er). They find wind direction by using a weather vane or windsock.

✔ **What affects the humidity of air?**

◄ This is a type of anemometer that also includes a weather vane. Wind speed is measured by counting how many complete turns the cups make in one minute. Usually, a machine counts the turns.

Daily Temperature Data for Weather City, Any State

	Daily High/ Daily Low (°F)	Record High/ Record Low (°F)	Daily Average Temperature (°F)
Sunday	89/72	101/44	81
Monday	90/74	100/50	82
Tuesday	85/65	99/42	75
Wednesday	88/69	103/40	79
Thursday	92/70	98/41	81
Friday	75/60	99/45	68
Saturday	79/62	102/44	71

▲ Charts like this are used to record daily weather conditions.

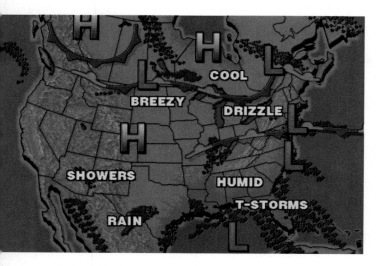

▲ Symbols on a weather map stand for fronts and weather conditions.

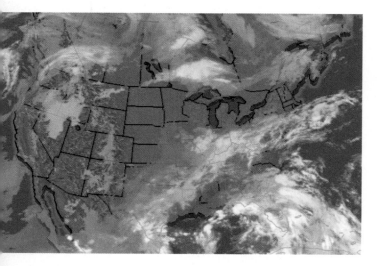

▲ A satellite photograph shows the positions of clouds and fronts. This satellite photograph matches the weather map above.

Mapping and Charting Weather

By watching and measuring weather conditions, scientists can keep track of moving air masses. Scientists record their measurements on charts and maps. Then they analyze the data to predict weather.

A weather map can be big or small. Large maps show how the weather differs across a country. Small maps show weather changes across a state or a smaller area. Satellite pictures and maps often show clouds and weather for a large part of Earth.

A weather map uses symbols to show weather conditions. Long lines marked with half-circles or triangles stand for fronts. Words or symbols describe the weather in an area. For example, small dashes may stand for rain, and small stars may stand for snow. Symbols also may show the type of clouds that are in the area.

✔ **How do weather charts and maps help scientists predict the weather?**

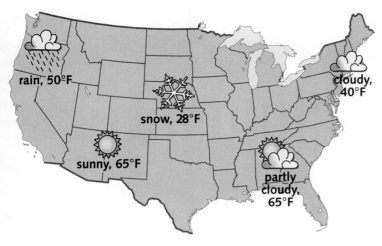

rain, 50°F

snow, 28°F

cloudy, 40°F

sunny, 65°F

partly cloudy, 65°F

▲ Simple weather maps like this are often printed in daily newspapers. What are the temperature and the weather in Nebraska?

Summary

Meteorologists are scientists who study and measure weather conditions. These conditions include air pressure, air temperature, humidity, and wind speed and direction. By measuring and studying weather conditions, meteorologists are able to predict the weather.

Review

1. What is a hygrometer?
2. What factors affect humidity?
3. What are two tools that meteorologists use to study and predict the weather?
4. **Critical Thinking** An air mass forms over Alaska. Describe what you think the temperature and humidity of this air mass will be like.
5. **Test Prep** Which instrument is used to measure air pressure?
   A thermometer
   B weather vane
   C hygrometer
   D barometer

LINKS

MATH LINK

Subtract Whole Numbers Make a chart like the one on page D22. In it, list the daily high and low temperatures of your area for one week. Find how much the temperature changed each day.

WRITING LINK

Expressive Writing—Friendly Letter Suppose you have a pen pal who lives in an area of the country very different from your area. Write a letter to your pen pal. Describe how the weather in your area changes when a cold front moves through.

DRAMA LINK

Be a Weather Forecaster Make a weather map showing imaginary weather conditions for your state. Present your forecast to the rest of the class. Make your presentation more interesting by using props.

TECHNOLOGY LINK

Learn more about tools for measuring weather conditions by joining a *Tornado Chase* on **Harcourt Science Explorations CD-ROM.**

Red Sprites, Blue Jets, and E.L.V.E.S.

Suppose you saw something completely new. How would you describe it? That was the challenge facing some airplane pilots and scientists. They tried to name unusual flashes they saw in the sky by calling them "upward lightning," "flames," and even "giant glowing doughnuts"!

Red sprite

T 04:00:20.00

UAF

Sprites, Jets, and ELVES

In 1989 scientists began trying to show that these light flashes are real. A videotape showed the unusual flashes during a thunderstorm. Nearly 20 were photographed during the early 1990s using video cameras that could work with very little light.

At least three types of flashes were identified. The scientists finally decided to name them sprites, jets, and ELVES.

ELVES stands for "*e*missions of *l*ight and *v*ery-low-frequency perturbations from *e*lectromagnetic-pulse *s*ources." You can see why the term is abbreviated. ELVES are very dim, quick red flashes. They move outward like ripples on a pond.

Sprites are red and seem to move in groups. They appear above a thunderstorm system, 65–75 kilometers (about 40–47 mi) above the ground. They have a "head" and strands coming down from the head. Sprites can occur over both sea and land.

Blue jets were once described as rocket lightning. Not until 1994 did weather scientists show, by using color video, that these glowing streaks are blue. Blue jets occur lower in the atmosphere than red sprites do, at 40–50 kilometers (about 25–30 mi) above the ground. Blue jets travel around 100 kilometers (about 62 mi) per second.

People in airplanes and on mountains could see blue jets and red sprites because the people were above storms. No one had ever seen ELVES because they last only a thousandth of a second. This is far too little time for the human eye to see. In 1990, videos taken from the space shuttle did show ELVES. Five more years passed before a second video of ELVES was made.

Finding Sprites, Jets, and ELVES

There are several reasons why it took so long to discover these unusual lights:

- They occur only above thunderstorms, so clouds usually block the view from the ground.
- They are dim and can be seen only after the eyes have adjusted to the dark. That adjustment is spoiled by bright lightning.
- Sprites last only about 3 ten-thousandths of a second (0.0003 second).

- Only about 1 in 100 lightning strikes produces these lights.

It took careful observation to find out that sprites, jets, and ELVES are real.

THINK ABOUT IT

1. What do you think scientists thought of the early reports of sprites and jets, before the videotape?
2. Why do scientists use low-light video cameras to take pictures of sprites, jets, and ELVES?

CAREERS
METEOROLOGIST

What They Do
Meteorologists study the atmosphere and the changes that produce different kinds of weather. Meteorologists may work for business or government. They may also research new uses for computer programs in the study of weather.

Education and Training
Someone who wants to be a meteorologist must study science in college. Many meteorologists get further training in weather research and technology after college.

WEB LINK
For Science and Technology updates, visit the Harcourt Internet site.
www.harcourtschool.com

El Niño water temperature maps

Denise Stephenson-Hawk

ATMOSPHERIC SCIENTIST

Dr. Denise Stephenson-Hawk always loved school and was especially good in math. She skipped her senior year in high school and entered Spelman College. While there, she received a scholarship to a summer program at the National Aeronautics and Space Administration (NASA). She worked on a project to test panels for the space shuttle to make sure the panels would withstand the high temperatures they experience upon reentry into Earth's atmosphere. Stephenson-Hawk was so excited by what she learned about the atmosphere that she decided to apply her math skills to the study of atmospheric science.

Stephenson-Hawk's first job was at AT&T Bell Laboratories. There she made computer models to learn how sound travels in the ocean. After teaching mathematical modeling at Spelman College, Stephenson-Hawk moved to Clark Atlanta University in Georgia. There she works as a senior research scientist and associate professor of physics.

Stephenson-Hawk is also a member of the Climate Analysis Center (CAC) at the National Oceanic and Atmospheric Administration (NOAA). The CAC uses computer models to analyze and predict climate changes that happen in a short time. Stephenson-Hawk's special project has been building computer models of the effects of El Niño, a series of events set off by warmer-than-normal surface-water temperatures in the Pacific Ocean. Stephenson-Hawk and the other scientists working on this project are trying to more accurately predict the impact of El Niño so that people can better prepare for unusual weather.

THINK ABOUT IT

1. Why else might scientists be interested in studying El Niño?
2. Why do you think atmospheric scientists use computer models?

RAIN GAUGE

What is a way to measure rain and other precipitation?

Materials
- 1-liter bottle, clear plastic
- scissors
- plastic ruler
- masking tape
- wire hanger
- water

Procedure

1. **CAUTION** **Be careful when using scissors.** Remove the cap, and cut the top off the bottle as shown.

2. Tape the ruler to the outside of the bottle. The zero mark should be about 1 cm above the bottom.

3. Bend the coat hanger to make a basket for the bottle. Make sure the bottle will hang straight up and down.

4. Fill the bottle with water to the zero mark on the ruler. Then turn the bottle top over like a funnel and put it inside the bottle bottom.

5. Hang the rain gauge out in the open and away from any roof edges or trees— for example, on a fence.

6. After a storm, measure the rainfall and empty the bottle to the zero mark.

Draw Conclusions
How did measuring rainfall help you measure weather?

WEATHER FRONTS

How can water model a weather front?

Materials
- tall, clear jar
- hot and cold tap water
- pitcher
- food coloring
- thermometer

Procedure

1. Fill the jar halfway with cold water.

2. Fill the pitcher with hot water. Add 10 drops of food coloring.

3. Tilt the jar of cold water. Then slowly trickle the hot water down the inside of the jar. Slowly put the jar upright. Observe what happens in the jar.

4. Use the thermometer to measure the temperature of the hot water in the jar. Carefully move the thermometer down to measure the cold water in the jar. Can you find the front by using the thermometer?

Draw Conclusions
How did the hot water and cold water interact? How were they like air masses?

Vocabulary Review

Use the terms below to complete the sentences. The page numbers in ( ) tell you where to look in the chapter if you need help.

atmosphere (D6)
air pressure (D7)
troposphere (D8)
stratosphere (D8)
greenhouse effect (D12)
air mass (D13)
front (D14)

cirrus (D15)
cumulus (D15)
cumulonimbus (D15)
stratus (D15)
barometer (D20)
humidity (D21)
hygrometer (D21)

1. The _____ is the thin layer of air that surrounds Earth.

2. The amount of water vapor in the air is called _____.

3. The warming caused when air traps some of the sun's energy is the _____.

4. _____ is the force with which the atmosphere presses down on Earth.

5. In the atmosphere, the _____ is the layer in which most weather occurs.

6. An _____ is a large body of air, and it forms and moves over land or water.

7. An instrument that measures air pressure is a _____.

8. A _____ forms when two air masses meet.

9. In the atmosphere, the layer that contains a lot of ozone is the _____.

10. An instrument that measures humidity is a _____.

11. Wispy _____ clouds are made up of ice crystals high in the atmosphere.

12. Low, gray _____ clouds form a layer and may bring light rain.

13. White, fluffy _____ clouds occur in fair weather, but they can become dark, towering _____ storm clouds.

Connect Concepts

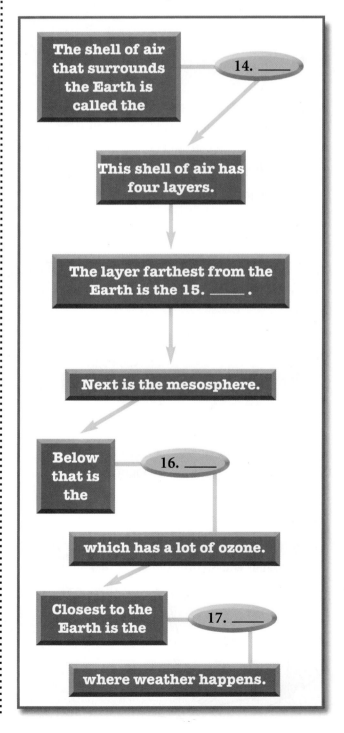

The shell of air that surrounds the Earth is called the **14. _____**

This shell of air has four layers.

The layer farthest from the Earth is the **15. _____** .

Next is the mesosphere.

Below that is the **16. _____** which has a lot of ozone.

Closest to the Earth is the **17. _____** where weather happens.

Check Understanding

Write the letter of the best choice.

18. As you get higher in the atmosphere, the space between air particles —
    A decreases
    B doesn't change
    C increases
    D masses

19. Energy from the _____ is trapped by gases in the air, causing the greenhouse effect.
    F Earth   H barometer
    G sun   J stratosphere

20. An air mass that forms over tropical waters would be —
    A warm and moist
    B cold and moist
    C cold and dry
    D warm and dry

21. A _____ front forms when two air masses meet and don't move.
    F cold   H stationary
    G warm   J pressure

22. _____ air can have more water vapor than _____ air.
    A Warm, cold
    B Dense, less dense
    C Cold, warm
    D Thermosphere, mesosphere

Critical Thinking

23. Why do mountain climbers use oxygen tanks?

24. You hear on a weather report that a cold front is coming. What weather changes can you expect?

25. Suppose you watch the weather report each day for five days. Each day the average temperature is the same and the air pressure doesn't change. What could be happening?

Process Skills Review

26. Remember the first investigation in this chapter. What did you **observe** that allowed you to **infer** that air is matter?

27. How is a **number** description of wind speed different from a word description of wind speed?

28. Suppose you will **measure** weather conditions over the next five days. What equipment will help you measure? Make a table to record your data. Include units of measure.

Performance Assessment

Weather Maps

With a partner, study the three maps your teacher gives you. Tell how the weather has changed in the map area over the past three days. Then predict what the weather will be for the next two days. Explain the reasons for your prediction.

The Oceans

Nearly three-fourths of Earth is covered with a great body of salt water. It is always moving and full of life. Its currents bring warm temperatures to otherwise cold areas. Its depths hide great mountain ranges. And its nutrient-rich waters are home to all sorts of living things.

Vocabulary Preview

water cycle
evaporation
condensation
precipitation
wave
storm surge
tide
deep ocean current
surface current
shore zone
continental shelf
abyssal plain
trench
mid-ocean ridge

Fast Fact

The oceans of the Earth are vast and deep. If Earth were a smooth ball with no mountains or valleys at all, it would be completely covered with water to a depth of more than 2 kilometers (about $1\frac{1}{4}$ mi).

Mount Everest

The deepest spot in the oceans is in the Mariana Trench in the Pacific—11,000 meters (about 36,000 ft) below sea level. If Mount Everest, Earth's highest mountain, were dropped into that spot, it would be covered with about $1\frac{1}{2}$ kilometers (about 1 mi) of water!

Fast Fact

The Pacific Ocean holds about half of Earth's ocean water, and it covers nearly a third of Earth's surface. Here's how three oceans compare:

Ocean Sizes		
Ocean	Size (Square kilometers)	Size (Square miles)
Pacific	181,000,000	70,000,000
Atlantic	94,000,000	36,000,000
Indian	74,000,000	29,000,000

What Role Do Oceans Play in the Water Cycle?

In this lesson, you can . . .

INVESTIGATE how to get fresh water from salt water.

LEARN ABOUT Earth's ocean water.

LINK to math, writing, social studies, and technology.

◄ Buoys float but are held in place by anchors. They mark paths where the water is deep enough for ships.

INVESTIGATE

Getting Fresh Water from Salt Water

Activity Purpose If you've ever been splashed in the face by an ocean wave, you know that sea water is salty. The salt in ocean water stings your eyes, leaves a crusty white coating on your skin when it dries, and tastes like the salt you put on food. In this investigation you'll evaporate artificial ocean water to find out what is left behind. From your **observations** you will **infer** how you can get fresh water from salt water.

Materials

- container of very warm water
- salt
- spoon
- cotton swabs
- large clear bowl
- small glass jar
- plastic wrap
- large rubber band
- piece of modeling clay
- masking tape

Activity Procedure   CAUTION

1 Stir two spoonfuls of salt into the container of very warm water. Put one end of a clean cotton swab into this mixture. Taste the mixture by touching the swab to your tongue. **Record** your observations. **CAUTION** Don't share swabs. Don't put a swab that has touched your mouth back into any substance. Never taste anything in an investigation or experiment unless you are told to do so.

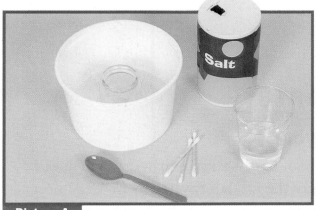

Picture A

Picture B

2 Pour the salt water into the large bowl. Put the jar in the center of the bowl of salt water. (Picture A)

3 Put the plastic wrap over the top of the bowl. The wrap should not touch the top of the jar inside the bowl. Put a large rubber band around the bowl to hold the wrap in place.

4 Form the clay into a small ball. Put the ball on top of the plastic wrap right over the jar. Make sure the plastic wrap doesn't touch the jar. (Picture B)

5 On the outside of the bowl, use tape to mark the level of the salt water. Place the bowl in a sunny spot for one day.

6 After one day, remove the plastic wrap and the clay ball. Use clean swabs to taste the water in the jar and in the bowl. **Record** your **observations.**

Draw Conclusions

1. What did you **observe** by using your sense of taste?

2. What do you **infer** happened to the salt water as it sat in the sun?

3. **Scientists at Work** The movement of water from the Earth's surface, through the atmosphere, and back to Earth's surface is called the water cycle. From what you **observed,** what can you **infer** about the ocean's role in the water cycle?

Investigate Further Put the plastic wrap and the clay back on the large bowl. Leave the bowl in the sun for several days, until all the water in the large bowl is gone. **Observe** the bowl and the jar. What can you **conclude** about ocean water?

> **Process Skill Tip**
>
> Observing and inferring are different things. You **observe** with your senses. You **infer**, or form an opinion, based on what you have observed and what you know about a situation.

Ocean Water

The Water Cycle

Oceans cover more of Earth's surface than dry land does. About three-fourths of the Earth is covered by water. Almost all of that water is ocean water. Even though ocean water is salty, it provides a large amount of Earth's fresh water. Earth's water is always being recycled. As the model in the investigation showed, heat from the sun causes fresh water to evaporate (ee•VAP•uh•rayt) from the oceans, leaving the salt behind. This evaporated water condenses to form clouds. Fresh water falls from the clouds to Earth's surface as rain. This constant recycling of water is called the **water cycle**. During the cycle, water changes from a liquid to a gas and back to a liquid. The diagram on these pages shows how the water cycle works. It includes the parts played by the sun, the water, the air, and the land.

✔ **What is the water cycle?**

FIND OUT

- about processes that make up the water cycle

- why ocean water is salty

VOCABULARY

water cycle
evaporation
condensation
precipitation

The sun warms the ocean, causing the water particles to move faster and faster. After a while, they have enough energy to leave the water and enter the air as water vapor. This is **evaporation**, the process by which a liquid changes to a gas. ▼

A cloud forms when water vapor condenses high in the atmosphere. **Condensation** (kahn•duhn•SAY•shuhn) happens when the water vapor rises, cools, and changes from a gas to liquid water. These drops of water in a cloud are so small that they stay up in the air.

Water vapor from an ocean can be carried a long way through the atmosphere. Water that evaporates from the Gulf of Mexico may fall back to Earth's surface far away in Georgia or Virginia.

In the cloud, some water drops bump into others and stick together. The drops get bigger. When they get too large to stay up in the air, they fall to Earth as rain, snow, sleet, or hail. Some of this precipitation (pree•sip•uh•TAY•shuhn) collects in lakes, rivers, and other bodies of water. Some precipitation soaks into the ground to become groundwater. Some falls directly back into the ocean.

What Is in Ocean Water

Ocean water is a mixture of water and many dissolved solids. Most of these solids are salts. Sodium chloride is the most common salt in ocean water. You probably know this substance by another name—table salt.

Where do you think the salts and other solids in the ocean come from? Most of the salts and other substances in the ocean come from the land. As rivers, streams, and runoff flow over the land, they slowly break down the rocks that make it up. Over time, flowing water carries substances from the rocks to the ocean.

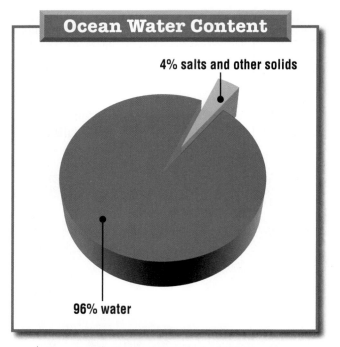

Ocean Water Content

4% salts and other solids

96% water

▲ Ocean water is made up of almost the same substances everywhere on Earth. Ocean water is about 96 percent water and 4 percent salts and other dissolved solids.

Dead Sea

Ocean

Salts and other dissolved substances in the ocean make ocean water denser than fresh water. So it is easier to float in water that is saltier. Look closely at these swimmers and the instruments shown next to them. One swimmer is in the Dead Sea, a body of water that is much saltier than the ocean, and the other is in the ocean. Which water is denser? How can you tell?

Near places where rivers empty into the ocean, the ocean water is less salty than it is farther from the shore. This is because the fresh water mixes with the salt water. Ocean water is a little saltier near the equator, where it is hot and water evaporates faster. And ocean water is a little less salty near the North and South Poles, where it is colder and water evaporates more slowly.

✓ **What is in ocean water?**

Summary

The waters of the ocean provide fresh water for Earth through the water cycle. As water moves through this cycle, it changes from a liquid to a gas and back to a liquid through the processes of evaporation and condensation. The water returns to Earth as precipitation. Sodium chloride is the most common salt in the ocean. The salts and other substances dissolved in ocean water make it denser than fresh water.

Review

1. What is the water cycle?
2. Explain how water changes from a liquid to a gas and back to a liquid in the water cycle.
3. What factors affect the saltiness or density of ocean water?
4. **Critical Thinking** How could you make salt water denser?
5. **Test Prep** Which of these processes occurs when a gas changes to a liquid?
   A evaporation
   B condensation
   C precipitation
   D salinity

LINKS

MATH LINK

Collect, Organize, and Display Data
Use library reference materials to find out more about the amounts of fresh water and salt water on Earth. Draw a large square on a sheet of paper, and divide it into fourths. Color the squares to show the amounts of land and ocean. Stack pennies or checkers on the squares to stand for the amounts of fresh water and salt water.

WRITING LINK

Narrative Writing—Story Suppose you are sailing alone around the world. For your teacher, write down some of your thoughts that describe the ocean and what it is like to have nothing but water all around you.

SOCIAL STUDIES LINK

El Niño Find out what El Niño is. Locate on a world map the places where this condition occurs. Write a report that explains what causes this situation and how it affected weather and crops around the world in 1998.

TECHNOLOGY LINK

Learn more about Earth's water systems by visiting the National Air and Space Museum Internet site.
www.si.edu/harcourt/science

 Smithsonian Institution®

What Are the Motions of Oceans?

In this lesson, you can . . .

INVESTIGATE water currents.

LEARN ABOUT the ways ocean water moves.

LINK to math, writing, social studies, and technology.

INVESTIGATE

Water Currents

Activity Purpose If you've ever gone swimming in the ocean, you've probably felt waves crash against your body. You may also have felt water moving against you below the surface. This movement below the water's surface is a *current*. In this investigation you'll **make a model** and **infer** one way currents form.

Materials

- clear, medium-sized bowl
- warm tap water
- colored ice cube
- clock

Activity Procedure

1. Put the bowl on a flat surface. Carefully fill the bowl three-quarters full of warm tap water.

2. Let the water stand undisturbed for 10 minutes.

◄ Ocean water moves in many ways. Both the rising water and the waves are washing away this sand castle.

3 Without stirring the warm water or making a splash, gently place the colored ice cube in the middle of the bowl. (Picture A)

4 **Observe** for 10 minutes what happens as the ice cube melts. Every 2 minutes, make a simple drawing of the bowl to **record** your observations.

Draw Conclusions

1. Describe what you **observed** as the ice cube melted in the bowl of warm water.

2. In your **model**, what does the bowl of water stand for? What does the ice cube stand for?

Picture A

3. Since the liquid in the bowl and the ice cube were both water, what can you **infer** about the cause of what happened in the bowl?

4. **Scientists at Work** In Chapter 1, you learned that cold air is denser than warm air. The same is true for water. Using this information and what you **observed** in the investigation, explain one way ocean currents form.

Investigate Further Mix up two batches of salt water. Use twice as much salt in one batch as in the other. Use the water to **model** another kind of ocean current. Fill a clear bowl three-fourths full with the less salty water. Add a few drops of food coloring to the saltier water. Along the side of the bowl, slowly pour the colored, saltier water into the clear, less salty water. Describe your **observations. Make a hypothesis** to explain what you observed. What **prediction** can you make based on the hypothesis? **Plan and conduct a simple investigation** to test your hypothesis.

Process Skill Tip

People make models to help them **observe** things in nature that are too small, too big, or too hard to see or understand. By observing a model, you can infer how things work.

Ocean Movements

Waves

FIND OUT

- about ocean waves and currents
- what causes tides

VOCABULARY

wave
storm surge
tide
surface current
deep ocean current

If you've ever been in the path of a wave in the ocean, in a lake, or in a wave pool, you know that even big waves don't move you either forward or back. You bob up and down, but you're still in about the same place after the wave passes. This is because a **wave** is the up-and-down movement of the water particles that make it up.

Water waves are caused by the wind. As wind blows over the water's surface, it pulls on the water particles. This causes small bumps, or ripples, of water to form. As the wind continues to blow, the ripples keep growing. Over time they become waves.

The height of a wave depends on three things: the strength of the wind, the amount of time the wind blows, and the size of the area over which the wind blows. Strong, gusty winds blowing

Waves drop and take away bits of rock and sand grains from a beach as they break on a rocky shore. ▶

Waves like these are caused by the wind. Waves break, or give up their energy, as they move onto the shore. ▼

▲ Waves erode a shore as the water carries sediment back toward the sea. What might happen to these houses if erosion continues?

over an area of many square kilometers can cause a group of very large waves called a **storm surge** to form. Storm surges often occur during hurricanes and can cause a lot of damage along a shore.

Waves change the shore in different ways. When waves break on a beach, water carries sand and other sediments as it flows back into the ocean. This carrying away of sediments is called *erosion*. Erosion along a shore causes beaches to become smaller. As waves give up their energy, they also deposit, or drop, sediments. This process is called *deposition* (dep•uh•ZISH•uhn). When waves deposit sediments near shore, a beach gets bigger.

The photograph at the bottom of this page shows a harbor during a hurricane. You probably know that a hurricane is a severe storm that has strong winds and a lot of rain. Storm surges during hurricanes cause erosion and deposition along a shore. Whole beaches can be washed away.

✔ **How do water waves change a shoreline?**

This is a harbor during a hurricane. Storm surges during hurricanes can be as high as 10 meters (more than 30 ft). ▼

Tides

If you watched a beach for 12 hours, you would probably notice that the waves don't always reach the same place. This is because of another type of ocean water motion called tides. **Tides** are the daily change in the local water level of the ocean.

At *high tide* much of the beach is covered by water. At *low tide* waves break farther away from shore. Less of the beach is under water. Every day most shorelines have two high tides and two low tides. High tide and low tide are usually a little more than six hours apart.

Tides are caused by gravity. *Gravity* is a force that causes all objects to be pulled toward all other objects. The force of gravity between two objects depends on two things: the sizes of the objects and the distance between them. Big objects have a greater pull than small objects. Objects that are closer together have a greater pull on one another than objects farther apart do.

Even though the moon is much smaller than the sun, the pull of the moon's gravity on Earth is the main cause of ocean tides. This is because the moon is much closer to Earth than the sun is.

▲ This photograph shows low tide in a harbor on the Bay of Fundy in Nova Scotia, Canada.

▲ This is the same harbor on the Bay of Fundy during high tide. Compare the positions of the ships with their positions in the photograph above.

◄ A tide pool is a small body of water on the shore. Parts of it may be out of the water during low tide. Sea animals such as starfish, crabs, and sea anemones (uh•NEM•uh•neez) live in these pools.

The moon pulls on everything on Earth. As the moon pulls on ocean water, the water forms a bulge that always faces the moon. Another water bulge forms on the side of Earth farthest from the moon, where the moon's pull is weakest. As Earth rotates, the bulges stay in the same places. High tide occurs as a point on Earth moves through a bulge. The water level rises on the shore. Low tide occurs as a point on Earth moves between the bulges. The water level on the shore gets lower.

At certain times each month, tides are very high or very low. Read The Inside Story to find out why.

✔ **What are tides?**

The Moon and Tides

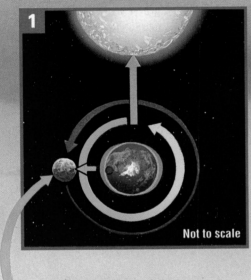

Not to scale

Not to scale

Even though the moon's pull on the oceans is greater than the sun's pull, the sun still affects tides. The pictures show how.

1 When the sun, Earth, and moon form a right angle, the bulge of water that forms high tides is smaller than usual. This causes *neap tides*, or only a small difference between high and low tides. Neap tides occur when the moon is in its first-quarter phase or in its third-quarter phase.

2 When the sun, moon, and Earth are in a straight line, the bulge of water that forms high tides is bigger than usual. This causes *spring tides*, or higher high tides and lower low tides. Two spring tides occur every month, when the moon is in its new-moon and full-moon phases.

Currents

Currents are rivers of water that flow in the ocean. A **surface current** forms when steady winds blow over the surface of the ocean. In the Northern Hemisphere, surface currents flow in a clockwise direction. In the Southern Hemisphere, surface currents flow in a counterclockwise direction.

Deep ocean currents form because of density differences in ocean water. You made a model of deep ocean currents in the investigation. The density of ocean water depends on two things—the amount of salt in the water and the temperature of the water. The more salt there is in water, the denser it will be. Cold ocean water also is

Scientists have mapped the paths of surface currents and deep ocean currents in the oceans. ▼

Cold water flows underneath warm water, forming a deep ocean current. The cold water can flow for great distances along the ocean floor. The green arrows on the globe show deep ocean currents. ▼

◄ Surface currents are caused by wind blowing mostly in the same direction over the ocean for a long time. The pink arrows on the globe show surface currents.

denser than warm ocean water. Deep ocean currents form when dense, cold water meets less dense water. The denser water flows under the less dense water, forcing the less dense water to rise.

✔ **What causes deep ocean currents?**

Summary

Ocean waves form as wind blows over the water's surface. Strong, gusty winds over a large area can cause a large wave called a storm surge. Tides are the rise and fall of ocean water caused by the pull of gravity between Earth, the moon, and the sun. Surface currents are caused by the blowing of steady winds. Deep ocean currents are caused by differences in saltiness or water temperature.

Review

1. How does an object floating in water move as a wave passes it?
2. What causes tides?
3. Why does the moon have a greater effect on tides than the sun has?
4. **Critical Thinking** Compare and contrast surface currents in the Northern and Southern Hemispheres.
5. **Test Prep** Which is caused by density differences?
   A surface currents
   B ocean waves
   C deep ocean currents
   D ocean tides

LINKS

MATH LINK

Find an Average Scientists estimate that sea level rose 10 to 15 centimeters between the years 1900 and 2000. They estimate that it will rise another 50 centimeters before 2100. What will the average yearly rate of sea level rise be for the years 2000 to 2100?

WRITING LINK

Informative Writing—Description Suppose you are a creature that lives in a tide pool. For a younger student, write a short description that explains how your life changes when the tide comes in and goes out.

SOCIAL STUDIES LINK

Trade Routes Find out about the triangle trade route that existed in colonial times in the United States. Mark this route on a copy of a world map, and explain how ocean currents and wind patterns made this route possible.

TECHNOLOGY LINK

Learn more about new ways to explore deep in the ocean by viewing *Robot Submarine* on the **Harcourt Science Newsroom Video.**

What Is the Ocean Floor Like?

In this lesson, you can . . .

INVESTIGATE the ocean floor.

LEARN ABOUT features of the ocean floor.

LINK to math, writing, social studies, and technology.

This is a sonar survey ship. Using a device called an echo sounder, the ship gathers data about ocean floor features. ▼

INVESTIGATE

Model the Ocean Floor

Activity Purpose The sonar ship in the picture uses an echo sounder to gather data about the ocean floor. This device sends sounds to the ocean floor. The sounds echo, or are reflected, back to the ship. The time for the signal to travel and return is measured. Using these times, a computer can calculate and display ocean floor depths. In this activity you will **use numbers** obtained by echo sounders to make a model of ocean floor features.

Materials
- grid paper
- shoe box
- clay

Activity Procedure

1 Set up a graph as shown at the top of page D47. Label the horizontal axis *Distance East of New Jersey (km)*. Label the vertical axis *Water Depth (m)*.

2 Look closely at the graph. Note that the top horizontal mark is labeled *0*. This mark stands for the surface of the ocean. The numbers beneath stand for depths below sea level.

3 Plot the chart data on the graph.

4 Connect the points on your graph. You have now made a profile of the Atlantic Ocean floor.

5 **Analyze** your graph. Determine how the ocean floor changes as you move eastward from New Jersey.

Distance (km)	Depth (m)
0	0
500	3500
2000	5600
3000	4300
4000	0
4300	3050
5000	5000
5650	0

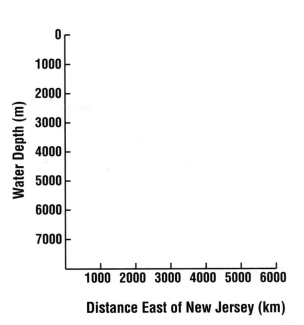

Distance East of New Jersey (km)

6 Use clay to **make a model** of your profile. Label the narrow end of the shoe box *Coastline*. Label the opposite end *6000 km*. Put the clay inside the box. Vary the height of the clay to model the changing depth of the ocean floor. (Picture A)

Draw Conclusions

1. Describe what you **observed** on the graph.

2. What does the clay in your **model** represent?

3. Based on your model, what can you infer about the ocean floor?

4. **Scientists at Work** Sound waves travel through ocean water at about 1525 meters per second. Suppose it takes two seconds for an echo to return. The sound takes one second to reach the ocean floor and one second to return, so the distance to the ocean floor is about 1525 meters. **Using the numbers** from the chart, at what distance from New Jersey would it take a sound wave four seconds to return to a ship?

Investigate Further Use numbers to make a chart of heights to profile one section of your classroom. Your chart should resemble the one shown in this activity. Exchange charts with a classmate and try to identify the exact location shown by the map.

Picture A

The Ocean Floor

FIND OUT

- about some ocean floor features

- how ocean floor forms

VOCABULARY

shore zone
continental shelf
abyssal plain
trench
mid-ocean ridge

Underwater Geography

What would you see if you somehow drained the water from the world's oceans? Many people think you would find a big, flat plain. In some places the ocean floor does look like that. But the ocean floor also holds the world's longest mountain range. This chain of mountains is four times longer than the Andes, Rockies, and Himalayas combined. Earth's tallest mountain is on the ocean floor. It is more than 1220 meters (about 4000 ft) taller than the tallest mountain on dry land. In some places, the ocean floor drops thousands of meters to form deep trenches, or canyons. One place in the Pacific Ocean is almost seven times as deep as the Grand Canyon.

In the investigation you made a profile of the floor of the Atlantic Ocean. The profile of the Atlantic Ocean shown on these pages was made in a similar way but with many more data points. Study the profile to learn more about the features of the ocean floor.

✔ **How is the ocean floor like Earth's surface?**

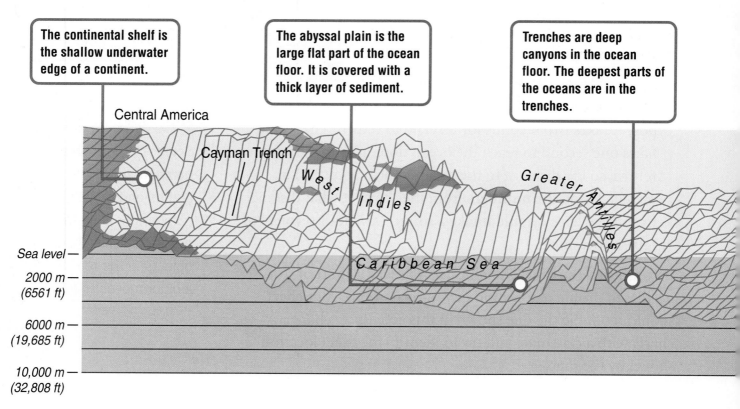

The continental shelf is the shallow underwater edge of a continent.

The abyssal plain is the large flat part of the ocean floor. It is covered with a thick layer of sediment.

Trenches are deep canyons in the ocean floor. The deepest parts of the oceans are in the trenches.

Central America

Cayman Trench

West Indies

Greater Antilles

Caribbean Sea

Sea level —
2000 m —
(6561 ft)
6000 m —
(19,685 ft)
10,000 m —
(32,808 ft)

Near the Shore

The **shore zone** is the place where land and ocean meet. The ocean floor of the shore zone is called the **continental shelf**. Here the continent slopes gently down beneath the water's surface. At the edge of a continental shelf, the ocean floor drops away rapidly.

The shore zone is an area rich in resources. Fish caught in the shore zone are an important food source. Oils and fertilizers are made from fish. Many types of salts are obtained from water in the shore zone.

Some parts of the shore zone contain oil deposits. Offshore rigs drill holes in the continental shelf to bring this valuable resource to Earth's surface.

✔ **What are some products of the shore zone?**

◄ Rocks and sand obtained from the shore zone are used to make roads and buildings.

◄ Dark masses of minerals form along the ocean floor. In the future these nodules may be mined for the metals they contain—manganese, copper, nickel, and cobalt.

The mid-ocean ridge is the world's longest mountain range. It extends across 65,000 km (about 40,000 mi) of the ocean floor.

This picture shows how the continental shelf slopes down under the ocean. ►

Continental Shelf

Atlantic Ocean

Cape Verde Islands

Africa

Mid-Atlantic Ridge

The abyssal plain is covered with sediments of clay, silt, sand, and rock carried into the ocean from the continents.

Steep-sided volcanic mountains called seamounts rise above the abyssal plain.

Undersea trenches are among the most dramatic features of the ocean floor. The deepest spot on Earth is located in the southwestern Pacific Ocean in the Mariana Trench.

Mid-Ocean Features

A steep slope leads from the continental shelf to huge flat areas of ocean floor called **abyssal** (uh•BIHS•uhl) **plains**. These plains are covered with thick layers of sediment that eroded from the continents and were carried into the oceans by rivers. Microscopic remains of ocean organisms also are a part of these sediments.

In some places the ocean floor suddenly plunges downward to form a deep, narrow **trench**. These trenches are the deepest parts of the ocean. Some of them are more than 10,000 meters (32,800 ft) below the ocean surface.

A vast chain of mountains crosses the center of Earth's oceans. Branches of this **mid-ocean ridge** stretch through the

> The island country of Iceland is one of the few places on Earth where the mid-ocean ridge rises above the ocean's surface.

> The continental shelf forms an area of shallower water around all the continents.

Earth's Surface

Most of Earth's surface is covered by water. In fact, only about 30 percent of Earth's surface is dry land. ▼

Atlantic, Pacific, and Indian Oceans. The chain's total length of 65,000 kilometers (about 40,000 mi) makes it Earth's longest mountain range. The peaks of the mid-ocean ridge rise an average of 2500 to 3000 meters (about 8,200 to 10,000 ft) above the ocean floor. The tallest of these mountains poke above sea level and form islands.

✓ **What are three features of the mid-ocean?**

The ocean floor is continually recycled through seafloor spreading. New crust forms in places where two ocean plates move apart. At other locations old crust is destroyed in ocean trenches. Scientists compare this movement of ocean floor to the motion of a conveyor belt. In both processes matter moves in a repeating pattern.

Basalt, a dark, heavy rock, forms from the magma that moves up to fill the crack formed by the plates moving apart. These ridges of basalt are what pile up to form mid-ocean ridges.

Changing Features

You may recall from Unit C, Chapter 1, that movement of Earth's plates produces many features of the ocean floor. Some underwater volcanoes form when a plate moves over a hot spot in Earth's mantle. An ocean trench forms when one plate slides beneath another.

Plate movement also produces the mid-ocean ridges and new ocean floor. At the ridges two plates are moving very slowly away from each other. As the plates move apart, magma from the mantle moves up between them. This cooled magma forms new ocean-floor crust. The new crust replaces older crust pushed deep into Earth at a trench. Sometimes the new crust collects to form a mountain.

✔ **What causes the formation of new ocean floor?**

Summary

Many of the features found on dry land also are found on the floors of Earth's oceans. In the shore zone, a continent slopes beneath the water's surface. This area of the ocean supplies humans with many valuable products. Far away from the shore zone, a long mountain ridge crosses the ocean floor. Other features of the ocean floor include vast abyssal plains and deep ocean trenches. The movement of Earth's plates forms many of these features. Plate movement also causes the formation of new ocean floor and the destruction of old ocean floor.

Review

1. How are the shore zone and continental shelf related?
2. What is unusual about Iceland?
3. How does new ocean floor form?
4. **Critical Thinking** What would happen if old ocean floor were not destroyed in deep trenches?
5. **Test Prep** Which ocean floor feature forms when one plate slides beneath another plate?
   - A abyssal plain   C shore zone
   - B trench   D volcano

LINKS

MATH LINK

Use Mental Math Ten liters of sea water weigh about 101 newtons. How much would a 4,000 liter tank weigh?

WRITING LINK

Informative Writing—Description Suppose you are a passenger in a deep-sea submarine. Write a letter to a friend describing your trip from the shore zone to the mid-ocean ridge.

SOCIAL STUDIES LINK

Ocean Profile Choose one of Earth's oceans. Research the unique features found on the floor of this ocean. Display your findings as a profile of that ocean.

PHYSICAL EDUCATION LINK

Scuba Diving Many people enjoy exploring the undersea world through the sport of scuba diving. Research the equipment and training needed to enjoy this activity. Share your findings in a pamphlet titled *Safe Scuba Diving Tips*.

GO ONLINE TECHNOLOGY LINK

Learn more about Earth's ocean floor by visiting this Internet site.

www.scilinks.org/harcourt

Deep Flight II

Deep Flight II is a submersible, or sub, that is being developed to explore the ocean depths. It will carry two pilots and will go to the deepest part of the ocean, the Mariana Trench.

Exploring the Deep Ocean

Only one mission with people has ever gone to the Mariana Trench. This trench in the Pacific Ocean is about 11,000 meters (about 7 mi) deep. From that depth, it would take more than 25 Empire State Buildings stacked on top of each other to reach the surface. In 1960 two men in a bathyscaph (BATH•uh•skaf) called the *Trieste* (tree•EST) went down for 20 minutes. The ship had none of the video cameras or computers we have today. And the *Trieste* could only go straight down and come straight back up.

Graham Hawkes, an engineer, and his business partner, Sylvia Earle, have been working to make deep-ocean subs, such as *Deep Flight II*. Scientists want better subs to help them investigate ocean-floor geology as well as deep-ocean plants and animals. Subs, however, can't meet all research needs. Robot, or remote-controlled, subs are often better for dangerous or long trips.

Built for Speed and Comfort

The time needed to go so deep is a problem, so Hawkes is designing a craft that "flies" through water like an airplane. It should reach the ocean floor in 90 minutes.

Another problem is the high pressure. The sub must support the weight of a column of water 11,275 meters high, so the hull of *Deep Flight II* is being built of strong, new ceramic materials. These materials are lighter than steel and won't break under high pressure. The ship will also protect

its crew from the near-freezing cold of the ocean water.

Hawkes is using shapes from nature for the design of *Deep Flight II*. Its smooth body and wings look like parts of dolphins, whales, and birds, as well as aircraft. It can skim forward below the ocean's surface or dive down into the depths. It can even do spins and rolls like a stunt airplane.

If the first voyage of *Deep Flight II* is a success, Hawkes and Earle may soon be designing and building more deep-sea subs.

THINK ABOUT IT

1. How will the pilot of *Deep Flight II* be like an astronaut landing on the moon?
2. Why do you think most of the ocean remains unexplored?

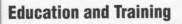

Graham Hawkes in a museum model of *Deep Flight I*

Rachel Carson
MARINE BIOLOGIST

"Science is part of the reality of living: it is the what, the how, and the why of everything in our experience."

Although Rachel Carson did not actually visit the ocean until she was 22 years old and a college graduate, she had been fascinated by it all her life.

Everything in nature thrilled Carson—flowers and birds, trees and rivers, animals and insects. She surprised many people at her college by changing from an English major to a biology major. At the time, science was seen as a career for men. No one expected her to do well.

Carson used both biology and writing in her work. She taught college classes after she graduated. Another of her early jobs was with the U.S. Bureau of Fisheries, writing scripts for radio broadcasts about life under the sea. She eventually moved up in the Bureau to become editor-in-chief of publications.

Carson was encouraged to write articles, which eventually were printed in one book, *Under the Sea-Wind*. Carson wrote other books about the sea, including *The Sea Around Us*, which became a best-seller.

Carson is best known for her book *Silent Spring*. She began it after a friend who had a bird sanctuary wrote a letter. Her friend wrote Carson that pesticides had killed all the birds at the sanctuary. It took Carson several years to collect information and write the book. She closely studied the dangers of DDT, a chemical used to kill insects. *Silent Spring* tells what a spring would be like without new life.

THINK ABOUT IT

1. Why was it important that Carson spend so much time collecting information for *Silent Spring*?

2. Why might it have been important that Carson had already published several books before writing *Silent Spring*?

MEASURING DENSITY

What are the relative densities of different solutions?

Materials

- unsharpened pencil with eraser
- tall, narrow glass or jar
- permanent marker
- safety goggles
- thumbtack
- water
- salt
- spoon

Procedure

① **CAUTION** **Put on your goggles.** Carefully push the thumbtack completely into the eraser.

② Fill the glass three-fourths full of tap water. Place the pencil, eraser end first, into the water. When it floats up on its own, grab the pencil at the point where it meets the surface of the water. Use the permanent marker to mark this point.

③ Add four spoonfuls of salt to the water. Stir until the salt dissolves. Place the pencil in the water, and mark it as you did in Step 2.

Draw Conclusions

Explain your observations in Steps 2 and 3.

MAKING WAVES

How does a wave move?

Materials

- safety goggles
- heavy washer
- 2-m length of rope

Procedure

① **CAUTION** **Put on your goggles.** String the washer onto the rope. It should fit loosely.

② Work with a partner. Each of you should hold one end of the rope. It should hang loosely with the washer in the center of the rope. The rope should not be stretched between you and your partner.

③ Shake one end of the rope by moving your arm while your partner holds the other end still. Observe the movement of the washer on the rope. Compare this movement to the movement of objects floating in ocean water.

Draw Conclusions

How did the washer move? How is the movement of the rope like the movement of a wave?

Vocabulary Review

Use the terms below to complete the sentences. The page numbers in ( ) tell you where to look in the chapter if you need help.

evaporation (D34)
water cycle (D34)
condensation (D34)
precipitation (D35)
wave (D40)
storm surge (D41)
tides (D42)

surface current (D44)
deep ocean
    current (D44)
shore zone (D49)
continental shelf (D49)
abyssal plain (D50)
trench (D50)
mid-ocean ridge (D50)

1. A large wave caused by strong winds is called a ＿＿＿.

2. ＿＿＿ is a process that changes a liquid to a gas.

3. A gas changes to a liquid by a process called ＿＿＿.

4. Blowing winds form a ＿＿＿, a river of water in the ocean.

5. Water vapor, clouds, rain, and the ocean are parts of the ＿＿＿.

6. Neap and spring ＿＿＿ are examples of changes in ocean level caused by the pull of the sun, moon, and Earth.

7. ＿＿＿ is any form of water that falls from clouds.

8. A ＿＿＿ forms when cold, dense ocean water meets and flows beneath warmer ocean waters.

9. The up-and-down motion of water is called a ＿＿＿.

10. The longest chain of mountains on Earth is the ＿＿＿.

11. The ＿＿＿ is the gently sloping part of the ocean floor near the shore.

12. When two of Earth's ocean plates collide, they can form a deep valley called a ＿＿＿.

13. An ＿＿＿ is a big, flat area of the ocean floor that is covered with a thick layer of sediments.

14. Many important resources are harvested from the ＿＿＿ of the oceans.

Connect Concepts

This diagram shows how water moves from the land and oceans to the atmosphere and back again. Label each section of the diagram, and write a title for it.

15. ＿＿＿

16. ＿＿＿

17. ＿＿＿

18. ＿＿＿

Check Understanding

Write the letter of the best choice.

19. The _____ provides the energy for the water cycle.
    A moon   C atmosphere
    B sun   D ocean wave

20. Ocean water is a mixture of water and many —
    F gases   H liquids
    G salts   J fluids

21. Wind causes an up-and-down movement of ocean water, called a —
    A deep ocean current
    B tide
    C surface current
    D wave

22. The part of the ocean floor nearest the shore is the —
    F abyssal plain
    G mid-ocean ridge
    H continental shelf
    J trench

23. The pull of _____ on Earth is the main reason for tides.
    A the moon
    B winds
    C the sun
    D currents

Critical Thinking

24. Would it be easier to float in the Great Salt Lake or in Lake Michigan? Explain your answer.

25. What do you think would happen to tides if the moon's gravity had a stronger pull than it does now?

Process Skills Review

26. Suppose there is a heavy rainstorm far out over the ocean. What can you **infer** about the density of the ocean water at the surface in that area right after the storm?

27. You **observe** clouds forming on a bright, sunny day. What can you **infer** is happening in the atmosphere? What may happen later in the day?

28. Sometimes people **use numbers** to compare very large natural objects to an everyday object. Pick an everyday object, estimate its size, and use it to describe one of the ocean floor features on pages D48–D53.

Performance Assessment

Currents

Completely fill a plastic cup with hot water. Add three or four drops of food coloring to the water. Cover the cup with plastic wrap. Hold the wrap in place with a rubber band.

Put the cup inside a bowl. Fill the bowl with cold water until it is almost full. There should be 2–3 cm of water over the cup. Use a pencil to poke a hole in the plastic wrap. Observe what happens. Explain what is happening inside the bowl. How could you make the same thing happen using salt water instead of hot water?

Planets and Other Objects in Space

Vocabulary Preview

satellite
orbit
phase
revolution
axis
rotation
solar system
star
planet
asteroid
comet
inner planet
outer planet
gas giant
telescope
space probe

From Earth you can study objects in space by just stepping outside on a clear night. Most of the objects you will see are stars, which are very, very distant suns. A few of the objects you will see are planets. Some are a little like Earth, and some are amazingly different.

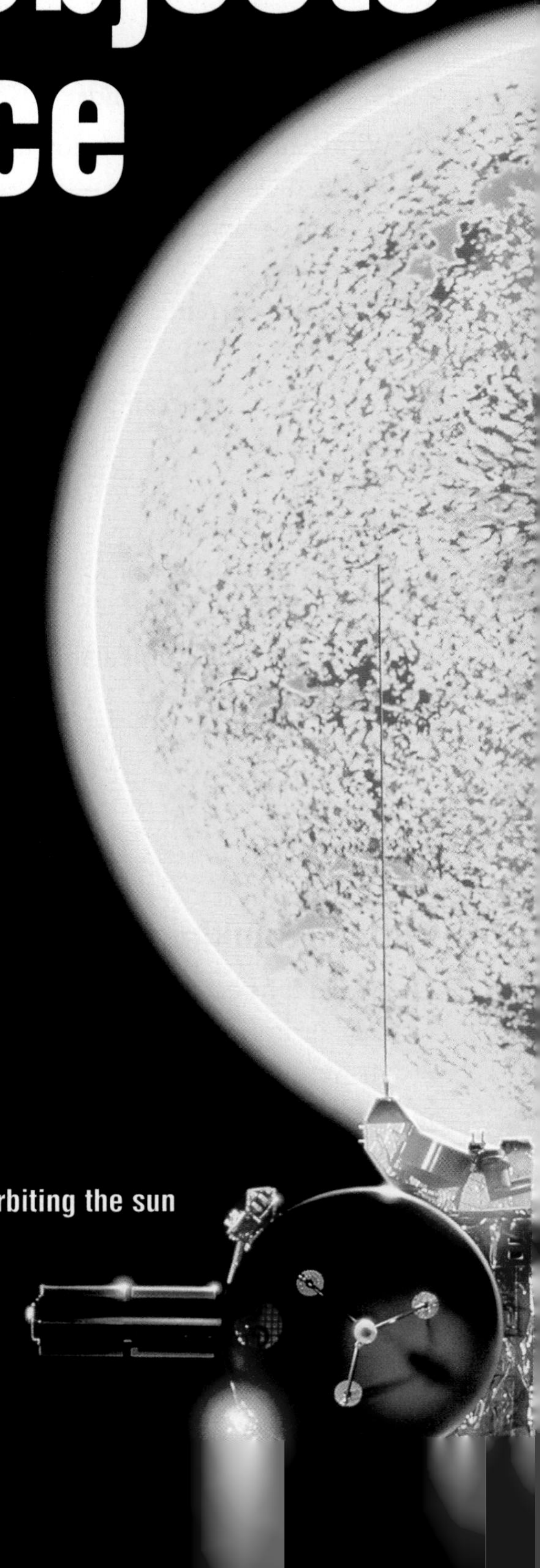

Ulysses orbiting the sun

Fast Fact

The sun is about 150,000,000 kilometers (93 million mi) from the Earth. It would take you about 193 years to travel this distance in a car at highway speed!

Fast Fact

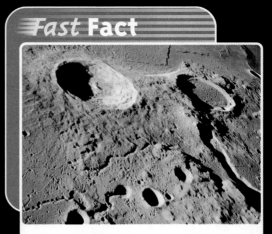

About 500,000 craters can be seen on the moon through telescopes on Earth. It would take you more than 400 hours to count them all. And this doesn't include the craters on the far side of the moon!

Fast Fact

Like most of the planets, Earth has seasons because it is tilted on its axis. But no planet is tilted like Uranus. Uranus is tilted so far that it is tipped over on its side! This gives Uranus a winter that lasts about 21 years!

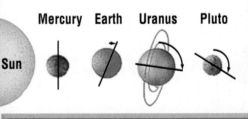

Sun   Mercury   Earth   Uranus   Pluto

How the Tilts of the Planets Compare

Planet	Degrees of Tilt
Mercury	0
Venus	177
Earth	23
Mars	25
Jupiter	3
Saturn	25
Uranus	98
Neptune	28
Pluto	122

How Do Earth and Its Moon Move?

In this lesson, you can . . .

INVESTIGATE the movements of Earth and the moon.

LEARN ABOUT the seasons.

LINK to math, writing, social studies, and technology.

Relative Size

Activity Purpose   The moon is about 384,000 km (238,613 mi) away from Earth. This makes the moon Earth's closest neighbor in space. On the other hand, the sun is a very distant neighbor. It is almost 400 times farther away from Earth than the moon is.

These distances in space affect the way the moon and the sun appear to viewers on Earth. In this investigation you'll **observe** various objects to determine how distance affects image.

Materials

- tennis ball
- basketball
- meterstick

Activity Procedure

1 Work with two other students. Two of you should stand side by side. One of these students should hold a tennis ball. The other should hold a basketball. Have the third student stand 3 to 4 m from the pair and **record** his or her **observations** of the two balls. (Picture A)

◀ Because of its closeness to Earth, the moon is the brightest object in the night sky. The moon is visible because it reflects light from the sun. So, a "moonbeam" is actually a reflected ray of sunshine.

Picture A

Picture B

2 Tell the person holding the basketball to move backward until the basketball appears to be the same size as the tennis ball. Use a meterstick to **measure** the distance between the two students. **Record** this distance. (Picture B)

3 Tell the person holding the basketball to continue to move backward until the basketball appears to be smaller than the tennis ball. Again use the meterstick to **measure** the distance between the two students. **Record** this distance.

Draw Conclusions

1. How did the size of the balls compare when held side by side?

2. At what distance did the balls appear the same size?

3. At what distance did the basketball appear smaller than the tennis ball?

4. The relationship between the sizes of the tennis ball and the basketball is similar to that between the sizes of the moon and the sun. From your **observations**, what can you infer about the size of these neighbors in space when viewed from Earth?

5. **Scientists at Work** How could you make sure that your **observations** of two objects show their actual traits?

Investigate Further Pluto is the farthest planet from the sun. **Hypothesize** how Pluto would appear when viewed from Earth's surface.

Process Skill Tip

You **observe** by using your senses. Scientists gather data by careful observations. They also note the conditions under which the observations were made. In this way, they can make more accurate inferences about what they have observed.

Moon and Earth Orbits

Motions of the Moon

FIND OUT

- how Earth and the moon move
- what causes seasons

VOCABULARY

satellite
orbit
phases
revolution
axis
rotation

The moon is a natural satellite of Earth. A **satellite** is an object that moves around another object in space. The moon moves around Earth in a certain path or **orbit**. It takes a little more than 28 days for the moon to complete its orbit.

When viewed from Earth, the moon appears to be almost the same size as the sun. As you saw in the investigation, these types of observations can be tricky. The moon is actually smaller than Earth, and Earth is much smaller than the sun. The moon looks as large as the sun because it is much closer to Earth.

The moon does not give off its own light. Instead, it reflects light from the sun. Half of the moon faces the sun and so it is lit. As the moon moves through its orbit, different amounts of its lit half can be seen from Earth. That's why the moon seems to have different shapes, or **phases**. The moon's cycle of phases takes just over 28 days to complete.

✔ **What are phases of the moon?**

It takes just over 28 days for the moon to complete one cycle of phases.

◀ During the last half of the moon's cycle (days 15 to 28), the amount of the lit side of the moon seen from Earth *wanes*, or decreases. Then the cycle begins again.

◀ During the first half of the moon's cycle (days 1 to 14), the amount of the lit side of the moon seen from Earth *waxes*, or increases.

D64

First quarter phase occurs about one quarter of the way through the cycle of phases, or about 7 days after new moon.

▲ Gibbous phase

During *new moon phase*, the lit part of the moon is not visible from Earth. ▶

▲ Full moon phase occurs about 14 days after the new moon.

After ▶ full moon, the lit portion of the moon seen from Earth shrinks. Between full moon and third quarter, a gibbous moon is seen again.

Third quarter phase ▶

Not to scale

Motions of Earth

Just as the moon moves around Earth, Earth moves around the sun. Just as the moon is a satellite of the Earth, Earth is a satellite of the sun. The movement of Earth around the sun is called its **revolution**. It takes Earth one year (365 days) to complete a revolution.

As Earth revolves around the sun, it is also spinning around an imaginary line. This imaginary line, or **axis**, runs through the center of Earth from the North Pole to the South Pole. It takes 24 hours, or one day, for Earth to complete one **rotation** on its axis. This rotation causes day and night.

✔ **What are two motions of Earth?**

It takes one year for Earth to revolve once around the sun. At the same time, Earth rotates on its axis once each day.

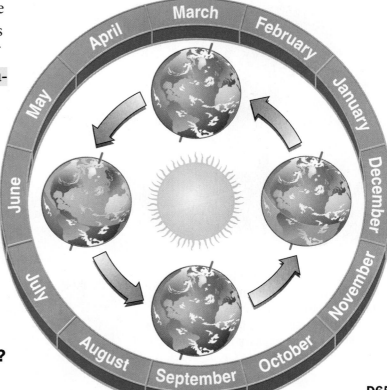

Earth and the Seasons

Earth's axis is slightly tilted. This tilt, along with the constant movement of Earth around the sun, causes seasons. For part of each year, the Northern Hemisphere tilts toward the sun. That part of Earth receives more direct energy from sunlight. We call this time of year summer. Six months later, when Earth has moved to the opposite side

SEPTEMBER 22 OR 23
Earth's axis is tilted neither toward nor away from the sun. All places on Earth have equal hours of daylight and night. Fall begins in the Northern Hemisphere, and spring begins in the Southern Hemisphere.

JUNE 21 OR 22
The Northern Hemisphere is pointed most directly toward the sun, causing more hours of daylight, shorter nights, and warmer weather. This marks the beginning of summer. The Southern Hemisphere has its shortest day and winter begins.

DECEMBER 21 OR 22
The Northern Hemisphere is tilted most directly away from the sun, causing fewer daylight hours, longer nights, and colder weather. This marks the beginning of winter. The Southern Hemisphere has its longest day

MARCH 20 OR 21
Earth's axis is tilted neither toward nor away from the sun. All places on Earth have equal hours of daylight and night. Spring begins in the Northern Hemisphere, and fall begins in the Southern Hemisphere.

of its orbit, the Northern Hemisphere tilts away from the sun. We call this time of year winter. That part of Earth receives less direct energy from sunlight.

✓ **When does winter occur in the Northern Hemisphere?**

Summary

The moon seems to change shape as it moves around Earth. These phases of the moon are caused by differences in the amount of lighted surface visible from Earth. As the moon orbits Earth, Earth is spinning on an imaginary axis. It takes one day for Earth to complete one rotation.

As Earth rotates it also revolves around the sun. It takes one year for Earth to complete a revolution. During its revolution some parts of Earth are titled toward the sun and other parts are tilted away from the sun. As a result, different locations on Earth receive different amounts of direct sunlight. This causes the seasons.

Review

1. Why would you classify the moon and Earth as satellites?

2. What are two ways that Earth moves?

3. What causes the seasons?

4. **Critical Thinking** How would day and night differ if Earth's axis were not tilted?

5. **Test Prep** What season would a town in the Southern Hemisphere have during January?

   A winter

   B spring

   C summer

   D fall

LINKS

MATH LINK

Solve a Problem The moon is about 384,000 kilometers from Earth. The average speed of an Apollo spacecraft was 38,600 kilometers per hour. At this rate, how long would it take to reach the moon?

WRITING LINK

Informative Writing—Identify the Phase Think about the characteristics of each phase of the moon. Write a letter to a friend, explaining how he or she can use observations of the moon to identify its phase.

SOCIAL STUDIES LINK

Apollo 11 On July 20, 1969, Neil Armstrong became the first human to set foot on the moon. Use reference materials to learn more about the historic flight of *Apollo 11*. Share your findings in a newspaper account of the mission.

GO ONLINE TECHNOLOGY LINK

Visit the Harcourt Learning Site for related links, activities, and resources.

www.harcourtschool.com

How Do Objects Move in the Solar System?

In this lesson, you can . . .

INVESTIGATE the ways planets move.

LEARN ABOUT our solar system.

LINK to math, writing, art, and technology.

Planet Movement

Activity Purpose Even though you can't feel it, Earth moves through space at nearly 30 kilometers (about 19 mi) per second. At this speed, our planet moves around the sun almost 100 times as fast as most jet planes cruise. You can't make anything move that quickly. So, in this investigation you'll **make a model** that shows how the planets in our solar system move.

Materials
- index cards
- scissors
- black marker

Activity Procedure

1 Label one of the cards *Sun.* Label each of the other cards with the name of one of the planets shown in the data table on the next page.

2 Put all of the cards face down on a table and shuffle them. Have each person choose one card.

3 Use the data table to find out which planet is closest to the sun. Continue **analyzing the data** and **ordering** the cards until you have all the planets in the correct order from the sun.

◀ This is Stonehenge, an ancient rock structure located in Britain. Stonehenge may have been used to study and predict the movement of Earth around the sun.

Planets and Distances from the Sun

Planet	Average Distance from the Sun (millions of km)	Planet	Average Distance from the Sun (millions of km)
Earth	150	Pluto	5900
Jupiter	778	Saturn	1429
Mars	228	Uranus	2871
Mercury	58	Venus	108
Neptune	4500		

4 In a gym or outside on a playground, line up in the order you determined in Step 3. (Picture A)

5 If you have a planet card, slowly turn around as you walk at a normal pace around the sun. Be sure to stay in your own path. Do not cross paths with other planets. After everyone has gone around the sun once, **record** your **observations** of the planets and their movements.

Picture A

Draw Conclusions

1. The sun and the planets that move around it are called the solar system. What is the order of the planets, starting with the one closest to the sun?

2. What did you **observe** about the motion of the planets?

3. **Scientists at Work** Why did you need to **make a model** to study how planets move around the sun?

Investigate Further Look again at the distances listed in the data table. How could you change your model to make it more accurate?

Process Skill Tip

Models are used when direct observations aren't possible. The huge size of the solar system is one reason scientists **make models** to study this complex collection of space objects.

Our Solar System

The Sun

FIND OUT

- **about the star we know as the sun**
- **the ways objects move in our solar system**

VOCABULARY

solar system
star
planet
asteroid
comet

In the investigation you made a model of our solar system. A **solar system** is a group of objects in space that move around a central star. Our sun is a **star**, a burning sphere (SFEER) of gases. This enormous fiery ball is more than 1 million kilometers (about 621,000 mi) in diameter. The sun is the largest object in our solar system. It is larger than the rest of the objects in the solar system put together.

The sun puts out a lot of energy in all directions. In fact, it is the source of almost all the energy in our solar system. Some of this energy reaches Earth as light, and some reaches it as heat.

Two features of the sun's surface are shown on this page. The dark areas, called *sunspots*, are cooler than the rest of the sun's surface and don't give off as much light. The red streams and loops of gases that shoot out from the sun are called *prominences* (PRAHM•ih•nuhn•suhs). These hot fountains often begin near a sunspot. They can be thousands of kilometers high and just as wide. Sunspots and prominences usually last for only a few days. Some can last for a few months.

✔ **What is the largest object in our solar system?**

The sun is the largest object in our solar system. The next largest object, Jupiter, is small compared to the sun. Earth is even smaller. ▼

Earth

Jupiter

Distances not to scale

The sun has 99.8 percent of the mass of our solar system. The planets, from nearest to farthest from the sun, are Mercury, Venus, Earth, Mars, Jupiter, Saturn, Uranus, Neptune, and Pluto. Each planet travels in its own orbit, a path around the sun. ▶

Not to scale

Other Objects in Our Solar System

As you saw in the investigation, our solar system is made up of the sun and nine planets. It also includes moons around the planets, and asteroids and comets.

A **planet**, such as Earth and its eight neighbors, is a large object that moves around a star. Most planets in our solar system also have at least one natural satellite, or moon. Earth and Pluto each have only one moon. Jupiter and Saturn, on the other hand, each have many moons.

Asteroids and comets are other objects that move around the sun. **Asteroids** are small and rocky. Most of them are scattered in a large area between the orbit paths of Mars and Jupiter. Some scientists hypothesize that these asteroids are pieces of a planet that never formed. All the asteroids

put together would make an object less than half the size of Earth's moon.

A **comet** is a small mass of dust and ice that orbits the sun in a long, oval-shaped path. When a comet's orbit takes it close to the sun, some of the ice on the comet's surface changes to water vapor and streams out to form a long, glowing tail.

✔ **Name the objects in our solar system.**

◀ As a comet orbits the sun, its tail always points away from the sun. Comet Hale-Bopp passed near Earth in April 1997. Its orbit is so big that it will not be seen from Earth again for 2380 years.

D71

Paths Around the Sun

In the investigation, student "planets" moved around a "sun." An object revolves as it moves around another object. The time for one complete orbit by a planet around the sun is its *year*. The orbits of the planets are not circles. Instead, they are a little bit elliptical, or oval, in shape.

Have you ever watched ice skaters spin? You may have noticed that as they bring their arms closer to their bodies, they spin faster. When they hold their arms out, they spin more slowly. The motion of the planets in their orbits is a little like the motion of the hands of a spinning ice skater. Planets with orbits closer to the sun move faster around the sun than those with orbits that are farther away.

Earth's rotation on its axis causes day and night. The side of Earth that faces the sun has day. At the same time, the opposite side of Earth has night. ▲

✔ **Where in our solar system are the planets that orbit fastest?**

Each planet follows an orbit, around the sun. How are the length of a planet's year and the planet's distance from the sun related? ▶

Length of Planet Years

Planet	Length of Year	Average Orbital Speed
Mercury	88 Earth days	about 48 km/s
Earth	$365\frac{1}{4}$ Earth days	about 30 km/s
Pluto	about 250 Earth years	about 5 km/s

Summary

Our solar system is made up of the sun, nine planets and their moons, asteroids, and comets. Each planet revolves in an elliptical orbit around the sun and rotates on its own axis.

Review

1. What is the sun?
2. In what way are the planets, comets, and asteroids alike?
3. How does a planet's distance from the sun affect its orbit speed?
4. **Critical Thinking** What might happen if the number of sunspots got much larger?
5. **Test Prep** What provides most of the heat and light to our solar system?

   A the comet Hale-Bopp

   B asteroids

   C the sun

   D Jupiter

LINKS

MATH LINK

Divide Whole Numbers The sun's diameter is about 1,392,000 km. About 109 Earths or 9 Jupiters would fit side by side across the sun. Use this information to figure out how many Earths would fit across Jupiter.

WRITING LINK

Expressive Writing—Poem Think about all the things you have learned about our solar system. Write a poem for your family describing how things move in our solar system or what makes up the solar system.

ART LINK

Drawing an Ellipse Tie the ends of a piece of string together to make a loop. Put the loop around two pushpins stuck several inches apart in a thick piece of cardboard. Place the point of a pencil inside the loop so the pencil touches the string. Keep the string tight as you draw around the pushpins. The shape you have drawn is an ellipse. What happens to the shape drawn if you move the pins closer together? Try it.

TECHNOLOGY LINK

Learn more about how asteroids move around the sun by visiting the National Air and Space Museum Internet site. **www.si.edu/harcourt/science**

 Smithsonian Institution®

What Are the Planets Like?

In this lesson, you can . . .

 INVESTIGATE distances between planets.

LEARN ABOUT the planets in our solar system.

LINK to math, writing, technology, and other areas.

INVESTIGATE

Distances Between Planets

Activity Purpose If you've ever used a map, you know what a scale model is. A scale model is a way to compare large distances in a smaller space. In this investigation you will **use measurements** to **make a scale model** that shows the distances between planets in our solar system.

Materials
- piece of string about 4 m long
- meterstick
- 9 different-colored markers

Activity Procedure

1 Copy the chart shown on the next page.

2 At one end of the string, tie three or four knots at the same point to make one large knot. This large knot will stand for the sun in your model.

3 In the solar system, distances are often measured in astronomical units (AU). One AU equals the average distance from Earth to the sun. In your model, 1 AU will equal 10 cm. Use your meterstick to accurately measure 1 AU from the sun on your model. This point stands for Earth's distance from the sun. Use one of the markers to mark this point on the string. Note in your chart which color you used. (Picture A)

◄ Europa (yoo•ROH•puh) is one of Jupiter's many moons. This natural satellite has a diameter of 3100 kilometers (about 1925 mi) and takes about $3\frac{1}{2}$ Earth days to orbit Jupiter.

Planetary Distances from the Sun

Planet	Average Distance from the Sun (km)	Average Distance from the Sun (AU)	Scale Distance (cm)	Marker Color	Planet's Diameter (km)
Mercury	58 million	$\frac{4}{10}$	4		4876
Venus	108 million	$\frac{7}{10}$	7		12,104
Earth	150 million	1			12,756
Mars	228 million	2			6794
Jupiter	778 million	5			142,984
Saturn	1429 million	10			120,536
Uranus	2871 million	19			51,118
Neptune	4500 million	30			49,532
Pluto	5900 million	39			2274

4 Complete the Scale Distance column of the chart. Then measure and mark the position of each planet on the string. Use a different color for each planet, and **record** in your chart the colors you used.

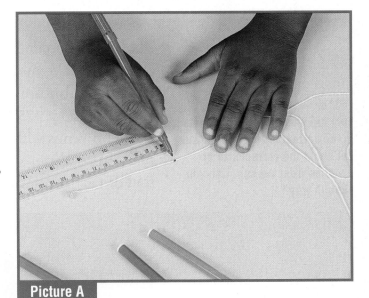

Picture A

Draw Conclusions

1. In your **model**, how far from the sun is Mercury? How far away is Pluto?

2. What advantages can you think of for using AUs to measure distances inside the solar system?

3. **Scientists at Work** Explain how it helped to **make a scale model** instead of trying to show actual distances between planets.

Investigate Further You can use a calculator to help make other scale models. The chart gives the actual diameters of the planets. Use this scale: Earth's diameter = 1 cm. Find the scale diameters of the other planets by dividing their actual diameters by Earth's diameter. Make a scale drawing showing the diameter of each planet.

Process Skill Tip

Models are made to study objects or events that are too small or too large to observe directly. A **scale model** shows large objects or areas in smaller sizes so that they can be more easily studied.

The Planets

The Inner Planets

The area of the asteroid belt can be thought of as a dividing line between two groups of planets, the inner and outer planets. The **inner planets**—Mercury, Venus, Earth, and Mars—lie between the sun and the asteroid belt. Like the asteroids, the inner planets are rocky and dense. Unlike the asteroids, these planets are large and, except for Mercury, have atmospheres.

Mercury, the planet closest to the sun, is about the size of Earth's moon. Mercury, which is covered with craters, even looks like the moon. Very small amounts of some gases are present on Mercury, but there aren't enough of them to form an atmosphere.

Venus, the second planet from the sun, is about the same size as Earth. But Venus is very different from Earth. Venus is dry and has a thick atmosphere that traps heat. The temperature at the surface is about 475°C (887°F). The thick atmosphere presses down on Venus with a weight 100 times that of Earth's atmosphere. Also, Venus spins on its axis in a direction opposite from that of Earth's rotation.

FIND OUT

- about the planets in our solar system
- how moons and rings may have formed

VOCABULARY

inner planets
outer planets
gas giants

This drawing shows the planets in the correct order from the sun but not at the correct size or distance from the sun. Can you explain why? ▼

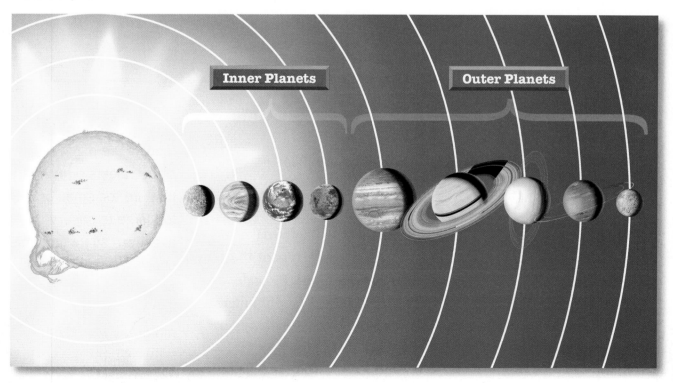

Inner Planets

Outer Planets

Mercury has a diameter of 4876 kilometers (about 3031 mi) and is 58 million kilometers (about 36 million mi) from the sun. This inner planet has no moons and takes about 59 Earth days to make one rotation, or turn once on its axis. Mercury orbits the sun in about 88 Earth days.

Venus has a diameter of 12,104 kilometers (about 7517 mi) and is 108 million kilometers (about 67 million mi) from the sun. This inner planet has no natural satellites. It takes Venus about 243 Earth days to make one rotation and 225 Earth days to orbit the sun.

Not to scale

Earth, the third planet from the sun, is the largest of the inner planets. It has one natural satellite, the moon. Earth is the only planet that has liquid water. It is also the only known planet that supports life. Earth's atmosphere absorbs and reflects the right amount of solar energy to keep the planet at the correct temperature for living things such as humans to survive.

Mars, the fourth planet from the sun, is sometimes called the Red Planet because its soil is a dark reddish brown. Mars has two moons and the largest volcano in the solar system—Olympus Mons (oh•LIHM•puhs MAHNS). Space probes have shown us that nothing lives on Mars. Dust storms can last for months and affect the whole planet. Although no liquid water has been found on Mars, it is believed that liquid water once existed there. This is because probes and satellites have found deep valleys and sedimentary rocks. These features probably were formed by flowing water.

✔ **List the inner planets in order from the sun.**

Earth has a diameter of 12,756 kilometers (about 7922 mi). Our planet is 150 million kilometers (about 93 million mi) from the sun. Earth has one moon and takes almost 24 hours to complete one rotation on its axis. It takes about 365 days to orbit the sun.

Mars has a diameter of 6794 kilometers (about 4230 mi) and is 228 million kilometers (about 142 million mi) from the sun. This inner planet has two moons. Mars completes a rotation in about 24.5 hours. Mars takes about 687 Earth days to complete one orbit around the sun.

The Outer Planets

On the other side of the asteroid belt are the **outer planets**—Jupiter, Saturn, Uranus, Neptune, and Pluto. Four of these planets—Jupiter, Saturn, Uranus, and Neptune—are large spheres made up mostly of gases. Because of this, these planets are often called the **gas giants**.

Jupiter is the largest planet in our solar system. A thin ring that is hard to see surrounds it. At least 16 moons orbit around it. Jupiter's atmosphere is very active. Its energy causes a circular storm known as the Great Red Spot. This weather, which is a lot like a hurricane, has lasted more than 300 years. It is so big around that three Earths would fit inside it.

Saturn is a gas giant known for its rings. Space probes have found that other planets also have rings. But Saturn's are so wide and so bright that they can be seen from Earth through a small telescope. Saturn has at least 18 named moons.

Not to scale

Uranus (YOOR•uh•nuhs), the seventh planet from the sun, is the most distant planet you can see without using a telescope. Uranus, a blue-green ball of gas and liquid, has at least 21 moons as well as faint rings around it.

Neptune, the farthest away of the gas giants, has at least eight moons and a faint ring. It also has circular storms, but none have lasted as long as the Great Red Spot on Jupiter.

In the investigation you saw that Pluto is the planet farthest from the sun. If you completed the Investigate Further, you also learned that Pluto is the smallest planet. From Pluto's surface the sun looks like a very bright star. Little heat or light reaches Pluto or its one moon. Unlike the other outer planets, Pluto is not a gas giant. Instead, Pluto has a rocky surface that is probably covered by frozen gases.

✔ **Which planets are gas giants?**

Uranus has a diameter of 51,118 kilometers (about 31,700 mi). This planet is 2870 million kilometers (1782 million mi) from the sun. Uranus makes one rotation in 17 hours and one orbit around the sun in about 84 Earth years.

Pluto has a diameter of 2300 kilometers (about 1430 mi) and is 5900 million kilometers (about 3664 million mi) from the sun. It takes Pluto about 7 days to complete one rotation and 249 Earth years to complete one revolution.

Neptune has a diameter of 49,532 kilometers (about 30,740 mi) and is 4500 million kilometers (about 2795 million mi) from the sun. Neptune completes one rotation in a little more than 16 hours and one revolution in about 165 Earth years.

▲ Titan, Saturn's largest moon, has a diameter of 5150 kilometers (about 3200 mi). Titan has no clouds in its atmosphere and is very cold.

▲ The rings around Saturn are made up of dust, ice crystals, and small bits of rock coated with frozen water. The rings are about 270,000 kilometers (about 167,700 mi) across but only about 10 kilometers (about 6 mi) thick.

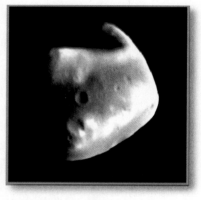

▲ Deimos (DY•muhs) is one of the two Martian moons. It has many craters and an uneven shape. It is about 14 kilometers (9 mi) in diameter.

Io (EYE•oh) is a moon of Jupiter. Io has a diameter of 3630 kilometers (about 2254 mi) and has several active volcanoes on its surface. The volcanoes are the big orange patches. ▶

Moons and Rings

Every planet except Mercury and Venus has at least one natural satellite, or *moon.* Earth's moon is round and rocky, and it has many craters. Others, like the two moons of Mars or the outer moons of Jupiter, are small and rocky and have uneven shapes. Jupiter and Mars orbit near the asteroid belt. So, their moons may be asteroids pulled in by the planets' gravity. The large moons of Jupiter and Saturn are almost like small planets. Io, one of Jupiter's larger moons, has active volcanoes. Titan (TYT•uhn), one of Saturn's moons, has a dense atmosphere that glows red-orange.

Besides having moons, each of the gas giants has a system of rings. These rings are made of tiny bits of dust, ice crystals, and small pieces of rock. Saturn's rings may have formed as a moon was pulled apart by gravity because it got too close to the planet.

✔ **What are planet rings made of?**

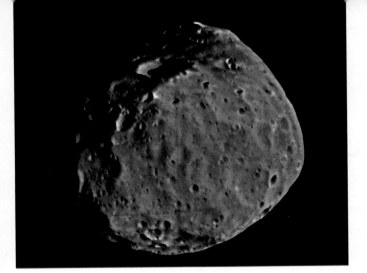

▲ Phobos (FOH•buhs) is the other moon that orbits Mars. Like Deimos, it is a small, rocky object. Its diameter is about 22 kilometers (14 mi). Phobos makes three trips around its planet each Martian day.

Summary

The inner planets—Mercury, Venus, Earth, and Mars—are small and rocky. Four of the five outer planets are gas giants. They are Jupiter, Saturn, Uranus, and Neptune. The outer planet that is farthest from the sun is Pluto, another rocky planet. Most of the planets have at least one moon. The gas giants also have rings.

Review

1. Name the inner planets, starting with the planet closest to the sun.

2. What can be thought of as the dividing line between the inner planets and the outer planets?

3. Which planets have no moons?

4. **Critical Thinking** Compare and contrast Venus and Earth.

5. **Test Prep** The outer planet that is **NOT** a gas giant is —

   A Jupiter

   B Saturn

   C Neptune

   D Pluto

LINKS

MATH LINK

Make a Bar Graph Make a bar graph showing the diameter of each planet. Use data from the table on page D75 and a computer program such as *Graph Links.*

WRITING LINK

Persuasive Writing—Opinion Suppose you are a real-estate agent trying to get adults to move to the planet of your choice. Write a newspaper ad pointing out all the benefits of living on your chosen planet.

ART LINK

View of a Planet Paint or draw a realistic landscape of the surface of another planet. Or paint the view of the planet as it would be seen from one of its moons.

LITERATURE LINK

The Wonderful Flight to the Mushroom Planet Read this book by Eleanor Cameron to find out what happens when two boys go on an adventure in space. Compare the planet with Earth.

GO ONLINE TECHNOLOGY LINK

Learn more about planets and other objects in space by visiting this Internet site.

www.scilinks.org/harcourt

How Do People Study the Solar System?

In this lesson, you can . . .

INVESTIGATE how to make a telescope.

LEARN ABOUT how people study objects in space.

LINK to math, writing, social studies, and technology.

INVESTIGATE

Telescopes

Activity Purpose Have you ever looked up into the sky at night and wished you could see some of the objects more clearly? Because distances in space are so great, scientists need to use instruments to study what is beyond Earth's atmosphere. In this investigation you will make a simple telescope and use it to **observe** some objects in space.

Materials

- small piece of modeling clay
- 1 thin (eyepiece) lens
- small-diameter cardboard tube
- 1 thick (objective) lens
- large-diameter cardboard tube

Activity Procedure

1 Press small pieces of clay to the outside of the thin lens. Then put the lens in one end of the small tube. Use enough clay to hold the lens in place, keeping the lens as straight as possible. Be careful not to smear the middle of the lens with clay. (Picture A)

2 Repeat Step 1 using the thick lens and large tube.

◀ This vehicle is the moon rover. Astronauts used it to travel over the surface of Earth's only natural satellite, the moon.

Picture A

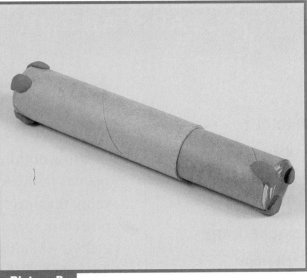

Picture B

3 Slide the open end of the small tube into the larger tube. You have just made a telescope. (Picture B)

4 Hold your telescope up, and look through one lens. Then turn the telescope around, and look through the other lens. **CAUTION** **Never look directly at the sun.** Slide the small tube in and out of the large tube until what you see is in focus, or not blurry. How do objects appear through each lens? **Record** your **observations.**

Draw Conclusions

1. What did you **observe** as you looked through each lens?

2. Using your observations, **infer** which lens you should look through to **observe** the stars. Explain your answer.

3. **Scientists at Work** Astronomers (uh•STRAWN•uh•merz) are scientists who study objects in space. Some astronomers use large telescopes with many parts to **observe** objects in space. How would your telescope make observing objects in the night sky easier?

Investigate Further Use your telescope to **observe** the moon at night. Make a list of the details you can see using your telescope that you can't see using only your eyes.

Process Skill Tip

When you **observe** an object, you use your senses to notice details about it. Using an instrument such as a telescope helps you observe objects that are too far away to be seen clearly using only your eyes.

Space Exploration

Telescopes

Using nothing more than your eyes, you can see most of the planets in the solar system. But what if you want to see them as more than just points of light in the sky? What if you want to see objects in space that are even farther away than the visible planets? Or what if you want to see smaller objects such as moons? To do any of these things, you need to use a telescope. A **telescope** is a device people use to observe distant objects.

Two very different types of telescopes are used to observe objects in space: *radio telescopes* and *optical telescopes,* or telescopes that use light. There are also two types of optical telescopes. A refracting telescope, which is what you made in the investigation, uses lenses to magnify an object, or make it appear larger. A reflecting telescope uses a curved mirror to magnify an object. Most large telescopes used today are reflecting telescopes.

FIND OUT

- about telescopes
- about missions into space

VOCABULARY

telescope
space probe

Even without using a telescope, you can see dark areas, bright areas, and some details on the moon. ▼

This telescope is very old. It uses two lenses to magnify objects that are far away. ▼

◀ Using a strong telescope lets you see more detail. Compare this photograph with the other one of the moon above.

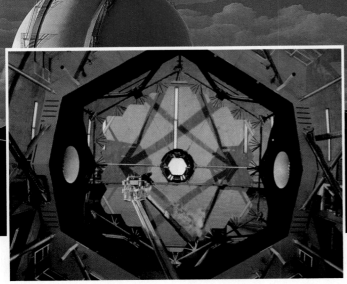

▲ The large mirror of the Keck telescope is made up of many smaller mirrors. They work together to gather light and magnify images of objects in space.

▲ This is a photograph of Keck Observatory in Hawai`i. An *observatory* is a building where scientists study the planets, the sun, and other distant objects in the sky. This observatory is at the top of an inactive volcano more than 4000 meters (about 13,130 ft) above sea level.

Telescopes that scientists use are much larger than the one you made in the investigation. Besides being large, telescopes that are used to study space objects are powerful. Many of them have cameras that constantly take pictures of space. Computers keep the telescopes pointed at the same place in the sky. This allows the powerful lenses and mirrors to collect more light so they can produce brighter and clearer pictures. Astronomers then study the pictures to find out about space objects.

Earth's atmosphere limits what optical telescopes can "see." Moving air causes the "twinkling" of stars. It also blurs pictures taken using optical telescopes. This is why observatories that use optical telescopes are often located high on mountains.

Scientists have found that stars and other objects in space give off more than just light energy that we can see. Radio telescopes work the way optical telescopes do. But instead of collecting and focusing light, they collect and focus invisible radio waves. Moving air, clouds, and poor weather don't affect radio waves. Computers process the data collected by radio telescopes. The computers then make "pictures" that astronomers can study.

A radio telescope collects radio waves with a large, bowl-shaped antenna. Scientists study images formed by these waves to learn about the objects that gave them off. This radio telescope is in Arecibo (ar•uh•SEE•boh), Puerto Rico. ▶

The telescopes you have seen so far in this chapter are Earth-based, or located on Earth's surface. Scientists have also built telescopes for use in space. These telescopes don't have any problems caused by the atmosphere. The Inside Story shows the parts of the most famous space-based telescope, the Hubble Space Telescope.

✔ **What is a telescope?**

THE INSIDE STORY

HUBBLE SPACE TELESCOPE

The Hubble Space Telescope, or HST, is a reflecting telescope. Its mirror, which has a diameter of 240 cm (about 94 in.), can "see" details ten times as clearly as telescopes on Earth.

The HST uses sunlight as its energy source. The instrument's solar panels change sunlight into electricity. Each panel is about $2\frac{1}{2}$ meters (about 8 ft) wide and 13 meters (about 42 ft) long.

The main cover tube of the HST protects the telescope as well as other instruments used to study space.

The main mirror of the HST is located near the back of the main cover.

▲ During some of the Apollo missions, astronauts explored our moon's surface. This spacecraft allowed astronauts to land on the moon. Later they could blast off and return to the main part of their ship, which was circling the moon.

Mir was a Russian *space station* in orbit above Earth. Aboard *Mir*, astronauts and scientists from many countries worked for months at a time. They experimented to find out how conditions in space affect things and people. ▼

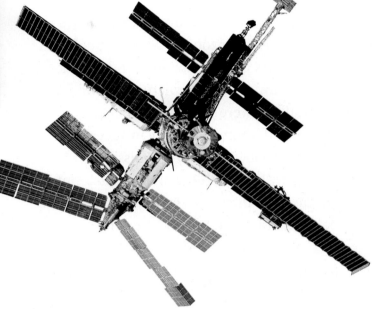

Crewed Missions

Another way to learn about space is to actually go there. Trips that people take into space are called *crewed missions.* Crewed missions are useful because people can actually find out for themselves what it is like to live and work in space.

The first person to be sent into space was a Russian, Yuri Gagarin, in 1961. Since then, astronauts from many countries have made trips into space. One of the most famous missions was carried out on *Apollo 11,* which was launched by the United States on July 16, 1969. On this mission Neil Armstrong and Edwin "Buzz" Aldrin spent two hours exploring the moon's surface. The United States sent five more crewed missions to the moon before the Apollo program ended in 1972.

Today the United States uses the space shuttle to carry crews, materials, and satellites to and from space. Astronauts on the shuttles do experiments, launch and get back satellites, and repair instruments.

✔ **What is a crewed space mission?**

Astronauts aboard the U.S. space shuttles also do experiments. These astronauts are working in Space Lab, which rides in the cargo area of a space shuttle. ▼

D87

Space Probes

We have learned much of what we know about the solar system by using space probes. **Space probes** are vehicles that carry cameras, instruments, and other tools. Probes are sent to explore places that are too dangerous or too far away for people to visit. Probes gather data and send it back to Earth for study. The pictures of Mars and Callisto were sent to Earth by probes millions of kilometers away in space.

Some probes have fly-by missions. That is, they fly by the object to be studied but do not land. As they pass the object, they gather data, including pictures. Other probes land on the surfaces of planets. These probes take pictures, collect and analyze rock samples, test for the presence of substances such as water, and collect other data.

✔ **What is a space probe?**

1000 km

1 km

▲ Information about this moon of Jupiter, Callisto, was gathered as the space probe *Galileo* flew past it.

Sojourner is a probe that was used to study the surface of Mars. *Sojourner* took thousands of photos of the surface as it gathered information about the Red Planet. It landed as part of *Pathfinder* on July 4, 1997. ▼

▲ The space probe *Galileo* was sent to Jupiter in 1989. Instruments launched from *Galileo* measured the sizes of particles that make up the clouds of Jupiter and the amounts of hydrogen and helium in Jupiter's atmosphere.

▲ *Voyager 2*, launched in 1977, flew by Jupiter in 1979, Saturn in 1981, and Uranus in 1986. The probe then headed on to Neptune.

Summary

A telescope is a device people use to observe distant objects. A refracting telescope uses lenses, and a reflecting telescope uses mirrors to magnify an object. Radio telescopes collect and focus radio waves. The Hubble Space Telescope is an optical telescope in orbit around Earth. Crewed missions and space probes are other ways to study objects in space.

Review

1. What are two types of telescopes?
2. What limits the things an Earth-based optical telescope can "see"?
3. What kind of work do astronauts on a crewed space mission do?
4. **Critical Thinking** What are the advantages of sending crewed missions instead of probes into space? The disadvantages?
5. **Test Prep** An instrument that uses lenses to magnify distant objects is a —
   A radio telescope
   B refracting telescope
   C reflecting telescope
   D space station

LINKS

MATH LINK

Solve a Problem When Earth and Jupiter are closest together, they are about 630 million km apart. *Voyager 2* took two years to reach Jupiter. About how far did it travel each year?

WRITING LINK

Informative Writing—Description Suppose you are an astronaut who will take part in the next space-shuttle mission. Find out about a typical day on the space shuttle. Then write a composition for a friend describing a typical day of your mission.

SOCIAL STUDIES LINK

International Space Station Find out which countries are building parts of the International Space Station. Locate each country on a map or globe. Make a chart that lists the name of each country, its continent, and which parts of the space station it is building.

TECHNOLOGY LINK

To learn more about pictures from space, watch *Hubble Images* on the **Harcourt Science Newsroom Video.**

Discovering the Planets

Five of the other eight planets in our solar system can be seen using just your eyes. These five—Mercury, Venus, Mars, Jupiter, and Saturn—were all known to astronomers before 1700. These early astronomers named the planets for gods and goddesses of Roman mythology.

Galileo and the Telescope

The invention of the telescope made astronomy a more complex science. Galileo, an Italian scientist and inventor who lived from 1564 to 1642, was the first person to use a telescope to view the stars and planets. Compared to telescopes now, his telescope wasn't very powerful. It magnified, or enlarged the view, only about 20 or 30 times. However, using just that weak telescope, Galileo was the first person to observe mountains on the moon, sunspots, and the phases of Venus. In 1610 Galileo was the first to see moons around Jupiter. His observations of planets and moons showed that not all bodies in space circled Earth, as many people at that time believed.

Discovering Uranus

Other scientists slowly improved on Galileo's telescope design. William Herschel, a British astronomer, discovered Uranus, the seventh planet from the sun. He used a telescope that his sister, Caroline, helped him build. On the night of March 13, 1781, Herschel saw something that he knew was not a star. He first thought it was a comet. Over time he mapped

Io, one of Jupiter's moons

The History of Planet Discoveries

Herschel and telescope

Uranus 1781
Uranus discovered

A.D. **1600**   A.D. **1700**

Jupiter 1610
Jupiter's moons discovered

the orbit of the object and realized it was a planet, which was later named Uranus. For a long time, others had a hard time seeing what Herschel had seen, because their telescopes weren't as good.

Using Math to Find New Planets

Two people, the English astronomer John C. Adams and the French astronomer Urbain Leverrier (oor•BAN luh•vair•YAY), found the location of the eighth planet at about the same time. They did not see the planet themselves. Using mathematics, they predicted its location. Then they sent their predictions to other scientists.

Adams sent his prediction to the Astronomer Royal of England, who paid little attention to it. Leverrier sent his prediction to the Urania (oo•RAHN•ee•uh) Observatory in Berlin, Germany. The director there, Johann Galle (YOH•hahn GAH•luh), and his assistant used Leverrier's research and found Neptune on September 23, 1846.

Pluto was also discovered through mathematics. In 1905 American astronomer Percival Lowell noticed that something seemed to be affecting the orbits of Uranus and Neptune. He hypothesized that a ninth planet was the cause. He searched unsuccessfully for it until his death in 1916.

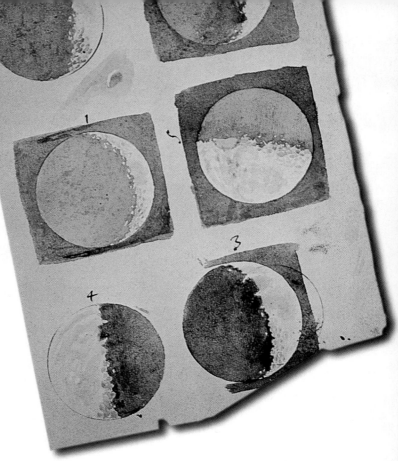

▲ These ink drawings are how Galileo recorded his telescope observations of Earth's moon.

In 1930 Pluto appeared as a small dot on three photographs Clyde Tombaugh took at Lowell Observatory, which was built by Percival Lowell.

THINK ABOUT IT

1. How have improvements in technology helped astronomers?

2. How did scientists Urbain Leverrier and Johann Galle work together?

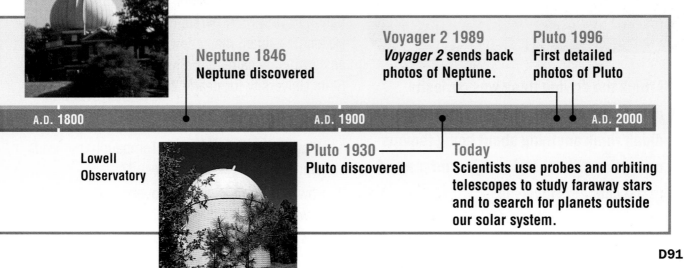

Urania Observatory

Lowell Observatory

Neptune 1846
Neptune discovered

Voyager 2 1989
Voyager 2 sends back photos of Neptune.

Pluto 1996
First detailed photos of Pluto

A.D. 1800   A.D. 1900   A.D. 2000

Pluto 1930
Pluto discovered

Today
Scientists use probes and orbiting telescopes to study faraway stars and to search for planets outside our solar system.

Telescope photo of Pluto, 1930

Clyde Tombaugh
ASTRONOMER, INVENTOR

Tombaugh in 1995 with his third telescope

"I think the driving thing was curiosity about the universe. That fascinated me. I didn't think anything about being famous or anything like that, I was just interested in the concepts involved."

Working on a farm in Kansas taught Clyde Tombaugh to be persistent and creative with materials at hand. He was always interested in astronomy. His uncle and father had a telescope, which they gave him when he was 9 years old. By the time Tombaugh was 20, he decided to build his own telescope. He used part of a dairy machine for the base and part of his father's 1910 Buick.

Later, Tombaugh's uncle asked Tombaugh to build a telescope for him. Tombaugh also built a better telescope for him. With that homemade telescope, he observed Mars and Jupiter. He drew what he saw and sent his sketches to the Lowell Observatory in Flagstaff, Arizona. The scientists at the observatory were impressed by Tombaugh's drawings. They invited him to come to Arizona and work there. He stayed for 14 years.

On February 18, 1930, Tombaugh discovered the planet Pluto. Other scientists had predicted its existence, but he was the first to locate it in the sky. During his life, he discovered asteroids and hundreds of stars.

After completing college, Tombaugh taught navigation to U.S. Navy personnel during World War II. He also designed many new instruments, including an astronomy camera. He taught at New Mexico State University for nearly 20 years.

THINK ABOUT IT

1. What have you read about Tombaugh that leads you to think he was resourceful?
2. How was Tombaugh's discovery of Pluto related to work by other scientists?

SUNDIAL

How can you make an instrument that uses the sun to tell time?

Materials

- small ball of clay
- short pencil
- cardboard, about 15 cm × 20 cm

Procedure

1. Use the lump of clay to stand the short pencil in the center of the cardboard. Make sure the sharpened end of the pencil is up.

2. Draw a half circle around the short pencil. The radius of the half circle should be the length of the pencil. The center of the half circle should be the lump of clay.

3. Put your sundial on a windowsill that gets sun all day. Each hour, trace the shadow of the pencil on the cardboard. Mark the time at the end of each line. Do this for six hours.

4. On the next sunny day, use your sundial to tell time.

Draw Conclusions

How does your sundial use Earth's movement to tell time?

SEASONS AND SUNLIGHT

How does the angle of light affect temperature?

Materials

- small 60-watt table lamp
- ruler
- graph paper
- black construction paper
- thermometer

Procedure

1. Darken the room. Place the lamp so that it shines directly down from 30 cm above a piece of graph paper. Draw an outline of the lighted area.

2. Repeat Step 1, this time placing the lamp so that it shines at an angle from the side.

3. Replace the graph paper with a sheet of black paper. Place the lamp as in Step 1. Then measure the temperature in the lighted area after 15 minutes.

4. Place the lamp as in Step 2. Measure the temperature in the lighted area after 15 minutes.

Draw Conclusions

How did moving the lamp change the area covered by the light? How did it affect the temperature? How is this activity related to the pictures shown on page D66?

Vocabulary Review

Use the terms below to complete the sentences. The page numbers in ( ) tell you where to look in the chapter if you need help.

satellite (D64)   **planet** (D71)

phases (D64)   **asteroid** (D71)

orbit (D64)   **comet** (D71)

revolution (D65)   **inner planets** (D76)

rotation (D65)   **outer planets** (D78)

axis (D65)   **gas giants** (D78)

solar system (D70)   **telescope** (D84)

star (D70)   **space probe** (D88)

1. A _____ is a group of planets and their moons that orbit a central star.

2. Venus is a _____ that revolves around the sun.

3. An _____ is an imaginary line around which a planet rotates, or spins.

4. Any object orbiting another object is a _____.

5. The four planets nearest the sun are called the _____.

6. An _____ is a rocky object that orbits the sun in a path between Mars and Jupiter.

7. A _____ is a vehicle sent into space in order to explore places too dangerous or too far away for people to visit.

8. The path a planet takes around the sun is its _____.

9. A _____ is a burning ball of gases.

10. Neptune is one of the four _____.

11. A _____ is an instrument used to observe distant objects.

12. A _____ is a space object made of ice, dust, and gases.

13. The five planets on the outer side of the asteroid belt are called the _____.

14. The moon seems to have different _____, or shapes, during a cycle of about 28 days.

15. A year is the time it takes Earth to make one _____.

16. A day is the time it takes Earth to make one _____.

Connect Concepts

List the planets, and classify them as to their position in the solar system. Be sure to list them in the correct order from the sun.

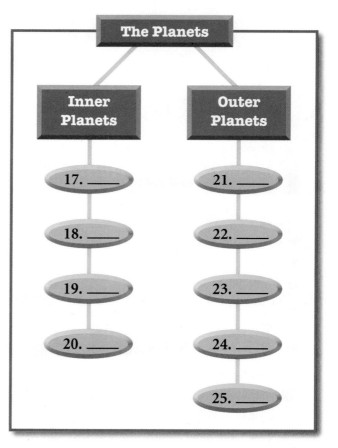

The Planets

Inner Planets

Outer Planets

17. _____
18. _____
19. _____
20. _____

21. _____
22. _____
23. _____
24. _____
25. _____

Check Understanding

Write the letter of the best choice.

26. The sun provides _____ of the energy to the solar system.

   A most   **C** none

   B little   **D** some

27. An imaginary line that runs through both poles of a planet is its —

   F star   **H** comet

   G orbit   **J** axis

28. _____ is the outer planet that is **NOT** a gas giant.

   A Saturn   **C** Uranus

   B Pluto   **D** Jupiter

29. This type of telescope never has problems seeing through Earth's atmosphere. It uses lenses to enlarge an object.

   F Earth-based telescope

   G reflecting telescope

   H refracting telescope

   J space-based telescope

30. Trips that people take into space are called —

   A crewed missions

   B uncrewed missions

   C space probes

   D observatories

Critical Thinking

31. Why do you think some stars in constellations look brighter than others?

32. Most asteroids are in the asteroid belt between the orbits of Mars and Jupiter. But some asteroids have "escaped" and have long, oval-shaped orbits like those of the comets. How do you think these asteroids escaped the asteroid belt?

Process Skills Review

33. In Lesson 1 you **observed** and compared the relative sizes of a basketball and a tennis ball. From a distance, you see buildings that seem to be the same height. What other **observations** would you make to confirm what you saw?

34. In Lesson 2 you **made a model** showing how planets rotate on their axes and revolve around the sun. How would you make a model to show the motions of Jupiter and its many moons?

35. In Lesson 3 you **made a model** to show the distances between the planets. What activity of planets would be modeled by cars racing around a racetrack?

36. In Lesson 4 you made a telescope to **observe** the night sky. Why did you need a telescope for this? What would you see if you didn't use a telescope?

Performance Assessment

Model Solar System

With a partner, draw a model of an imaginary solar system. Include one star, five planets, and two comets. Also include at least one more object that would be found in a solar system. Compare your model solar system with the one we live in.

There are many places where you can learn about patterns on Earth and in space. You can learn about weather and the exploration of space by visiting the places below. You'll also have fun while you learn.

Fernbank Science Center

WHAT A science center that has a meteorology lab along with its other exhibits

WHERE Atlanta, Georgia

WHAT CAN YOU DO THERE? Tour the science center, see the exhibits, and visit the Meteorology Lab, where you can find current weather data.

U.S. Space & Rocket Center

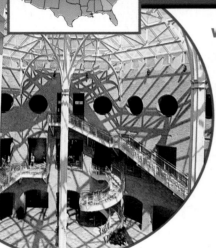

WHAT A collection of rockets, spacecraft, and space exhibits

WHERE Huntsville, Alabama

WHAT CAN YOU DO THERE? Tour Rocket Park, visit the space exhibits, and explore the collection of hands-on exhibits and simulators.

GO ONLINE Plan Your Own Expeditions

If you can't visit the Fernbank Science Center or the U.S. Space & Rocket Center, visit a museum near you. Or log on to The Learning Site at **www.harcourtschool.com** to visit these science sites. Learn more about Earth and space.

Matter and Energy

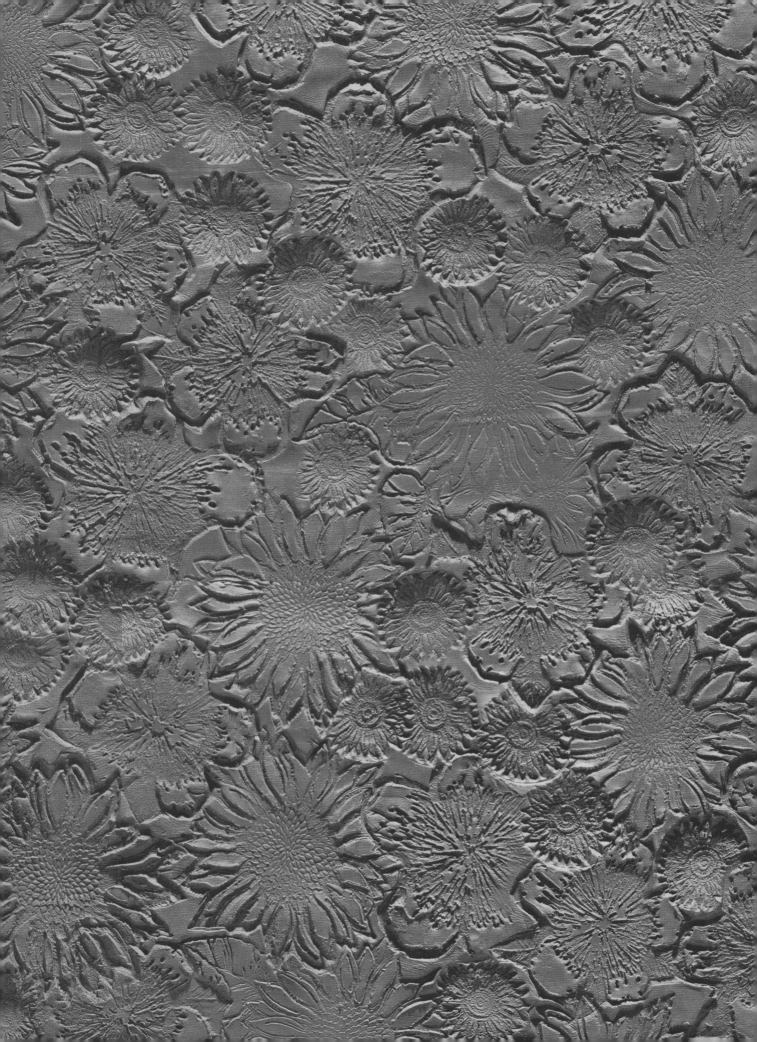

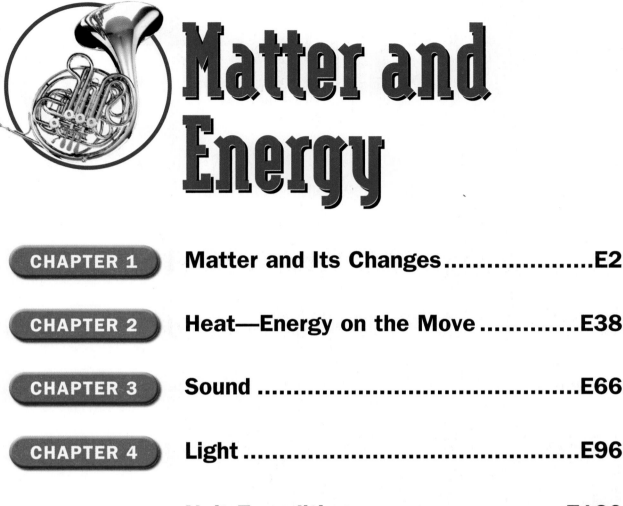

Matter and Energy

UNIT EXPERIMENT

Color and Energy Absorption

Everything around you is made of matter. Part of science is studying properties of matter, such as how matter and energy interact. While you study this unit, you can conduct a long-term experiment about color and light energy. Here are some questions to think about. How does color affect the amount of energy absorbed from light? Does one color warm up or cool down faster than others? Do different light sources produce different results? Does insulation affect the results? Plan and conduct an experiment to find answers to these or other questions you have about matter and energy. See pages x–xix for help in designing your experiment.

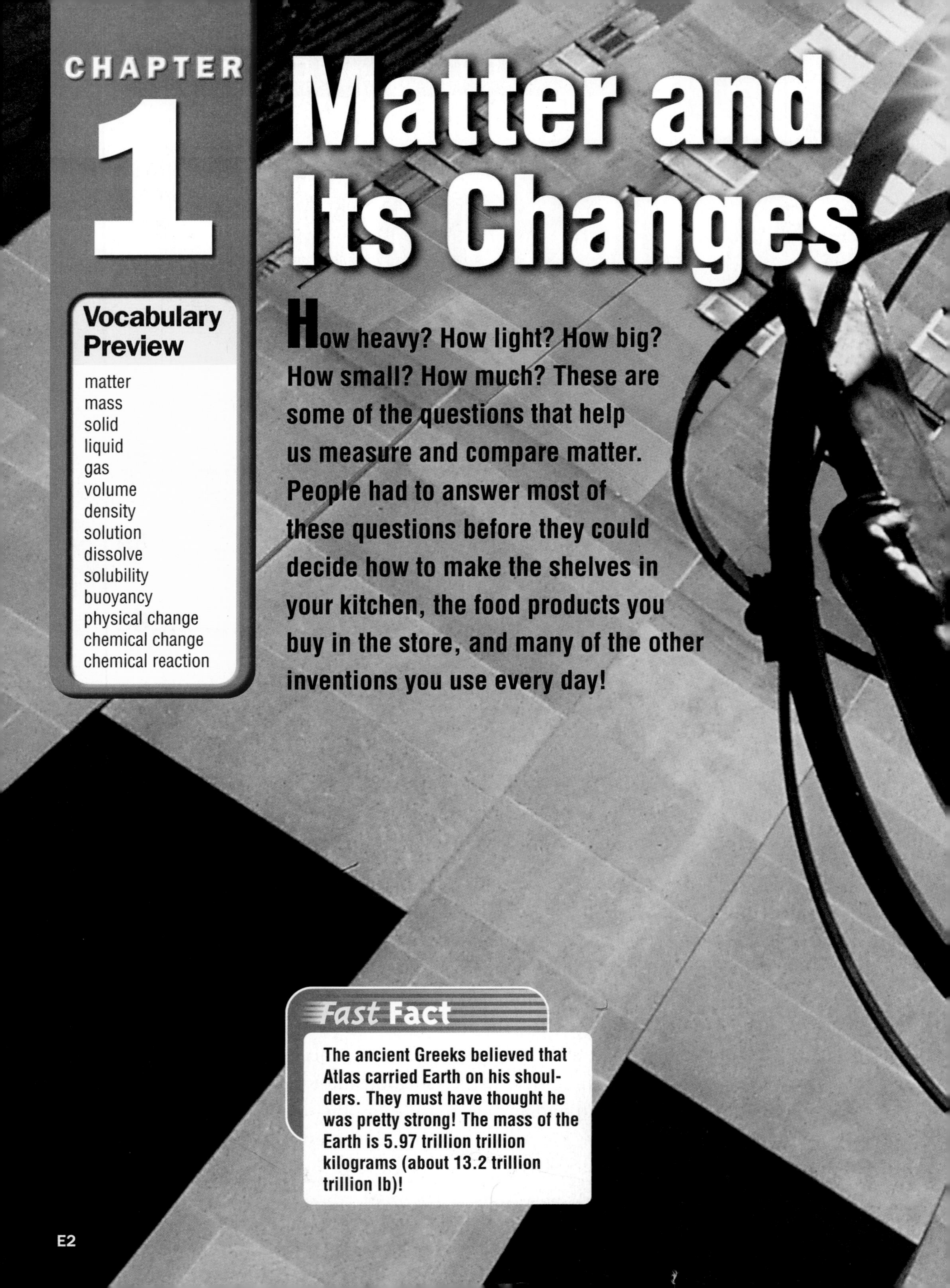

Matter and Its Changes

Vocabulary Preview

matter
mass
solid
liquid
gas
volume
density
solution
dissolve
solubility
buoyancy
physical change
chemical change
chemical reaction

How heavy? How light? How big? How small? How much? These are some of the questions that help us measure and compare matter. People had to answer most of these questions before they could decide how to make the shelves in your kitchen, the food products you buy in the store, and many of the other inventions you use every day!

Fast Fact

The ancient Greeks believed that Atlas carried Earth on his shoulders. They must have thought he was pretty strong! The mass of the Earth is 5.97 trillion trillion kilograms (about 13.2 trillion trillion lb)!

If all the ice in the world melted (a volume of 60 million cubic kilometers or 14.3 million cubic miles), the oceans would rise 55–80 meters (180–262 ft or 18–27 stories)! In New York City's harbor, the entire Statue of Liberty would be under water except for her crown and torch!

Which is denser, gold or lead? To figure out how dense a material is, scientists compare an object's density to the density of water. Water has a density of 1 g/cubic centimeter. How dense are some other common materials?

Densities

Materials	Density (g/cm³)
Aluminum	2.7
Copper	9.0
Gold	19.3
Ice	0.9
Iron	7.9
Lead	11.4
Mercury	13.6

Atlas Statue in
New York City

What Are Three States of Matter?

In this lesson, you can . . .

INVESTIGATE a physical property of matter.

LEARN ABOUT solids, liquids, and gases.

LINK to math, writing, technology, and other areas.

Physical Properties of Matter

Activity Purpose You can't see it. Often you can't even feel it. But air is all around you. In this investigation you will **observe** one way air behaves and you will **infer** a property of matter.

Materials
- plastic bag
- plastic drinking straw
- book

Activity Procedure

1 Wrap the opening of the plastic bag tightly around the straw. Use your fingers to hold the bag in place. (Picture A)

2 Blow into the straw. **Observe** what happens to the bag.

◀ After a while this horse carving made of ice will melt into a puddle of water. How are the carving and a puddle alike? How are they different?

Picture A

Picture B

3 Empty the bag. Now place a book on the bag. Again wrap the opening of the bag tightly around the straw and use your fingers to hold the bag in place. (Picture B)

4 **Predict** what will happen when you blow into the straw. Blow into it and **observe** what happens to the book.

Draw Conclusions

1. What happened to the bag when you blew air into it? What happened to the book?

2. What property of air caused the effects you observed in Steps 2 and 4?

3. **Scientists at Work** Scientists **draw conclusions** after they think carefully about observations and other data they have collected. What data supports your answer to Question 2 above?

Investigate Further In a sink, place a filled 1-L bottle on an empty plastic bag. Use a tube connected to a faucet to slowly fill the bag with water. What happens to the bottle when the bag fills with water? What property of water do you **observe**?

Process Skill Tip

When you **draw a conclusion,** you make a statement of what you know based on all the data you have collected. Unlike an inference, a conclusion is supported, or shown to be likely, by results of tests.

States of Matter

Solids

One way you know about the world around you is from your sense of touch. A tree trunk stops your finger. Water changes its shape as you poke your finger into it. You feel the moving air of a breeze. By touch you know that wood, water, and air have different properties. Yet they are all matter. Everything in the universe that has mass and takes up space is classified as **matter**.

In the investigation you saw that air takes up space. Matter also has mass. **Mass** is the amount of matter something contains. A large, heavy object such as an elephant has a lot of mass. A small, light maple leaf has much less mass. Even though an elephant and a leaf are very different, each is an example of matter.

All matter is made up of small bits called *particles*. The particles are so small that they can be seen only with the strongest microscopes. These tiny particles are always moving quickly.

The arrangements of particles give matter properties. Each arrangement is called a *state of matter*. A door key is an example of matter in the solid state. When you touch a door key, it stops your finger. A **solid** is matter that has a definite shape and takes up a definite amount of space. The particles in a solid are close together, like neat and even stacks of tiny balls. Each particle moves back and forth around one point. This arrangement of particles gives a solid its definite shape.

✔ **How are particles arranged in a solid?**

FIND OUT

• how particles are arranged in matter

• how three states of matter are different

VOCABULARY

matter
mass
solid
liquid
gas

This old key is a solid. It keeps its shape when you put it into a lock. ▶

▼ The particles in this metal key are arranged in a tight, regular pattern.

Liquids

A frozen ice cube keeps its shape. But when you heat the ice cube in a pan, the ice becomes liquid water. The water changes shape and fills the bottom of the pan. If you spill the water onto a table, the water will spread out to cover the tabletop. The water still takes up the same amount of space as in the pan. It just has a new shape. A **liquid** is matter that takes the shape of its container and takes up a definite amount of space.

When matter is a liquid, its particles slip and slide around each other. The particles don't keep the same neighbors, as particles in a solid do. They move from place to place. But they still stay close to each other.

As the particles in a liquid move, they bump into the walls of their container. The solid walls of the container don't change shape. The particles of the liquid can't move past the walls, and the liquid particles stay close together. So, the liquid takes the shape of its container.

If you pour a liquid from one container into another, the amount of matter in the liquid stays the same. The amount of space the liquid takes up also stays the same.

✔ **Why does a liquid have the same shape as its container?**

▲ The particles in a liquid move past each other easily. They are still close together but are not in a neat, even arrangement, as particles in a solid are.

As these straws show, a liquid always takes the shape of its container. ▶

Water vapor is a gas that you can't see. Its particles fly out the whistling teakettle spout. Some particles cool and clump together to form tiny water drops. The drops are the white mist that you can see.

Gases

A **gas** is matter that has no definite shape and takes up no definite amount of space. Like particles in liquids, the particles in gases are not arranged in any pattern. Unlike particles in liquids, however, particles in gases don't stay close together. This is because particles in gases are moving much faster than particles in liquids.

The amount of space a gas takes up depends on the amount of space inside its container. A gas always fills the container it is in. If the container is open, the gas particles move out.

Most matter can change state from a solid to a liquid to a gas. You can see this when you leave an ice cube in a pan on a hot stove. In a few minutes, the cube changes from a solid to a liquid. Minutes later the liquid is gone—the water has become a gas called *water vapor*. The gas particles have moved off in all directions.

Heating matter makes particles move faster. When ice is heated, some particles begin to move fast enough to break away from their neighbors. As the regular arrangement of particles breaks down, the ice melts. Heated particles of liquid water move faster and faster. After a while they move fast enough to bounce away from each other. The liquid boils, or changes quickly into a gas.

✔ **How does heating matter change its state?**

◄ A lot of air is squeezed into the tank carried by this diver. The tank valve is open. Particles of gases move out of the tank as the diver breathes in.

A gas completely fills this balloon. The gas particles push out against the balloon's sides.

Summary

Matter takes up space. Matter is made up of particles. Particles in solid matter stay close together and move back and forth around one point. Particles in liquid matter stay close together but move past each other. Particles in a gas are spread far apart.

Review

1. What are three states of matter?
2. Which state of matter keeps its shape?
3. Which states of matter take the shapes of their containers?
4. **Critical Thinking** How can matter be changed from a liquid to a solid?
5. **Test Prep** Which sentence describes a liquid?
   A Particles slide past each other.
   B Particles stay near their neighbors.
   C Particles are arranged in a pattern.
   D Particles bounce away from each other.

LINKS

MATH LINK

Solve a Problem Mercury is a metal that becomes a solid at 39° *below* 0°C. It becomes a gas at 357° *above* 0°C. What is the total number of degrees Celsius at which mercury is a liquid?

WRITING LINK

Narrative Writing—Story Suppose that you are a particle in a solid that melts and then becomes a gas. Write a story for your teacher about your experiences.

HEALTH LINK

States of Matter in the Body Find out which organ in the body is a liquid. Name some of the organs that bring a gas into the body. Plan and make a model of one body system that uses a liquid or a gas.

ART LINK

Using Matter in Art Find and describe in your own words one example each of a work of art that uses a solid, a liquid, and a gas.

GO ONLINE TECHNOLOGY LINK

Visit the Harcourt Learning Site for related links, activities, and resources.
www.harcourtschool.com

WELCOME TO THE LEARNING SITE

LESSON **2**

How Can Matter Be Measured and Compared?

In this lesson, you can . . .

 INVESTIGATE the densities of some types of matter.

 LEARN ABOUT measuring and comparing matter.

 LINK to math, writing, health, and technology.

Density

Activity Purpose Some objects have more matter packed into a smaller space than other objects. In this investigation you will **measure** the mass of raisins and of breakfast cereal. Then you will **compare** their masses and the amounts of space they take up.

Materials
- 3 identical plastic cups
- raisins
- breakfast cereal
- pan balance

Activity Procedure

1 Fill one cup with raisins. Make sure the raisins fill the cup all the way to the top. (Picture A)

2 Fill another cup with cereal. Make sure the cereal fills the cup all the way to the top.

3 **Observe** the amount of space taken up by the raisins and the cereal.

 The gold coin is only slightly larger than the quarter. However, it has more then five times the quarter's mass.

E10

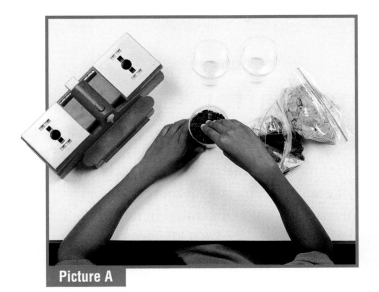

Picture A

Picture B

4 Adjust the balance so the pans are level. Place one cup on each pan. **Observe** what happens. (Picture B)

5 Fill the third cup with a mixture of raisins and cereal. **Predict** how the mass of the cup of raisins and cereal will compare with the masses of the cup of raisins and the cup of cereal. Use the pan balance to check your predictions.

Draw Conclusions

1. **Compare** the amount of space taken up by the raisins with the space taken up by the cereal.

2. Which has more mass, the cup of raisins or the cup of cereal? Explain your answer.

3. Which cup has more matter packed into it? Explain your answer.

4. **Scientists at Work** It is important to know the starting place when you measure. What would happen if you **measured** without making the balance pans equal? Explain your answer.

Investigate Further Write step-by-step directions to **compare** the masses of any two materials and the space they take up. Exchange sets of directions with a classmate. Test the directions and suggest revisions.

Measuring Matter

Measuring Mass

You can compare the amount of matter in two objects by measuring the mass of each. The object with more mass has the greater amount of matter. Mass is measured in units called grams and kilograms (KIL•uh•gramz). Half a kilogram, or $\frac{1}{2}$ kg, is about the same mass as four sticks of margarine. A medium-sized paper clip has a mass of about 1 gram, or 1 g.

One way to compare two masses is by using a pan balance. Put an object in each pan. When the pans of the balance are level, the matter in the two pans has the same mass. In the investigation, you used a pan balance to find out that a cup of raisins has more mass than a cup of cereal.

If you know the mass of the matter in one pan, you can find the mass of the matter in the other pan. This is one way scientists measure mass. They have objects with masses that are known—for example, 50 grams, 200 grams, and 1 kilogram. These objects are known as *standard masses*. Scientists put an object whose mass they don't know in one pan and put standard masses in the other pan. Then they add or remove standard masses until the two pans balance. The total of the standard masses equals the mass of the object.

✔ **Name one way you can measure mass.**

FIND OUT

- about mass and volume and how to measure them

- a way to use measurements of mass and volume to describe density

VOCABULARY

volume

density

When the pans of a balance are level, the pieces of matter on the two pans have the same mass. These cotton balls have the same mass as the wood block. ▼

◀ It is easy to measure the volume of a liquid by using this container marked in milliliters, or mL. This container is called a beaker, and it has about 400 mL of red liquid.

▲ You can find the volume of odd-shaped solid objects, such as these marbles, by sinking them in water. They push away some of the water, and the water level rises. The change in water level gives the volume of the solids.

▲ The level in this graduate changed from 250 mL to 285 mL when the marbles were added. Therefore, the volume of the marbles is 285 mL − 250 mL = 35 mL.

Volume

Matter has mass and takes up space. The amount of space that matter takes up is called its **volume** (VAHL•yoom). You can measure the amount of space a solid or liquid takes up. You also can measure a container such as a box and calculate its volume. Volume often is measured in cubic centimeters. A *cubic centimeter* is the space taken up by a cube that has each side equal to 1 centimeter. A cubic centimeter is the same as a milliliter.

Cooks use measuring cups and measuring spoons to find the volume of ingredients for a recipe. Scientists measure volume with a beaker or a graduate, a tall cylinder with measuring marks on the side.

A solid keeps its shape, so it is easy to see that its volume stays the same. A liquid changes shape to match its container. But it does not change its volume. A gas has no definite volume. However, the mass of a gas sample doesn't change when the volume of the gas changes.

✔ **What is volume?**

To find the volume of a box, first measure its height, width, and length. Then multiply the three numbers together. This box is about 6 cm thick, 20 cm wide, and 30 cm tall. Its volume is 6 cm × 20 cm × 30 cm = 3600 cubic centimeters. ▶

Density

Some matter takes up a large space but has a small mass. A balloon filled with gas may take up 10,000 cubic centimeters. But it may have such a small mass that it floats in the air. Other matter takes up very little space and has a large mass. A brick is smaller than the balloon, but it has much more mass.

The property of matter that compares the amount of matter to the space taken up is called **density** (DEN•suh•tee). The gas in a balloon has a low density. The density of a brick is much higher.

You can find the density of an object by dividing the mass of the object by its volume. For example, an apple may have a mass of 200 grams and a volume of 200 cubic centimeters. Its density is 200 grams ÷ 200 cubic centimeters, or 1 gram per cubic centimeter.

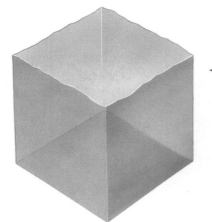

◄ One cubic centimeter of water has a mass of 1 gram. The density of water is 1 gram per cubic centimeter.

In the investigation you saw that cereal is less dense than raisins. You also found that a mixture of cereal and raisins is denser than cereal and less dense than raisins. Whenever you mix two kinds of matter, the density of the mixture is between the densities of the two separate materials.

✔ **Which material in the table has the greatest density?**

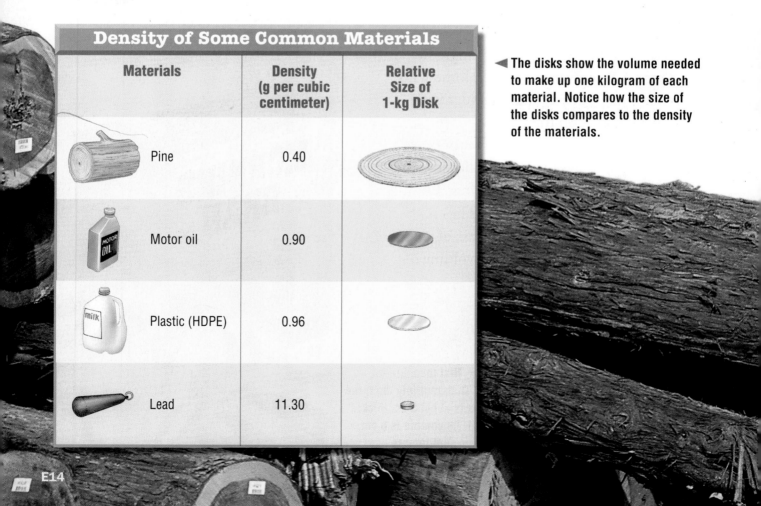

Density of Some Common Materials

Materials	Density (g per cubic centimeter)	Relative Size of 1-kg Disk
Pine	0.40	
Motor oil	0.90	
Plastic (HDPE)	0.96	
Lead	11.30	

◄ The disks show the volume needed to make up one kilogram of each material. Notice how the size of the disks compares to the density of the materials.

Summary

All matter has mass and volume. Mass is the amount of matter in an object. The space that matter takes up is called volume. Density compares the amount of matter in an object to the amount of space it takes up. You can find the density of an object by dividing its mass by its volume.

Review

1. What is one way to measure mass?
2. What word is used to describe the amount of space that matter takes up?
3. What property of matter compares the amount of matter to the space that the matter takes up?
4. **Critical Thinking** You are shopping for cereal. How does estimating density help you find a good buy?
5. **Test Prep** If a black ball is denser than a white ball of the same size, the black ball has —
   A less volume
   B more volume
   C more matter taking up the same space
   D less matter taking up the same space

LINKS

MATH LINK

Compare Volumes Use a pan balance and three cups to measure 100 g, 200 g, and 300 g of water. Use a beaker or a graduate to measure and compare the volumes of water.

WRITING LINK

Informative Writing—Narration You are making a short video for younger students. It will show how to measure volume and mass. Decide what you will show. Then, write a script to explain what you are showing.

HEALTH LINK

Your Density Find out how to measure and compare the mass of a person's muscles and body fat. Make a comic strip that shows how this is done.

GO ONLINE TECHNOLOGY LINK

Learn more about measuring matter by visiting this Internet site.
www.scilinks.org/harcourt

SCiLINKS
THE WORLD'S A CLICK AWAY

LESSON **3**

What Are Some Useful Properties of Matter?

In this lesson, you can . . .

INVESTIGATE what happens to some solids in water.

LEARN ABOUT ways to group kinds of matter.

LINK to math, writing, technology, and other areas.

INVESTIGATE

Floating and Sinking

Activity Purpose Some solids sink in liquid water, and others float. But even solids that sink can be made to float. In this investigation you will see what happens to two solid materials when they are placed in water. Then you will make boats from the materials. You will **infer** some of the things that affect floating and sinking.

Materials

- plastic shoe box
- water
- sheet of aluminum foil
- modeling clay

Activity Procedure

1 Fill the plastic shoe box halfway with water.

2 Take a sheet of aluminum foil about 10 cm long and 10 cm wide. Squeeze it tightly into a ball. Before placing the ball in the shoe box, **predict** whether it will sink or float. Test your prediction and **record** your **observations.**

3 Take a thin piece of modeling clay about 10 cm long and 10 cm wide. Squeeze it tightly into a ball. Place the ball in the shoe box. **Observe** whether it sinks or floats.

◀ This sailing ship is made to float, but its black metal anchor is made to sink.

Picture A

Picture B

4. Uncurl the foil. Use it to make a boat. (Picture A) Before placing the boat on the water, **predict** whether it will sink or float. Test your prediction and **record** your **observations.**

5. Make a boat out of the modeling clay. Before placing the boat on the water, **predict** whether it will sink or float. Test your prediction and **record** your **observations.** (Picture B)

Draw Conclusions

1. Which objects floated? Which objects sank?

2. Which do you think has the greater density, the ball of aluminum foil or the ball of modeling clay? Explain.

3. **Scientists at Work** Scientists often look at two situations in which everything is the same except for one property. What property was the same in Step 3 as in Step 5? What property was different in Step 3 and Step 5? What can you **infer** about how that difference changed the results?

Investigate Further How fast do you think each boat would sink if you put a hole in the bottom of it? **Form a hypothesis** about how the size and material of a boat affect its rate of sinking. Then **plan and conduct an experiment** to test your hypothesis. Be sure to **control,** or keep the same, all the variables except the one you are changing and the one you are observing.

Process Skill Tip

Usually in an investigation, only one property is changed at a time. This makes it easier to **infer** the causes of the results. This is called controlling variables.

How Water Interacts with Other Matter

Water and Sugar

FIND OUT

- **how solids dissolve in water**
- **why objects float or sink**

VOCABULARY

solution
dissolve
solubility
buoyancy

If you put a spoonful of solid sugar into a glass of liquid water and stir, what happens? The sugar seems to disappear. The glass still contains a clear liquid. Where did the sugar go?

The answer is that the sugar and the water formed a kind of mixture called a solution. A **solution** (suh•LOO•shuhn) is a mixture in which the particles of different kinds of matter are mixed evenly with each other. In this case the sugar particles mixed with the water particles. You can't see the sugar, but you can tell it is there because the solution tastes sweet. Another way to show that the sugar is still there is to let the water evaporate, or dry up. After all the water is gone, solid sugar will be left at the bottom of the glass.

When you mix sugar and water, they form a solution. What is happening to the sugar as you stir the water? ▼

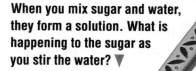

1. When a lump of sugar dissolves in water, water particles pull sugar particles away from the solid sugar.

2. Moving water particles spread sugar particles to all parts of the solution.

3. After a while all the sugar particles are pulled away by water particles. The sugar is completely dissolved. It can't be seen because the particles are too small and spread out.

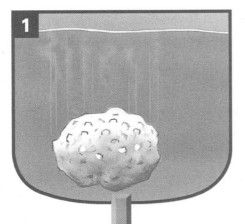

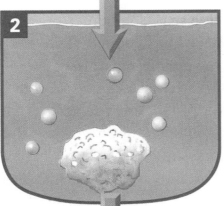

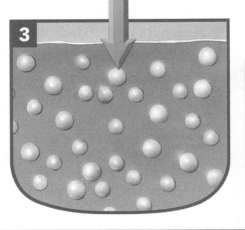

When one material forms a solution with another material, we say it **dissolves** (dih•ZAHLVZ). As sugar dissolves in water, particles of solid sugar are pulled away from each other by water particles. The water particles bump into and move the sugar. Very quickly the sugar particles spread to all parts of the solution. You can no longer see the sugar because the very small sugar particles are mixed evenly with the water particles.

If you add more and more sugar to a glass of water, at some point the sugar particles can't mix evenly with the water particles. The extra sugar doesn't dissolve. When you stop stirring, the extra sugar falls to the bottom of the glass.

Some solids dissolve in water. Other solids do not. Try stirring sand into water. While you are stirring, the sand mixes with the water but does not dissolve. When you stop stirring, the sand falls to the bottom of the jar. **Solubility** (sahl•yoo•BIL•uh•tee) is a measure of the amount of a material that will dissolve in another material. The solubility of sand in water is zero. No amount of sand dissolves in water.

✔ **What happens to a solid when it forms a solution with water?**

Solubility in Water		
Material	**Volume of Water (mL)**	**Mass of Materials That Can Be Dissolved in Water at 25°C (g)**
Sugar	100	105
Salt	100	36
Baking soda	100	7
Sand	100	0

E19

Floating and Sinking

If you put a coin, such as a penny, into water, it doesn't dissolve. It sinks. A chip of wood doesn't dissolve in water, either. It floats. The ability of matter to float in a liquid or gas is called **buoyancy** (BOY•uhn•see).

A solid object denser than water sinks in water. Lead is more than 11 times as dense as water, so a lead fishing weight rapidly sinks. A solid object less dense than water floats in water. Pine wood is about half as dense as water. So a plank of pine floats.

▲ Most humans have a density that is a little less than 1 gram per cubic centimeter, so they float in water.

If you tied several pine planks together to form a raft, the raft would float because it is made of a material that is less dense than water.

Liquids can also float or sink. Have you ever seen rainbow streaks on puddles on a road or sidewalk? Motor oil floating on the water causes the streaks. The oil floats because it is less dense than water.

Some liquids sink in water. Maple syrup is mostly a sugar solution. It is denser than pure water. Maple syrup sinks to the bottom when you pour it into a glass of water.

Gases can also sink or float. All the gases in the air you breathe are much less dense than liquid water. When you blow through a drinking straw into water, air bubbles are pushed up, or buoyed up, by the water. They rise to the top of the glass. Helium is another gas that is less dense than air. When you fill a balloon with helium, it is buoyed up by the air and rises.

◄ A scuba diver wears a belt or vest with dense pieces of lead. This makes the diver's density about the same as that of water. With the belt on, the diver can swim up or down easily.

The density of the cup and air is less than water so the cup floats.

Most rocks sink. But pumice (PUHM•is) is a kind of rock that contains a lot of air, so pumice floats.

Diet soft drink is less dense than water, so this can of diet soft drink floats. A can of regular soft drink would sink.

Most wood floats, but most metal, like this can opener, sinks.

Remember from Lesson 2 that you can change the density of a material by mixing it with material that has a different density.

Air is not very dense. A good way to lower the density of an object is to add air to it. If you add enough air, the object will become less dense than water. Then it will float. Clay is denser than water. In the investigation you got clay to float by making it into a boat. A boat contains air. The sides and bottom of a boat keep water out and hold air in. The clay boat floated because it contained a lot of air. Even a heavy metal boat will float if it contains enough air.

Most human bodies are a little less dense than water. So, most people float on water. Scuba divers don't want to float or sink. If they floated, they would have to swim hard to stay under water. If they sank, they would have to swim hard to get back to the water's surface. Scuba divers control their buoyancy by wearing a belt or vest loaded with dense lead pieces. While wearing the lead weights, a diver has about the same density as water.

✔ **What is buoyancy?**

Each liquid layer in this beaker has a different density. The densest layer is liquid mercury on the bottom. Even a steel bolt floats on mercury. The less dense materials float on the more dense materials. ▶

Floating Transportation

Humans use machines to control buoyancy and to move from place to place. Submarines, hot-air balloons, and blimps all use buoyancy to help move people. Hot-air balloons are buoyed up by air, so they rise.

This is because hot air is less dense than cool air. Blimps are big, football-shaped balloons. They are filled with helium, a gas that is less dense than air. Submarines control their density to float and to sink in the water.

✔ **How is buoyancy used for travel?**

THE INSIDE STORY

How Submarines Work

Submarines can float on top of the ocean or dive down and travel deep under water. They do this by adding or removing water to control their density.

1. When a submarine floats on the surface of the water, it is like any other metal boat. It is filled with enough air to make it float.

2. Tanks inside the submarine have air in them when the submarine is at the surface. To make the submarine float just below the surface, some of the air is taken out and the tanks are partly filled with water. The combination of the submarine, the water, and the air has about the same density as water.

3. The submarine can dive to the bottom by squeezing air in its tanks into smaller tanks. Because the air's volume is now smaller, its density is greater. The original tanks are then filled with water. This makes the metal submarine denser than water. To allow the submarine to return to the surface, water is pumped out of the tanks. Air is allowed to expand back into them. The submarine becomes less dense than water. It is buoyed up and rises to the surface.

Summary

Solutions are mixtures in which the particles are mixed evenly. Some matter dissolves in water and some does not. Matter that is less dense than water floats on water. Buoyancy can be controlled by changing density.

Review

1. What changes happen to sugar when it dissolves in water? What stays the same?
2. What happens when you add more of a material to water than the water will dissolve?
3. How can you float a piece of solid material that is denser than water?
4. **Critical Thinking** What could you do to make an object float in air?
5. **Test Prep** Any material that floats in water —
   A is denser than water
   B has the same density as water
   C is less dense than water
   D is made of metal

LINKS

MATH LINK

Use Mental Math The greatest amount of sugar you can dissolve in 100 milliliters of water is 105 grams. How much sugar can you dissolve in 1000 milliliters of water?

WRITING LINK

Informative Writing—Explanation Find out what the ancient Greek scientist Archimedes discovered about density. Write an explanation of what you learn for a younger student.

PHYSICAL EDUCATION LINK

Floating and Swimming Find out what survival floating is. Use a model to demonstrate it for your class, or make a poster that explains it.

LITERATURE LINK

Submarine Predictions Read *20,000 Leagues Under the Sea* to find out what French science-fiction writer Jules Verne predicted about the modern submarine.

TECHNOLOGY LINK

Learn more about physical properties of matter by viewing *Peep Science* on the **Harcourt Science Newsroom Video.**

What Are Chemical and Physical Changes?

In this lesson, you can . . .

INVESTIGATE a chemical change.

LEARN ABOUT physical and chemical changes.

LINK to math, writing, art, and technology.

◄ The bright colors and booming sounds of fireworks are caused by chemical changes.

INVESTIGATE

Changes in a Penny

Activity Purpose A bright, shiny new bicycle looks great. An older, used bicycle looks dull, scratched, and may be rusty. The bicycle looks different because of changes to metal, paint, and other materials. In this activity, you will investigate a change of another metal object. You will **observe, compare,** and **predict** changes of a penny.

Materials

- safety goggles
- 2 paper clips
- foam cup
- vinegar
- 3 pennies
- plastic wrap

CAUTION

Procedure

1. **CAUTION** **Put on the safety goggles.** Make a coin holder. Bend the paper clip into the shape shown in Picture A.

2. Place one penny flat on the bottom of the cup at one side. Use the second paper clip to attach a penny to the top of the coin holder. Put the coin holder on the bottom of the plastic cup.

3. Carefully pour vinegar down the side of the cup until the flat penny is just covered. The vinegar should be about 1 cm deep at most. (Picture B)

4. Cover the cup tightly with a piece of plastic wrap. Lay the third penny on top of the plastic wrap. Place the cup where it will not be bumped or spilled.

5. **Observe** each penny carefully. Record your observations.

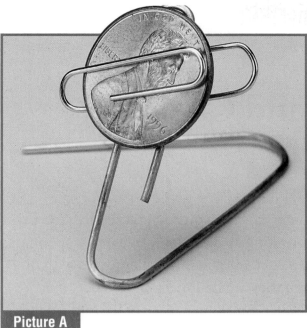

Picture A

Picture B

6. **Observe** each penny after four hours. **Record** your observations.

7. **Predict** what will happen to each penny after one day.

8. Test your prediction and **record** your observations.

Draw Conclusions

1. **Compare** your observations of the pennies in Steps 5 and 6.

2. Do your observations in Step 8 match the prediction you made in Step 7? Explain.

3. What is the purpose of the penny on the top of the plastic wrap?

4. **Scientists at Work** Scientists **predict** new observations using what they have learned from their past observations. Explain how you used past observations to make your prediction in Step 7.

Investigate Further What will happen if the pennies are replaced by dimes? **Form a hypothesis** about the effect of vinegar on dimes. Then **design and conduct an experiment** to test your hypothesis.

> ### Process Skill Tip
> You can tell that a substance has changed by **comparing observations** made at different times. If the observations are different, then the substance has changed.

E25

Physical and Chemical Changes

Physical Changes

To cool a glass of water quickly, you add cracked ice. You can make cracked ice by breaking an ice cube with a heavy spoon. The ice changes from a cube into many smaller pieces with different shapes. Although they are no longer an ice cube, the pieces still are frozen water. Breaking a piece of ice into smaller pieces is an example of a change in shape.

An ice cube can change in another way—you can melt it in your hand. In Lesson 1, you learned that melting is a change of state. The melted ice still is water. If you wanted, you could refreeze it and make a new ice cube. These changes of state are physical changes. Any change in the size, shape, or state of a substance is called a **physical change**.

✔ **What is a physical change?**

How do you change a sheet of paper when you cut it, fold it, or wad it up? Does it change colors? Does it become a piece of cloth? No, of course not. You change only the shape and size of the paper. These changes are examples of physical changes.

Sugar can undergo many physical changes. Even though each form is different, they are all still sugar.

▲ Rock candy is a large crystal of sugar. It is a clear solid with many smooth, flat surfaces.

▲ Sugar cubes are made by pressing together many small grains of sugar. The cubes are not clear or smooth like rock candy, but they still taste sweet.

▲ Table sugar is made up of many separate, tiny crystals. Unlike rock candy or cubes, you can pour and scoop it. It is still sugar.

▲ Confectioners' sugar is made by grinding sugar crystals into powder. It looks different than rock candy, cubes, or grains but it is still sugar.

Heat from the waffle melts the butter. In cold butter, the butter particles move slowly. As butter warms, the particles move faster and can slide past each other. The change from a solid to a liquid is a physical change. ▼

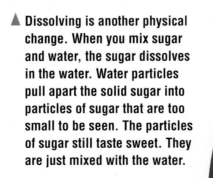

▲ Dissolving is another physical change. When you mix sugar and water, the sugar dissolves in the water. Water particles pull apart the solid sugar into particles of sugar that are too small to be seen. The particles of sugar still taste sweet. They are just mixed with the water.

▲ Here is the glass of sugar solution after it has stood for several days. The water has evaporated, or dried up. Evaporation is a physical change because the water has changed state. As the water evaporates, sugar particles are left behind in the glass.

Chemical Changes

Did you ever bite into an apple and then lay it down? When you picked it up later, parts of it were brown. A change of color is a sign that a new substance formed. A change that produces one or more new substances and may release energy is called a **chemical change**. Remember the color change of the penny in the activity? The dark material was a new substance formed by a chemical reaction. **Chemical reaction** is another term for chemical change.

The sweet smell of baking bread is another sign that a chemical reaction is taking place. The odor is a property of a new substance. The substance forms as the bread dough is cooked. If you watch the dough bake, you also can see it change color from pale white to brown.

When someone strikes a match, you can see light and feel warmth as the match head burns and slowly turns black. Light, energy release, and color change are all signs of a chemical change. Where does the light energy come from? A match head has *potential*, or stored, energy because of the arrangement of its particles. This stored energy is changed to light and heat when the match head burns. Potential energy that can be released by a chemical change is called *chemical energy*. Fuels such as gasoline have chemical energy.

✔ **What are some signs of a chemical change?**

The dark areas on the teapot are a thin layer of a new substance called tarnish. The tarnish is not bright and shiny like silver. A new substance formed when silver and substances in the air combined. Polishing rubs away the tarnish and uncovers the shiny silver again. ▶

◄ The bottle contains vinegar. The snugly fitting balloon contains some baking soda. When vinegar and baking soda mix, the balloon fills with a gas. The filled balloon shows that a new substance formed. A chemical reaction made a gas called carbon dioxide.

◄ The burning gas in a Bunsen burner produces warmth, light, carbon dioxide, and water vapor.

Rust results from a slower chemical change than burning. It is made by a chemical reaction between the metal iron and oxygen, a gas in the air. Rust is a different color and weaker than iron. A new anchor is strong, but this rusty anchor crumbles easily. ▼

◄ Burning is a chemical change. Light and warmth are released. Smoke, ash, and hot gases are produced.

E29

Using Physical and Chemical Changes

Making steel is an important industry because steel is a useful substance. Steel sheets are used to make the outside of washers, dryers, stoves, and refrigerators. Steel beams help support buildings and bridges. Metal spoons, forks, and knives are made of a kind of steel.

The steel industry uses physical and chemical changes. Steel is made in a large furnace. Burning fuel heats iron and other materials until they melt. The melted materials mix to form liquid steel.

Liquid steel is poured into smaller containers, where it cools. The cooled steel is slowly moved into a giant machine. Rows of large, heavy rollers squeeze the steel into long slabs. Sprays of water cool the steel. It slowly hardens.

To make thin sheet steel, the hardened slabs are reheated. Then the hot slabs move through another rolling machine. These rollers squeeze the slabs, making them thinner and thinner. Finally, the thin sheet steel is cut and rolled up for shipment.

✔ **How is a chemical change used to make steel?**

▲ Burning provides the energy to melt the iron and other substances that form steel. The light and thermal energy released show chemical changes are taking place.

To form these rolls of thin sheet steel, large steel bars were heated, partially melted, and rolled thinner and thinner (below left). These changes of state and changes of size and shape are physical changes. ▼

Summary

Physical changes are changes to the size or shape of a substance such as cutting or folding; and changes of state such as melting, freezing, and boiling. During physical changes, no new substances are formed. Chemical changes, or chemical reactions, form new substances. Changes in color or releases of energy show chemical changes have taken place. Burning and rusting are examples of chemical changes.

Review

1. What changes happen to a substance during a physical change?
2. What is a chemical change?
3. Describe one physical change in the production of steel.
4. **Critical Thinking** Is an explosion a slow or fast chemical reaction? Explain your thinking.
5. **Test Prep** Which of the following is a chemical change?

   A boiling some water

   B frying a hamburger

   C sawing a board

   D grinding wheat into flour

LINKS

MATH LINK

Solve a Two-Step Problem Some knife blades are made of hard, high-carbon steel, which can be made very sharp. High-carbon steel is made up mostly of iron with a little carbon. Suppose a block of high-carbon steel contains 396 grams of iron and 4 grams of carbon. What fraction of the block is carbon?

WRITING LINK

Expressive Writing—Song Lyrics You see physical and chemical changes happening all around you. Set them to music. Choose a tune you know. Then write words for a song that will help someone else see these changes, too.

HEALTH LINK

Food Changes Food gives your body energy. To get this energy, your body must change food physically and chemically. Use library resources to find out more about one of these changes. Then report to the class to share what you learned.

GO ONLINE TECHNOLOGY LINK

Visit the Harcourt Learning Site for related links, activities, and resources. **www.harcourtschool.com**

WELCOME TO THE LEARNING SITE

Plastics You Can Eat

The two inventors of edible plastic

Plastics are artificial materials, or substances that are made by people. They can be shaped into different objects, such as bottles, chairs, or notebook covers. There are hundreds of different plastics, each with its own properties. One new type has an unusual property for a plastic. It dissolves in a special way, so it can be eaten!

Why Would Anyone Want to Eat Plastic?

You wouldn't want to eat regular plastic. It could be harmful. But the people who invented plastic that can be eaten weren't thinking about making it edible. Two students were trying to make green slime in their high-school laboratory for a Halloween trick. But something went wrong.

There was a small explosion. Green slime flew everywhere, covering the laboratory floor, ceiling, and walls. The students cleaned up the mess before anyone found out. But they missed a little bit of slime that landed in a jar.

The next day, their teacher found the green slime in the jar. It was stuck to a glass stirring rod. It looked like a lollipop. It even looked edible, and it really was.

Plastic Coated Medicine

It turned out that the green slime dissolves in the saliva in your mouth, but it doesn't dissolve in just water. This makes it perfect as a coating for pills. It protects the medicine in the pills from moisture in the air, but still is digested easily in the stomach. Other pill coatings take in moisture from the air. This can make the medicine less effective.

Green slime works well for coating medicine that can be absorbed in the stomach. But some medicines, such as the insulin needed by people who have diabetes, are destroyed by the digestive juices in the stomach. For that reason, these medicines are usually given as shots instead of pills. But no one likes to get shots.

Another Edible Plastic

Scientists have invented another kind of edible plastic that won't dissolve in the mouth, the stomach, or even the small intestine. Medicine that has been coated with this plastic gets all the way to the large intestine. There, the plastic absorbs water and

gets larger. Tiny holes in the plastic open up as that happens. The medicine gets out through the holes, and the patient gets the medicine without getting a shot.

THINK ABOUT IT

1. What other uses can you think of for edible plastic?
2. Do you know of any other medicines that can't be swallowed that edible plastic could be used for?

CAREERS
INDUSTRIAL ENGINEER

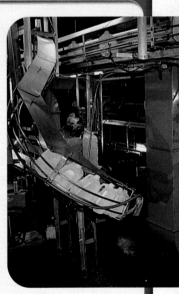

What They Do Industrial engineers design and build machines for factories. They solve problems to help people make things and put things together easily and quickly. For example, they might design the machines to make pills and coat them with plastic. They also might decide what shapes work best for plastic or metal car parts.

Education and Training

Industrial engineers need a college degree. They may be licensed as a professional engineer by the state they live in. For that, they will need four years of experience and a passing grade on a state test.

 WEB LINK
For Science and Technology updates, visit the Harcourt Internet site.
www.harcourtschool.com

E33

Shirley Ann Jackson

PHYSICIST

This is a view downward into the core of a nuclear reactor.

As a little girl in Washington, D.C., Shirley Jackson collected live hornets, bumblebees, and wasps to study. She kept the animals in old mayonnaise jars under the back porch. She also studied fungi and molds around her home. Her father helped her with these science projects. She won first place at a science fair with an experiment on how different environments affect the growth of bacteria.

Jackson graduated first in her class at Roosevelt High School. She won scholarships for college and decided to go to the Massachusetts Institute of Technology (MIT). She became the first African-American woman to receive a doctoral degree, or advanced degree, from MIT.

From 1995 to 1999, she was chairperson of the five-member U.S. Nuclear Regulatory Commission (NRC). NRC makes sure nuclear reactors and radioactive materials are used safely.

In 1998, Jackson was inducted into the National Women's Hall of Fame. She was included because of her work in education, science, and public policy.

In 1999, Jackson became president of Rensselaer Polytechnic Institute, a university in Troy, New York.

THINK ABOUT IT

1. What areas of science first interested Jackson when she was young? What area of science most interests her now?

2. What skills and talents do you think a person needs to work for NRC?

LIQUID LAYERS

How does density help you predict which liquids float?

Materials

- 3 clear plastic cups
- water
- corn oil
- maple syrup

Material	Density
water	1 g/mL
corn oil	< 1 g/mL
maple syrup	> 1 g/mL

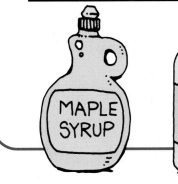

Procedure

❶ Fill one cup about one-fourth full of water.

❷ Repeat Step 1 for the corn oil and for the maple syrup.

❸ Slowly pour the maple syrup down the inside of the cup containing water. Observe what happens.

❹ Predict what will happen when you pour the corn oil into the same cup. Slowly pour the corn oil down the side of the cup. Observe what happens.

Draw Conclusions

What can you conclude about the buoyancy of these liquids?

SOLUBILITY

How can you determine solubility?

Materials

- safety goggles
- rubber gloves
- 200-mL beaker
- water
- balance
- 40 g alum
- small scrap of paper
- stirring stick

Procedure

❶ **CAUTION** Put on the goggles and gloves.

❷ Fill the beaker to the 100-mL mark with cold tap water.

❸ Measure 25 g of alum on the paper. Use the paper to pour the alum into the water.

❹ Stir until the alum dissolves.

❺ Measure 1 g of alum, and add it to the beaker. Stir. Observe the solution.

❻ Repeat Step 5 until no more alum will dissolve.

Draw Conclusions

What is the solubility of alum?

Vocabulary Review

Use the terms below to complete the sentences. The page numbers in ( ) tell you where to look in the chapter if you need help.

matter (E6)	**solution** (E18)
mass (E6)	**dissolve** (E19)
solid (E6)	**solubility** (E19)
liquid (E7)	**buoyancy** (E20)
gas (E8)	**physical change** (E26)
volume (E13)	**chemical change** (E28)
density (E14)	**chemical reaction** (E28)

1. The ____ of a solid cube is the amount of space it takes up.

2. In a ____, the particles are far away from each other and move quickly.

3. You can't see a solid when you ____ it, because its particles become separated by water particles.

4. If the particles of matter move back and forth around one point, the matter is in the ____ state.

5. The amount of matter in an object is its ____.

6. ____ is a measure of whether an object floats or sinks in a gas or liquid.

7. Particles of matter in the ____ state can slip and slide past each other.

8. When the particles of a mixture are evenly mixed and can't be seen, the mixture is a ____.

9. Air and pine wood each have a ____ that is less than that of water.

10. ____ is a measure of the amount of a material that will dissolve in another material.

11. ____ is anything that takes up space and has mass.

12. Melting is an example of a ____ change.

13. Rusting is an example of a ____ change, which is another name for a ____.

Connect Concepts

Some of the substances and objects mentioned in the chapter are listed in the Word Bank. In the table below, list each substance or object under each of its properties. Use each item as often as necessary.

air	lead weight	water vapor	brick
wood	sugar cube	ice	water

Properties of Matter		
Dissolves in Water	**Floats in Water**	**Density About 1 g/mL**
14. _____	15. _____	17. _____
	16. _____	
Takes Shape of Container	**Sinks in Water**	**Has No Definite Volume**
18. _____	21. _____	23. _____
19. _____	22. _____	24. _____
20. _____		

Check Understanding

Write the letter of the best choice.

25. A boat made from matter that is denser than water can float on water if it is filled with enough —
    A water
    B air
    C salt
    D salt water

26. When two materials are mixed, the ＿＿ of the mixture is between those of the separate materials.
    F mass
    G volume
    H density
    J state

27. Which of the following properties of sugar does **NOT** change when sugar dissolves in water?
    A color
    B shape
    C texture
    D taste

28. The volume of a ＿＿ depends on the size of its container.
    F liquid
    G solid
    H gas
    J solution

29. Formation of a new substance shows that a ＿＿ has happened.
    A physical change
    B change of state
    C solution
    D chemical reaction

Critical Thinking

30. Compare the relationships between particles in ice, water, and water vapor.

31. When a solid dissolves completely in water, what happens to the particles that made up the solid?

Process Skills Review

32. You measure the temperature of four pans of boiling water. Your measurements are 99°C, 100°C, 100°C, and 101°C. What **conclusion** can you **draw** about the temperature at which water boils? Explain your answer.

33. You use the same pan balance to **measure** the mass of a rock on two days. Your measurement is larger on the second day. The rock hasn't changed. How do you explain the difference in measurements?

34. You take a sip from a glass of clear water, and it tastes salty. What can you **infer** about what is in the glass?

35. Suppose that you **observe** a fresh scratch on a bicycle. A few weeks later, you notice that the area under the scratch has changed color. What are two things you can infer by **comparing** your observations?

Performance Assessment

Maximum Float

Use a piece of aluminum foil to make a shape that will float in water. Experiment to find the boat shape that will support the largest number of pennies. Explain the reasons you changed the boat's shape.

Heat—Energy on the Move

Vocabulary Preview

energy
kinetic energy
thermal energy
temperature
heat
conduction
convection
radiation
infrared radiation
fuel
solar energy

You push and shove! Finally the door opens! In summer, doors often stick. This is because materials expand and contract as they get hot and cold. For the same reason, if you put a jar with a stuck lid under hot water, the lid will loosen!

Fast Fact

If you add enough heat, almost anything will boil. If you take away enough heat, things freeze. Water freezes at 0°C (32°F) and boils at 100°C (212°F). Substances freeze and boil at different temperatures.

Freezing and Boiling

Substance	Freezes at °C (°F)		Boils at °C (°F)	
Iron	1538	(2800)	2862	(5184)
Mercury	-39	(-38)	357	(675)
Nitrogen	-209	(-344)	-196	(-321)
Oxygen	-218	(-360)	-183	(-297)

Molten iron

When a light bulb is on, the temperature of the glowing wire inside is a sizzling 2500°C (about 4500°F). That's why the outside of a light bulb gets hot while the bulb is on. The empty space around the wire keeps the bulb from melting and the wire from burning up.

Fast Fact

The temperature of a lightning bolt is estimated to be 30,000°C (54,000°F)! If people could harness the energy from a single lightning bolt, they could light up an average-size town for a year.

How Does Heat Affect Matter?

In this lesson, you can . . .

INVESTIGATE how heat affects air in a balloon.

LEARN ABOUT thermal energy.

LINK to math, writing, social studies, and technology.

◄ Icicles form when water melts, flows, and freezes again.

INVESTIGATE

Changes in a Heated Balloon

Activity Purpose Have you ever wondered why a hot-air balloon rises? Or how a thermometer measures temperature? The answers have something in common—a property of matter. In this investigation you will **measure** changes in a balloon as it is heated. Then you'll **infer** what caused the changes.

Materials

- desk lamp
- bulb
- safety goggles
- stopwatch or clock with second hand
- 3 rubber balloons
- string
- ruler

CAUTION

Activity Procedure

1 Turn on the lamp, and let the light bulb get warm.

2 **CAUTION** **Put on your safety goggles.** Blow up a rubber balloon just enough to stretch it. Tie it closed.

3 **Measure** the length of the balloon with the ruler. **Record** the measurement. (Picture A)

4 Carefully hold the balloon by its tied end about 3 cm above the lamp. Hold it there for two minutes. (Picture B) **CAUTION** **The light bulb is hot. Do not touch it with your hands or with the balloon. Observe** what happens to the balloon. **Record** your observations.

E40

Picture A

Picture B

5 **Measure** the length of the balloon while it is still over the lamp. **Record** the measurement.

6 Repeat Steps 2 through 5 using a new balloon each time.

Draw Conclusions

1. What did you **observe** as you warmed the balloons?

2. **Compare** the lengths of the heated balloons with the lengths of the unheated balloons.

3. What can you **infer** happened to the air inside the balloons as you heated it?

4. **Scientists at Work** Scientists often **measure** several times to make sure the measurements are accurate. In this investigation you measured the lengths of three different balloons. Were the measurements all the same? Explain.

Investigate Further Fill a balloon with water that is at room temperature. Put the balloon on a desk and **measure** its length. Heat the balloon by putting it in a bowl of hot tap water for 15 minutes. Take the balloon out of the bowl and measure its length. **Compare** these lengths with those you measured with the air-filled balloons in the investigation.

Process Skill Tip

Scientists often observe and **measure** an object or an event several times. Patterns among measurements may show something important in an investigation.

Matter and Energy

Thermal Energy

Have you ever thrown a ball? Pushed a grocery cart? Run in a race? All these activities need energy. **Energy** is the ability to cause a change. In each of these cases, you transferred energy to the object and its motion changed. The ball flew through the air. The grocery cart rolled through the store. You moved along the racetrack. Each of these three objects gained **kinetic** (kih•NET•ihk) **energy**, or energy of motion.

The much smaller particles in matter are always moving from one place to another at random. The particles in a solid jiggle back and forth like balls on a spring. The particles in a liquid slide past each other. The particles in a gas move quickly in many directions. All of this movement requires energy. The kinetic energy of particles in matter is called **thermal energy**. The word *thermal* means "heat." We feel the thermal energy of the particles in matter as heat.

✔ **What is thermal energy?**

FIND OUT

• what thermal energy is

• the difference between thermal energy and temperature

VOCABULARY

energy
kinetic energy
thermal energy
temperature

Water boils when its particles are moving so fast that many begin to fly away from its surface. This happens when the water's temperature is 100°C (212°F). ▼

When liquid water freezes, its particles settle into an arrangement as a solid. This happens when the temperature of the water is 0°C (32°F). The ice cubes and lemonade are at 0°C. ▼

1 These balls stand for particles in a solid. The springs stand for the forces holding the solid together. Particles in a solid keep their arrangement, but they move back and forth around a point.

2 When you add thermal energy, the particles move faster. The solid gets hotter.

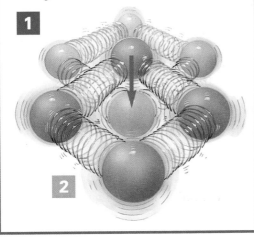

▲ The water in this cup is the same temperature as the nearly boiling water in the hot spring. But the water in the spring has more thermal energy because it has more water and, therefore, more moving particles of matter.

Temperature

Most people think that temperature is a measure of heat. Actually, **temperature** is a measure of the average energy of motion of the particles in matter. At 50°F (about 10°C) the particles in the air move more slowly than they do at 80°F (about 27°C). They have less thermal energy.

In the investigation you heated a balloon and observed how its volume changed. You can measure temperature by observing how the volume of a liquid changes as it is heated or cooled. One kind of thermometer has liquid in a narrow tube. When the liquid gets hotter, its volume changes and it moves up the tube. When it gets colder, it moves back down the tube.

✔ **What does temperature measure?**

Temperature and Thermal Energy

Two pieces of matter can be at the same temperature but not have the same amount of thermal energy. Temperature measures the *average* amount of motion of the particles in a piece of matter. Thermal energy is the *total* energy of motion of the particles in a piece of matter. More matter equals more particles. More particles equals more energy of motion.

When a drop of cold water falls into a hot pan or skillet, the water boils away in a second or two. Its particles speed up and fly off. Little thermal energy is needed to warm the drop to 100°C (212°F). A pan full of cold water has many more particles. It takes much more thermal energy to boil the water.

✔ **What is the difference between temperature and thermal energy?**

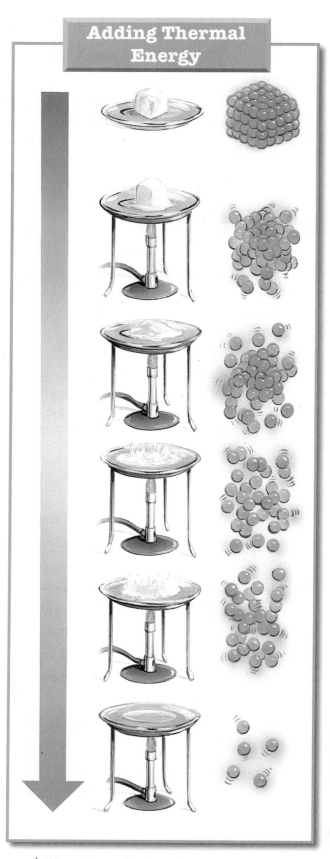

▲ When thermal energy is added to frozen water, the water slowly changes from a solid to a liquid and then from a liquid to a gas. When thermal energy is removed from water vapor, this process is reversed.

Adding Thermal Energy

When thermal energy is added to matter, the particles in the matter move faster. Below 0°C (32°F) water is solid ice. The particles move back and forth around one point. As you add thermal energy, the particles move faster and faster. At 0°C (32°F) the particles begin to move past and around each other. The ice melts.

After ice melts, adding energy causes the particles of liquid water to move faster and faster. The temperature of the liquid water rises. After a while, particles begin to fly away from the water's surface. The water boils, or rapidly becomes a gas.

✔ **What happens to matter when you add thermal energy?**

Water vapor in the air loses energy to the cold air outside the window. First, it becomes small water droplets on the glass. Then, it becomes a solid and forms these ice crystals. ▼

Summary

Energy is the ability to cause change. Energy is needed to move something from one place to another. The total energy of motion of the particles in matter is thermal energy. More particles mean more total thermal energy. Temperature is a measure of the average motion of the particles in matter. Adding thermal energy causes the particles of matter to move faster.

Review

1. What does temperature measure?

2. If all particles in a metal spoon start moving faster, how has the spoon's temperature changed?

3. When you add thermal energy to matter, what happens?

4. **Critical Thinking** The water in two glasses has the same average energy of motion. One glass holds 250 mL, and one holds 400 mL. Which glass of water has more thermal energy? Why?

5. **Test Prep** The particles in two pieces of chocolate have the same average energy of motion. One piece has more mass than the other. Which piece is at a higher temperature?

   A the piece with more mass

   B the piece with less mass

   C the piece with more thermal energy

   D They are the same temperature.

LINKS

MATH LINK

Measure Temperature On a Fahrenheit temperature scale, water freezes at 32°F and boils at 212°F. How many Fahrenheit degrees are between the two temperatures? Now think about the boiling and freezing temperatures in Celsius degrees. Are Celsius degrees bigger or smaller units of measure than Fahrenheit degrees?

WRITING LINK

Expressive Writing—Poem Write a poem for your family that describes a hot day and a cold day. You could describe how your neighborhood looks, things people do, and how you feel.

SOCIAL STUDIES LINK

Early Thermometers Find out who invented the first thermometers and temperature scales and how the thermometers worked. Make a time line that shows what you learned.

GO ONLINE TECHNOLOGY LINK

Visit the Harcourt Learning Site for related links, activities, and resources.
www.harcourtschool.com

WELCOME TO
THE
LEARNING
SITE

LESSON 2

How Can Thermal Energy Be Transferred?

In this lesson, you can . . .

INVESTIGATE one way thermal energy is transferred.

LEARN ABOUT the three ways thermal energy is transferred.

LINK to math, writing, art, and technology.

Hot Air

Activity Purpose Have you ever watched a hawk soaring high in the sky? The hawk rides on air that is moving up. But what makes the air move up? In this investigation you will **observe** the effects of air moving up and **infer** why the air is moving up.

Materials

- sheet of construction paper
- scissors
- straight pin
- 20-cm piece of thread
- desk lamp
- bulb

CAUTION

Activity Procedure

1. **CAUTION** **Be careful when using scissors.** Cut out a spiral strip about 2 cm wide from the sheet of construction paper. (Picture A)

2. **CAUTION** **Be careful with the pin.** With the pin, carefully make a small hole through the center of the paper spiral. Tie the thread through the hole.

◄ A glass blower uses a tube to blow air into hot glass. The long tube keeps heat from the glass away from his face. How can you tell the glass is hot?

E46

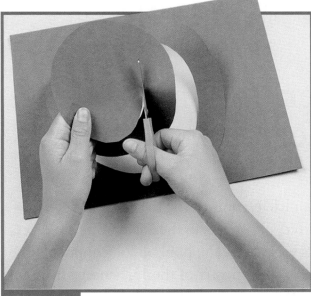
Picture A

Picture B

3 Hold the spiral above your head by the thread. Blow upward on it. **Observe** the spiral.

4 Carefully hold the spiral a few centimeters above the unlighted desk lamp. **Observe** the spiral.

5 Turn on the desk lamp. Let the bulb warm up for a few minutes.

6 Carefully hold the spiral a few centimeters above the lighted desk lamp. **Observe** the spiral. (Picture B)

Draw Conclusions

1. What did you **observe** in Steps 3, 4, and 6?

2. What caused the result you **observed** in Step 3?

3. What was different about Steps 4 and 6?

4. **Scientists at Work** Scientists often **infer** from **observations** a cause that they can't see directly. What do you think caused the result you observed in Step 6?

Investigate Further Hold the spiral a few centimeters away from the side of the lighted desk lamp. **Observe** the spiral. What can you **infer** from your observation?

Process Skill Tip

You need to **observe** what an object does in different situations before you can **infer** the causes of what it does.

How Thermal Energy Is Transferred

Heat

FIND OUT

- what heat is
- three ways thermal energy is transferred

VOCABULARY

heat
conduction
convection
radiation
infrared radiation

When you touch an icicle, some of the thermal energy in your hand is transferred, or moved, to the icicle. Your hand gets colder. The icicle gets warmer. If you hold on long enough, the icicle melts completely. This transfer of thermal energy from one piece of matter to another is called **heat**.

Thermal energy is transferred naturally from hot matter to cold matter. When you walk in warm sand, some of the thermal energy from the sand moves to your feet. The soles of your feet get warmer. When your lips touch a cold can of soft drink, thermal energy is transferred from your lips to the can. Your lips lose thermal energy and get cooler. The can gains thermal energy and gets warmer.

Thermal energy is transferred in three ways—conduction, convection, and radiation. You will learn more about these processes on the next pages.

✔ **What is heat?**

◄ The burning gases from the artist's torch are very hot. A large amount of thermal energy moves to the metal where the gases touch it. The metal glows and quickly melts.

Conduction

You can tell if tap water is hot by touching the metal faucet it is running through. This works because the particles of hot water are moving fast and bump into the particles of the faucet, causing them to start moving fast as well. In other words, the particles of hot water transfer thermal energy to the faucet. Soon the faucet and the water are the same temperature. The transfer of thermal energy by particles bumping into each other is called conduction (kuhn•DUHK•shuhn).

Conduction is how thermal energy moves from an electric stove burner to a metal pan. Conduction is also how you can get a painful burn if you touch the pan.

Most metals conduct thermal energy well. They are good *conductors*. But some kinds of matter do not conduct thermal energy so well. A foam cup, for example, is a very poor

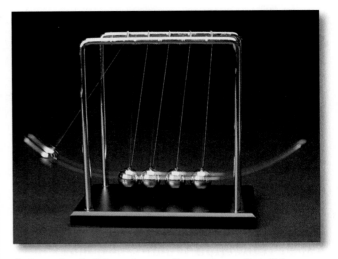

▲ A moving ball transfers motion energy when it bumps into its neighbor. A particle in matter transfers motion energy when it bumps into a nearby particle.

conductor of thermal energy. If a foam cup were filled with hot cocoa, the cocoa would get cold long before the outside of the cup became hot to the touch. Materials that don't conduct thermal energy well are called *insulators*.

✔ **What is conduction?**

As the burner gets hotter, the particles in it move faster because they have more thermal energy. ▼

◀ Thermal energy moves from the burner to the pot to the water by conduction.

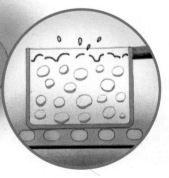

▲ The particles in the pot bump into nearby particles of water. The bumping makes the water particles move faster. The water gets hotter. The pot transfers thermal energy to the water.

The particles in the burner bump into particles in the bottom of the pot. The bumping causes the particles in the pot to move faster. The pot becomes hotter. ▶

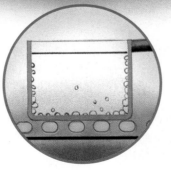

Convection

Unlike particles in solids, particles in liquids and gases move from one place to another. In the investigation, you held a paper spiral above a lighted bulb. The heated air above the light bulb moved enough to cause the spiral to twirl. In this case, a large group of hot particles of air moved and transferred thermal energy. This type of energy transfer in a liquid or a gas is called **convection** (kuhn•VEK•shuhn).

As the air near a hot object gets hot, it takes up more space, or expands. You saw a balloon expand in the investigation on pages E40–E41. Because the hot air is less dense, it is forced up by the cooler, denser air around it.

As the hot air is forced up, it warms the air around it. As the hot air cools, its density increases, and it sinks. This process can repeat. The air can move in a circle—warming, being pushed up, cooling, sinking, and then warming again. This pattern of movement is called *convection current*.

✔ **What is convection?**

The air above the stove gets warm. Cool air pushes in and forces the warm air up. The warm air moves through the room and transfers energy to the things around it.

◄ As cooler air pushes up air warmed by a campfire, sparks, smoke, and soot are pushed up also.

The warm air slowly cools and sinks to the floor.

Cool air moves toward the stove and forces up the warm air near the stove. Then the cool air is heated. This cycle of convection currents transfers thermal energy from the stove to the rest of the room.

A Hot-Air Balloon

1 A hot-air balloon is a large empty sack that is placed with its opening above a burner. The burner heats the air. The density of the heated air decreases. It is pushed up into the balloon by cooler air. The balloon soon fills with warm air.

2 Convection keeps air inside the balloon hot. As the warm air is forced upward by the cooler air below, it cools. The cooled air sinks and is warmed again by the burner.

3 The density of the warm air inside the balloon is less than the density of the cooler air outside the balloon. The balloon filled with hot air is pushed up. When the balloon is floating, the push of the cool air upward equals the weight of the filled balloon and its passengers.

Radiation

The sun produces great amounts of thermal energy. But there's no matter between Earth and the sun to which it can transfer that energy. So energy can't reach Earth by conduction or convection. The sun transfers bundles of energy that can move through matter and empty space. Bundles of energy that move through matter and empty space are called **radiation** (ray•dee•AY•shuhn).

You sense some bundles of energy with your eyes. This radiation is visible light. You sense other bundles of energy with your skin. These bundles of energy are carrying heat. Bundles of energy that carry heat are called **infrared** (in•fruh•RED) **radiation**. Outside on a sunny day, your skin feels warm because of infrared radiation from the sun.

Some things can transfer energy by conduction, convection, and radiation at the same time. For example, the air above a

campfire is warmed by convection. This hot air quickly warms your hands by conduction. You can warm your hands around the sides of a campfire, too. But it is radiation, not hot air, that is warming them.

✔ **How is thermal energy transferred from the sun?**

▼ A gila (HEE•luh) monster warms its body by moving to a sunny place where its skin absorbs infrared radiation.

Not to scale

◄ The sun's energy moves as infrared radiation through 150 million kilometers (about 93 million mi) of empty space before reaching Earth.

Summary

Heat is the transfer of thermal energy from one piece of matter to another. Thermal energy naturally moves from warm matter to cool matter. Conduction and convection need moving particles of matter to transfer thermal energy. Energy is transferred as infrared radiation through matter and empty space.

Review

1. Which type of thermal-energy transfer requires moving liquids and gases?

2. How is energy transferred through empty space?

3. How is thermal energy transferred when particles are touching?

4. **Critical Thinking** Which type of thermal-energy transfer is prevented when a baker uses a potholder to remove hot cookie sheets from an oven?

5. **Test Prep** What property must be different between two pieces of matter for thermal energy to be transferred between them?
   A density
   B mass
   C temperature
   D volume

LINKS

MATH LINK

Solve a Two-Step Problem The ability of air conditioners to cool air is rated in British thermal units (Btus). It takes about 12,000 Btus to cool a room that measures 500 square feet. How many Btus are needed to cool a room with 100 square feet of floor space?

WRITING LINK

Persuasive Writing—Business Letter Imagine that you are selling a furnace for a house to a homeowner. Write a letter describing the furnace and giving reasons for the homeowner to buy it.

ART LINK

Icons A "don't walk" sign that shows a walking person inside a circle with a slanted line across it is an icon. So is a smiley face. Design icons that show (1) heating by conduction, (2) heating by convection, and (3) heating by radiation.

TECHNOLOGY LINK

Learn more about how thermal energy is used to shape glass by viewing *Glass Blowing* on the **Harcourt Science Newsroom Video.**

E53

How Is Thermal Energy Produced and Used?

In this lesson, you can . . .

INVESTIGATE temperatures in a solar cooker.

LEARN ABOUT ways to produce and use thermal energy.

LINK to math, writing, literature, and technology.

◄ Most people like pizza best when it is crisp and fresh from the oven. This pizza oven burns wood to produce thermal energy for baking. In what other ways is thermal energy produced and used?

INVESTIGATE

Temperatures in a Solar Cooker

Activity Purpose You know that heat from a campfire can cook hot dogs. Heat from the sun can cook them, too. A solar cooker uses a mirror to reflect, or bounce, infrared radiation from the sun to the food. In this activity you will make a mirror to reflect infrared radiation onto a thermometer. You will then **gather, record, display,** and **interpret data** about the temperatures in the cooker.

Materials

- 2 sheets of graph paper
- shoe-box lid
- aluminum foil
- thermometer
- clock or watch
- scissors
- poster board
- glue
- string

Activity Procedure

1 Label the two sheets of graph paper like the example shown on page E55.

2 Place the thermometer in the shoe-box lid. (Picture A)

3 Place the lid in sunlight. **Record** the temperature immediately. Then record the temperature each minute for 10 minutes.

4 In the shade, remove the thermometer from the shoe-box lid.

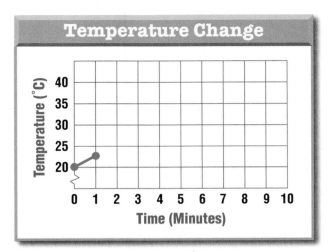

Temperature Change

Picture A

5. Cut a rectangle of poster board 10 cm by 30 cm. Glue foil to one side. Let the glue dry for 10 minutes.

6. **CAUTION** **Be careful when using scissors.** Use scissors to punch a hole about 2 cm from each end of the rectangle. Make a curved reflector by drawing the poster board ends toward each other with string until they are about 20 cm apart. Tie the string.

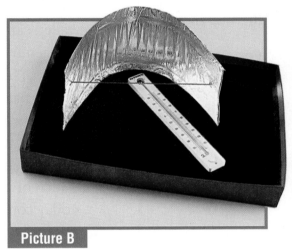
Picture B

7. Put the curved reflector in the shoe-box lid. Put the thermometer in the center of the curve. Repeat Step 3. (Picture B)

8. Make a line graph of the measurements in Step 3. Make another line graph of the measurements in Step 7.

Draw Conclusions

1. Describe the temperature changes shown on each graph.

2. **Compare** the temperature changes shown on the two graphs.

3. **Infer** what may have caused the differences in the temperatures on the two graphs.

Investigate Further Use what you observed in the activity to **form a hypothesis** about how quickly a different size cooker would warm up. **Plan and conduct an experiment** to test your hypothesis.

Process Skill Tip

When scientists **interpret data** shown on graphs, they look at the slants of the lines on the graphs. In your graphs a line with a steep slant means a fast change in the temperature. A line with a less steep slant means a slower temperature change.

Using Thermal Energy

Burning Fuel

FIND OUT

- ways to produce thermal energy
- uses of the sun's energy
- examples of wasted thermal energy

VOCABULARY

fuel
solar energy

When something burns, it gets hot. Burning releases thermal energy and light. Many homes are heated by furnaces that burn oil or natural gas. Some cooking stoves burn natural gas. Any material that can burn is called a **fuel**. Wood was the first fuel people used, and it is still used today. Wood contains a substance called carbon. When wood burns, the carbon combines with oxygen from the air. A new substance called carbon dioxide forms. Plants use carbon dioxide to make food. Carbon dioxide is also part of the *greenhouse effect*, which helps keep Earth warm. (See page D12.)

Many fuels contain carbon. Coal is mainly carbon. Fuel oil and natural gas both contain carbon. Much of the thermal energy people use today comes from burning fuels that contain carbon.

✔ **What happens when a fuel burns?**

Burning coal releases thermal energy. In some houses the energy is used to warm air directly. In others it is used to heat water in radiators. Like the burner below the coal, a gas stove burns natural gas. The thermal energy released from the flame is used for cooking and baking.

Most of the electricity used in the United States is produced by energy stations that burn fuels.

Solar Energy

The energy given off by the sun is called **solar energy**. People use solar energy to heat water. They put solar panels on top of their roofs. The panels absorb infrared radiation from the sun. The radiation heats water flowing through the panels. The hot water can be used for washing. Solar energy also heats some homes and businesses.

Solar energy can also be used to cook. A solar cooker gathers infrared radiation from the sun and reflects it onto food. You know this works because you measured temperature change in a solar cooker in the investigation.

The sun is the source of most energy on Earth. Even the thermal energy in fossil fuels, such as coal and oil, came from the sun. These fuels have stored energy from plants and animals that lived long ago. The plants used the sun's energy to make food by photosynthesis. The animals got their energy by eating plants or other animals.

✔ **What is solar energy?**

Rooftop solar panels like these are used to heat water.

An electric water heater contains a tank of water. Under the tank is an electric heating coil.

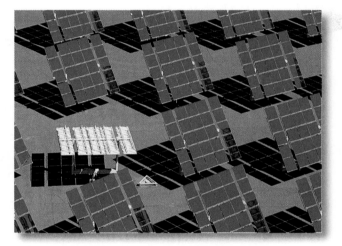

▲ These mirrors focus the sun's thermal energy on a target. The thermal energy gathered in the target is used to produce electricity.

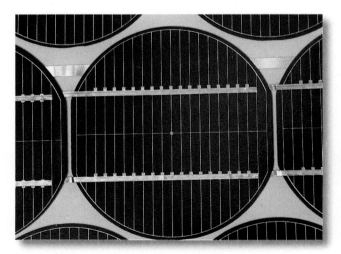

▲ Small appliances such as calculators and watches often use solar cells such as these to supply electricity. Solar cells can also keep batteries charged.

E57

Waste Heat

Using fuel for energy has a side effect. It often makes thermal energy that no one wants or needs. This unneeded thermal energy is called *waste heat*. For example, a campfire produces thermal energy even if the campers need it only for light. Even a campfire used for warmth sends most of its thermal energy straight up, where it is not useful to campers.

Common light sources such as candles and bulbs also make waste heat. So do car engines, electric energy stations, computers, and people. Almost any time energy is produced or used, thermal energy is a part of the process. Much of that thermal energy is not useful, and it can even be harmful. It must be gotten rid of. For example, cars have radiators to carry thermal energy that is not needed away from the engine.

✔ **What is waste heat?**

▲ Light bulbs give off both light and heat. But most of the thermal energy from light bulbs in your home is waste heat.

A candle produces less light than a light bulb but can produce more thermal energy. Most of the thermal energy from candles is not used. ▶

Electric energy stations can't change all thermal energy from fuel into electricity. There is always some waste heat produced. One way to remove this waste heat is to let it heat water. The hot water then cools in towers or ponds. ▼

Fans and radiators carry waste heat away from a car engine. If either the fan or the radiator stops working, the engine soon overheats and stops working as well. ▼

Radiator

▲ Large, very fast computers need special cooling systems such as this one to get rid of waste heat from wiring and circuits.

Summary

Much of the thermal energy used by people today comes from burning fuels that contain carbon. Energy given off by the sun is called solar energy. Solar energy can be used to heat homes and businesses, heat water, and cook food. Most processes that use energy also produce thermal energy. If this thermal energy isn't useful, it is waste heat.

Review

1. What is a fuel?

2. What happens when a fuel burns?

3. What do we call energy given off by the sun?

4. **Critical Thinking** What happens to most waste heat?

5. **Test Prep** Which of the following removes waste heat?

   A car radiator

   B solar cell

   C stove burner

   D windmill

LINKS

MATH LINK

Solve a Two-Step Problem A water heater produces a total of 500 Btus of thermal energy each hour. Only 400 Btus go to heat water. How much waste heat is produced per hour? How much waste heat is produced in a 24-hour day?

WRITING LINK

Persuasive Writing—Opinion A new kind of light bulb, called a compact fluorescent bulb, produces less waste heat than an incandescent light bulb. Write an ad telling consumers why you think they should use this new bulb.

LITERATURE LINK

A Cold Time in the North In Jack London's short story "To Build a Fire," a man lost in the wilderness has a lot of trouble getting thermal energy. Read the story and suggest other ways the man might have kept warm.

GO ONLINE TECHNOLOGY LINK

Learn more about fossil fuels and thermal energy by visiting this Internet site.

www.scilinks.org/harcourt

REFRIGERANTS

Hot weather and high humidity can be unpleasant. For some people, such as older people or those with lung diseases, heat can even be dangerous. Their bodies don't work well enough to stay cool. They need to be kept cool by air conditioning.

Air Conditioning

You already know that when thermal energy moves from one place to another, the place it moves *to* gets hotter. The place it moves *from* gets colder. That's part of what makes air conditioners work.

An air conditioner is a machine that uses energy to move heat in the opposite direction from where it would flow on its own. An air conditioner moves heat from inside a house to the outdoors, where it's hotter. To do this, an air conditioner uses a material called a *refrigerant* (ree•FRIJ•er•uhnt).

In an air conditioner, liquid refrigerant is pumped under pressure through tubes. In the part of the air conditioner that is inside

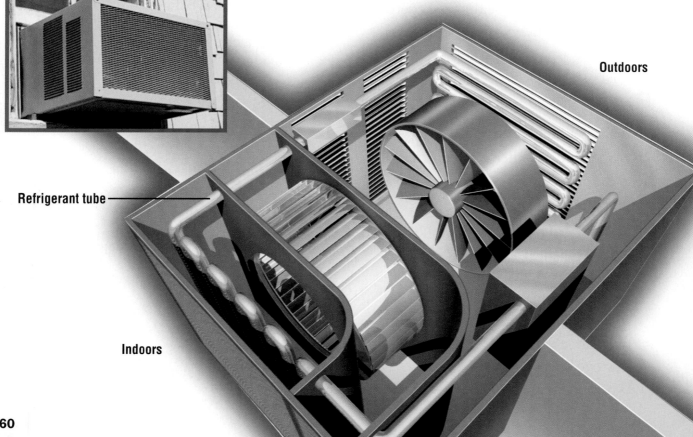

Outdoors

Refrigerant tube

Indoors

the house, the refrigerant gets thermal energy from the air. This causes it to boil. The refrigerant, which is now a gas, is pumped to the part of the air conditioner that is outside the house. There the gas is squeezed and changed back to a liquid. It must lose thermal energy to do this. The thermal energy moves to the outside air.

The first refrigerant used was ammonia (uh•MOHN•yuh). It's still used for large refrigerators in factories. It has an unpleasant smell, however, and it is a poison. Leaks of ammonia, common in the first air conditioners, can cause breathing problems for any people nearby. The second refrigerant used was methyl chloride (METH•uhl KLOR•eyed). But when methyl chloride leaked into the air, it exploded.

Freon

Freon (FREE•ahn) is a colorless, tasteless, odorless gas that doesn't explode or make people ill. It also boils at a temperature that works best for refrigerants. So when Thomas Midgley discovered Freon, he thought he'd found the perfect refrigerant.

Freon made home air conditioners and modern refrigerators possible. From its discovery in the 1930s until the 1990s, Freon was almost the only refrigerant used. In the 1970s, however, scientists discovered that Freon and similar refrigerants harm Earth's protective ozone layer. So the use of Freon as a refrigerant was banned in the United States. Scientists started looking for other materials to use.

Old and New Refrigerants

Ammonia and other "old" refrigerants may be used to replace Freon in refrigerators and home air conditioners. New machines use less ammonia and are sealed more tightly. Other substances that are like Freon but are less damaging are being developed. However, none of these materials work very well in cars, where refrigerants sometimes must both heat and cool the air. Scientists at the University of Illinois are testing ordinary carbon dioxide gas as a refrigerant for cars. So, some of the gas that you breathe out may end up cooling you off!

THINK ABOUT IT

1. Why do you think refrigerant leaks were so common in early air conditioners?
2. Where does the thermal energy that leaves an air-conditioned home go?

CAREERS
HVAC TECHNICIAN

What They Do HVAC (heating, ventilation, and air conditioning) technicians install, repair, and maintain heating and cooling systems. These systems may be in buildings, vehicles, or machinery such as the refrigerator in your home.

Education and Training Most HVAC technicians need a high-school education that includes math, electricity, and technical drawing. Most employers prefer technicians to have also finished either a two-year apprenticeship or a technical program.

WEB LINK For Science and Technology updates, visit the Harcourt Internet site.
www.harcourtschool.com

Frederick McKinley Jones
INVENTOR

Modern refrigerated truck

Frederick Jones was an orphan by the age of nine and quit school after sixth grade. He was sent to live with a Catholic priest in Kentucky. As an older teenager, he moved to Minnesota and began a job fixing farm machinery. He studied electricity and mechanical engineering when he wasn't working.

Jones served in World War I. When he came back from the war, he built a radio transmitter in his town. He also invented machine parts so that movies with sound could be run on small projectors. During the early 1930s, he heard a man who owned trucks telling his boss that a whole shipment of chicken had spoiled because of the heat. Jones began to design a refrigeration unit for trucks.

Earlier ways to keep trucks cold took up too much room. Most also fell apart quickly because of being shaken during travel. Jones built his first refrigeration unit by using odds and ends of machine parts. It was small, shake-proof, and lightweight. But it was made to go beneath the truck and broke down often because mud and dirt from roads got inside.

After a time, Jones designed and made a unit that went on top of a truck. He and his boss formed a partnership to build the trucks. Jones was vice-president of the company.

The refrigerated trucks could ship more than food. During World War II, Jones's invention saved lives. Because the units were portable, badly needed blood and medicine could be shipped safely to battlefields.

Jones continued to work on his inventions. He eventually received more than 60 patents. More than 40 of them were for refrigeration products.

THINK ABOUT IT

1. What were some design problems that Jones solved to make a working truck-refrigerator?
2. What foods do you eat that might be shipped in a refrigerated truck?

COMPARE CONDUCTORS

Which material conducts thermal energy fastest?

Materials

- 3 thermometers
- warm tap water
- tape
- jar
- plastic, wood, and metal spoons of about the same size

Procedure

❶ Carefully tape the bulb of a thermometer to the handle of each spoon.

❷ Fill the jar with warm tap water to a level that will cover only the bottoms of the spoons. Carefully place the spoons in the jar.

❸ Measure and record the temperature of each spoon every minute for 5 minutes.

Draw Conclusions

Which spoon conducted thermal energy most quickly? How do you know?

THERMAL ENERGY

How do different amounts of water affect melting?

Materials

- warm tap water
- 2 jars, 1 large and 1 small
- 4 ice cubes that are the same size
- clock or watch

Procedure

❶ Fill each container almost full with warm tap water.

❷ Put two ice cubes in each container.

❸ Measure the time it takes for each pair of cubes to melt completely.

Draw Conclusions

Did one pair melt faster than the other pair? Why were the times different?

Vocabulary Review

Use the terms below to complete the sentences. The page numbers in ( ) tell you where to look in the chapter if you need help.

energy (E42)   **conduction** (E49)

kinetic energy (E42)   **convection** (E50)

thermal   **radiation** (E52)
  energy (E42)   **infrared radiation** (E52)

temperature (E43)   **fuel** (E56)

heat (E48)   **solar energy** (E57)

1. ＿＿ is the transfer of thermal energy.

2. The ability to cause a change is ＿＿.

3. A material that is burned to produce thermal energy is ＿＿.

4. ＿＿ is a measure of the average energy of motion of particles in matter.

5. The total energy of motion of particles of matter is ＿＿.

6. ＿＿ is the transfer of thermal energy by particles bumping into each other.

7. Radiation that carries thermal energy is called ＿＿.

8. ＿＿ is bundles of energy that can travel through empty space.

9. Energy given off by the sun is called ＿＿.

10. ＿＿ is the transfer of thermal energy that can occur only in a liquid or gas.

11. Because an object such as a bicycle is moving, it has ＿＿.

Connect Concepts

Fill in the blanks in the diagram below to correctly describe some of the main concepts of this chapter.

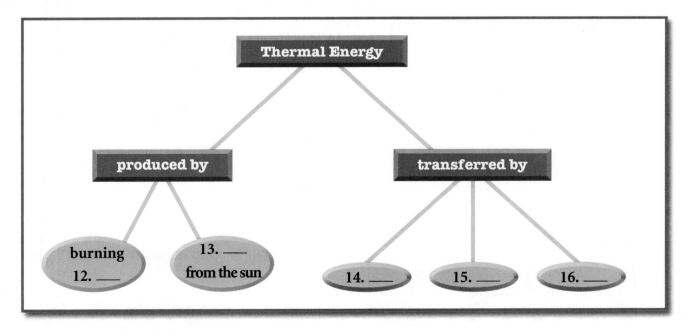

Thermal Energy

produced by — burning 12. ＿＿ — 13. ＿＿ from the sun

transferred by — 14. ＿＿ — 15. ＿＿ — 16. ＿＿

Check Understanding

Write the letter of the best choice.

17. Most thermometers work because matter ____ when it is heated.
    A disappears
    B collects radiation
    C expands
    D loses mass

18. A thermometer measures the ____ energy of motion of particles of matter.
    F total
    G long-term
    H solar
    J average

19. Two pieces of the same kind of matter have the same temperature. The one with the larger mass has more —
    A conduction
    B thermal energy
    C convection
    D solar energy

20. When thermal energy moves from one piece of matter to another, the transfer is called —
    F solar energy
    G heat
    H temperature
    J fuel

21. Thermal energy can be transferred by conduction from one piece of matter to another only if the two pieces are —
    A liquids   C solids
    B touching   D fuel

22. Convection takes place only in liquids and —
    F gases   H solids
    G energies   J states

23. Energy that travels from the sun to Earth is being transferred by —
    A conduction   C convection
    B fuel   D radiation

Critical Thinking

24. You put a pot of water on the burner of an electric stove and turn the burner on high heat. The water soon boils. Describe how the heat from the stove gets to the water in the pot.

25. A solar panel on a roof collects solar energy to warm water for a house. Describe how the heat is transferred from the sun to the panel, and then from the panel to the water.

Process Skills Review

26. What property of particles of matter do you **measure** with a thermometer?

27. Suppose a thermometer is hanging from a thread inside a jar completely empty of gases or liquids. You **infer** that infrared radiation is falling on the thermometer. What observation would lead you to this inference? Explain.

28. A line graph has the temperature scale on the left and the time scale on the bottom. If the line is level, what can you conclude by **interpreting** the temperature **data** shown?

Performance Assessment

Temperature Balance

Your teacher will give you a thermometer, a straw, a full glass of warm water, a full glass of cool water, and an empty glass. Your goal is to use the materials to end up with a glass that is half full of water that is about room temperature. You can't wait for the two full glasses to cool and warm naturally. Explain what you did and why it worked.

Sound

Have you ever heard nothing at all? Probably not. Even in a space suit while orbiting Earth, you can still hear the sound of your blood flowing and your heart beating!

Vocabulary Preview

sound
compression
sound wave
amplitude
wavelength
loudness
pitch
speed of sound
echo
sonic boom

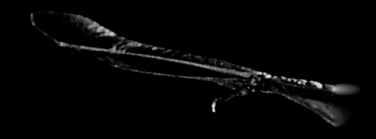

Fast Fact

Bats don't use their eyes to catch prey. They use their ears! Bats send out high-pitched squeaks and clicks that bounce off objects. The returning echoes direct them to their prey. Using echoes, some bats can find an insect as thin as a human hair in total darkness!

Fast Fact

SUMATRA

Jakarta

JAVA

When a volcano on the island of Krakatau, Indonesia, erupted in 1883, it made the loudest natural sound ever observed. Heard 4500 km (2796 mi) away, the eruption was so strong that it blew the island apart!

Fast Fact

Every type of animal has a different hearing and voice range. When the Canadian Pacific Railroad switched to air-driven horns, large numbers of female moose were killed by trains. Biologists determined that the low-pitched horns sounded like the calls of male moose! Changing the pitch of the horns has greatly reduced the number of moose on the tracks.

Sound and Hearing

	Hearing Range (Vibrations per Second)	Voice Range (Vibrations per Second)
Bats	1,000–120,000	10,000–120,000
Cats	60–65,000	750–1500
Dogs	15–50,000	452–1080
Dolphins	150–150,000	7000–120,000
Humans	20–20,000	80–1500
Robins	250–20,000	2000–15,000

What Is Sound?

In this lesson, you can . . .

INVESTIGATE making and hearing sounds.

LEARN ABOUT the way sound travels.

LINK to math, writing, social studies, and technology.

Sound from a Ruler

Activity Purpose Sit still a moment and listen. What do you hear? People talking, car horns honking, dogs barking, the refrigerator humming? We hear different kinds of sounds all day long. In this investigation you will **observe** how a sound is made. You will also observe some ways to change sound.

Materials

- plastic ruler

Activity Procedure

1. Place the ruler on a tabletop. Let 15 to 20 cm stick out over the edge of the table.

2. Hold the ruler tightly against the tabletop with one hand. Use the thumb of your other hand to flick, or strum, the free end of the ruler. (Picture A)

3. **Observe** the ruler with your eyes. **Record** your observations.

4. Repeat Step 2. **Observe** the ruler with your ears. **Record** your observations.

◄ Hitting cymbals together produces a loud sound that can be heard over that of an entire band or orchestra.

Picture A

Picture B

5 Flick the ruler harder. **Observe** the results. **Record** your observations.

6 Change the length of the ruler sticking over the edge of the table, and repeat Steps 2 through 5. **Observe** the results. **Record** your observations. (Picture B)

Draw Conclusions

1. What did you **observe** in Step 3?

2. What did you **observe** in Step 4?

3. **Make a hypothesis** to explain what you **observed** in Steps 3 and 4. How could you test your explanation?

4. **Scientists at Work** When scientists want to learn more about an experiment, they change one part of it and **observe** the effect. What did you change in Step 6? What effect did you observe?

Investigate Further Place one ear on the tabletop. Cover the other ear with your hand. Have a partner repeat Steps 1 and 2. What do you **observe? Plan and conduct an experiment** to test this **hypothesis**: Sounds are louder if you listen through a solid material than if you listen through air.

Process Skill Tip

When people use the word *observe*, they usually think of seeing. But you can use all your senses to **observe**. In this investigation you also used your sense of hearing to observe the effects of the movements of the ruler.

E69

Characteristics of Sound

FIND OUT

- **causes of sounds**
- **how sound travels**
- **how your ears help you hear**

VOCABULARY

sound
compression
sound wave
amplitude
wavelength

Vibrations

In the investigation, you saw the ruler make quick back-and-forth movements after you snapped it. These back-and-forth movements are called *vibrations* (vy•BRAY•shuhnz). After you strum a guitar string, it vibrates for a while and slowly stops. You hear the guitar note start and then slowly fade away. When you hum, you can feel the vibrations of your larynx (LAIR•inks), or voice box, by putting your fingers on the outside of your throat. When you stop humming, the vibration also stops. **Sound** is vibrations that you can hear. An object vibrates to make sounds. This vibration causes particles in the air around the object to vibrate as well. You can see and feel the object vibrate, but not the particles in the air.

✔ **What is sound?**

As the ruler vibrates, the particles in air are pushed closer together. The areas where air is pushed together are called compressions (kuhm•PRESH•uhnz). ▶

When one end of the ruler is snapped, it vibrates, or moves back and forth. The ruler pushes against the air around it. ▼

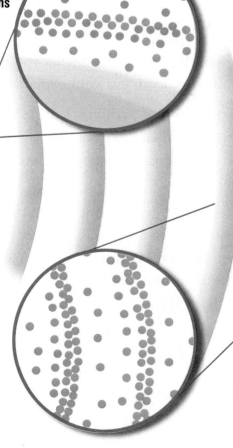

Each compression moves away from the ruler, in the same way that ripples move away from a pebble thrown into a pond. ▶

Traveling Waves

The vibrations of the guitar string, the ruler, and your voice box push and then pull on the particles of air around them. As they push, they increase the pressure in the air. The area where air is pushed together is called a **compression**. As the vibrations pull, they decrease the pressure in the air. This results in alternating areas of high and low pressure in the air. **Sound waves** are quickly moving areas of high and low pressure. All sound is carried through matter as sound waves.

Sound waves move out in all directions from a vibrating object. You can hear something making sound all around you, above you, or below you. As the sound waves move away from their source, their energy is spread over a larger area. The farther you are from the source of a sound, the softer the sound will be.

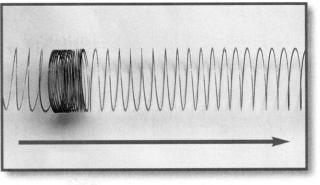

▲ A wave travels through this spring toy just as a sound wave travels through the air. The places where the springs are close together are like compressions, or areas of high pressure, in the air. The places where the springs are far apart are like areas of low pressure in the air.

Most of the sound we hear travels through the air. In the investigation you found that sound waves travel through other materials, too. Sound waves can move through each state of matter.

✔ **In what direction do sound waves travel?**

1 Each instrument in a marching band makes a sound by vibrating something. For example, the head of a bass drum vibrates when it is hit. The vibrations cause sound waves in the air. The audience watching and listening to the parade hears the drumbeat.

2 Sound waves can also travel through liquids. These underwater swimmers could hear the band play if it marched by the pool.

3 Someone behind a closed door could hear the band, too, because sound waves can also travel through solids.

E71

Waves

Ka-plunk—you hear a rock fall into a pond. You turn toward the sound and see ripples on the water. You put your hand in the water and feel the ripples lap against your fingers. The small ripples in water are an example of a wave.

How did the rock form the ripples? The rock transferred kinetic energy to the water as it fell into the pond. This caused a wave to form. As the energy moved through the water, it made the water's surface rise and fall.

You can use how a wave rises and falls to describe it. The greatest distance that the water rises from its rest, or calm, position is called **amplitude** (AM•pluh•tood). The more energy a wave carries, the greater its amplitude. **Wavelength** is the distance in a straight line from one place on a ripple to the same place on the next ripple.

✔ **What causes a wave to form?**

▼ This picture shows a snapshot of a wave on a pond. When a rock falls into a calm pond, it pushes the nearby water particles. These particles then push on their neighbors. The movement of the particles is a wave that moves through the water.

When you drop a rock into a calm pond, it causes ripples. Each ripple forms a ring that gets wider as it moves through the water. The source of the rings is the place where the rock was dropped into the water. ▼

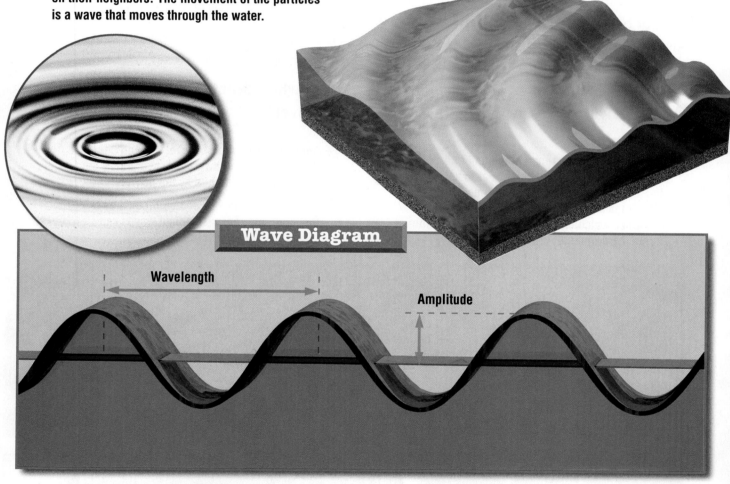

Wave Diagram

Wavelength

Amplitude

▲ The straight, dark-red ribbon shows where the calm, smooth surface of the pond would normally be. It is called the *rest position* of the water. As you can see, part of the wave is above the rest position and part of the wave is below it. A drawing of the ripple shape is called a wave diagram. You can use a wave diagram to show wavelength and amplitude.

The jangle of an alarm clock is a sound. The sound wave moves out from the alarm in all directions, much like ripples on a pond. ▶

The ripples of this wave model the areas of high and low pressure in the sound wave further below. The peaks, or high points, show where pressure is greatest. The valleys, or low points, show where pressure is lowest. ▼

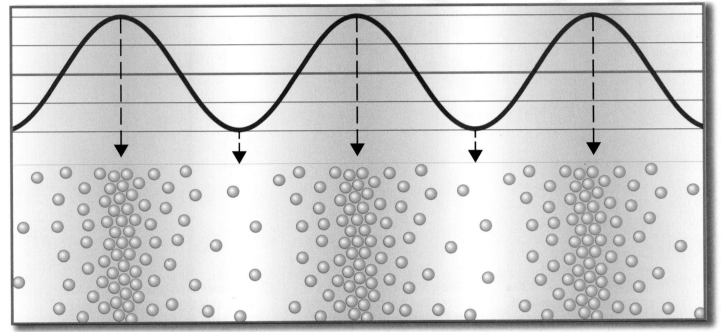

▲ A sound wave is moving areas of high and low pressure. The high pressure occurs where particles are bunched together. The low pressure occurs where they are spread apart. Suppose you could stack the particles in each thin slice of this sound wave. The stacks would form a pattern of peaks and valleys just like the wave shown above.

Waves and Sound

Waves on a pond are like sound waves. They both move out in all directions from the source. When you trace the ripple shape of a wave with your finger, your finger's back and forth movements are like the vibrations that cause sounds. In fact, scientists use the ripple shapes of waves to model sound waves.

The peaks and valleys of a wave stand for the areas of high and low pressure in a sound wave. The peaks match where pressure is highest. The valleys match where pressure is lowest. If the source of the sound is vibrating faster, the peaks will be closer together.

The amplitude, or tallness, of a wave stands for the loudness of a sound. A taller wave stands for a louder sound.

✔ **What part of a wave diagram models a low pressure part of a sound wave?**

A human ear has three main parts— the outer ear, the middle ear, and the inner ear. Each plays a role in helping you hear.

1 The outer ear is like a funnel. It collects sounds and guides them to the eardrum.

2 The middle ear is made up of three tiny bones that connect the outer ear to the inner ear. The three bones are called the hammer, the anvil, and the stirrup because of their shapes.

3 The inner ear is shaped like a snail shell. It is a tube filled with liquid. Tiny hairs on the inside are connected to nerves. Sounds move the hairs, which then send signals along nerves to the brain. Your brain figures out the signal, and you hear a sound.

Hearing Sounds

We hear sound when sound waves reach our ears. Our ears take in the sound waves and turn them into signals that go to our brains. Our brains figure out these signals and tell us what the sound is.

The first part of the ear that a sound wave hits is the outer ear. The outer ear is like a funnel that collects sound waves and guides them to the eardrum.

The eardrum is made of thin material that bends easily. It is about 1 centimeter ($\frac{1}{2}$ in.) across. It works like the top of a drum. The eardrum vibrates when sound waves hit it. As the eardrum moves back and forth, it moves a tiny bone at the outside end of the middle ear.

The middle ear is about the size of the tip of your little finger. In it, vibrations pass through three tiny bones. The bones connect the eardrum to the inner ear.

The inner ear is shaped like a snail shell. It is filled with liquid. The walls of the inner ear are lined with tiny hairs. These hairs are connected to nerves.

The third bone of the middle ear vibrates one end of the inner ear. These vibrations cause waves in the liquid. The waves move the tiny hairs. This causes nerve cells to send signals to your brain. Your brain interprets the signals as sounds.

✔ **Which part of the ear connects it to the outside world?**

Summary

Sound is made by vibrating objects. The vibrations travel through matter as areas of high and low pressure called sound waves. A wave diagram is a way to model the amplitude and wavelength of a sound wave. Sound waves move through the three parts of the ear. You sense the vibrations as sound.

Review

1. What is sound?

2. What are sound waves?

3. Which part of the ear is connected to nerves that send signals to the brain?

4. **Critical Thinking** Sometimes you can hear and feel the rumble of a passing truck. What are you feeling?

5. **Test Prep** The middle ear contains —
   A liquid
   B the eardrum
   C three bones
   D hairs

LINKS

MATH LINK

Find a Rule Some music scale notes can be found by shortening the length of a string to a fraction. For example, if the base pitch is played on a length of 1, an *octave* (AHK•tiv) higher would be played on a length of $\frac{1}{2}$. What would be the length of the second octave higher? The third octave?

WRITING LINK

Informative Writing—Description Suppose that you are a sound wave traveling through someone's ear. Write a description for your classmates of what happens to you as you move from the outer ear to the inner ear.

SOCIAL STUDIES LINK

Flutes and Drums In many countries traditional music is played on flutelike and drumlike instruments. Choose a country. Find pictures of these types of musical instruments from that country. Make a map showing the location of the country. Add labeled pictures of the instruments.

GO ONLINE TECHNOLOGY LINK

Learn more about early recorders by visiting the Jerome and Dorothy Lemelson Center for Invention and Innovation Internet site.
www.si.edu/harcourt/science

Smithsonian Institution®

LESSON 2

Why Do Sounds Differ?

In this lesson, you can . . .

INVESTIGATE
making different sounds.

LEARN ABOUT
differences in sounds.

LINK to math, writing, music, and technology.

Making Different Sounds

Activity Purpose If you pluck a guitar string, you hear a sound. If you pluck another guitar string, you hear a different sound. How are the sounds different? What causes the difference? In this activity you will **observe** sounds made by a vibrating rubber band. You will **compare** observations and **infer** what causes differences in sounds.

Materials

- safety goggles
- foam cup
- long rubber band
- paper clip
- ruler
- masking tape

CAUTION

Activity Procedure

1. **CAUTION** **Put on the safety goggles.** With a pencil, punch a small hole in the bottom of the cup. Thread the rubber band through the paper clip. Put the paper clip inside the cup, and pull the rubber band through the hole. (Picture A)

2. Turn the cup upside down on a table. Stand the ruler on the table next to it, with the 1-cm mark at the top. Tape one side of the cup to the ruler. Pull the rubber band over the top of the ruler, and tape it to the back. (Picture B)

3. Pull the rubber band to one side and let it go. **Observe** the sound. **Record** your observations.

◄ The word *piano* is short for *pianoforte* (pee•ah•noh•FOR•tay). *Piano* is the Italian word for "soft." *Forte* is the Italian word for "loud." Why do you think this instrument is called a pianoforte?

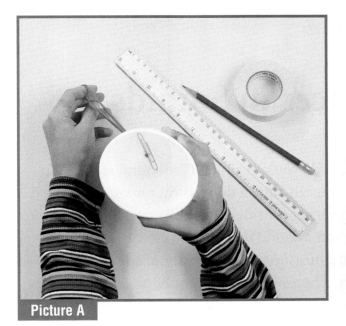
Picture A

Picture B

4 Repeat Step 3, but this time pull the rubber band farther. **Observe** the sound. **Record** your observations.

5 With one finger, hold the rubber band down to the ruler at the 4-cm mark. Pluck the rubber band. **Observe** the sound. **Record** your observations.

6 Repeat Step 5, but this time hold the rubber band down at the 6-cm mark. Then do this at the 8-cm mark. **Observe** the sounds. **Record** your observations.

Draw Conclusions

1. **Compare** the sounds you observed in Steps 3 and 4.

2. **Compare** the sounds you observed in Steps 5 and 6.

3. When was the vibrating part of the rubber band the shortest?

4. **Scientists at Work** Scientists use their observations to help them **infer** the causes of different things. Use your observations from Steps 5 and 6 to infer what caused the differences in the sounds.

Investigate Further Try moving your finger up and down the ruler as you pull on the rubber band. Can you play a scale? Can you play a tune? What cause and effect relationship do you **observe? Form a hypothesis** to explain that relationship. **Plan and conduct an experiment** to test the hypothesis.

Process Skill Tip

Scientists use their observations to **infer** the causes of their results. In this investigation your observations helped you infer the causes of different sounds.

Differences in Sounds

FIND OUT

- the difference between loud and soft sounds
- the difference between high and low sounds

VOCABULARY

loudness
pitch

Loudness

You can whisper and you can shout. One sound is soft, and the other is loud. You can close a door softly, or you can bang it shut so hard that everyone inside the building can hear. You can hear how loud or soft a sound is. This property is called loudness. **Loudness** is a measure of the amount of sound energy reaching your ears. The amplitude of a sound wave shows how loud the sound is.

The loudness of a sound depends on how far the vibrating object is moving as it goes back and forth. In the investigation the sound was louder when you pulled the rubber band farther. You added more energy to the rubber band by stretching it more. In the same way, if you hit a drum harder or slam a door harder, you make a louder sound.

✔ **What does loudness measure?**

A bluebird's song is pretty, but it is not loud. The amplitude of the sound wave from the bluebird is small. ▶

◀ Noise from an amplified bass guitar is much louder than a bluebird's song. It's so loud that it can injure your ears if you don't protect them. The amplitude of the sound wave from the bass guitar amplifier is large.

A tuba makes low sounds. The compressions of a tuba's sound wave are far apart. It has a long wavelength. ▼

◀ Piccolo music reminds some people of the high sounds of singing birds. A piccolo makes fast vibrations. The compressions of a piccolo's sound wave are close together. It has a short wavelength.

Pitch

You can make loud sounds and soft sounds. You can also make high sounds and low sounds. When you growl like a dog, you are making a low sound. When you squeak like a mouse, you are making a high sound.

A sound's **pitch** is a measure of how high or low it is. Pitch depends on how fast the source of the sound is vibrating. The faster the vibrations, the higher the pitch. Pitch is related to wavelength. The longer the wavelength, the lower the sound you hear.

You can change how fast a string or rubber band vibrates by changing its length. In the investigation, when you made the vibrating part of the rubber band shorter, it vibrated faster. The sound it made got higher in pitch.

✔ **What does the pitch of a sound depend on?**

The keys at the right-hand end of a piano make high sounds. The keys to the left make lower sounds. The lowest note on a modern piano vibrates about $27\frac{1}{2}$ times a second. The highest note on a piano vibrates about 4224 times a second. Humans can hear sounds from about 20 to about 20,000 vibrations a second. ▶

Changing Pitch

Many musical instruments can be played at different pitches by changing the length of certain parts. A guitar or violin player puts his or her fingers down on the strings in different places. This changes the lengths of the vibrating strings. As a result, the violin or guitar plays different pitches.

Another way to make a different pitch is to change the thickness of the material that vibrates. A thin string vibrates faster than a thick string. Low-pitched guitar and piano strings have wire wrapped around them to make them thicker.

✔ **Name two ways you can change the pitch of a vibrating object.**

A trombone is a long tube. To play a note, a trombone player's lips vibrate. This makes the air inside the tube vibrate. ▼

When a trombone player pushes the slide out, the tube gets longer. This makes the pitch of the sound lower than before. Notice that the wavelength of the sound is longer. ▼

The cone-shaped object in the trombone is a mute (MYOOT). It makes a trombone note softer because the mute absorbs sound energy. With the mute the sound wave made by the trombone has less energy. Notice that the amplitude of the wave is smaller than the first wave, above, but the wavelength is the same. ▼

A voiceprint is an electronic "picture" of a voice. It shows the changing pitch and loudness of the voice as a person speaks. ▼

Summary

Loudness is a measure of the sound energy reaching your ears. It depends on the size of the vibrations. Pitch is a measure of how high or low a sound is. Pitch depends on how fast an object vibrates. You can change pitch by changing the length or the thickness of a vibrating object.

Review

1. What is the loudness of a sound?
2. What is the pitch of a sound?
3. What happens to sound as it gets farther away from the object making the sound?
4. **Critical Thinking** How do you think the finger holes on the side of a piccolo control the pitch of its sound?
5. **Test Prep** If you put your finger down on a guitar string to make the string shorter, the sound the string makes will get —

   A lower   **C** louder
   B higher   **D** softer

LINKS

MATH LINK

Calculate a Difference The highest note on a piano vibrates 4224 times a second. The lowest note on a piano vibrates $27\frac{1}{2}$ times a second. What is the difference between these two pitches?

WRITING LINK

Informative Writing—Description Sit still and listen for one minute. Time yourself. As you're listening, make a list of every sound you hear. Then write a paragraph for your teacher describing all the sounds. Be sure to include loudness and pitch in your descriptions.

MUSIC LINK

High and Low Two of the families of instruments in an orchestra are the brass instruments and the woodwind instruments. Find out the names of the instruments in each of these families. Then find out the highest and lowest pitches each instrument family can play.

TECHNOLOGY LINK

Learn more about how scientists and engineers are using sound energy by viewing *Sound Wave Energy* on the **Harcourt Science Newsroom Video.**

LESSON 3

How Do Sound Waves Travel?

In this lesson, you can . . .

INVESTIGATE ways sound is reflected.

LEARN ABOUT how sound waves travel.

LINK to math, writing, health, and technology.

Hearing Sounds

Activity Purpose Have you ever made a sound and heard it come back to you? In this investigation you will **gather and record data** while making a sound and listening to find out if it comes back to you.

Materials

- large metal spoon
- metal pot
- red crayon

Activity Procedure

1 Find a playing field with a scoreboard or building at one end. Use a pencil to make a drawing of the playing field.

2 Walk out onto the playing field. Use a pencil to record on your drawing where on the playing field you are standing and which way you are facing.

3 Bang the spoon against the pot once. Wait and observe whether or not the sound comes back to you. If the sound comes back to you, use a red crayon to mark that place. (Picture A)

◀ When the space shuttle reenters the atmosphere and coasts toward a landing, it is traveling much faster than the speed of sound.

4 Move to another location on the playing field. Again, use a pencil to record where on the playing field you are standing and which way you are facing.

5 Repeat Step 3. If the sound comes back to you, be sure to use a red crayon to mark the spot on your drawing.

6 Move forward and back. Move from side to side. Each time you move, mark your position on your drawing, bang the pot once, and wait to see whether or not the sound comes back to you. Each time use the crayon to mark the places where the sound came back to you.

7 Keep moving to different places on the playing field until you have gathered information from 20 locations.

Picture A

Draw Conclusions

1. Look at your drawing. How many different positions did you show? At how many different places did the sound come back to you?

2. Look at all the places marked in red on your drawing. Do they have anything in common?

Picture B

3. **Scientists at Work** Each mark that you made on your drawing was a piece of data. When scientists do investigations, they **gather and record** as much **data** as they can. All the data helps them draw conclusions. How could you gather more data in an organized way?

Investigate Further Move to each of the places on the field where you heard the sound come back to you. Blow a whistle loudly in each place. Does the sound come back to you? Describe a simple **experiment** to test this **hypothesis**: Only short, loud sounds come back to you.

Process Skill Tip

Scientists often use drawings when they **gather and record data**. Their drawings help them see patterns in the information they gather. They use the patterns to help them draw conclusions.

How Sound Travels

Speed

VOCABULARY

speed of sound
echo
sonic boom

Have you ever been to a baseball game and watched a batter hit a home run? If you were sitting all the way across the ballpark, you saw the batter hit the ball a split second before you heard the crack of the bat. This is because sound waves take more time to move through the air than light does. Even so, it took less than a second for the sound wave to travel from the bat to your ears.

The speed at which a sound wave travels is called the **speed of sound**. Sound waves move at different speeds through different materials. In dry, cool air, sound waves travel 340 meters (about 1115 ft) per second. The speed of sound traveling through steel is 5200 meters (about 17,060 ft) per second.

In hard, solid materials, sound waves move very fast. This is because the particles in solids are close together and bump into each other often. The particles in liquids don't bump into each other as often as particles in solids do. So vibrations take longer to move through liquids. Sound moves more slowly through liquids than through most solids.

 When it first enters Earth's atmosphere, the space shuttle is traveling 25 times as fast as sound travels through air. Another way to say that speed is Mach (MAHK) 25. Just before the shuttle touches down, it travels at Mach 1, the speed of sound. Mach 1 is almost two times as fast as a normal plane flies.

Sound moves even more slowly in gases. The particles in gases are far apart. They don't bump into each other as often as particles in liquids, so vibrations take longer to move through gases. But what if there were no particles at all, or very few particles? In that case, there would be no sound at all. This is very much like the conditions in space. Suppose you are in a spacesuit outside a space shuttle. No matter how loudly you shouted, no one in the shuttle would hear you. You could talk back and forth only by using a radio.

✓ **What does the speed of sound measure?**

1 In air, sound travels about 1 mile in 5 seconds. You can use this to find the distance to a thunderstorm. Light travels so fast that you see a lightning bolt almost as it happens. Start the stopwatch when you see the flash, and wait to hear the thunder.

2 When you hear the thunder, you stop the stopwatch. It reads 10 seconds.
10 sec ÷ 5 sec/1 mi = 2 mi
The storm is about 2 miles away.

Sound waves travel at different speeds in different materials. The arrangement of particles in materials affects how the waves move. ▼

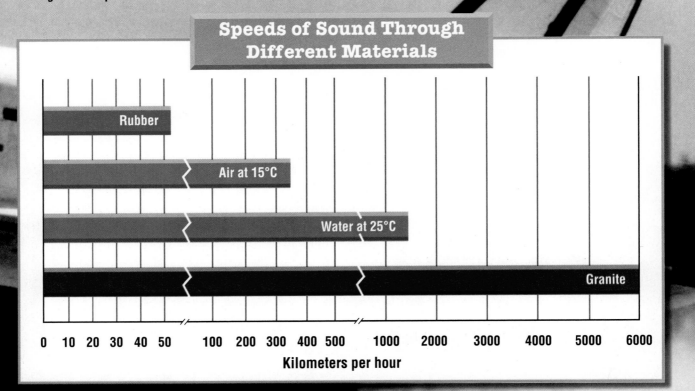

Speeds of Sound Through Different Materials

Rubber

Air at 15°C

Water at 25°C

Granite

0 10 20 30 40 50   100 200 300 400 500   1000   2000   3000   4000   5000   6000
Kilometers per hour

Reflection

As sound waves travel through the air, an object such as a wall may be in their path. In this case, the sound waves hit the object and bounce, or reflect, off it. A sound reflection is called an **echo**. In the investigation, you heard an echo when you faced the scoreboard or building, hit the pot with the spoon, and heard the sound come back to you.

Not all echoes are clear or easy to recognize. A line of trees, for example, doesn't reflect a clear echo. That is because the surfaces of the trees are uneven. Each sound wave hits a different surface and is reflected in a different direction.

It is very much like what happens to your reflection in a pool of water. If the water is smooth and still, you can see yourself clearly. But if the surface of the pond ripples, your reflection gets broken up. Rough or uneven surfaces do the same thing to sound waves.

✔ **What is an echo?**

THE INSIDE STORY

"Seeing" with Sound

Dolphins see with their eyes. They also "see" underwater by using echoes. Dolphins use sound to find their way around rocks and other things in their way. They also use sound to find food such as small fish and squid.

1 Dolphins make sounds that have high pitches. The sounds are called clicks. Scientists aren't sure how dolphins make the clicks. The click sound waves travel through the water.

2 The click sound waves reflect off the rocks and fish. Some echoes return to the dolphin.

Sound waves reflect straight from a smooth, flat surface, just as a ball bounces off a wall. Most of the sound energy goes in one direction, so there is a clear echo. ▶

When sound waves hit a rough, uneven surface, they are reflected in many different directions. The sound energy is spread out, so there is no clear echo. ▶

3 Dolphins have an organ called a melon on the tops of their heads. It senses the echoes of the clicks. The melon absorbs the sound and helps the dolphin avoid rocks and find its food.

Sonic Booms

Some jet airplanes can fly faster than sound. Their powerful engines produce loud sounds. What happens to these sounds when the plane is moving faster than they are?

An airplane traveling faster than sound makes sound waves that move away in all directions. But the airplane is moving faster than the sound waves moving away in front of it. When the plane catches up to these sound waves, they are squeezed closer together. All the energy of the sound waves becomes one strong wave. This strong wave is called a shock wave. You can hear this shock wave as a loud "boom-boom." People call the double boom a **sonic boom**. Any object moving faster than sound makes such a shock wave. You hear the "crack" of a rifle shot because the bullet is moving faster than sound.

A plane is always making sound waves. So if it is flying faster than sound, its sonic boom travels with it, much like the plane's shadow does.

▲ A supersonic jet is allowed to fly faster than sound only over the ocean or deserts. Because of this, most of the time people don't hear its sonic booms.

A sonic boom is a large, quick air pressure increase followed by a large quick decrease. Then the pressure returns to normal. ▶

Suppose you and 20 of your friends were to stand in a line down the length of a football field. You stand on a goal line. Each of your friends stands on a different yard line. Coming from the direction nearest you, an airplane flies down the field going faster than sound. You will be the first to hear its sonic boom. Then, one by one, each of your friends will hear it. Finally, the person standing on the far goal line will hear it.

✔ **What is a sonic boom?**

Summary

Sound waves travel at different speeds through different materials. They travel fastest through hard, solid materials. Sound waves reflect off objects in their paths. An echo is a sound reflection off a smooth, hard surface. Objects traveling faster than the speed of sound cause shock waves that we hear as sonic booms.

Review

1. What does the speed of sound measure?

2. Why is there no sound in outer space?

3. Where does the energy of a sonic boom come from?

4. **Critical Thinking** Why don't you hear echoes in a forest?

5. **Test Prep** In which material would sound waves probably travel the fastest?

   A cotton

   B milk

   C iron

   D oxygen

LINKS

MATH LINK

Compare Whole Numbers The speed of sound in air is 340 meters per second. In water it is 1497 meters per second. About how many times as fast is the speed of sound in water as in air?

WRITING LINK

Informative Writing—Narration Suppose you are at home and a thunderstorm is going on outside. By watching the lightning and listening to the thunder, you track the storm. Write a story for a younger child telling what you see and hear, and where the storm is going.

HEALTH LINK

Ultrasound Doctors use ultrasound in medical tests. Find out what ultrasound is and how it works. Then find out about some of the tests it's used for. Make a poster or display to show what you learned.

TECHNOLOGY LINK

Learn more about sound wave differences by exploring *Waves of Music* on **Harcourt Science Explorations CD-ROM.**

Active NOISE CONTROL

Sound can be beautiful, as some music is. Sound can give information, as in the case of warning bells or someone speaking to tell you how to fix your bicycle. But sometimes sound is just noise.

Noise

Some noise is unwanted sound. It upsets people and makes them angry. Think of how listening to a jackhammer or a chainsaw outside your window all day long would make you feel. A sound that one person thinks is pleasantly loud may be an unwanted noise to another person. Still, any loud sound, whether or not you like it, can cause permanent damage to your ears.

Noise Reduction

Most ways of reducing noise involve absorbing sound or spreading out sound energy. For example, inside a car muffler, sound waves bounce off many walls and dividers. Each bounce takes a little energy out of the sound wave. As a result, the car makes less noise. Rugs, curtains, and ceiling tiles work in much the same way. All these ways of reducing noise are *passive*—they don't need energy to make them work.

For several years now, scientists have been working on a process called active noise control (ANC). ANC makes sounds to cancel out noise. It does this by making sound waves that are the exact opposite of the noise waves. Where a noise wave has a compression, the ANC wave doesn't. When the two waves meet, their areas of high and low pressure cancel each other out.

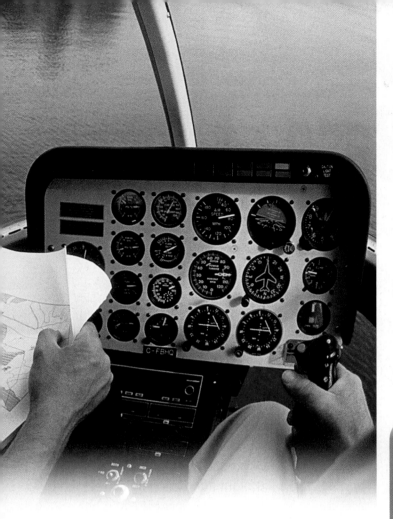

Another way ANC ideas could be used is to reduce vibrations while making lenses for cameras and telescopes. For example, it's important that lenses be as smooth as possible to give a clear image. Most lenses now are ground by a robot using a grinding tool. The tool vibrates, so the surface of the lens isn't completely smooth. A person must do the final polishing. This adds time and cost. If the grinder did not vibrate, no human polisher would be needed. This would lower the cost of lenses.

THINK ABOUT IT

1. Why do you think ANC works best indoors?
2. Do you think ANC could be used to block out noise from your neighbor's stereo?

An ANC system is made up of microphones to pick up the noise, a computer to analyze the noise, and speakers to make the sound waves that cancel other sounds.

ANC works best indoors on noise that repeats, for example inside airplanes and cars, where you might hear the sound of tires on the road or propellers turning. ANC headphones for use in helicopters are one success story. They allow the person wearing them to hear people talking and sounds of warning sirens, but they cancel out the low-pitched sounds from the rotor blades.

Other Uses for ANC

What works for noise may also work for other unwanted vibrations. ANC technology might help prevent or lessen earthquake damage. When a building begins to shake, opposing vibrations made by an ANC system could help stop the shaking.

Amar Gopal Bose
SOUND ENGINEER

To celebrate finishing his college research, Amar Bose treated himself to a new sound system. But he didn't like the way the speakers sounded. He began to study acoustics (uh•KOOS•tiks), the science of sound, so he could build better speakers.

The speaker in a stereo system changes electric signals to vibrations. The vibrations create sound waves. Most sound systems need two speakers to play sounds correctly. One speaker makes high sounds, and one makes low sounds. Each speaker is usually put into a wooden box. The size and shape of the box affect how the speaker sounds.

Bose graduated from the Massachusetts Institute of Technology (MIT) and went to Delhi, India, to teach at the National Physics Laboratory. He later returned to teach at MIT. During this time, he continued experimenting with sound. Starting in 1959, Bose received a number of patents for designs of sound systems, including loudspeakers. Five years later, Bose started his own company with a former student.

At the beginning, Bose wasn't paid a salary and he worked at night after teaching classes at MIT. Now, his company is successful and has more than 2,500 workers.

Bose still listens to music. He took violin lessons when he was younger but decided to study science instead. When he has time, he listens to classical music, including classical music of India.

THINK ABOUT IT

1. The speaker that handles low-pitched sounds is called a woofer. The speaker that handles high-pitched sounds is called a tweeter. Why might this be so?

2. With an adult's permission, look at a sound system in your school, home, or family car. What size and shape are the speakers? How do they sound?

SOUNDS OF WATER GLASSES

How do water glasses make sounds with different pitches?

Materials

- 4 or 5 identical water glasses
- water
- metal spoon

Procedure

① Put a different amount of water in each glass.

② Predict which glass will have the highest pitch and which will have the lowest pitch.

③ Tap each glass lightly with the back of the spoon and listen.

Draw Conclusions

Were your predictions correct? What relationship did you observe between pitch and water level?

SOUNDS AND MATTER

Can you hear sounds through a solid, a liquid, and a gas?

Materials

- tuning fork
- board eraser
- metric ruler
- balloon
- water

Procedure

① **Listen to a sound through a gas.** Hold the tuning fork about 20 cm from one ear. Strike the fork with the eraser.

② **Listen to a sound through a solid.** Place one ear on a desk. Cover your other ear with your hand. Have a partner strike the tuning fork with the eraser and hold the base of the tuning fork against the desktop about 20 cm from your ear.

③ **Listen to a sound through a liquid.** Fill the balloon with water until it is about 20 cm long. Place one end of the balloon against your ear. Cover your other ear with your hand. Have your partner strike the tuning fork and hold its base against the opposite end of the balloon.

Draw Conclusions

Was the tuning fork loudest when you heard it through the air, through the water, or through the desk? Explain.

Vocabulary Review

Use the terms below to complete the sentences. The numbers in ( ) tell you where to look in the chapter if you need help.

sounds (E70)   **loudness** (E78)

sound waves (E71)   **pitch** (E79)

compression (E71)   **speed of sound** (E84)

amplitude (E72)   **echo** (E86)

wavelength (E72)   **sonic boom** (E88)

1. The _____ of a sound describes how high or low a sound is.

2. Moving areas of high and low pressure that carry sound are _____.

3. Vibrations that you hear are _____.

4. The amount of sound energy reaching your ears is _____.

5. A reflection of sound is an _____.

6. How fast sound moves is the _____.

7. The sound of a shock wave produced by an object moving faster than the speed of sound is a _____.

8. A _____ is a place where particles are squeezed closer together by a sound wave.

9. The height of a wave above rest position is its _____.

10. The distance from one point on a wave ripple to the same point on the next ripple is its _____.

Connect Concepts

Use the terms in the Word Bank to complete the diagram.

pitch   **sound wave**   **sound**   **echo**
loudness   **vibrates**   **reflect**

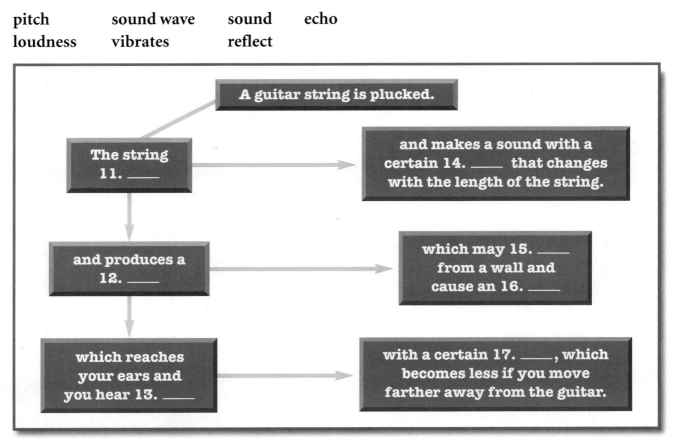

A guitar string is plucked.

The string 11. _____

and makes a sound with a certain 14. _____ that changes with the length of the string.

and produces a 12. _____

which may 15. _____ from a wall and cause an 16. _____

which reaches your ears and you hear 13. _____

with a certain 17. _____, which becomes less if you move farther away from the guitar.

Check Understanding

Write the letter of the best choice.

18. Sound waves cannot travel through —

  A a solid   **C** empty space

  B gases   **D** liquids

19. What we hear as pitch is related mostly to —

  F reflection

  G how far away the source of the sound is

  H the speed of sound

  J how fast the source of the sound is moving back and forth

20. You can make the sound louder if you pluck a guitar string by —

  A moving the string farther before letting go

  B stopping the string when it starts to move

  C shortening the string

  D lengthening the string

21. A sound wave has areas called _____ where particles are squeezed together.

  F echoes   **H** sonic booms

  G compressions   **J** pitches

22. If the _____ of a wave changes, you will hear a softer sound because less energy is reaching your ears.

  A pitch

  B wavelength

  C amplitude

  D echo

23. You are more likely to hear an echo when standing —

  F close to a short wall

  G facing a tall, smooth wall

  H in a large, open field

  J in a very small room

24. A _____ is the sound you hear when something is moving faster than the speed of sound.

  A vibration

  B pitch wave

  C high pitch

  D sonic boom

Critical Thinking

25. Explain how the vibrations you cause by hitting a drum move from the drum to your brain, where they are interpreted as sound.

26. How does a sonic boom form?

Process Skills Review

27. What features would you use to describe a sound that you **observed**?

28. What is the difference between **observing** a vibration and **inferring** how the vibration affects air particles?

29. Why do scientists sometimes use drawings to **record** the **data** they **gather**?

Performance Assessment

Sound Vibrations

Strike a tuning fork. After you hear the sound of the fork, place its base on a tabletop. Observe and report what happens. Explain your observations in terms of vibrations and sound waves. You may use a drawing as part of your explanation.

Light

Flick! Bounce, reflect, bounce! That's what happens to the light from a flashlight if you turn it on and shine it at your image in a mirror. The light goes so fast it seems to hit the mirror and you at the same instant you turn the flashlight on!

Vocabulary Preview

reflection
refraction
absorption
opaque
translucent
transparent
prism
visible spectrum

Fast Fact

We see stars as they were when their light left them. This table shows how long it takes the light from some space objects to reach us.

The Speed of Light		
Object in Space	**Distance from Earth**	**Light Reaches Us In**
Moon	384,462 km	$1\frac{1}{3}$ seconds
Venus	41.2 million km	$2\frac{1}{3}$ minutes
Sun	149.7 million km	$8\frac{1}{2}$ minutes
Alpha Centauri	40.2 trillion km	$4\frac{1}{3}$ years
Sirius	81.7 trillion km	$8\frac{1}{2}$ years
Andromeda Galaxy	21.2 billion billion km	$2\frac{1}{4}$ million years

Have you ever seen your reflection in a pool of water? This three-meter mirror is a pool of mercury, a liquid metal. It is part of a telescope. The whole pool is spun to give the mirror a smooth curve like a saucer.

Andromeda Galaxy

Light travels at the speed of 299,330 kilometers per second (186,000 mi per sec). If you could run that fast, you would be able to circle the Earth more than seven times in just one second!

How Does Light Behave?

In this lesson, you can . . .

INVESTIGATE how light travels.

LEARN ABOUT things light can do.

LINK to math, writing, drama, and technology.

How Light Travels

Activity Purpose Have you ever noticed how the shadow of a tree changes during the day? It's long in the morning, short at noon, and long again in the late afternoon. These changes happen because the tree blocks the light and the position of the sun in the sky changes. In this investigation, you will change the position of index cards and use a light bulb to **observe** how light travels.

Materials

- 3 index cards
- ruler
- pencil
- clay
- small, short lamp without a lampshade

Activity Procedure

1 Make a large X on each card. To draw each line, lay the ruler from one corner of the card to the opposite corner. (Picture A)

2 On each card, make a hole at the place where the lines of the X cross. Use the pencil to make the holes.

3 Use the clay to make a stand for each card. Make sure the holes in the cards are the same height. Stack the cards on top of each other. Line up the edges. Then, hold them tightly together and use a pencil to make sure the holes are the same size and at the same height. (Picture B)

◀ Late in the day, the position of the sun causes long shadows.

4 Turn on the light. Look through the holes in the cards. Move the cards around on the table until you can see the light bulb through all three cards at once. You may have to pull down the blinds or dim the room lights to help you see the light bulb. Draw a picture showing where the light is and where the cards are.

5 Move the cards around to new places on the table. Each time you move the cards, draw a picture showing where the cards are. Do not move the light! **Observe** the light through the holes each time.

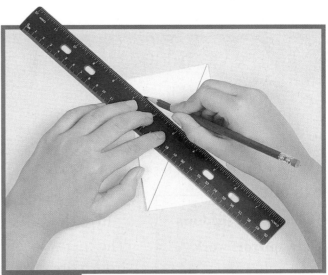
Picture A

Draw Conclusions

1. Where were the cards when you were able to see the light?

2. Were there times you couldn't see the light? Where were the cards then?

3. **Scientists at Work** Scientists **observe** carefully and then **record** what they observe. Often they draw pictures to **communicate** what they observe. Did drawing pictures help you describe what you saw? Explain.

Picture B

Investigate Further Do you **predict** you will get the same results if the cards are at an angle to the lamp? Use the clay to attach the cards to a meterstick. Put a stack of books near the light. Rest the meterstick on books and hold it at an angle to the table. Test your prediction.

Process Skill Tip

Scientists can learn many things about the world just by **observing**. Then they **record** what they see. After they observe the same thing many times, they **communicate** by telling other scientists what they have observed.

Light

FIND OUT

- what makes shadows
- how mirrors work
- how water affects the path of light.

VOCABULARY

reflection
refraction
absorption
opaque
translucent
transparent

Light Energy

You know that energy is the ability to cause things to change. The energy in a fire changes a sheet of paper into ashes. The heat from a fire can change your hands from cold to warm. Bacteria use energy to change a dead log into soil for plants.

Light is also a kind of energy. Light energy can make many changes. Without light energy, you could not see anything. Light energy gives things colors. The sun shines on the soil, and plants grow. Doctors use the light energy of lasers to perform some operations. Light energy can make cars move. In space, satellites and the space station use solar cells to change light energy into electricity. If all satellites depended on batteries instead, the added weight would make them too expensive to launch into orbit.

✔ **What are three changes light energy can cause?**

Plants can't live in complete darkness. They need light energy to carry out photosynthesis to make food. ▼

▲ Scientists are finding new ways to use light. The solar panels on the rear of the roof change light energy from the sun into electricity. Some of the energy is used right away. The rest is stored in batteries to be used later.

Shadows

When you put your hand in front of a lamp, you make a shadow on the wall. The shadows move and change shape as you move your hand. Shadows move and change because of the way light travels.

Light travels in straight lines. When you put your hand in front of a lamp, some of the straight lines of light hit your hand. The shadow on the wall shows where the light is blocked by your hand. When you move your hand, the shadow moves because your hand blocks different lines of light.

In the investigation you could see the light bulb only when the holes in the three cards were in a straight line. When one of the holes wasn't in line with the others, it blocked the line of light. How did this show that light travels in a straight line?

When you stand in the sun, you block some of the lines of sunlight. As the sun moves in the sky, you block different lines of light. When the sun is low in the sky, in the morning and in the afternoon, your shadow is long. When the sun is high overhead, your shadow is short.

Long ago, people figured out that they could predict the pattern of changing shadows during a day. They used that pattern to tell time. A device used to do so is called a sundial. It is made up of a triangular pointer called a *gnomon* (NOH•mahn) and a circular dial marking the hours of the day. As the sun moves across the sky, the shadow of the gnomon moves from left to right and points to the hours of the day.

✔ **How does light travel?**

▲ Early in the morning, the sun is rising in the east. The shadow of the gnomon on this sundial points to eight o'clock on the far left side of the dial.

▲ Later in the day, the sun is in the west. The shadow of the gnomon has moved to point to two o'clock on the dial.

Bouncing Light

Look in a mirror. What do you see? You probably see yourself and some of the things around you. You are looking in front of you at the mirror. But the things you see in the mirror are next to you or even behind you. How is this possible?

Hold a lamp in front of a mirror, and you will see the lamp in the mirror. The light from the lamp moves in a straight line to the mirror. When it hits the mirror, it bounces off. It is still traveling in a straight line. But now it's going in a new direction. It is com-ing straight back to you. The bouncing of light off an object is called **reflection** (rih•FLEK•shuhn). You see objects in a mirror because their light is reflected straight back to you.

Light bounces from a mirror like a ball bounces from a wall. If you roll a ball straight at a wall, it bounces straight back to you. If you roll a ball toward a wall at an angle, it bounces away from the wall at an angle. This is why you can use a mirror to look around a corner. The light strikes the mirror at an angle and bounces to your eyes.

◀ When light bounces off a mirror, the light changes direction. The letters on the sign are backward. This is because a mirror reverses an image from left to right.

Light travels in straight lines. Even if it bounces off many mirrors, you can still see the object. If the mirrors are lined up exactly right, you can see many reflections of the object. ▼

Light bouncing off a smooth surface gives an image you can see. A mirror is very smooth. So are shiny metal and still water. You can see yourself in these things. But most things aren't as smooth as mirrors. Most things are bumpy. When light hits a bumpy surface, each straight line of light goes off in a different direction. Then you don't see any image.

A mirror can also have a smooth, curved surface. Mirrors like this make your reflection seem bigger or smaller than you really are. Carnival fun-houses and science museums often have such mirrors on display.

✔ **What is reflection?**

◀ If the water is rippling, each wave reflects light in a different direction. Since the light is traveling in so many directions, it is hard to see a clear picture on the surface of the water.

The water on the lake is so still that it acts like a mirror. ▼

Bending Light

Light doesn't bounce off every surface. There are some things light goes through. That's why you can see through air, water, and glass.

Light travels at different speeds in air, water, and glass. So when light goes from one thing to another, such as from air to glass, it changes speed. Any time light goes from one kind of matter to another, it changes speed. If light hits the new matter straight on, it keeps going straight. But if light hits the new matter at a slant, the light bends. The bending of light when it moves from one kind of matter to another is called **refraction** (rih•FRAK•shuhn).

Light moving from air to glass is like an in-line skater moving from a sidewalk to the grass. If the skater is going straight into the grass, both front wheels hit the grass at the same time. The skater slows down because grass is softer than concrete. But he or she continues to go straight. If the skater does not go straight into the grass, one wheel hits the grass first. The other is still on the sidewalk. The wheel that hits the grass first slows down first. This makes the skater turn toward the grass. If the skater were moving at an angle from the grass onto concrete, his or her path would bend closer to the grass for the same reason.

Scientists use refraction to study objects and to fix problems. The thick hand lenses that you use to observe small objects use refraction to make an object seem larger than it really is. Eye doctors make lenses to correct people's eyesight. Both eyeglasses and contact lenses are designed to control refraction.

✔ **What is refraction?**

Half of this toy diver is in the water. You see the bottom half through the water. The light bends when it hits the water. You see the top half through air. This light isn't bending. So the toy diver looks as if it is broken in two. ▼

Here the light hits the glass at an angle. This time the light bends and changes direction. ▲

Light travels through air and glass. This light hits the glass straight on and keeps going straight. ▶

Here the light is refracted three times. So the pencil looks as if it is broken into four pieces. ▶

E105

Stopping Light

You have learned that you can see through air, water, and glass. Light travels through these forms of matter. But most matter doesn't let light pass. When light hits a wall, the wall stops, or absorbs, the light. Stopping light is called **absorption** (ab•SAWRP•shuhn). Have you ever watched rain falling on grass? The soil absorbs the water. Most matter absorbs light in the same way.

When light hits most objects, some of the light bounces off and the rest is absorbed. Smooth, shiny objects reflect almost all the light that hits them. Other objects absorb most of the light that hits them and reflect the rest. If an object doesn't produce its own light, what you see when you look at it is the light that bounces off it.

There are three ways an object can interact with light. Scientists have a name for each of them. An **opaque** (oh•PAYK) object reflects or absorbs all light. If you try to look through an opaque object, you see only light reflecting from the object. A wood door is opaque.

A **translucent** (trans•LOO•suhnt) object reflects and absorbs some light. You can see a blurry or fuzzy image when you look through a translucent object. Some light is reflected from the object and some goes through. A fogged-over window is translucent.

A **transparent** (trans•PAIR•uhnt) object does not reflect or absorb much light. You can see a clear image when you look through a transparent object. Windows and plastic wrap are transparent. Colored, clear glass is also transparent.

✔ **What is absorption?**

▲ You can't see through this opaque, blue plate.

▲ The boy's hand and face are blurred behind this translucent plate.

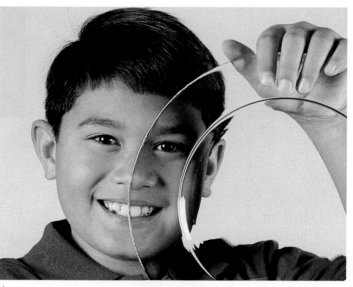

▲ You can see a clear image through this transparent plate.

E106

Summary

Light energy can cause things to change. Plants require light to make food. Some machines use energy from light to generate electricity. Light travels in a straight line unless it is reflected, refracted, or absorbed. Mirrors produce clear images because their surfaces are smooth. Bumpy surfaces don't produce clear images. Objects can be classified as opaque, translucent, or transparent based on how they interact with light.

Review

1. What does a mirror do?

2. Your shadow is shorter than you at 10:00 in the morning. How do you predict its length will change over the next two hours?

3. Give one example each of an object that is opaque, translucent, and transparent. Then use *reflection* and *absorption* to explain why each object matches its description.

4. **Critical Thinking** You stick your hand into an aquarium to get something out. Why does your hand look as if it is cut off from your arm?

5. **Test Prep** Which is an example of light energy being used?

    A water boiling

    B a plant growing

    C a ball bouncing

    D a girl lifting a chair

LINKS

MATH LINK

Elapsed Time How many hours of daylight are there if the sun rises at 6:15 A.M. and sets at 7:15 P.M.? If it rises at 7:00 A.M. and sets at 5:30 P.M.?

WRITING LINK

Informative Writing—Description Write a short story for your classmates that describes a building reflected in a puddle. Include one description each for when the water is smooth and when it is rippling.

DRAMA LINK

Shadow Puppets Make a screen out of a cloth sheet. Shine a light behind it. Make shadow animals on the sheet. Use them to tell a story to the class.

ART LINK

Stained Glass Stained glass art uses properties of light and materials. Use library resources to find an example of stained glass art such as a window, lamp, or sculpture. Explain for your classmates how the artist used properties of light.

TECHNOLOGY LINK

Learn more about how light can be used by watching *Using Natural Light* on the **Harcourt Science Newsroom Video.**

How Are Light and Color Related?

In this lesson, you can . . .

INVESTIGATE rainbows.

LEARN ABOUT light and color.

LINK to math, writing, art, and technology.

INVESTIGATE

Making a Rainbow

Activity Purpose
Grass and leaves from trees appear in many colors of green when you see them in daylight. At night under moonlight, you see them only in shades of gray. The daytime world is a colorful place. You know that you can see colors only when the light is shining. In the dark you can't see color. So is color in the objects or in the light? In this investigation you can **observe** where colors come from.

Materials
- small mirror
- clear glass
- water
- flashlight

Activity Procedure

1 Gently place the mirror into the glass. Slant it up against the side.

2 Fill the glass with water. (Picture A)

3 Set the glass on a table. Turn out the lights. Make the room as dark as possible.

◀ You can see many, many more than twelve colors. But, the colors of these twelve pencils can be mixed to draw much of the colorful world around you.

Picture A

Picture B

4. Shine the flashlight into the glass of water. Aim for the mirror. Adjust your aim until the light hits the mirror. If necessary, adjust the mirror in the water. Make sure the mirror is slanted.

5. **Observe** what happens to the light in the glass. Look at the light where it hits the ceiling or the wall. **Record** what you observe. (Picture B)

Draw Conclusions

1. What did the light look like as it went into the glass?

2. What did the light look like after it came out of the glass?

3. **Scientists at Work** Scientists **draw conclusions** based on what they **observe**. What conclusions can you draw about where color comes from?

Investigate Further Change the angles of the mirror and the flashlight. Which setup gives the best result? Draw a picture of the best arrangement.

Process Skill Tip

You **draw conclusions** when you have gathered data by observing, measuring, and using numbers. Conclusions tell what you have learned.

Light and Color

FIND OUT

- how many colors are in light
- what makes a rainbow

VOCABULARY

prism
visible spectrum

Prisms

Have you ever drawn a picture of the sun? Did you color it yellow? People often do. But sunlight is really made of many different colors. Yellow is only one of them. The sunlight you see is really white light. White is the color of all the sun's colors mixed together.

Different colors of light travel at different speeds in water and in glass. So when white light moves from air to glass or from air to water, the different colors of light bend at different angles. They separate into each individual color.

In the investigation you used water and a mirror to break white light into different colors. Scientists use glass triangle prisms to experiment with light. A **prism** (PRIZ•uhm) is a solid object that bends light. When white light hits the prism, each color of light bends at a different angle. Red light is bent the least. Blue light is bent the most. Light that passes through a prism separates into a rainbow. The colors of a rainbow make up the visible spectrum. The **visible spectrum** (SPEHK•truhm) is made up of all the colors of light that people can see.

✔ **What is a prism?**

◀ White light is made up of many different colors of light. When a beam of white light passes through a prism, it is refracted twice—once when it passes from air into glass and again when it passes from glass into air. The colors of light are refracted different amounts each time, so the beam spreads out into rainbow bands of color.

How Rainbows Form

You can sometimes see a rainbow in the sky during a summer rain when the sun is out. Because of the way raindrops refract and reflect white sunlight, you can see a rainbow only when the sun is behind you. ▷

Each drop of falling water in a rainstorm is like a tiny prism and mirror. Sunlight enters a drop, is reflected from the back wall, and then passes out through the front. So, it is refracted twice, just as it is in a prism.

There are more colors in a rainbow than anyone could count. However, most people use just six colors to remember the order in which the bands always appear: red, orange, yellow, green, blue, and violet.

Adding Colors

A prism breaks white light into colors. You can also add colors together. When you add different colored lights together, they form other colors. Shining a red light and a green light onto the same spot will make a yellow light. Shining a blue light and a red light onto the same spot will make a purple light. You can add red light, blue light, and green light in different ways to make all other colors.

Televisions and computer monitors add light colors. The inside of a TV screen is coated with millions of tiny dots of red, green, and blue. Dots that are near each other are made to glow in different patterns and brightnesses. Your eyes combine the colors to make the pictures you see.

✔ **What is one method for making colors?**

Seeing Colors

All the colors of light, called white light, hit every object you see. Most objects absorb most of the light, but not all of it. The light that is not absorbed is reflected and is the color you see. For example, green grass absorbs all of the white light except the green part. The green part reflects back to your eyes, and you see green grass.

Mixing paint colors is a way of controlling absorption and reflection. Yellow paint reflects yellows and absorbs other colors. Blue paint reflects blues and absorbs other colors. When you mix yellow and blue, all the colors are absorbed, or subtracted out, except greens. So, you see shades of green when you mix blue and yellow paint. When you mix all paint colors, almost all light is absorbed. So you see very dark brown or black.

✔ **Why do you see color?**

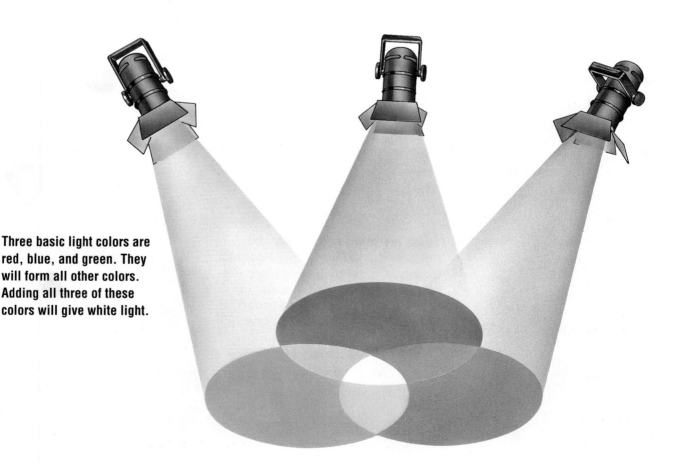

Three basic light colors are red, blue, and green. They will form all other colors. Adding all three of these colors will give white light.

◄ The red rose absorbs all parts of white light except red. Red light is reflected, and we see a red flower.

Summary

White light is made up of many colors mixed together. A prism separates the colors. Raindrops act like prisms to form rainbows. You can make colors by adding different colored lights. The colors of objects you see are the colors of light that the objects reflect.

Review

1. Describe how a prism works.
2. Name the colors that make up white light.
3. What happens if you add different colors of light?
4. **Critical Thinking** Why don't you see a rainbow during most rainstorms?
5. **Test Prep** Which light colors are absorbed and which are reflected by a yellow tulip?(HINT: Look at the lights on page E112.)
   A Absorbed—red, reflected—blue and green
   B Absorbed—blue, reflected—red and green
   C Absorbed—green, reflected—red and blue
   D Absorbed—red, reflected—red and green

LINKS

MATH LINK

Identify Solid Figures The bases of a triangular prism are triangles. What are the bases of a rectangular prism?

WRITING LINK

Informative Writing — Narration Find five different words that describe colors of red. Write a paragraph for your teacher, describing a scene that includes each of these colors.

ART LINK

Color Wheel Find out what a color wheel is and how an artist might use one. Draw one, and explain it to a classmate.

SOCIAL STUDIES LINK

Sources of Dyes Before artificial dyes were invented, people used natural materials to dye cloth. Colors made by such dyes were often named after the source of the dye. Use library resources to find out the sources of these colors: tyrean purple, cochineal red, and indigo. Make a poster to share what you learned.

GO ONLINE TECHNOLOGY LINK

Visit the Harcourt Learning Site for related links, activities, and resources.
www.harcourtschool.com

WELCOME TO THE LEARNING SITE

◄ Optical fibers

Discovering Light and Optics

We use our eyes to see. A curved lens inside the eye bends light, focusing an image on the retina. This image is sent to the brain, which interprets the image.

Using Lenses

Lenses in tools such as microscopes, telescopes, and even eyeglasses work the same way. All lenses have at least one curved surface. The curve of the lens bends and focuses the light. The image formed by the lens might be smaller than, larger than, or the same size as the original object.

People have worn eyeglasses for hundreds of years. The Italian explorer Marco Polo saw people in China wearing glasses around 1275. After books became common in the late 1400s, glasses became common for reading. During the 1600s, people discovered that using lenses would correct nearsightedness. Nearsighted people have difficulty seeing objects far away. More than 125 million people in the United States now have corrected vision.

Today, many people correct their eyesight with contact lenses. The first glass contact lenses were made in the 1930s. They were expensive, uncomfortable, and hard to make. In 1961, a Czechoslovakian scientist patented a flexible plastic lens that absorbed water. His soft contact lenses were first sold in 1970. They have become more and more popular ever since then.

Lasers—Light in a Straight Line

If you've ever shone a flashlight into a dark room, you've seen a property of most light beams. In most cases, a beam spreads apart as it leaves its source. Lasers turn a regular beam of light into a narrow, straight beam of bright light. Laser light is very focused and has only one color.

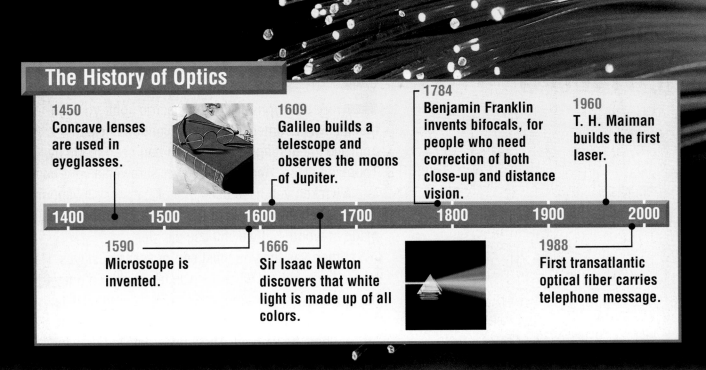

The History of Optics

1450
Concave lenses are used in eyeglasses.

1609
Galileo builds a telescope and observes the moons of Jupiter.

1784
Benjamin Franklin invents bifocals, for people who need correction of both close-up and distance vision.

1960
T. H. Maiman builds the first laser.

1400   1500   1600   1700   1800   1900   2000

1590
Microscope is invented.

1666
Sir Isaac Newton discovers that white light is made up of all colors.

1988
First transatlantic optical fiber carries telephone message.

The word *LASER* stands for *l*ight *a*mplification by *s*timulated *e*mission of *r*adiation. This phrase describes how a laser works. Energy is added to a material. Adding energy stimulates, or causes, light radiation. The light that results is amplified, or made stronger, by the shape of the laser.

Laser light is used in many ways. Lasers are used to scan bar codes on products. Laser light has been bounced off the moon to accurately measure its distance from Earth. Physicians use lasers to do surgery. The most common use of lasers is in compact disc (CD) and digital video disc (DVD) players. A laser beam cuts information onto the discs. The narrow beam allows a disc to hold more information than a tape. Lasers are then used to read and play back the recorded information. Besides music, entire encyclopedias have been put on CDs.

Telephones have long used electric current and copper wire to carry messages. Flashes of light can be used to send messages, too. Laser beams can carry many different messages along very thin glass fibers called optical fibers. Many fibers, each carrying a different message, can be squeezed into a single cable. Fiber-optic telephone lines are now used between many cities. Lines were laid across the Atlantic and Pacific Oceans in the late 1980s.

Fiber optics are also used in medicine to make surgery easier. Doctors can use the fibers to see inside the body while making only small cuts—or no cuts at all.

THINK ABOUT IT

1. How can lenses change an image?
2. What are two uses of optical fibers?

Lewis Howard Latimer
INVENTOR, ENGINEER

Every time you turn on an electric light, you can thank Lewis Latimer. His many inventions helped improve the first light bulb, which had been made by Thomas Edison. And if you've ever screwed a light bulb into a socket, you have used one of Latimer's inventions. He designed the threads of the socket. His model was made of wood, but we still use his idea.

Latimer was the youngest son of escaped slaves. He had to leave school when he was ten to earn money for his family. He never stopped learning, though. He taught himself mechanical drawing by watching the men in the office where he worked. They made detailed drawings of inventions for patent applications. (Having a patent means the inventor "owns" the idea and the invention.) Latimer's office was near the office of Alexander Graham Bell, who invented the telephone. When Bell applied for a patent, he asked Latimer to make the drawing.

Later Latimer worked with the Edison Pioneers, a group of 80 inventors. He was the only African American in the group. He helped install lighting systems in New York, Philadelphia, Montreal, and even London.

THINK ABOUT IT

1. What do inventing and writing poetry have in common?

2. How is teaching yourself something, perhaps by watching others, different from learning in a classroom?

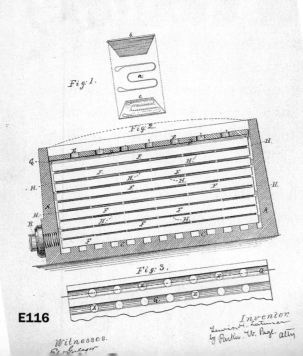

L. H. LATIMER.
PROCESS OF MANUFACTURING CARBONS.
Patented Jan. 17, 1882.

No. 252,386.

Fig. 1.

Fig. 2.

Fig. 3.

Witnesses.

Inventor
Lewis H. Latimer
by Parker W. Page, atty

COLORS

What colors are reflected off different colors of paper?

Materials

- glue
- strips of colored construction paper
- prism

Procedure

1. Glue strips of construction paper together in the order of the colors of the rainbow: red, orange, yellow, green, blue, and violet.

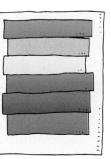

2. Use a prism to separate the colors in sunlight. Aim the colors from the prism at the different colors of construction paper.

3. Observe how the light from the prism is reflected by the different colors of construction paper.

Draw Conclusions

What colors from the prism are reflected from the green strip of construction paper? Explain.

MAKE A PERISCOPE

How can you see around a corner?

Materials

- glue
- aluminum foil
- 2 index cards
- shoe box
- black construction paper
- flashlight

Procedure

1. Glue aluminum foil, shiny side out, to the index cards to make mirrors. Make the foil as smooth as possible.

2. Line the inside of the box with black paper. Cut out a hole in the

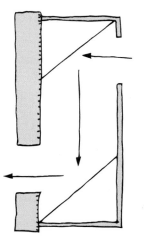

bottom of the box, about 3 cm from one end. Cut out a hole in the lid about 3 cm from one end.

3. Fold the ends of the aluminum foil mirrors to make tabs. Then glue the aluminum-foil mirrors to the inside of the box as shown.

4. While the glue is still damp, shine a flashlight straight into one of the openings. Look into the second opening and adjust one of the mirrors so that you can clearly see the flashlight. Let the glue dry.

5. Put the lid back on the box, and look through your periscope.

Draw Conclusions

How could you use a periscope to see around a corner?

Vocabulary Review

Use the terms below to complete the sentences 1 through 8. The page numbers in ( ) tell you where to look in the chapter if you need help.

reflection (E102)   **translucent** (E106)

refraction (E104)   **transparent** (E106)

absorption (E106)   **prism** (E110)

opaque (E106)   **visible spectrum** (E110)

1. The bending of light is called _____.

2. A _____ breaks white light into colors.

3. All the colors that you can see make up the _____.

4. You can't see through aluminum foil at all, so it is _____.

5. The bouncing of light off objects is called _____.

6. A window is _____ because you can see a clear image through it.

7. Stopping light and holding it in is _____.

8. A fogged-over window is _____. You see a blurry image through it.

Connect Concepts

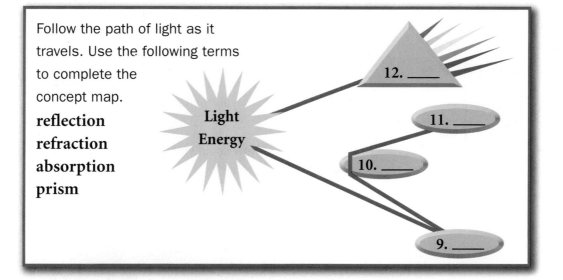

Follow the path of light as it travels. Use the following terms to complete the concept map.

reflection
refraction
absorption
prism

Light Energy

12. _____

11. _____

10. _____

9. _____

Check Understanding

Write the letter of the best choice.

13. Suppose you drop a penny into a shallow pool of water. You try to grab it but cannot seem to get your fingers in the right place. This happens because of —

    A reflection
    B absorption
    C refraction
    D light energy

14. Suppose you are standing at a pond. Your friend tries to sneak up on you, but you see him coming. You see him in the pond because of —

    F refraction
    G reflection
    H noise in the grass
    J absorption

15. White light is really —

    A all colors of light mixed
    B a mixture of yellow and white light
    C bright in the morning
    D a mixture of red and green light

16. Light travels —
    F through walls
    G around objects
    H in straight lines
    J in a curvy pattern

17. Most light bulbs have a coating inside the glass that makes them look white. Light still passes through the coating, so it is —
    A opaque
    B transparent
    C translucent
    D a prism

18. A bright, yellow raincoat looks yellow because —
    F it absorbs yellow light and reflects all other colors
    G it reflects a mix of blue and red light
    H it absorbs blue light and reflects a mix of red and green light
    J it refracts yellow light differently than other colors

Critical Thinking

19. A skylight has water drops on it from a rainstorm. The sun comes out, and you see a rainbow on the wall. What is happening?

20. Describe how you could use a mirror to signal your friend in the house across the street.

21. You go to see a play. The light on the stage is yellow. You look up at the lights. They are red and green. Explain.

22. For art class, your teacher has you draw a bowl of fruit. The bowl contains a red apple, an orange, and a banana. After you have finished, your teacher puts a green spotlight on the fruit and asks you to draw it again. Why do you need to draw a new picture?

Process Skills Review

Write *True* or *False*. If the statement is false, correct it to make it true.

23. When you **observe** what is happening in an experiment, you use only your eyes.

24. Scientists sometimes draw pictures to help them **draw conclusions** about their experiments.

Performance Assessment

Make a Model Prism

With a partner, use construction paper to make a large model of a prism breaking a ray of white light into its colors. Be sure to show the colors in the right order. Label each color. Make a hole in the model and add some string so it can be hung up in the classroom. You will need construction paper, glue, scissors, string, and a pencil.

There are many places where you can learn about matter and energy. By visiting the places below, you can learn more about how matter changes and how heat affects matter. You'll also have fun while you learn.

The Discovery Center of Science & Technology

WHAT A learning center with exhibits and hands-on activities

WHERE Bethlehem, Pennsylvania

WHAT CAN YOU DO THERE? Visit the learning center, see the exhibits, and find out more about science through the many activities they offer.

The United States Mint

WHAT A facility where all kinds of United States coins are made

WHERE Denver, Colorado

WHAT CAN YOU DO THERE? Tour the mint and learn what properties a metal must have before it can become a coin.

 Plan Your Own Expeditions

ONLINE If you can't visit the Discovery Center of Science & Technology or the United States Mint, visit a science center or a mint near you. Or log on to The Learning Site at **www.harcourtschool.com** to visit these science sites and see what more you can learn about energy and changes in matter.

Forces
and Motion

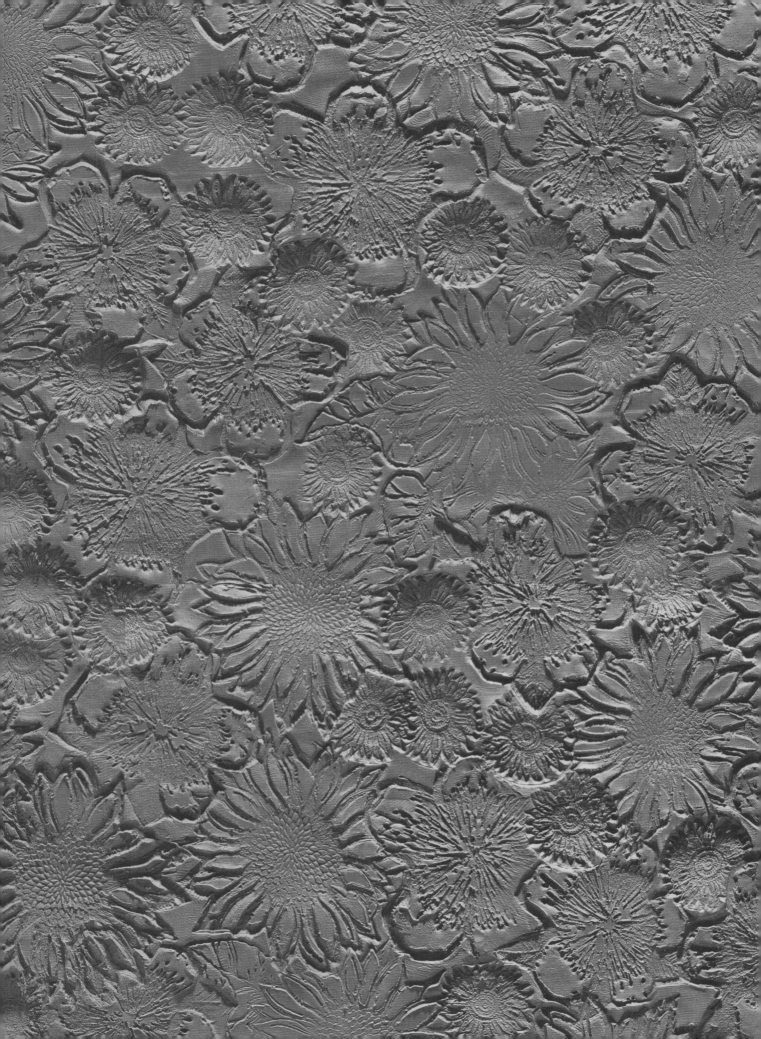

Forces and Motion

UNIT EXPERIMENT

Strength of Electromagnets

Forces enable you to affect the world around you. You push and pull to walk, eat, and do homework. When you use appliances, you are using electric and magnetic forces. While you study this unit, you can conduct a long-term experiment about a type of magnet and its force. Here are some questions to think about. What affects the strength of an electromagnet? How does a different wire or battery size affect the magnet? Plan and conduct an experiment to find answers to these or other questions you have about forces and motion. See pages x–xix for help in designing your experiment.

1

Electricity and Magnetism

Vocabulary Preview

charge
static electricity
electric field
electric current
circuit
electric cell
conductor
insulator
resistor
series circuit
parallel circuit
magnet
magnetic pole
magnetic field
electromagnet

Snap! Crackle! Pop! Your socks crackle and spark when you separate them from your freshly dried sweater! This kind of electricity is called static electricity. You can become charged with static electricity just by dragging your feet when you walk across carpet. Then ZAP! you'll get a "charge" out of opening the next door you come to!

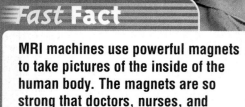

Fast Fact

MRI machines use powerful magnets to take pictures of the inside of the human body. The magnets are so strong that doctors, nurses, and patients can't carry any metal into the room where the machine is working.

Photocopiers make images by using static electricity! A large charged drum inside a photocopier pulls powdered ink to it. The ink goes to wherever dark spots on the original are reflected on the drum. The powder pattern is put on a piece of paper. Then the paper is heated and the ink melts, making a permanent copy.

Electricity use is measured in kilowatt-hours. Every home has a meter that measures how many kilowatt-hours have been used. A 60-watt light bulb uses 0.06 kilowatt-hours in one hour. Here's a list of the number of kilowatt-hours different appliances use in an hour:

Electricity Use

Appliance	Kilowatt-Hours Used in One Hour
Color television	0.23
Toaster	1.2
Hair dryer	1.5
Microwave oven	1.5
Clothes dryer	4.0
Refrigerator/freezer	5.0–7.0

LESSON 1

What Is Static Electricity?

In this lesson, you can . . .

INVESTIGATE rubbing balloons with different materials.

LEARN ABOUT causes of static electricity.

LINK to math, writing, health, and technology.

◀ It's not the wind that's making this boy's hair stand on end. It's static electricity. You may be surprised to learn what else static electricity can do.

INVESTIGATE

Balloons Rubbed with Different Materials

Activity Purpose Have you ever opened a package that had something breakable inside? There may have been little foam pieces in the box, and you may have noticed the strange way they acted. They jumped away from each other but stuck to almost everything else. You can make balloons act this way, too. In this investigation you will rub balloons with different materials. Then you'll **compare** your **observations** to **infer** why the balloons behaved the way they did.

Materials

- two small, round balloons
- string
- tape
- scrap of silk cloth
- scrap of wool cloth
- paper towel
- plastic wrap

Activity Procedure

1 Blow up the balloons, and tie them closed. Use string and tape to hang one balloon from a shelf or table.

2 Rub the silk all over each balloon. Slowly bring the free balloon near the hanging balloon. **Observe** the hanging balloon. **Record** your observations. (Picture A)

Picture A

Picture B

3 Again rub the silk all over the hanging balloon. Move the silk away. Then slowly bring the silk close to the balloon. **Observe** the hanging balloon, and **record** your observations. (Picture B)

4 Repeat Steps 2 and 3 separately with the wool, a paper towel, and plastic wrap. **Record** your **observations.**

5 Rub the silk all over the hanging balloon. Rub the wool all over the free balloon. Slowly bring the free balloon near the hanging balloon. **Observe** the hanging balloon. **Record** your observations.

Draw Conclusions

1. **Compare** your observations of the two balloons in Step 2 with your observations of a balloon and the material it was rubbed with in Steps 3 and 4.

2. **Compare** your observations of the hanging balloon in Step 2 with your observations of it in Step 5.

3. **Scientists at Work** Which of your observations support the **inference** that a force acted on the balloons and materials? Explain your answer.

Investigate Further When you rubbed the balloons, you caused a charge to build up. Like charges repel. Opposite charges attract. Review your results for each trial. Tell whether the balloons or material had like charges or opposite charges.

> **Process Skill Tip**
>
> A force is a push or a pull. You can **infer** a force between two objects by observing whether the objects are pulled toward each other or pushed away from each other.

F5

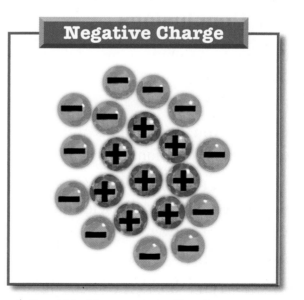
Static Electricity

FIND OUT

- about a property of matter called charge
- how charges move from one piece of matter to another
- how electric fields cause forces

VOCABULARY

charge
static electricity
electric field

Two Kinds of Charge

Remember that matter is made of particles that have mass and volume. Particles of matter also have a property called *electric charge*. A particle can have a positive (+) charge, a negative (−) charge, or no charge at all.

Matter in an object normally has equal numbers of positive and negative particles. It is *neutral*. Rubbing two objects together, however, can move negative particles from one object to the other. That is exactly what happened in the Investigation. The result was that the number of positive charges on each balloon was different from the number of negative charges. **Charge** is a measure of the extra positive or negative particles that an object has. Rubbing gave one object an overall *positive charge*, and it gave the other an overall *negative charge*.

The charge that stays on an object is called **static electricity** (STAT•ik ee•lek•TRIS•ih•tee). *Static* means "not moving." Even though the charges moved to get to the object, once there they stayed.

✔ **What are the two types of charges?**

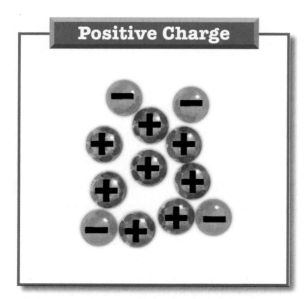

▲ A single positive charge is labeled +. A single negative charge is labeled −. When an object has more positive charges than negative charges, its overall charge is positive.

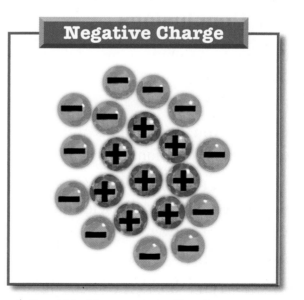

▲ If an object has more negative charges than positive charges, its overall charge is negative. How many extra negative charges are shown here?

Separating Charges

Most of the time, you, a balloon, and a doorknob have neither an overall negative charge nor an overall positive charge. You and the objects are neutral. To see the effects of forces between charges, you must separate negative charges from positive charges.

You can separate the negative and positive charges of many objects by rubbing them together. Rubbing pulls negative charges off one object onto the other. Note that only negative charges move in this way.

When you comb dry hair, the teeth of the comb rub negative charges from the hair. The comb gets extra negative charges, so it has an overall negative charge. Your hair loses negative charges. It now has an overall positive charge.

✔ **Which kind of charge moves to make a static charge?**

As clothes tumble in a dryer, different fabrics rub against each other. Negative charges move from one piece of clothing to another. When this happens the clothes stick together. ▼

▲ If you hold a piece of wool next to a balloon, nothing happens. So you know that neither the wool nor the balloon is charged. The numbers of positive and negative charges on the balloon are equal. The charges are also equal on the wool. Both items have a neutral charge.

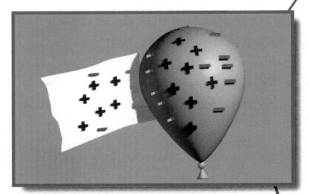

▲ Rubbing wool on a balloon separates charges. Negative charges move from the wool to the balloon. The balloon now has more negative charges than positive charges. The balloon is negatively charged. The wool loses negative charges. Now it has more positive charges than negative charges. It is positively charged.

Electric Forces

In the investigation you saw how a charged balloon pushed or pulled another charged balloon. The push or pull between objects with different charges is an *electric force.* An electric force causes two objects with opposite charges to *attract,* or pull, each other. An electric force causes two objects with like charges to *repel* (rih•PEL), or push away from, each other.

The space where electric forces occur around an object is called an **electric field**. The electric field of a positive charge attracts a nearby negative charge. The electric field of a positive charge repels a nearby positive charge.

In diagrams, arrows are used to show an electric field. They point the way one positive charge would be pulled by the field. The pictures here show the electric fields of two pairs of balloons. One pair has opposite charges. The other pair has the same charges.

✔ **What is an electric field?**

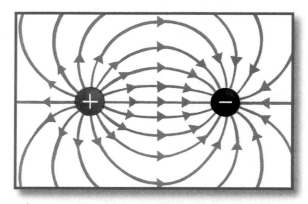

▲ One balloon has a positive charge. The other has a negative charge. Their electric fields form a closed pattern of field lines. Balloons with opposite charges attract each other.

Both balloons have negative charges. Their electric fields do not form a closed pattern of field lines. Balloons with the same type of charge repel each other.

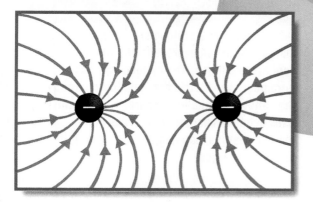

After you comb your hair, your comb has a negative charge. Its electric field repels the negative particles in the stream of water. Negative particles are pushed to the opposite side of the stream. That leaves extra positive charges on the side near the comb. The stream bends toward the comb.

Summary

Objects become electrically charged when they gain or lose negative charges. A charge causes an electric field. The electric fields of charged objects interact to produce electric forces. Objects with like charges repel each other. Objects with unlike charges attract each other.

Review

1. What is static electricity?

2. What is charge?

3. What is an electric field?

4. **Critical Thinking** How can you make a piece of rubber that has an overall positive charge neutral again?

5. **Test Prep** A plastic ruler can get a positive charge by —
    A gaining a single negative charge
    B losing a single negative charge
    C gaining a single positive charge
    D losing a single positive charge

LINKS

MATH LINK

Use Addition Properties The two pictures on page F6 show charges. How many single negative charges must each object gain or lose to become neutral? Use numbers and math symbols to show how you found your answer.

WRITING LINK

Informative Writing—Description Suppose you are a balloon. Write a paragraph for a classmate describing what happens to you as you gain a negative charge from a piece of wool.

HEALTH LINK

Lightning Safety Lightning is a big movement of charged particles. It can kill people and animals, and it can start fires. Find out the safety rules you should follow during a thunderstorm. Make a poster illustrating the rules.

GO ONLINE TECHNOLOGY LINK

Learn more about early use of electricity by visiting the National Museum of American History Internet site.
www.si.edu/harcourt/science

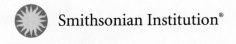 Smithsonian Institution®

What Is an Electric Current?

In this lesson, you can . . .

INVESTIGATE using a battery to light a bulb.

LEARN ABOUT electric current.

LINK to math, writing, health, and technology.

INVESTIGATE

Making a Bulb Light Up

Activity Purpose Can a flashlight work without batteries? You would be right if you said *no.* The batteries produce the electricity that makes the bulb shine. But how does the electricity get from the batteries to the bulb? You can **plan and conduct a simple investigation** to find out how materials need to be arranged to make a bulb light.

Materials

- D-cell battery
- insulated electrical wire
- miniature light bulb
- masking tape

Activity Procedure

1. Make a chart like the one shown on the next page. You will use it to **record** your **observations**.

2. **Predict** a way to arrange the materials you have been given so that the bulb lights up. Make a drawing to **record** your prediction. (Picture A)

3. Test your prediction. **Record** whether or not the bulb lights up. (Picture B)

◄ The lights of a Ferris wheel shine in the night as the wheel goes round and round. The electricity that makes the bulbs glow and moves the wheel also goes round and round.

Picture A

Picture B

Predictions and Observations

Arrangement of Bulb, Battery, and Wire	Drawing	Observations

4 Continue to work with the bulb, the battery, and the wire. Try different arrangements to get the bulb to light. **Record** the results of each try.

Draw Conclusions

1. What did you **observe** about the arrangement of materials when the bulb lighted?

2. What did you **observe** about the arrangement of materials when the bulb did NOT light?

3. **Scientists at Work** To find out more about bulbs and batteries, you could **plan an investigation** of your own. To do that, you need to decide the following: What question do you want to answer? What materials will you need? How will you use the materials? What will you observe?

Investigate Further **Conduct your investigation.**

> ### Process Skill Tip
>
> When you **plan and conduct a simple investigation**, you work to find the answer to a question or to solve a problem. By doing many tests and observing their outcomes, you can draw conclusions about how something works.

Electric Currents

Moving Charges

You know that a static charge stays on an object. But even a static charge will move if it has a path to follow. The snap and crackle of a static electric shock are the result of a moving charge.

Have you ever gotten a small electric shock from touching a doorknob? Here's how it happens. Walking on a carpet rubs negative charges off the carpet and onto your feet. The charges spread out on your body. Your whole body becomes negatively charged. When you touch the doorknob, all the extra negative charges move at once from your hand to the doorknob. You get a small "zap." The static, or unmoving charge, has become a *current*, or moving charge. A flow of electric charges is called an **electric current**. Current is measured in amperes (AM•peers).

In the investigation you arranged a wire, a bulb, and a battery to make a path in which negative charges could flow. A path that is made for an electric current is called a **circuit** (SER•kit). The battery was an important part of the circuit you made. A battery is an **electric cell**, which supplies energy to move charges through a circuit. The energy a battery can provide is measured in volts.

✔ **What does an electric current need in order to flow?**

◀ **FIND OUT**

• how electric charges can move

• ways different materials control electric current

• differences between series and parallel circuits

VOCABULARY

electric current
circuit
electric cell
conductor
insulator
resistor
series circuit
parallel circuit

◀ An electric current in a circuit moves like a bike wheel. When you pedal, you give energy of motion to the whole wheel at once. When you connect a circuit, a battery moves energy to all parts of the circuit at the same time.

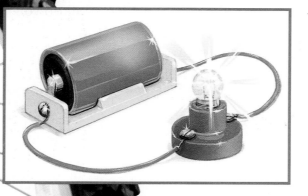

◀ Use your finger to trace the path of the current through each part of the circuit. What do you notice?

Symbols stand for the various circuit parts. A long and a short line next to each other stand for an energy source. You can see this symbol near the batteries. Opposite ends of a battery are marked with a − and a +. Current flows from the + end toward the − end.

The symbol for a switch is an opening in the line. It looks like a gate that can be pushed open and closed.

▲ The diagram around this flashlight shows how a circuit is drawn. The black line around the flashlight stands for the conductor that connects all the circuit parts.

The wire in the bulb acts as a resistor. When the switch is closed, the wire glows and gives off light. The symbol for a resistor is a zigzag line.

Controlling Current

A circuit with a battery, bulb, and wires contains different materials such as copper and plastic. You can classify these materials by the way they control the flow of charges through them.

A **conductor** is a material that current can pass through easily. Most metals are good conductors of electric current. Electric wires are made of metal, often copper. The base of a light bulb is made of metal because it must conduct an electric current.

A material that current cannot pass through easily is called an **insulator** (IN•suh•layt•er). The black band between the metal tip and the screw-in part of a light bulb is an insulator. A plastic covering insulated the wire you used in the investigation. Plastic keeps the metal of the wire from touching other metal.

A flashlight has a switch to turn it on and off. A *switch* uses conductors and insulators to make and break a circuit. When the switch is on, two conductors touch. When they touch, the path is complete. Current flows through the circuit. When the switch is off, air separates the two conductors, breaking the path. No current can flow.

Some materials cut down, or resist, the flow of charges. A material that resists but doesn't stop the flow of current is called a **resistor** (rih•ZIS•ter). A flashlight bulb contains a tiny coil of metal. The coil is a resistor. As charges move through the resistor, they transfer thermal energy to it. The metal becomes hot. The glowing coil transfers some of its thermal energy to the air as radiation. It gives off light.

✔ **What does a switch do in a circuit?**

Series Circuits

When you turn on a flashlight, there is one path for the current to follow through the circuit. A circuit that has only one path for the current is called a **series circuit**. The pictures below show a series circuit with two bulbs. Note that the current runs from the battery to one bulb, then to the next bulb, and then back to the battery. What happens if you remove one bulb or a bulb burns out? The single path is broken. No current moves through the circuit. As a result, the second bulb will go out.

✔ **How does current travel in a series circuit?**

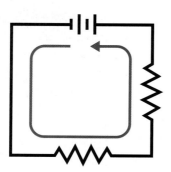

▲ As the arrow shows, there is only one path for current in a series circuit. Disconnecting a light bulb opens the whole circuit, so both bulbs go out.

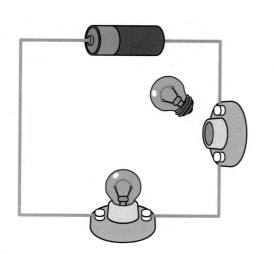

Parallel Circuits

A **parallel** (PAIR•uh•lel) **circuit** has more than one path for current to travel. With your finger, trace the path of the current in the parallel circuit shown below. Part of the current moves through each path of the circuit. What happens when a bulb is removed from this circuit? The current still moves through the other path. The second bulb stays lit. If one bulb in a parallel circuit burns out, the other bulbs will stay on.

✔ **Which type of circuit has more than one path for current?**

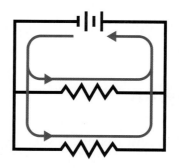

▲ Notice how the arrow splits in two. There are at least two paths for current in a parallel circuit. Disconnecting a bulb opens only one path. The other bulb stays lit.

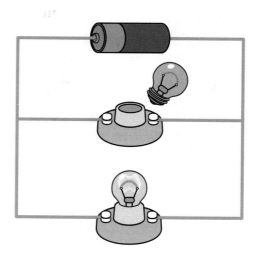

▲ Circuits inside appliances are a mix of many parallel and series circuits.

Summary

Electric current is a flow of charges through a path called a circuit. A material in a circuit can be classified as a conductor, an insulator, or a resistor. If a circuit has one path for current, it is a series circuit. A parallel circuit has more than one path for current.

Review

1. What is an electric current?
2. Describe what has to be in place for a circuit to work.
3. Contrast conductors and insulators.
4. **Critical Thinking** Most wall outlets in your home have places for two plugs. Infer which type of circuit an outlet is part of. How do you know?
5. **Test Prep** What supplies energy in an electric circuit?
   A conductors
   B electric cells
   C resistors
   D switches

LINKS

MATH LINK

Solve a Problem Electric energy is measured in a unit called a kilowatt-hour, or kWh. With a parent's permission, read the electric meter at your home twice, one week apart. Use the readings to calculate how many kWh were used. If each kWh costs 10 cents, how much did a week of electricity use cost?

WRITING LINK

Descriptive Writing—Personal Story In the United States, electricity is a part of almost everyone's life. Suppose you woke up one morning and electricity no longer worked anywhere. Write a story describing what a day completely without electricity would be like.

HEALTH LINK

Electricity Safety The batteries you have been using are safe because they are low voltage. Higher voltage household current can hurt people or start fires. Use library resources to find out more about home electricity safety. Then share what you learned with your family and conduct an electricity safety survey of your home.

TECHNOLOGY LINK

Learn more about controlling large circuits by viewing *L.A. Traffic Control* on the **Harcourt Science Newsroom Video.**

What Is a Magnet?

In this lesson, you can . . .

INVESTIGATE how a compass works.

LEARN ABOUT the ways magnets interact.

LINK to math, writing, social studies, and technology.

The compass is an important tool that helps sailors find their way across the oceans.

INVESTIGATE

A Compass

Activity Purpose If you are like most people, you have papers stuck with magnets to your refrigerator. A *magnet* is an object that attracts certain materials, mainly iron and steel. The material in your refrigerator magnet attracts the steel in your refrigerator door. The attraction is strong enough that it works through paper. In this investigation you will make your own magnet and, based on your **observations, infer** how a compass works.

Materials
- safety goggles
- small bar magnet
- small objects made of iron or steel, such as paper clips
- large sewing needle or straight pin (4–5 cm long)
- small piece of foam tray
- cup of water

CAUTION

Activity Procedure

1 **CAUTION** **Put on your safety goggles.** Hold the bar magnet near a paper clip. **Observe** what happens. Now hold the needle near the paper clip. Observe what happens.

2 **CAUTION** **Be careful with sharp objects.** Hold the needle by its eye and drag its entire length over the magnet 20 times, always in the same direction. (Picture A)

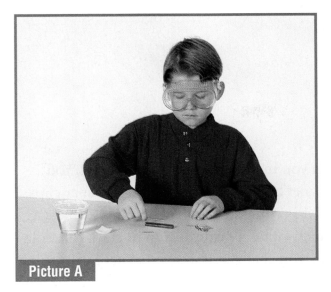

Picture A

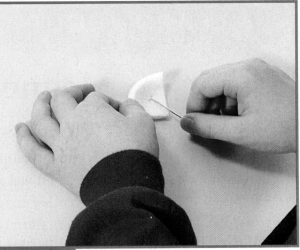

Picture B

3 Repeat Step 1. **Observe** what happens.

4 Hold the foam on a flat surface. From one side, slide the needle into the foam with the point away from your fingers. **CAUTION** Be careful with sharp objects. (Picture B)

5 Move the bar magnet at least a meter from the cup. Float the foam in the water. **Observe** what happens to the needle.

6 Carefully and slowly turn the cup. **Observe** what happens to the needle.

7 Hold one end of the bar magnet near the cup. **Observe** what happens to the needle. Switch magnet ends. What happens?

Draw Conclusions

1. Describe what happened when you floated the foam with the needle in water. What happened when you turned the cup?

2. What happened when you brought the bar magnet near the floating needle?

3. **Scientists at Work** What **hypothesis** can you make based on your observations of the needle? What predictions can you make by using your hypothesis?

Investigate Further **Plan and conduct an experiment** to test your hypothesis from Question 3, above.

> **Process Skill Tip**
>
> When you **hypothesize**, you carefully explain all your observations. A hypothesis is more detailed than an inference. Unlike an inference, a hypothesis can be used to make predictions that you can test.

Magnets

Two Poles

FIND OUT

- **about magnetic poles**
- **how magnetic fields cause magnetic forces**
- **how to use Earth's magnetic field to find directions**

VOCABULARY

magnet
magnetic pole
magnetic field

In the investigation you made a needle into a magnet. You could tell it was a magnet because it attracted metal paper clips, just as other magnets do. A **magnet** is an object that attracts certain materials, usually objects made of iron or steel. A needle isn't a natural magnet. You changed it into a magnet by dragging it along the bar magnet.

A magnet has two ends called **magnetic poles**, or just *poles* for short. A magnet's pull is strongest at the poles. If a bar magnet can swing freely, one end, called the *north-seeking pole*, will always point north. The opposite end, called the *south-seeking pole*, will always point south. A magnet's north-seeking pole is usually marked *N*. Its south-seeking pole is marked *S*.

✔ **What is each end of a magnet called?**

A magnet has a north-seeking pole on one end and a south-seeking pole on the opposite end. ▼

▲ If you cut a magnet in half, each half will be a magnet with a pole at each end.

▲ No matter how many times you cut a magnet, each piece will be a magnet with a pole at each end.

Magnetic Forces

If you've ever played with magnets, you've probably felt them pull toward each other. At other times they seem to push away from each other. The forces you felt are magnetic forces caused by magnetic fields.

A **magnetic field** is the space all around a magnet where the force of the magnet can act. You can't see the field. However, a magnet can move iron filings into lines. The pattern made by the iron filings shows the shape of the magnet's field.

Forces between magnet poles are like forces between electric charges. Opposite magnetic poles attract, and like poles repel. If the N pole of one magnet is held toward the S pole of another magnet, their fields form a closed pattern. This closed pattern of lines shows a force that pulls the magnets together.

If two magnets are held with their N poles near each other, their magnetic fields form an open pattern of lines. Just as with electric charges, this pattern shows a force that pushes the magnets away from each other.

✔ **Where is the pull of a magnet strongest?**

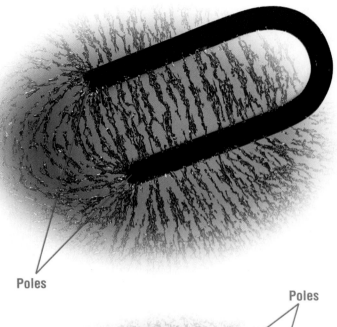

Poles

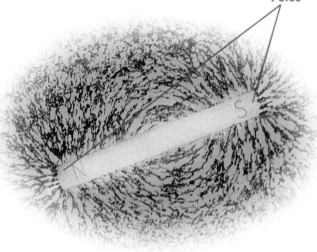

Poles

▲ The shape of a magnetic field depends on the shape of the magnet. The bunching of iron filings on the end of a magnet shows that the magnetic force is strongest at a magnet's poles.

▲ Opposite poles of two magnets attract. The pattern of iron filings is closed. This shows a magnetic force that attracts, or pulls, the magnets together.

▲ Like poles of two magnets repel. The field lines are open, showing lines of force that push the magnets apart.

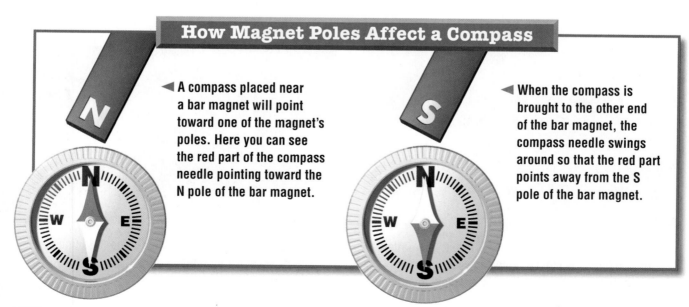

A magnetic field fills the space around Earth. Earth's magnetic poles and the "true" poles made by Earth's axis are not identical.

Compasses

The north-seeking and south-seeking property of magnets is useful. For hundreds of years, people have used magnets to find direction. The first magnets used were made of a heavy natural material called *lodestone.* Today geologists know this material as the mineral magnetite.

A compass today uses a lightweight magnetic needle that is free to turn. This is much like the needle you made into a magnet in the investigation. A compass needle points along an imaginary line connecting the North and South Poles. This is because Earth is like a giant magnet.

How Magnet Poles Affect a Compass

N

◀ A compass placed near a bar magnet will point toward one of the magnet's poles. Here you can see the red part of the compass needle pointing toward the N pole of the bar magnet.

S

◀ When the compass is brought to the other end of the bar magnet, the compass needle swings around so that the red part points away from the S pole of the bar magnet.

The field lines of Earth's magnetic field come together close to the planet's North and South Poles. This pattern is like the one shown by the iron filings around the bar magnet on page F19. Indeed, Earth's magnetic field is like the field of a giant bar magnet.

✔ **How does a compass work?**

Summary

Magnets are objects that attract materials such as iron. Every magnet has two magnetic poles. Magnetic forces are caused by the interaction of magnetic fields. Earth's magnetic field is like the field of a bar magnet. A compass needle interacts with Earth's magnetic field.

Review

1. How can you find the poles of a magnet?

2. What is a magnetic field?

3. Which type of magnet has a field that is about the same shape as the magnetic field of Earth?

4. **Critical Thinking** Describe the field lines formed if the south poles of two magnets are brought close together.

5. **Test Prep** How many poles does a magnet have?

   A none

   B one

   C two

   D four

LINKS

MATH LINK

Make a Bar Graph Decide on a way to measure the strength of different bar magnets or different magnet shapes. Test some magnets. Then use a computer program such as *Graph Links* to make a bar graph to show what you measured.

WRITING LINK

Informative Writing—How-to Write a paragraph telling a classmate how to use a compass to find the direction in which he or she is traveling.

SOCIAL STUDIES LINK

Earth's Moving Magnetic Poles Earth's north magnetic pole is constantly moving. Find out how the pole's location is shown on topographical (tahp•uh•GRAF•ih•kuhl) maps, which show the land's surface features, and on navigational charts. Find the current location of the north magnetic pole on a globe. Measure the distance between the true North Pole and the magnetic north pole.

GO ONLINE TECHNOLOGY LINK

Learn more about Earth's magnetic field by visiting the National Air and Space Museum Internet site.
www.si.edu/harcourt/science

Smithsonian Institution®

LESSON 4

What Is an Electro-magnet?

In this lesson, you can . . .

INVESTIGATE the magnetic field around a wire that carries current.

LEARN ABOUT uses of electromagnets.

LINK to math, writing, language arts, and technology.

Strong magnetic forces lift this train slightly from the tracks and push it forward. ▽

How Magnets and Electricity Can Interact

Activity Purpose The pictures at the bottom of page F20 show how a bar magnet affects a nearby compass. Have you ever tried this yourself? In this investigation you will **observe** how a bar magnet affects a compass needle. You'll **compare** it with the way a current in a wire affects a compass needle. You can then **infer** some things about electricity moving through wires.

Materials

- bar magnet
- small compass
- sheet of cardboard
- tape
- insulated wire, about 30 cm long, with stripped ends
- D-cell battery

Activity Procedure

1 Try several positions of the magnet and compass. **Record** your **observations** of how the magnet affects the compass needle.

2 Place the compass flat on the cardboard so the needle is lined up with north. Tape the middle third of the insulated wire onto the cardboard in a north-south line.

3 Tape one end of the wire to the flat end of a D-cell battery. Tape the battery to the cardboard. (Picture A)

4 Without moving the cardboard, put the compass on the taped-down part of the wire.

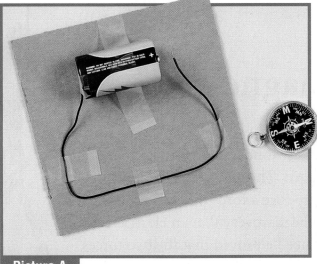

Picture A

Picture B

5 Touch the free end of the wire to the (+) end of the battery for a second. (Picture B) **Observe** the compass needle. Repeat this step several more times. **Record** your observations.

6 Carefully remove a piece of tape. Place the compass underneath the wire so that both line up along a north-south line. **Predict** what will happen if you repeat Step 5.

7 Repeat Step 5. **Record** your observations.

Draw Conclusions

1. **Compare** your observations in Step 5 with those in Step 7. Was your prediction accurate? Explain.

2. Using what you know about compasses in magnetic fields, what can you **infer** about currents in wires?

3. **Scientists at Work** Just as you predicted what would happen in Step 7, scientists often **predict** the outcome of an experiment based on their observations and inferences. Based on your observations, what would you predict will happen in this experiment if the current is made to move in the opposite direction?

Investigate Further Test your **prediction**. Remove the battery from the cardboard. Turn it so that its ends are pointing in the opposite direction. Attach the wire again. **Record** your observations.

Process Skill Tip

When you **predict**, you tell what you expect to happen. A prediction is based on patterns of observations. If you think you know the cause of an event, you can predict when it will happen again. Predictions aren't always correct.

Electromagnets

Currents Make Magnets

FIND OUT

- **how electricity and magnetism are related**

- **ways to change the strength of an electromagnet**

- **uses of motors and generators**

VOCABULARY

electromagnet

In the past, scientists wondered if electric charge and magnetism were related. They knew that charged objects and magnets both produce a force that can pull or push without touching. The discovery that an electric current can turn a compass needle proved that the two forces are related.

A current in a wire produces a magnetic field around the wire. You saw evidence of this in the investigation. The magnetic field produced by current moved the compass needle.

If you could see them, the field lines around a wire that carries current would look different from those around a bar magnet. They circle around the wire instead of looping out from the wire ends. A compass needle moves to point along magnetic field lines. So, it moves to point at right angles to the wire.

When current flows in the wire, it produces a circular magnetic field. The compass needle lines up with the field lines by turning at right angles to the wire. ▶

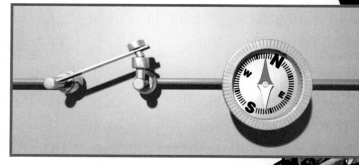

When the switch is open, current no longer flows and the magnetic field goes away. The compass needle swings back to its original position. ▶

This coil of wire is carrying an electric current. Iron filings show the shape of the magnetic field inside the coil. The lines of filings are closest together where the field is strongest. ▶

Compared with bar magnets, current-carrying wires produce weak magnetic fields. But there's a way to put a lot of wire in one place. When a current-carrying wire is coiled, the fields of the loops overlap. The strengths of the fields add up. The more loops you put together, the stronger the field gets.

The fields produced by many wire coils add up to make a field like that of a bar magnet. Iron filings line up along the middle of the coil. Outside the coil, the magnetic field lines loop out from one open end and back to the other.

Alone, a coil of wire easily bends. To make it stiffer and easier to use, the coil is wrapped around a solid material called a *core*. This arrangement of wire wrapped around a core is called an **electromagnet** (ee•LEK•troh•mag•nit). An electromagnet is a temporary magnet. There is a magnetic field only when there is an electric current in the wire.

If the core of an electromagnet is made of iron, the core also becomes a magnet when there is current in the wire. This makes the electromagnet stronger.

✔ **Why is an electromagnet a temporary magnet?**

◀ This big electromagnet on a crane can lift a heavy load of scrap metal. It has an iron core and many wire coils, and it carries a strong current. What will happen when the current to the electromagnet is turned off?

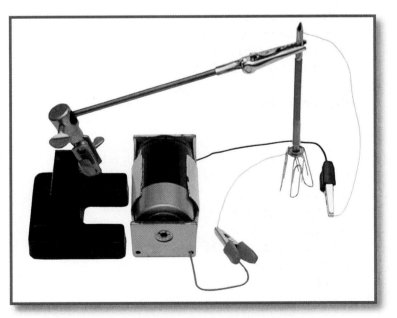

▲ When current flows through an electromagnet, the electromagnet acts like a bar magnet. This one is strong enough to hold three paper clips.

Controlling Electromagnets

A magnet and an electromagnet have one main difference. An electromagnet is a temporary magnet. You can turn it on and off with a switch. A bar magnet is a permanent magnet. It doesn't have an *off* switch. Electromagnets are a useful tool because you can control them. You can learn how one is used in The Inside Story.

Turning an electromagnet on and off is one way to control it. You can also control the strength of an electromagnet. One way to do this is to add or remove coils of wire. The more coils an electromagnet has, the stronger it is.

The amount of current also affects the strength of an electromagnet. The more current that is flowing, the stronger the electromagnet is.

Electromagnets today are made to use large amounts of current to lift large amounts of weight. Smaller and weaker ones are also made. Small electromagnets work out of sight inside computer disk drives, video players, television screens, and other electronic devices.

✔ **What is the main difference between a bar magnet and an electromagnet?**

THE INSIDE STORY

Alarm Bell

The bells used in fire alarms, doorbells, and telephones work because electromagnets can be turned off and on very quickly. The picture and diagram on the right show you how an electric bell works.

❶ When the bell is turned on, current flows in the electromagnet. The electromagnet pulls the long iron rod into the coils.

❷ The hammer is connected to the rod. It moves and strikes the bell, making a sound.

❸ The strip of metal with the hammer acts like a switch. As the hammer moves to strike the bell, the switch opens. No current flows in the circuit. The electromagnet is turned off. The hammer returns to its original position.

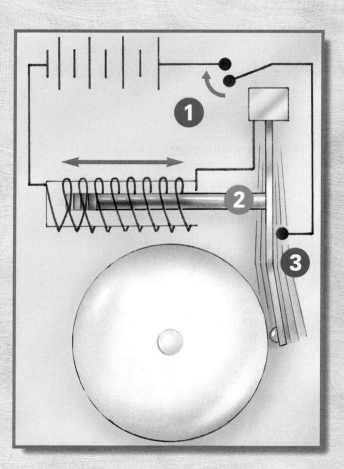

The strength of an electromagnet depends on the number of coils. Count the paper clips and the coils. ▼

▲ This electromagnet is the same as the one above to the left except that it has more coils. There are two layers of coils. Count the paper clips and coils.

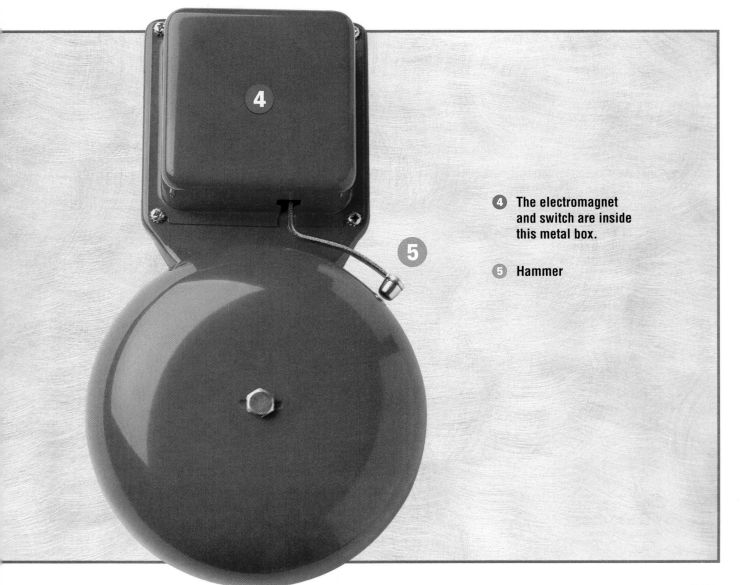

④ The electromagnet and switch are inside this metal box.

⑤ Hammer

Motors and Generators

If electricity can produce a magnetic field, can a magnetic field produce electricity? Yes! If you move a coil of wire near a magnet, current flows in the wire. Current flows as long as the wire is moving through magnetic field lines. This is how an electric generator works.

A coil of wire, a magnet, and electricity can also be used to cause motion. That's how an electric motor works. The coil of an electromagnet is pushed and pulled by the poles of other magnets. The coil turns. This turning motion is used in machines such as kitchen appliances, toys, and tools.

✔ **What things do generators and motors have in common?**

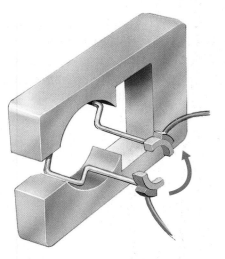

▲ One simple electric motor contains an electromagnet and a permanent magnet. When the motor is on, the direction of current is changed in a pattern. As it changes, the coil is pushed and then pulled by the permanent magnet. The coil turns.

In this hand mixer, a small electric motor turns the beaters. ▼

◀ A small, simple generator uses a hand crank to turn a magnet around a loop of wire. Generators that supply electric power for homes and factories are much bigger, about the size of a bus. They usually use steam or water power to turn a coil.

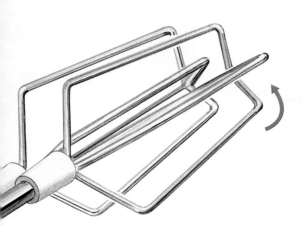

Summary

Wires carrying an electric current become magnets. An electromagnet is a core wrapped with wires that carry current. The ends of the electromagnet's coil are its poles. An electromagnet is magnetic only when there is a current in the wire. Generators use electromagnets to produce current from motion. Motors use electromagnets to produce motion from current.

Review

1. What do magnets and electric charges have in common?

2. Name two ways that you can make an electromagnet stronger.

3. What is a motor?

4. **Critical Thinking** Why is it useful to have a magnet that can be turned on and off?

5. **Test Prep** The ends of an electromagnet that are useful are called —

   A cores
   B loops
   C poles
   D wires

LINKS

MATH LINK

Find a Rule An electromagnet with 10 loops of wire can pick up 5 paper clips. With 20 loops it can pick up 10 paper clips. Predict how many paper clips the electromagnet can pick up if it has 40 loops. Write a procedure to find out how many paper clips this electromagnet can pick up if you know the number of loops of wire.

WRITING LINK

Informative Writing—Description Think of an appliance in your home that has an electric motor. Write a description for a younger child, telling what the appliance does. If there were no electric motors, how would you do what the appliance does?

LANGUAGE ARTS LINK

Making Words The word *electromagnet* was made by joining two words. What are they? Research these two words to find out where they came from and how old they are. Why do you think this word is used to describe the device you learned about in this lesson?

GO ONLINE TECHNOLOGY LINK

Visit the Harcourt Learning Site for related links, activities, and resources.
www.harcourtschool.com

WELCOME TO THE LEARNING SITE

Discovering
ELECTROMAGNETISM

Have you used a computer today? Answered the telephone or the doorbell? Watched television? These are just a few examples of everyday machines that work because of electromagnetism.

The First Discoveries

The early Greeks were the first people to observe and describe static electricity. They noticed that rubbing amber, a yellowish gemstone, with a cloth caused the amber to attract bits of straw or feathers. The Greek word for amber is *elektron*. Our words *electron* and *electricity* come from this Greek word.

The Greeks were also the first to observe and describe magnetism. Thales (THAY•leez), a Greek philosopher, lived in a town called Magnesia. Some of the rocks near his town seemed to pull at the shepherds' walking sticks, which had iron tips. Thales noted that the rocks also pulled toward each other and toward all iron objects that were close to them. These rocks were magnetite, a natural magnet. Later, people in Europe called this natural magnet *lodestone* (LOHD•stohn), which means *leading stone.*

The Chinese may have been the first to use magnets as compasses. Sailors and other travelers found that lodestone always turns to point along a north-south line. Compasses could be made by putting a thin piece of lodestone on a piece of wood floating in water. Later, lodestone was used to magnetize iron compass needles.

Learning More About Electricity

In the 1700s scientists began experimenting with electricity and magnetism, which they thought might be related. One of the scientists, Alessandro Volta (ah•leh•SAHN•droh VOHL•tah), discovered that he could make electricity by using pieces of two different metals. He made the first battery, which was called a voltaic (vohl•TAY•ik) pile. Using this battery moved electricity steadily through a conductor,

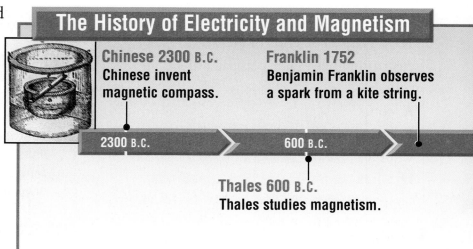

The History of Electricity and Magnetism

Chinese 2300 B.C.
Chinese invent magnetic compass.

Franklin 1752
Benjamin Franklin observes a spark from a kite string.

2300 B.C.   600 B.C.

Thales 600 B.C.
Thales studies magnetism.

such as a salt solution, instead of giving off the electricity all at once, like a lightning bolt or a spark caused by static electricity.

The key to understanding the connection between electricity and magnetism came from a chance observation. While giving a demonstration for a class, Hans Oersted (HAHNZ ER•stuhd) noticed that when he put a compass over a wire carrying electricity, the compass needle moved. He went on to prove that an electric current always produces a magnetic field.

Other scientists built on Oersted's discovery. Michael Faraday invented a generator, a machine that produces electricity. The generator makes electricity from a moving magnet and a coil of wire.

James Clerk Maxwell also studied Oersted's work. Maxwell hypothesized that electric and magnetic fields work together to make radiant energy, or light. About 20 years after Maxwell's experiments, Heinrich (HYN•rik) Hertz proved Maxwell was right.

Amber and feathers

Superconductors

In 1911 Dutch scientist Heike Onnes (HY•kuh AW•nuhs) discovered super-conductors. At very low temperatures, near ⁻273°C (⁻459°F), these metals or mixtures of metals conduct electrical current without any resistance. Superconductors are part of MRI machines, which are used by doctors to make images of the inside of the human body. In the early 2000s, trains that float above their tracks using superconducting magnets were being built and tested in Japan.

THINK ABOUT IT

1. How did observation and curiosity help Oersted?
2. How has the research of Thales, Volta, Faraday, and others affected your life?

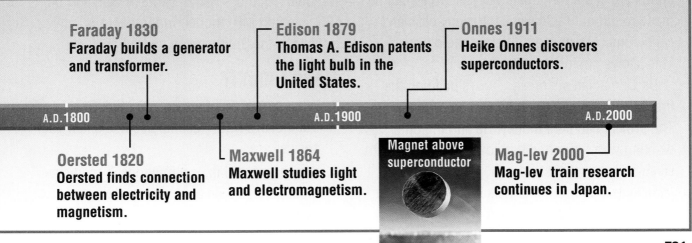

Faraday 1830
Faraday builds a generator and transformer.

Edison 1879
Thomas A. Edison patents the light bulb in the United States.

Onnes 1911
Heike Onnes discovers superconductors.

A.D.1800   A.D.1900   A.D.2000

Oersted 1820
Oersted finds connection between electricity and magnetism.

Maxwell 1864
Maxwell studies light and electromagnetism.

Magnet above superconductor

Mag-lev 2000
Mag-lev train research continues in Japan.

F31

Raymond V. Damadian
INVENTOR

"I think the thing that matters is not so much what you are doing but the spirit in which you are doing it."

▼ Modern open MRI machine

Dr. Raymond Damadian had many interests besides science as he was growing up. He was an accomplished violinist by the time he was eight. He attended The Juilliard School of Music before becoming a doctor. He also was a professional tennis player.

Dr. Damadian and his co-workers invented the magnetic resonance imaging machine (MRI). An MRI machine uses very strong magnets to take pictures of the inside of the body. When certain atoms are in a strong magnetic field, they can be made to put out radio waves. Healthy cells and cancerous cells give off different radio waves. This allows doctors to detect cancer.

Dr. Damadian spent eight years building the first MRI machine, which he named *Indomitable*. The project had little money. He and the others working with him often had to buy equipment at electronics surplus stores.

Testing the first model took many years. First, the team tested mice who had cancer. Finally, they tried to test it on Damadian himself, but he was too big for the machine! They found a smaller man to test the machine, and produced the first human body MRI scan in 1977.

MRI has many good qualities. It is safer than many other tests. No surgery is needed. A patient gets no dangerous radiation. MRI "sees" through bone and can produce a clearer picture than X rays.

In 1989 Damadian was inducted into the National Inventors Hall of Fame in Washington, D.C. His first MRI model, *Indomitable*, is now housed at the Smithsonian Institution.

THINK ABOUT IT

1. What sort of magnets do you think Dr. Damadian's MRI machine used? Explain your answer.

2. Why do you think new methods in medicine must be tested on animals and then on humans?

TEST CONDUCTIVITY

How can you test for conductors and insulators?

Materials

- wire, 3 pieces
- light bulb
- D-cell battery
- Test objects such as aluminum foil, coins, salt, distilled water, salt water, rubber balloon, Mylar balloon, plastic wrap, craft stick, steel wool, paper

Procedure

❶ Build a series circuit like the one shown. Touch the two wire ends together to make sure your circuit works.

❷ Try to complete the circuit by touching both wires to one of the test objects. Observe the bulb carefully. Record your observations.

❸ Repeat Step 2 for each of the test objects.

❹ Try again, this time holding the wire ends farther apart when they touch each object.

Draw Conclusions

Which materials were good conductors of electricity? How do you know?

MAKE A GENERATOR

How can you use a magnet to produce a current?

Materials

- bar magnet
- tape
- cardboard
- compass
- insulated wire, 100 cm with ends stripped

Procedure

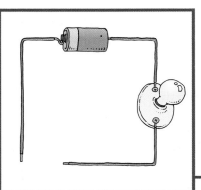

❶ Wrap 20 loops of the wire loosely around the bar magnet.

Twist the stripped ends of the wire tightly together.

❷ Tape a length of the unlooped section of wire to the cardboard. Tape the compass under the wire so the needle lines up with the wire.

❸ Move the magnet back and forth inside the loops of wire. Observe what happens to the compass needle.

Draw Conclusions

Describe how the compass needle behaves. Explain why this happened.

Vocabulary Review

Use the terms below to complete the sentences. The page numbers in ( ) tell you where to look in the chapter if you need help.

charge (F6)   resistor (F13)
static electricity (F6)   series circuit (F14)
electric fields (F8)   parallel circuit (F14)
electric current (F12)   magnet (F18)
circuit (F12)   magnetic pole (F18)
electric cell (F12)   magnetic fields (F19)
conductor (F13)   electromagnet (F25)
insulator (F13)

1. A pathway for current is called a ____.

2. ____ and ____ are similar because they are both areas where forces can act without objects touching.

3. Current passes easily through a ____ but doesn't pass easily through an ____.

4. A core wrapped in a wire that is carrying current is called an ____.

5. A measure of the extra charges that are on an object is called ____.

6. A material that resists the flow of current is called a ____.

7. An ____ is a flow of charges.

8. In a ____, taking out one light does not turn off the whole circuit.

9. The charge that stays on an object is called ____.

10. A ____ attracts objects made of iron or steel.

11. A ____ has only one path for the current.

12. Energy to move current through a circuit is supplied by an ____.

13. A ____ is where a magnet's pull is strongest.

Connect Concepts

Use the terms in the Word Bank to complete the concept map.

poles
negative
charges
attract
north
repel
positive
south

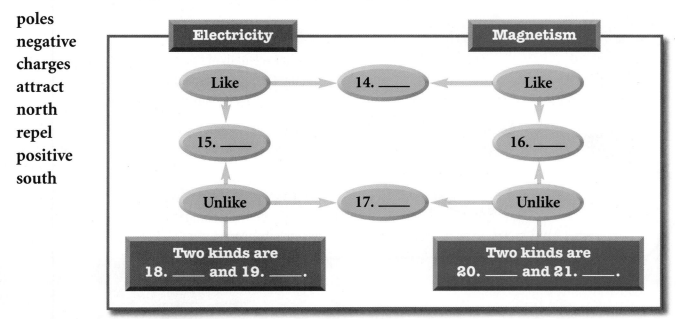

Check Understanding

Write the letter of the best choice.

22. An object has a ____ charge if it has extra positive charges.
    A large   C negative
    B neutral   D positive

23. If the electric fields of two charged objects form a closed pattern of field lines, the objects are ____ charged.
    F negatively   H neutrally
    G positively   J oppositely

24. If one bulb is removed from a series circuit, the other bulbs will —
    A dim   C flicker
    G get brighter   D go out

25. The strip of material that glows in a light bulb is —
    F a charge   H a conductor
    G an insulator   J a resistor

26. A device that produces motion energy from electrical energy is —
    A a compass   C an electromagnet
    B a generator   D a motor

Critical Thinking

27. Look at the circuit below. What will happen to each bulb if Switch 1 is off and Switch 2 is on?

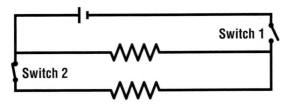

28. Why will chalk dust sprinkled on a plastic sheet placed over a bar magnet **NOT** show the shape of the magnetic field?

Process Skills Review

29. You **observe** that the north pole and south pole of two magnets attract each other when there is a piece of paper between them. What can you **infer** about magnetic fields and paper?

30. **Plan a simple investigation** to show the results of wrapping more coils of wire around a core. Be sure to include a description of the observations you would make and the conclusions you might draw. Use the following materials: a battery, a long piece of insulated copper wire with the ends stripped, an iron nail, a pile of paper clips.

31. Suppose you observe in the investigation you planned for Question 30 that the magnet picks up 5 paper clips with 10 coils of wire, 10 paper clips with 20 coils of wire, and 15 with 30 coils of wire. What would you **predict** will happen when you test the electromagnet with 40 coils of wire? How could you test your prediction?

Performance Assessment

Make a Circuit

Make a diagram of a parallel circuit with wires, three light bulbs, and two batteries. Show where to put a switch to turn all the lights off and on. Explain why you chose that switch location. Build and test the circuit.

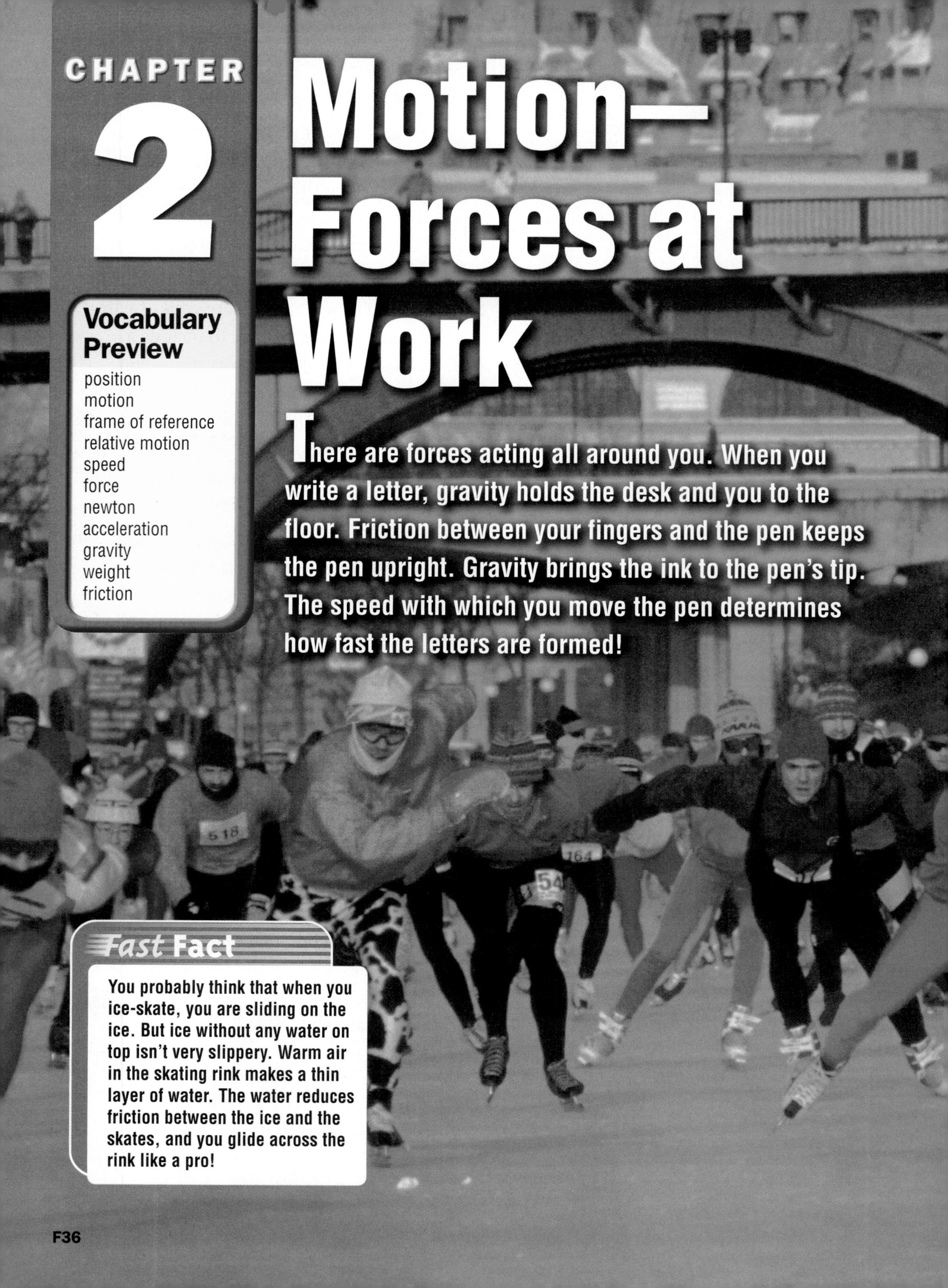

Motion— Forces at Work

Vocabulary Preview

position
motion
frame of reference
relative motion
speed
force
newton
acceleration
gravity
weight
friction

There are forces acting all around you. When you write a letter, gravity holds the desk and you to the floor. Friction between your fingers and the pen keeps the pen upright. Gravity brings the ink to the pen's tip. The speed with which you move the pen determines how fast the letters are formed!

Fast Fact

You probably think that when you ice-skate, you are sliding on the ice. But ice without any water on top isn't very slippery. Warm air in the skating rink makes a thin layer of water. The water reduces friction between the ice and the skates, and you glide across the rink like a pro!

On the bottoms of their feet, geckos have hairs that increase friction. These tiny hairs let the lizards grip very smooth surfaces, even glass!

Friction slows a car when a driver brakes. It takes about 1.5 seconds for an alert driver to react to an emergency. It takes even longer to stop the car after the driver brakes. This table shows how far a car travels while a driver is reacting and braking and the total distance it takes to stop.

Car Braking			
Speed (mi/hr)	A Reaction Distance (ft)	B Braking Distance (ft)	Total Stopping Distance [A+B]
20	44	25	69
30	66	57	123
40	88	101	189
50	110	158	268
60	132	227	359
70	154	310	464

What Is Motion?

In this lesson, you can . . .

INVESTIGATE giving directions.

LEARN ABOUT motion and speed.

LINK to math, writing, language arts, and technology.

INVESTIGATE

Giving Directions

Activity Purpose When you give directions to get to a place, you tell someone when to turn and where to move. So, giving directions is a way to describe movement and position. For example, you might tell a new neighbor how to get to the grocery store, or you might tell a visiting family member how to find the school office. In this investigation you will write directions to get to a place you have chosen in your school.

Materials
- paper
- pencil

Activity Procedure

1 Choose a place in the school, such as a water fountain or an exit door. A person going there should have to make several turns. Tell your teacher the place you chose.

▲ Do you think the pitcher has thrown a fastball or a curveball? *Fast* and *curve* describe the movement of a ball. How else can you describe the motion of the ball?

2 After your teacher has approved your place, start walking to it. As you walk, **record** where and how you are moving. For example, you might include the distance you walk, about how long it takes for each part of the trip, where you turn, and any landmarks you use to tell where you are. (Picture A)

3 Go back to your classroom. On a separate sheet of paper, write directions to the place you chose. Use your notes to add details about time, distance, and position. Don't name the place on the directions page. Give the directions to a classmate and ask him or her to follow them. (Picture B)

4 When your partner comes back, talk about any problems he or she had with your directions. Underline the parts of the directions that caused the problems.

5 Walk with your partner as he or she follows the directions again. Decide together how to make the directions clearer. **Record** the reasons for any changes.

6 Switch roles with your partner and repeat Steps 1–5.

Picture A

Picture B

Draw Conclusions

1. How did your partner know where to start following the directions?

2. How did your partner know how far to walk, which direction to walk, and where to turn?

3. **Scientists at Work** Directions **communicate** the way to get from one place to another. **Compare** your directions to the procedure of an experiment.

Investigate Further Using your notes and directions, draw a map showing the way to the place you chose. Trade maps with a new partner. Is the map easier to use than written directions? Explain your answer.

Process Skill Tip

Often scientists repeat experiments that were done by others. So, it is important to **communicate** clearly all the parts of an experiment. These parts include how to do the experiment, the data collected, and the results and conclusions.

Motion

Changing Places

FIND OUT

- **ways to describe motion**
- **what speed measures**
- **how to calculate speed**

VOCABULARY

position
motion
frame of reference
relative motion
speed

How do you tell someone where you are? Are you behind a desk? Under a light? Are you 2 meters (about 6 ft) to the left of the bookshelf? Each of these describes a certain place, or **position**. In the investigation, you chose a certain place. Then you wrote directions to tell someone how to move to get there, or how to change position. Good directions gave your partner a lot of ways to know his or her positions along the way and to find the next position.

As your partner followed your directions, he or she was in motion. **Motion** is any change of position. Your partner started in one position, moved to another, and kept changing position until he or she reached the final position—the place you chose. The photo below shows runners in motion around a track.

✔ **How do you know a runner is in motion?**

In a race the position of the runner on the track changes from moment to moment. The race will be won by the person who moves, or changes position, fastest. ▼

Point of View

Look around you. Are you moving? You probably would say that you're not. You don't sense any change in your position. You answer questions about your motion by checking, or referring to, the things around you. Together, all the things around you that you can sense and use to describe motion make up your **frame of reference**.

You know that Earth is rotating on its axis and revolving around the sun. So, even when you sit at your desk, you actually *are* moving. But you can't sense that movement. You can't tell you are moving by using your frame of reference—the classroom and what you can sense from your seat.

Suppose an astronaut is watching your school from space far away from Earth. His or her answer about your movement on Earth will be different because the frame of reference is different. From space, the astronaut sees Earth rotate. Motion that is described based on a frame of reference

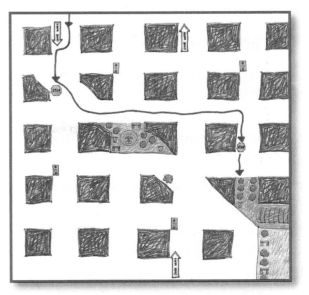

▲ To describe your position, you need a frame of reference. On a map you find your position by looking for landmarks or street names. How would you give directions to the park shown on the map? How would you check your position if you were following the directions?

is called **relative motion**. When you're sitting at your desk, your movement relative to the classroom is nothing. But your movement relative to the astronaut in space is very fast.

✔ **What is a frame of reference?**

▲ Jim watches Sarah and Rosa ride by on their bicycles. His frame of reference is what he sees by standing still on the sidewalk. Relative to him, the two girls are moving and the buildings and street are not moving.

Rosa's frame of reference is what she sees from her bike. Relative to Rosa, Sarah is not moving because the two girls are riding at the same speed. To Rosa, the buildings and street seem to be speeding by. Jim and Rosa describe Rosa's motion differently because they have different frames of reference.▼

Speed

Did you ever hear someone say that his or her house was only a five-minute bike ride from school? When you hear that, you know that the house and school are not too far apart. But what if someone said, "My house is only a five-minute spaceship ride away from school?" Then you would know that the house and school were very far apart. Why? You know that a spacecraft travels a lot faster than a bike. So it could go a lot farther in five minutes than a bike could.

Speed is one way to describe how fast something is moving. **Speed** is a measure of an object's change in position during a unit of time. For example, a racing swimmer has a speed of 1 meter (about 3 ft) per second. From this information, you know the swimmer is moving a distance of 1 meter (about 3 ft) during each second. So during 3 seconds, he or she will travel 3 meters (about 9 ft).

To find a swimmer's speed, you need two measurements. One measurement is change in position, or distance moved. Remember, you can't describe motion without a frame of reference. So you would measure how far the swimmer traveled from the end of the pool.

▲ A stopwatch is often used to measure time during track and swimming events.

How Fast Can You Go?			
Activity	**Distance (km)**	**Time (h)**	**Speed (km/h)**
Flying in a jet plane	1000	1	1000
Riding in a car	240	3	80
Riding a bike	30	2	15
Walking	3	1	3

In a race each swimmer goes the same distance. The one who goes that distance in the least amount of time wins the race. That person has the greatest speed. ▼

◀ In some track and swimming events, distance is measured in meters.

The other measurement needed is time. You would start timing as the swimmer left the edge of the pool. The swimmer's speed is the distance moved divided by the time it took to move that distance. The table on page F42 shows how distance, time, and speed are related.

✓ **What is speed?**

Summary

Motion is any change from one position to another. A frame of reference is a point of view from which to describe motion. The same motion can look different from different frames of reference. Motion described from one frame of reference is called relative motion. Speed is a measure of motion. Speed describes the distance an object travels in a unit of time.

Review

1. What is position?
2. What is motion?
3. What is relative motion?
4. **Critical Thinking** Give two different frames of reference from which to describe a roller-coaster ride.
5. **Test Preparation** What is the speed of a cat that runs 6 meters in 3 seconds?
   A $\frac{1}{2}$ meter per second
   B 2 meters per second
   C 3 meters per second
   D 9 meters per second

LINKS

MATH LINK

Collect, Organize, and Display Data Use reference books to find the speeds of different land animals. Use a computer program such as *Graph Links* to make a bar graph of the speeds of some of the faster ones and some of the slower ones.

WRITING LINK

Expressive Writing—Poem Write a poem for your teacher. Describe the motion of running horses as you pass them while riding a passenger train.

LANGUAGE ARTS LINK

Moving Words Make a set of cards for matching. On one group of cards, write words describing motion, such as *fluttering, twirling,* and *dangling.* On another set of cards, write the names of different objects, such as *dog, leaf,* and *kite.* Turn the cards face down, and choose a card from each set. Turn the two cards face up. Write a sentence using the two words. Read your sentence to the class.

GO TECHNOLOGY LINK
ONLINE

Visit the Harcourt Learning Site for related links, activities, and resources.
www.harcourtschool.com

WELCOME TO THE LEARNING SITE

What Effects Do Forces Have on Objects?

In this lesson, you can . . .

INVESTIGATE forces measured by spring scales.

LEARN ABOUT forces acting on objects.

LINK to math, writing, physical education, and technology.

INVESTIGATE

Pairs of Forces Acting on Objects

Activity Purpose When you push a bicycle or a grocery cart, you expect it to move. But what happens if two people pull a grocery cart in opposite directions? What happens if they pull in the same direction? In this investigation you will **plan and conduct an investigation** to learn how pulling in two directions at the same time moves a toy car.

Materials

- safety goggles
- toy car
- 2 pieces of string, each 1 m long
- 2 spring scales
- ruler

Activity Procedure

1. **CAUTION** Wear safety goggles to protect your eyes. The spring scale hooks or string may slip loose and fly up. Work with a partner. Tie the ends of each string to the toy car. Pull on the string to make sure it won't come off easily. Attach a spring scale to each loop of string.

◀ This rock climber has strong arm and leg muscles that pull and push him up the rock face.

Picture A

2 With a partner, try different ways and directions of pulling on the spring scales attached to the toy car. (Picture A)

3 **Plan a simple investigation.** Your goal is to **describe** how the toy car moves when two spring scales pull it at the same time. Plan to include a chart and a diagram to **record** your data and **observations.**

4 With your partner, carry out the investigation you planned.

Draw Conclusions

1. How did pulling in different directions affect the toy car?

2. How did pulling in the same direction affect the toy car?

3. **Scientists at Work** Scientists use what they know to help them **plan and conduct investigations**. What knowledge did you use to help you plan and conduct this investigation?

Investigate Further What will happen if you pull on the car with a third string and spring scale? **Form a hypothesis** that explains how the three forces interact. Then **plan and conduct an experiment** to test your hypothesis.

Forces

Pushes and Pulls

FIND OUT

- what a force is
- how an object moves when no force is acting on it
- how forces are added and subtracted

VOCABULARY

force
acceleration
newton

Think of all the times in a day you push or pull on something. You may push open doors, pull on a grocery cart, or push a pencil across paper. In the investigation you pulled a toy car. Every time you push or pull something, you use a force. A **force** is a push or a pull. Forces transfer energy. When you throw a ball, the force of your muscles moves your arm to push the ball into the air. When you pick up a book, the force of your muscles moves your arm to pull the book off the desk.

You're not the only source of forces. Other forces are pushing and pulling things all around you. The force put out by a car's engine turns the wheels to push the car down the road. The force of the wind pushes flags and tree branches, making them flap and rustle. The force of a magnet pulls it to a refrigerator door.

✔ **What is a force?**

◄ This archer pulls on the bowstring. When she lets go, the string will push the arrow away from the bow and toward the target.

Starting Motion

Many of the things around you are probably motionless, or not moving. The books on your desk are motionless. So are the pictures on the wall. Objects stay in place unless a force starts them moving. If something is moving, you know that a force started it moving.

How a force affects an object depends on the object's mass. Suppose you push with equal force on a toy car and a wagon filled with books. When you stop pushing, the toy car will be moving much faster than the wagon. That is because the toy car has less mass than the wagon. A force affects an object with less mass more than it affects an object with more mass.

The force needed to start an object moving also depends on other forces that are acting on the object. Suppose your coat is fastened closed with Velcro. In that case the force needed to open your coat must be more than the force of the Velcro that's holding it closed.

▲ You have to pull to keep a sled moving uphill. If you stop pulling, the weight of the sled will pull it back down.

Once an object is moving, it moves until a force stops it. Sometimes it's easy to see where the stopping force comes from, such as when a soccer goalie stops a kicked ball. At other times, the stopping force is harder to name. You know that even if no other player stops a kicked soccer ball, the ball will stop rolling at some time. You can't see what stops the ball. It's a force called *friction* (FRIK•shuhn).

✔ **What do you have to do to start motion?**

◄ It's easy to start an empty grocery cart moving at a walking speed. After the cart is full, you must push it much harder to start it moving at a walking speed.

Changing direction is another kind of change in motion. It always takes a force to change the direction an object is moving. To turn, this in-line skater changes the angle of her skates. The skates push sideways to the left against the ground, and she skates around the curve. ▼

▲ When you stop, you change your motion. You slow down until you are not moving. It always takes a force to change motion. This in-line skater uses the force of the brake against the ground to make herself stop.

Changing Motion

It takes a force to start motion. Starting is a change from no motion to some motion. A force is needed to change motion in other ways, too. Speeding up, slowing down, turning, and stopping all are motion changes that need a force.

If you've ridden a bicycle on a smooth, level surface, you know that you can coast. Once you start moving, you can keep going for a while without pedaling. But to speed up, you have to pedal. The force of your feet pushing on the pedals speeds up the bicycle. To slow down or stop, you squeeze, or put force on, the brake handles.

Suppose you are riding a bicycle and want to turn left. You turn the handlebars to the left. The front wheel pushes sideways against the pavement and the bicycle moves left. If you were riding on icy pavement, turning would be harder. The front wheel couldn't push sideways against the pavement without slipping.

Starting and slowing to a stop are examples of changing speed. Turning is an example of changing direction. Starting, slowing, and turning are all accelerations. An **acceleration** (ak•sel•er•AY•shuhn) is any change in the speed or the direction of an object's motion. It always takes a force to cause an acceleration.

✔ **What is needed to make an object change its motion?**

Changing Speed

A larger force causes a larger acceleration. This means that the harder you push something, the more quickly it speeds up. When you pedal your bicycle harder, it goes faster. If you squeeze harder on the brake handles, you will stop faster.

Pushing for a longer time also causes a larger acceleration. If you get on a bicycle and pedal hard for 2 seconds, you will be moving slowly. If you pedal just as hard for 20 seconds, you will be moving much faster.

✔ **What is needed to give an object a greater acceleration?**

At the start of a race, the push of the bobsled team starts the bobsled moving. The push of the team increases the speed of the sled from 0 to 15 kilometers (about 10 mi) per hour.

Force accelerating bobsled

◄ As the bobsled slides down the curving course, its weight accelerates it bit by bit. The longer the bobsled moves down the hill, the faster it goes. The sled's final speed may be 145 kilometers (about 90 mi) per hour or more.

F49

▲ Both dogs are pulling with the same force. The forces on the rope are balanced. There is no acceleration, and the rope doesn't move. The arrows stand for the forces. When you put them side by side, you can see they are balanced.

Adding Forces

Suppose you push on a box from one side and your friend pushes on it from the opposite side. What happens? If your friend pushes just as hard as you do, the box won't move. The forces are balanced. When all forces acting on an object are balanced, the motion of an object does not change. It does not accelerate.

If you push harder than your friend pushes, the box will move toward your friend. But if your friend pushes harder than you do, the box will move toward you.

When forces on an object are in opposite directions, you subtract the smaller force from the larger force. The force that remains will accelerate the object.

When two forces on an object are in the same direction, they add together. The force that results is in the same direction as the two forces and is larger than either of them. The photo below shows how forces can add together to move a piano easily.

✔ **What happens to an object when the forces acting on it are balanced?**

◀ When three people push together, the piano moves easily. Their forces add together to make one larger force. The arrows show how the three forces add together.

Measuring Forces

You used spring scales in the investigation to help you observe the effects of two forces on a toy car. The numbers on the spring scale showed you the size of the force in units called newtons. The **newton** is the metric, or Système International (SI), unit of force. It's abbreviated as *N*. A newton is a small amount of force. It's about as much force as you need to lift a medium-sized apple.

A spring scale can show how accelerating an object depends on the object's mass. Suppose you hook a spring scale to an empty wagon. Then you take two steps to pull the wagon up to your walking speed. As you pull, the scale reads 10 N. Next, you put your dog in the wagon. Again, you take two steps to pull the wagon up to walking speed. This time the scale reads 20 N. Putting the dog in the wagon added mass. Because of the added mass, it took a larger force to accelerate the wagon to the same speed in the same amount of time.

▲ A spring scale measures force. The greater the force that is pulling on the scale, the more the spring stretches. The pointer on the scale moves with the end of the spring.

To measure the force of his pull, the boy connected the hook of the spring scale to the handle of the wagon. Then he pulled the wagon by pulling the top of the spring scale. ▼

As its name suggests, a spring scale has a spring in it. When you pull on the scale, you stretch the spring. The pointer on the scale moves as you pull. To measure the force you are using, you have to be able to lift or pull on the spring scale. Holding the scale and pushing won't give you a reading on the scale.

Other kinds of scales also measure forces. You've probably seen a bathroom scale or the scale at a grocery store checkout lane.

✔ **What does the stretch of a spring scale measure?**

THE INSIDE STORY

Two Scales

These are two other kinds of scales. They also measure force, but they work differently from a simple spring scale.

This is a dial spring scale. Dial spring scales are often found in the produce sections of grocery stores. The push of an object placed in the pan stretches a spring that has a gear attached to it. As the gear moves down, it causes a needle to turn. The tip of the needle points to the amount of force with which the object pushes on the pan. ▶

◀ In this electronic scale, the force of the food placed on the pan pushes a rod on the bottom of the pan into a magnet. An electric current in the coil around the rod makes an electromagnet. Like poles of the magnet and electromagnet interact. The two forces balance exactly when the pan is lifted to its original position. When the pan stops moving, the number you see shows the force of the food on the pan.

▲ Scales can also be very large. This scale measures the weight of trucks full of gravel and asphalt.

Summary

A force is a push or a pull. Starting, stopping, slowing down, and turning are all changes in motion, or kinds of acceleration. An object does not accelerate unless a force acts on it. Forces can add together, subtract, or balance each other. When all the forces on an object are balanced, it does not accelerate. Forces are measured in newtons (N).

Review

1. What is a force?
2. What is the name of the SI unit of force?
3. What is acceleration?
4. **Critical Thinking** What happens to a door if you push on one side and someone else pushes with the same amount of force on the other side?
5. **Test Preparation** What happens when you are riding your bicycle on a smooth, level surface and you stop pedaling?
   A You stop right away.
   B You go faster.
   C You slowly slow down.
   D You turn to the right.

LINKS

MATH LINK

Draw a Picture to Solve a Problem
Two students are pushing on a piano. One student can push with a force of 30 newtons. The other can push with a force of 50 newtons. What is the greatest force they can use to push on the piano? What is the smallest force that they can put on the piano if they both push hard?

WRITING LINK

Expressive Writing—Song Lyrics
Choose a tune you know. Then write words to go with that tune. The words should describe for a younger child ways to use forces to move an elephant from the zoo to your house. You might want to include a verse about what you will do with the elephant once you get it home.

PHYSICAL EDUCATION LINK

Sports and Motion Make a list of at least five different sports. Then make a chart to identify objects that change motion while each sport is being played.

TECHNOLOGY LINK

Learn more about forces and accelerations by viewing *Coaster Physics* on the **Harcourt Science Newsroom Video.**

What Are Some Forces in Nature?

In this lesson, you can . . .

INVESTIGATE forces on a sliding box.

LEARN ABOUT four different types of forces.

LINK to math, writing, art, and technology.

Forces on a Sliding Box

Activity Purpose Have you ever slipped on a patch of ice? To make ice on a sidewalk less slippery, you can put sand on it. In this investigation you will **measure** the force that you need to slide a box across several different materials. You will **order** the measurements and use them to **compare** the materials.

Materials
- shoe box
- spring scale
- books

Activity Procedure

1 Make a table to **record** your **observations.**

2 Put the hook of the spring scale through the two openings on the end of the box. Place several books in the box. (Picture A)

3 Use the spring scale to slowly drag the box across the top of a desk or table. Be sure to pull with the spring scale straight out from the side of the box. Practice this step several times until you can pull the box at a steady, slow speed. (Picture B)

◀ The force of gravity is pulling this snowboarder down the hill. The force of friction is holding him back. But the snowboard is made to slide on the snow with as little friction as possible. So its speed is quite fast.

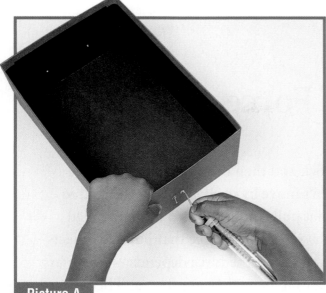

Picture A

Picture B

4 When you are ready, **measure** the force of your pull as you drag the box. **Record** the force measurement and the surface on which you dragged the box. **Observe** the texture of the surface.

5 Repeat Steps 3 and 4, dragging the box across other surfaces, such as the classroom floor, carpet, tile, and cement. **Predict** the force needed to drag the box on each surface.

Draw Conclusions

1. Make a new table. In this table, list the forces you used in order from the smallest to the largest. What was the least amount of force you used?

2. In your new table, write the name of each surface next to the force you used on it. On which surface did you use the greatest amount of force?

3. How did a surface affect the force needed to drag the shoe box across it?

4. **Scientists at Work** After scientists gather data, they often put it in some kind of **order** to help them understand their results. How did putting your data in order help you in this investigation?

Investigate Further **Predict** how much force it would take to pull the shoe box across a patch of ice. If possible, find a place, and test your prediction.

> **Process Skill Tip**
>
> When scientists measure many things in the same way, they usually put the data in **order.** Often they start with the smallest measurement and end with the largest. This helps them compare data and makes any patterns easier to see.

Kinds of Force

FIND OUT

- **what gravity is**
- **what holds atoms together**
- **how friction slows down motion**

VOCABULARY

gravity
weight
friction

Gravity

If you pick up a rock and then drop it, it will fall to the ground. The rock can't move by itself. A force is needed to move it. The force that pulls things toward Earth is called gravity. **Gravity** (GRAV•ih•tee) is a force that pulls all objects toward each other. The size of the force depends on the mass of the objects and how far apart they are. The pull between objects that have a large mass is stronger than the pull between objects that have a small mass. For example, the mass of Earth is large, so its pull on you is strong. But you have much less mass than Earth has, so the pull of your gravity on other objects is much too small to notice.

The greater the distance between objects, the weaker the pull of gravity is. The pull of gravity is strong between Earth and everything near its surface, including you. Space satellites orbit far from Earth. The pull between Earth and a satellite orbiting over one place on Earth's equator is small. It is only about $\frac{2}{100}$ of what the pull would be at Earth's surface.

✔ **What is gravity?**

The force of gravity between the sun and Earth pulls them toward each other. The pull between Earth and the sun holds Earth in its orbit around the sun. ▼

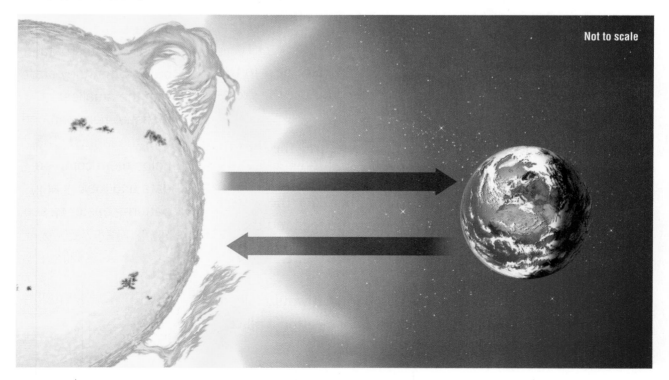

Not to scale

The girl's weight is a measure of the force of gravity between Earth and the girl. ▼

Weight on Planets in Our Solar System

Planet	Weight	
Mercury	102 N	(23 lb)
Venus	245 N	(54 lb)
Earth	270 N	(60 lb)
Mars	102 N	(23 lb)
Jupiter	638 N	(142 lb)
Saturn	247 N	(55 lb)
Uranus	240 N	(53 lb)
Neptune	304 N	(68 lb)
Pluto	18 N	(4 lb)

◄ This arrow stands for the girl's weight on Earth.

The force of gravity between Mars and the girl is about one-third the force of gravity between Earth and the girl. On Mars her weight would be about one-third her weight on Earth. ►

Weight

How many times have you had your weight measured? You probably know what your weight is now. **Weight** is a measure of the force of gravity on an object. Your weight is a measure of the force of gravity between you and Earth.

If you go to a place where the force of gravity is different, your weight will be different, too. The force of gravity on the moon is less than on Earth. That's mostly because the moon has less mass than Earth. The moon's gravity is about one-sixth of Earth's gravity. So on the moon your weight would be one-sixth of your weight on Earth. The force of gravity near Jupiter is much larger than it is near Earth. On Jupiter your weight would be more than twice what it is on Earth.

✔ **Why would you weigh less on the moon than you do on Earth?**

F57

Friction

In the investigation you pulled a shoe box filled with books across a desktop. As you were pulling the shoe box forward, another force was pulling it back. That force was friction. **Friction** (FRIK•shuhn) is a force that keeps objects that are touching each other from sliding past each other easily. As you observed in the investigation, the rougher a surface is, the more friction it has.

Sometimes friction is useful. Without friction, walking on a sidewalk would be like slipping on perfectly smooth ice. Friction also can stop motion. When you use a bicycle brake, pieces of rubber rub against the wheel rims. The friction between the rubber and the rims slows and stops the wheels. The harder you squeeze, the faster the bicycle stops.

Often people want to make the force of friction smaller. Friction can wear away machine parts that rub against each other. To reduce friction, people put oil on the machine parts to make them more slippery. This is why car engines need oil.

✔ **What is friction?**

When the wheel of this grinder touches the sculpture, it drags away little pieces of metal. Some of the energy from the grinder makes the metal red-hot. ▼

▲ An in-line skater pushes the heel stop of the skate against the ground to slow down or stop. Friction reduces the skater's speed.

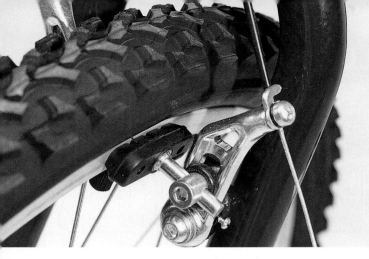

▲ The friction caused by the brake rubbing against the bicycle wheel stops the wheel.

Summary

Forces in nature include gravity and friction. Gravity keeps you on Earth. Friction is a force that keeps things from sliding past each other easily.

Review

1. Would you expect the force of gravity one kilometer above the moon to be stronger or weaker than the force of gravity at its surface?

2. If the mass of Earth doubled, how would your weight change?

3. What is the force between two objects that keeps one object from sliding past the other easily?

4. **Critical Thinking** Where do you think the pull of gravity is stronger—at the surface of Earth or at the surface of the sun? Explain.

5. **Test Preparation** The direction of the force of friction on a book sliding to the right on a table is —
   A down
   B to the left
   C to the right
   D up

LINKS

MATH LINK

Solve a Two-Step Problem A rock that weighs 18 newtons on Earth weighs 3 newtons on the moon. What would a rock that weighs 12 newtons on Earth weigh on the moon?

WRITING LINK

Expressive Writing—Friendly Letter Suppose you are an astronaut who has landed on a planet that has a force of gravity two times as strong as Earth has. Write a letter to a friend on Earth, describing how it feels to walk and to lift tools.

ART LINK

See the Force Look at the things around you. Choose one object and then think of the different forces that are acting on it. Make a drawing, painting, or sculpture that shows the object and the forces acting on it.

TECHNOLOGY LINK

Learn about friction, gravity, and motion by investigating *Build a Model Race Car* on **Harcourt Science Explorations CD-ROM.**

High-Speed HUMAN-POWERED VEHICLES

Engineers who develop high-tech bicycles work with forces, accelerations, and friction every day. Their job is to build Human Powered Vehicles (HPVs) that are as fast and as easy to ride as possible.

What's the big idea?

Most people in the United States who ride bikes do it for fun, not because they need them for transportation. When you want to travel long distances quickly, you often go in a car. But teams of scientists and engineers who work on HPVs have developed bikes that can go even faster than some cars.

How fast are they?

One of the best-known HPVs is called the Cheetah. It was built by a team of college students at the University of California. In 1992, scientists recorded the Cheetah traveling as fast as 112 kilometers (70 mi) per hour. The fastest that most regular bikes can go is 40–48 kilometers (25–30 mi) per hour.

The fastest HPV that has been built so far is the Ultimate Bike. Because its engineers understood ideas such as friction, force, and weight, they were able to design a bike that can reach speeds as fast as 332.64 kilometers (206.7 mi) per hour. The Ultimate Bike is made from the same super-lightweight material used in jet planes. But even though it weighs only about $4\frac{1}{2}$ kilograms (about 10 pounds), the Ultimate Bike is stronger than any bike made from metal.

How do they work?

You've probably noticed from the photos that these bikes don't look like the bikes you see in your neighborhood. That's because they need to be built differently to reach such high speeds. For example, most HPVs have a gear system that's different from the one on regular bikes. The front crank that is turned by the pedals is much bigger than the crank on most bikes. This allows small movements of the pedals to make the wheels turn a large distance quickly.

Wind resistance can greatly reduce bicycle speed. That's why these HPVs have the pedals in front of the rider. The rider sits close to the ground, so less of his or her body is hit by the wind. See if you can feel the wind resistance the next time you ride a bicycle. What can you do safely to reduce this resistance?

You probably won't see HPVs like these in a bike store soon. But the problems HPV scientists and engineers are solving may make ordinary bicycles faster and easier to ride.

THINK ABOUT IT

1. How could an HPV be useful to the average person?
2. In addition to that of an engineer, what are some jobs where ideas like acceleration, force, and friction are important?

CAREERS
BICYCLE MECHANIC

What They Do Bicycle mechanics usually work for bike shops or sporting goods stores. They repair broken bikes and build new ones. HPVs like the Cheetah and the Ultimate Bike need mechanics to keep them running.

Education and Training Most bike shops will train their workers to be mechanics. Some high schools offer bike repair classes.

GO ONLINE

WEB LINK For Science and Technology updates, visit the Harcourt Internet site. **www.harcourtschool.com**

Ellen Ochoa
ASTRONAUT

> "Only you put limitations on yourself about what you can achieve, so don't be afraid to reach for the stars."

Ellen Ochoa puts no limitations on herself. She became the first Hispanic woman in space. Chosen in 1990 by the National Aeronautics and Space Administration, Ochoa was a mission specialist on the 9-day-long *Discovery* mission in April 1993. On this mission she studied the sun and Earth's atmosphere to find out how the sun affects Earth's climate. She also flew on an 11-day mission in November 1994. She has spent almost 500 hours in space.

The most challenging part of space travel is remembering details. Every astronaut is trained to run all shuttle systems, such as computer, communication, air and water, and other equipment. All astronauts learn about the experiments and other jobs that are part of a shuttle mission. Ochoa says that astronauts must work very hard in space, because they have little time.

Model of completed International Space Station

Ochoa dreams of helping to build a space station. She thinks it is needed for human exploration in space to advance. For two years, she directed all Astronaut Office support for the International Space Station program.

Ochoa believes that education is key to success in life. She learned this from her mother. Ochoa believes students, especially girls, should study math and science. Another role model for Ochoa was Sally Ride, the first American woman in space. "Sally made it possible for anyone to become an astronaut," Ochoa has said. Ride was in space when Ochoa was in college and first thinking of becoming an astronaut.

THINK ABOUT IT

1. How could studying math and science be helpful to you?
2. Who in your life has taught you that education is important?

OBSERVING MOTION

How does motion result from changing position?

Materials

- pad of small self-stick notes
- ruler
- pencil

Procedure

❶ Hold the pad so that the sticky band is across the top. On the first note, draw a dot 1 cm from the bottom of the pad and 1 mm from the left side. Lift the note, but do not remove it from the pad.

❷ On the second note, draw a dot 1 cm from the bottom and 2 mm from the left side.

❸ On separate notes, continue drawing dots, each one 1 mm to the right of the previous one until the last dot is at the right side. Remove any notes that were not used.

❹ Hold the note pad by the top, and flip the pages with your thumb. Observe the dots.

Draw Conclusions

How do the dots show a change in position over time? What happens if you flip the pages faster?

MARBLES ON A RAMP

Which marbles go faster?

Materials

- masking tape
- 2 metersticks
- books
- meter tape or ruler
- 10 marbles
- stopwatch

Procedure

❶ Tape the two metersticks together at a right-angle as shown. Prop up one end of the meter-sticks with books to make a ramp.

❷ Put the meter tape on the floor, with the zero mark at the low end of the ramp. Make a table for your data, with columns labeled *Starting Position* and *Time*.

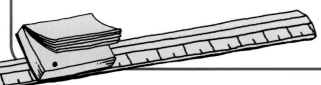

❸ Roll the marbles down the ramp one at a time. Start the marbles from different positions on the ramp. In your table, record the starting position for each marble.

❹ Use the stopwatch to measure the time it takes the marble to travel the length of the meter tape. Record the time in your table. Graph your results.

Draw Conclusions

What force pulled the marbles down the ramp? Which height made the speed of the marbles the fastest as they left the ramp? The slowest?

Vocabulary Review

Use the terms below to complete the sentences. The page numbers in ( ) tell you where to look in the chapter if you need help.

position (F40)   acceleration (F48)

motion (F40)   newton (F51)

frame of reference (F41)   gravity (F56)

relative motion (F41)   weight (F57)

speed (F42)   friction (F58)

force (F46)

1. The force that pulls all objects together is called ____.

2. Meters per second is a unit of ____, or the distance an object travels in a unit of time.

3. A certain place is called ____.

4. A ____ is a push or a pull.

5. A unit called a ____ is used to measure pulls and pushes.

6. ____ is a change in position.

7. Your ____ is the measure of the force of gravity on you.

8. A ____ is a point of view from which to describe motion.

9. Stopping your bike is an example of an ____.

10. Motion described from a frame of reference is called ____.

11. ____ is a force that keeps objects that are touching each other from sliding past each other easily.

Connect Concepts

Match the following effects with their causes.

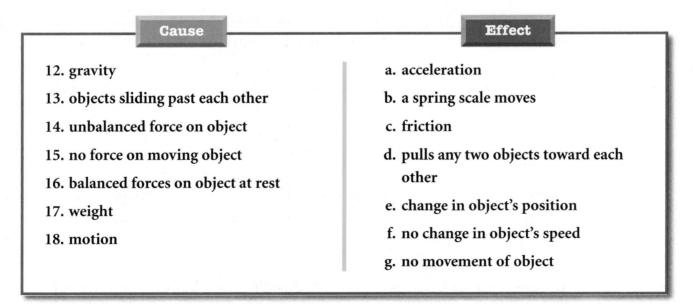

Cause	Effect
12. gravity	a. acceleration
13. objects sliding past each other	b. a spring scale moves
14. unbalanced force on object	c. friction
15. no force on moving object	d. pulls any two objects toward each other
16. balanced forces on object at rest	e. change in object's position
17. weight	f. no change in object's speed
18. motion	g. no movement of object

Check Understanding

Write the letter of the best choice.

19. If you are standing in an elevator that is moving up at a steady speed of 1 meter per second, your motion relative to the elevator is at a speed of —

A 0 meters per second

B 1 meter per second down

C 1 meter per second up

D 2 meters per second up

20. Each of the following is an example of acceleration **EXCEPT** —

F resting

G starting

H stopping

J turning

21. The ____ pulls the moon toward Earth.

A electric force

B friction

C force of gravity

D magnetic force

Critical Thinking

22. Suppose you are riding in a car and you pass a truck going in the same direction you are. You can easily read the words printed on the side of the truck. But then the same truck passes you going the same speed in the opposite direction. This time the words are hard to read. Why?

23. Your push on a hockey puck moving toward you stops it. What will the same push do to a hockey puck moving away from you?

24. A monkey that weighs 270 newtons is hanging from the branch of a tree. What is the size and direction of the monkey's force on the tree branch?

Process Skills Review

25. A student measured the force needed to pull a wagon across a wood floor, a heavy rug, and grass. He decided to **communicate** the results with a bar graph. The three bars on the graph each had the same width but different heights. What did the height of a bar show?

26. Look at the data in the table on page F57. How is the data **ordered**? Think of another possible order, and put the data in that order. Explain the new order.

27. A student decided to find out if a change in speed changes the force of friction. Help her **plan an investigation** to find this out. Include tips she could use as she **conducts** the **investigation**.

Performance Assessment

Force Drawing

Use a spring scale to measure the force needed to pull a book across a desktop at a steady speed. Identify and give the direction of three forces on the book as it slides. Make and label a drawing to show the forces.

CHAPTER 3

Simple Machines

In an old comedy movie, movers try to get a piano into a fifth-floor apartment. First the piano rolls down a truck ramp and on down a hill. Then they use pulleys to lift the piano into the apartment through a window, and the piano crashes back to the ground. What makes all this comedy possible? Acting talent and simple machines!

Fast Fact

With a long enough lever your weight could lift almost any object! In fact, with a lever 4800 meters long you could lift a whale!

Object One Meter from Fulcrum	Mass of Object (kg)	Your Distance from Fulcrum (m)
Student	27	1
Adult	68	2.5
30 Friends	810	30
Elephant	4995	185
Whale	129,600	4800

The first computer was designed by Charles Babbage in 1832. It was to be entirely mechanical and would use more than a thousand levers!

Can you guess what kind of machine was first called a wooden ox or a gliding horse? This useful machine, made up of two levers connected by a wheel, lets one person carry a load that would normally require two. The machine was invented around A.D. 200 by the Chinese. It's a wheelbarrow!

This drawbridge in Mystic, Connecticut, is a large lever. The weight of the bridge is balanced by the large concrete blocks at the top on the right.

How Does a Lever Help Us Do Work?

In this lesson, you can . . .

INVESTIGATE how one kind of lever works.

LEARN ABOUT how levers help us do work.

LINK to math, writing, music, and technology.

INVESTIGATE

Experimenting with a Lever

Activity Purpose You may have played on a seesaw, or teeter-totter. A seesaw is a type of lever. A *lever* is a bar that turns on a point that doesn't move. In a seesaw the board is the bar and the center pipe is the point that doesn't move. A person sits near each end of the board. Each person takes a turn lifting a weight (the other person) at the other end of the board. As the people take turns using their legs and weight to lift each other, the board goes up and down. But what if the weight you were trying to lift were in the middle of the lever instead of at the end? In this investigation you will **observe** and **measure** to find out what happens.

Materials
- 2 wooden rulers
- 2 identical rubber bands, long
- safety goggles

CAUTION

Activity Procedure

1 **CAUTION** **Put on your safety goggles.** Put a rubber band 2 cm from each end of the ruler. One band should be at the 2-cm mark, and the other should be at the 28-cm mark.

◄ A boat oar is a lever—a type of simple machine made up of a bar and a point on which the bar moves. The wood oar is the bar. It moves around a point, called an oarlock, on the side of the boat.

Positions and Rubber Band Lengths

Finger Position	Observations	Length of Rubber Band on 2-cm Mark	Length of Rubber Band on 28-cm Mark
15-cm mark			
17-cm mark			
19-cm mark			
21-cm mark			

2 Have a partner lift the ruler by holding the rubber bands. Place your index finger at the 15-cm mark, and press down just enough to stretch the rubber bands. Your partner should lift hard enough on both rubber bands to keep the ruler level. (Picture A)

3 Have a third person **measure** the lengths of the two bands. **Record** your **observations** and measurements in a chart like the one above.

4 Move your finger to the 17-cm mark. Your partner should keep the ruler level. Again **measure** the length of the rubber bands, and **record** your **observations** and measurements.

5 Repeat Step 4, this time with your finger at the 19-cm mark and then the 21-cm mark.

Picture A

Draw Conclusions

1. Describe what happened to the ruler each time you moved your finger away from the center of it.

2. **Compare** the ruler and rubber bands to a seesaw. What was the ruler? What were the forces of the rubber bands?

3. **Scientists at Work** Look at the **measurements** you recorded. How do they support your other observations? Is there a pattern?

Investigate Further For the same ruler setup, **predict** what will happen if you put your finger on the 9-cm mark. Try it and see if your prediction is correct.

Process Skill Tip

Measuring is one type of observation. Measurements can sometimes more clearly show a pattern. They also are a good way to communicate to other people what you observed.

Levers

Parts of a Lever

You may picture a machine, such as a washing machine or a sewing machine, as a device that has many parts. But these machines are built from smaller parts that are also machines. The basic machines that make up other machines are called **simple machines**. There are six simple machines. They are the lever, pulley, wheel and axle, inclined plane, screw, and wedge. All these machines help us move things by changing the size of the force applied, the direction of the force, or both at once.

One simple machine is the lever. As you saw in the investigation, a **lever** is made up of a bar that turns on a fixed point. The fixed point, or one that doesn't move, is called the **fulcrum** (FUHL•krem).

When you push or pull a lever, you put a force, called the **effort force**, on one side of the bar. This force causes the bar to turn on the fulcrum. The other end of the bar moves. The resulting force on that end is what you use to move a load, or do work. In the investigation, the length of each stretched rubber band showed the force on each end of the lever.

✔ **What are the parts of a lever?**

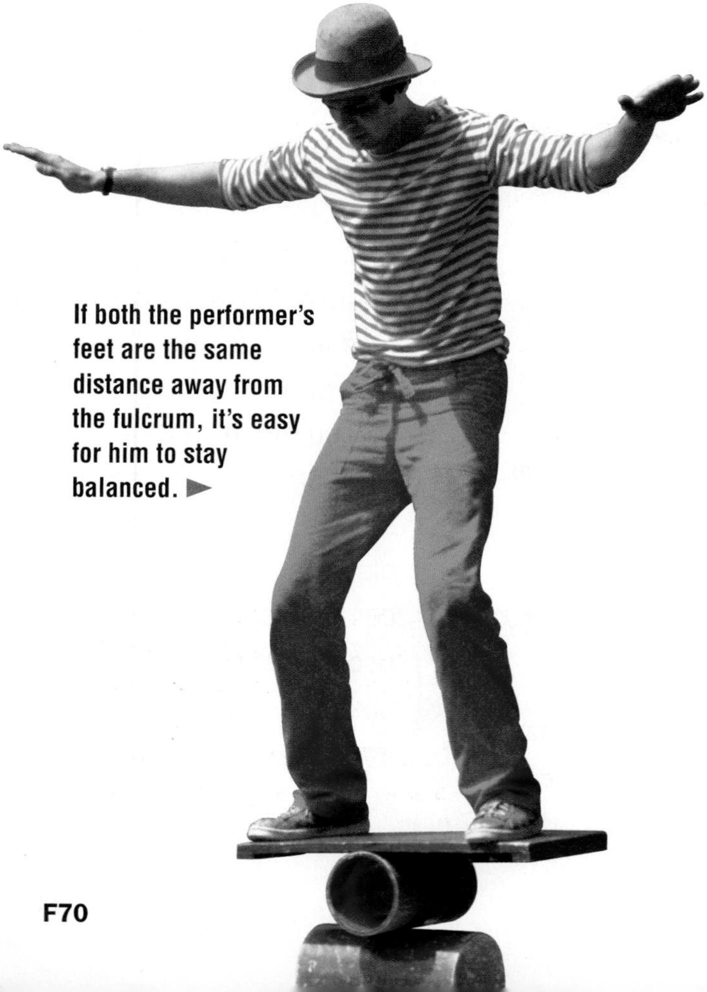

If both the performer's feet are the same distance away from the fulcrum, it's easy for him to stay balanced. ▶

This diagram shows how the performer is balancing on the lever. The blue arrow stands for the effort force, the red arrow is the resulting force, and the small dot is the fulcrum. The effort and resulting forces are balanced, so the lever doesn't move. ▼

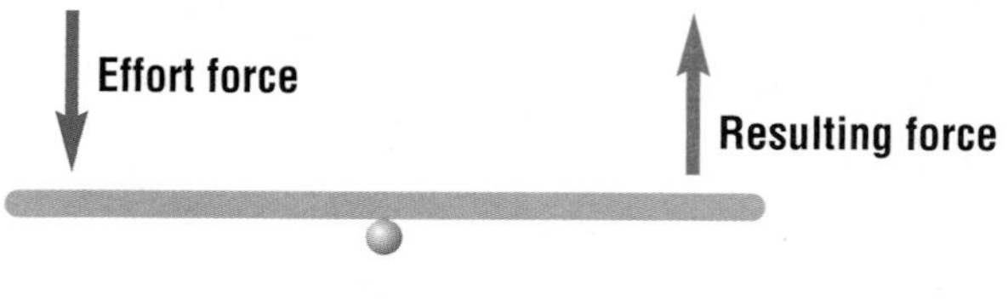

Effort force

Resulting force

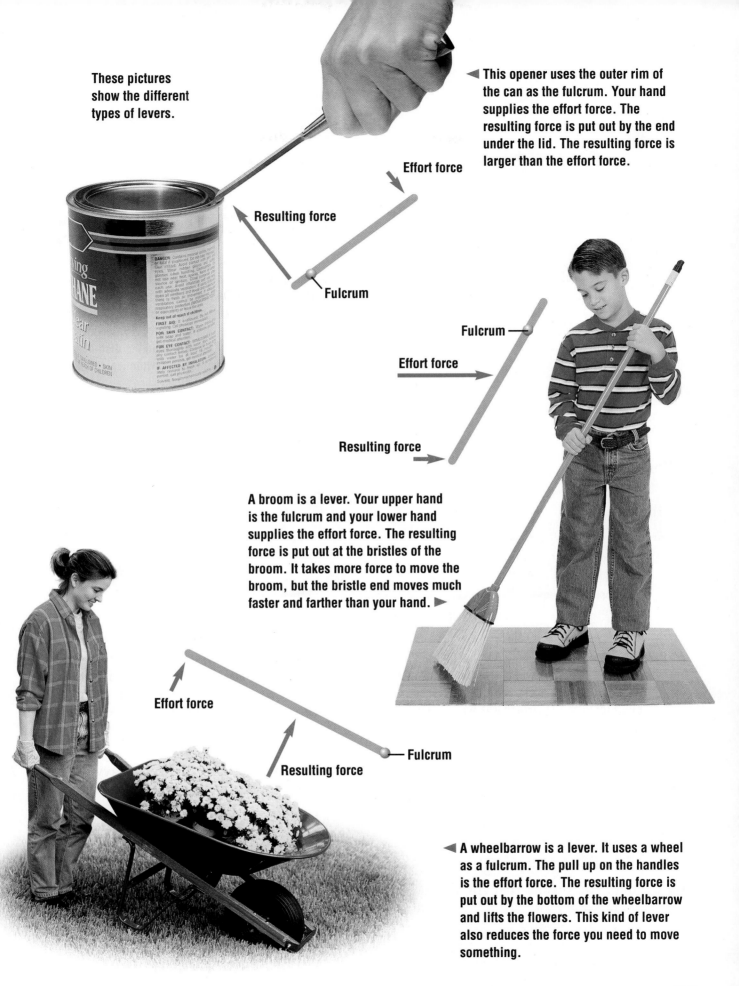

These pictures show the different types of levers.

This opener uses the outer rim of the can as the fulcrum. Your hand supplies the effort force. The resulting force is put out by the end under the lid. The resulting force is larger than the effort force.

Effort force

Resulting force

Fulcrum

Fulcrum

Effort force

Resulting force

A broom is a lever. Your upper hand is the fulcrum and your lower hand supplies the effort force. The resulting force is put out at the bristles of the broom. It takes more force to move the broom, but the bristle end moves much faster and farther than your hand. ▶

Effort force

Resulting force

Fulcrum

A wheelbarrow is a lever. It uses a wheel as a fulcrum. The pull up on the handles is the effort force. The resulting force is put out by the bottom of the wheelbarrow and lifts the flowers. This kind of lever also reduces the force you need to move something.

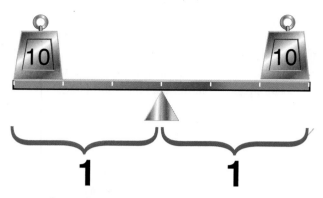

▲ A lever is often compared to a seesaw. If the weights are the same and the distances from the fulcrum are the same, the seesaw balances.

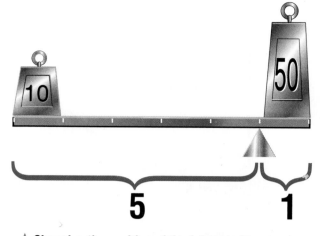

▲ Changing the position of the fulcrum changes the balance of the lever. Now a small effort force makes a larger resulting force. The distance from the fulcrum to the 10-newton weight is five times larger than the distance from the fulcrum to the 50-newton weight.

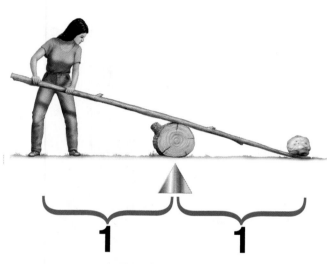

▲ The balanced lever above has the fulcrum in the center. If you move one end of the branch down, the other end moves up the same distance. An effort force of 10 newtons lifts a rock weighing 10 newtons.

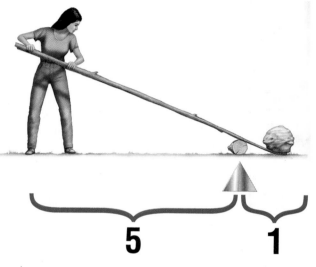

▲ When this lever moves, the long end travels five times farther down than the short end travels up. To lift a 50-newton rock would take an effort force of only 10 newtons. But you have to push five times farther down than the rock is lifted up.

Levers and Forces

The kind of lever shown above changes the direction of the force applied to it. A force down on one side pushes the other side up. On a seesaw the weight of a person on the high end pushes that end down. This lifts the person sitting on the other end.

When the fulcrum of this kind of lever is not in the middle of the bar, a light weight on the long side can balance a heavy weight on the short side.

On a seesaw you can balance a heavier person if the fulcrum is closer to him or her. Your smaller weight is on the long side of the lever. It balances the larger weight on the other end.

✔ **How does a lever change the force applied to it?**

Levers in Tools

Many hand tools are levers. A pry bar is a lever that has a long handle and a short end for prying. A small force on the handle becomes a much greater force on the prying end. Sewing scissors have long, wedge-shaped blades and short handles. The fulcrum is the bolt in the middle. A large movement of the handles causes a small movement of the blades close to the bolt. Fingernail scissors have long handles and short blades. They make it easier to cut hard fingernails.

✔ **Name three tools that include levers.**

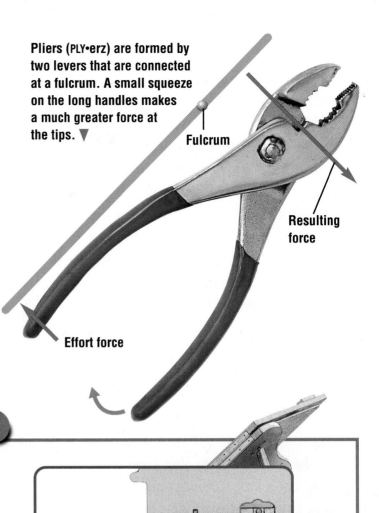

Pliers (PLY•erz) are formed by two levers that are connected at a fulcrum. A small squeeze on the long handles makes a much greater force at the tips. ▼

Fulcrum

Resulting force

Effort force

THE INSIDE STORY

Piano Keys

A piano makes a sound when the part called a hammer hits a string that then vibrates. The force on a piano key moves through a series of levers to cause the string to be hit. The levers form a compound machine, a machine made up of two or more simple machines.

Here's how it works.

① Pushing a piano key down lifts up the other end of a long lever (Lever 1). The direction of the effort force on the key is changed.

② Lever 1 pushes up on Lever 2. The direction of the force stays the same, but Lever 2 moves farther than Lever 1. This is because of the location of the fulcrum of Lever 2.

③ Lever 2 pushes up on Lever 3. A padded hammer is on the end of Lever 3. Again, because of the position of its fulcrum, Lever 3 increases the distance the hammer moves. The hammer moves up fast and strikes the string. Then the hammer is caught as it bounces off the string, before it hits the string again.

④ A pianist moves each finger only a small distance—about 1 centimeter (less than $\frac{1}{2}$ in.)—to produce a strong hit on a piano string.

Work

Machines are used to do work. You may think that as you read this sentence, you are doing work, but a scientist would say you're not. In science, the word *work* has a special meaning. **Work** is done on an object when a force moves the object through a distance. The force and motion *must* be in the same direction. By this definition, thinking isn't work. Just holding a book isn't doing work on the book. But lifting a book is doing work on the book. Carrying a basketball isn't doing work on the basketball. This is because the force holding the ball up and its motion aren't in the same direction. Shooting the basketball, however, is doing work on the ball.

Levers help you do work. You could pick up a heavy rock using just your arms, or you could use a lever to help you. Either way the same amount of work gets done. The rock is lifted the same distance.

Work can be measured and described mathematically. To find the work done on an object, multiply the force used to move the object by the distance the object moves.

$$Work = Force \times distance$$

Here's the work done to lift a 10-newton rock 2 meters.

$$Work = 10 \text{ N} \times 2 \text{ m}$$
$$Work = 20 \text{ N-m (newton-meters)}$$

✓ **In science, when is work done?**

In this type of lever, the amount of work done is about the same on either side of the fulcrum. It takes only a small force to push down the long end, but that end moves through a large distance. On the short end, a large force pushes up, but that end moves only a small distance. ▼

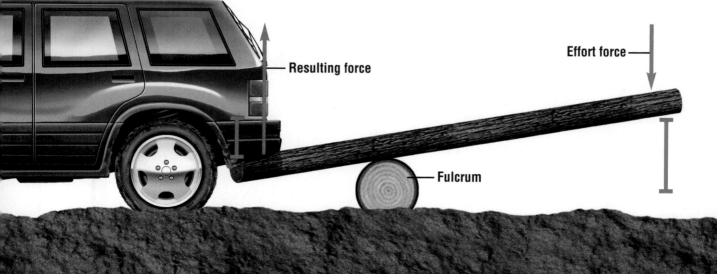

Resulting force

Effort force

Fulcrum

◄ At work or at play? You may think that the adult dressed in black is working and the students are playing. Look again, but this time use a scientist's definition of *work*. The supervisor isn't moving any objects. So she isn't doing any work on anything. The students to the right, on the other hand, are applying forces to lift a ball. So they are actually doing work on the ball.

Summary

The basic machines that make up all other machines are simple machines. A lever is a simple machine that changes the direction or size of a force. Work is done on an object when a force moves an object through a distance.

Review

1. What are the parts of a lever?
2. How does a pry bar help you do work?
3. What is work?
4. **Critical Thinking** Why do you think it is important that the bar of a lever not bend?
5. **Test Prep** An example of a lever is a —
   A wheelbarrow
   B wheel
   C screw
   D wrench

LINKS

MATH LINK

Measure Length Measure and compare the lengths of the effort force and resulting force arrows shown with the wheelbarrow on page F71. Which arrow is longer? About how many times as long is it? Which force is greater—the effort force or resulting force? How many times as great?

WRITING LINK

Informative Writing—Description Some apes, including chimpanzees and orangutans, use levers. Other animals, including crows and sea otters, also use very simple tools. Find an example of how an animal uses a tool. Write an article describing how the animal uses the tool to help meet its needs.

MUSIC LINK

Instrument Keys Many musical instruments use keys, including almost all the woodwinds and many of the brasses. As with piano keys, the keys on these instruments are levers. Choose an instrument and find out how the keys work the levers. What do the levers do?

GO ONLINE TECHNOLOGY LINK

Learn more about levers and other simple machines by visiting this Internet site.
www.scilinks.org/harcourt

2

How Do a Pulley and a Wheel and Axle Help Us Do Work?

In this lesson, you can . . .

INVESTIGATE how pulleys work.

LEARN ABOUT pulleys and about wheels and axles.

LINK to math, writing, physical education, and technology.

INVESTIGATE

How a Pulley Works

Activity Purpose Have you ever seen someone raise or lower the flag? Together the rope and wheel on the flagpole make up a pulley (PUHL•ee). Like a lever, a pulley can change the direction of a force. Can a pulley change forces in other ways as levers do? In this investigation you'll **compare** forces to find out.

Materials
- 2 broom handles
- strong rope, 6 m or longer

CAUTION

Activity Procedure

1 Firmly tie one end of the rope to the center of one of the broom handles. This will be Handle 1.

2 Have two people face each other and stand about 30 cm apart. Have one person hold Handle 1. His or her hands should be about 40 cm apart—20 cm on either side of the rope. Have the other person hold the other broom handle (Handle 2) in the same way. (Picture A)

3 Loop the rope around Handle 2 and back over Handle 1. (Picture B)

◀ A pasta maker includes a simple machine— a wheel and axle. As you turn the crank (the wheel), it turns a post (the axle) inside the machine. Blades connected to the axle cut the pasta to the width you want.

4 Stand behind the person holding Handle 1. Have your partners try to hold the broom handles apart while you slowly pull on the free end of the rope. **CAUTION** **Don't let fingers get caught between the handles.** **Observe** and **record** what happens.

5 Repeat Steps 3 and 4. This time, loop the rope back around Handles 1 and 2 again. (Picture C) **Observe** and **record** what happens.

6 Add more loops around the broom handles. Again pull on the free end of the rope to try to bring the handles together. **Observe** and **record** what happens.

Picture A

Picture B

Draw Conclusions

1. **Compare** your observations in Steps 4, 5, and 6. Which way of looping the rope made it hardest to pull the handles together? Which way made it easiest?

2. Reread the description of a pulley in the Activity Purpose. What in this investigation worked as wheels do?

3. **Scientists at Work** How did the handles and rope change your effort force? **Compare** this to how levers work. How is it like levers? How is it different?

Picture C

Investigate Further How do you think adding loops of rope will change the way the broom handles and rope work? **Form a hypothesis** that explains how adding rope loops will change your results. **Plan and conduct an experiment** to test your hypothesis. Plan to use a spring scale to measure forces.

Process Skill Tip

Scientists often **compare** a new observation to what they know already. When you compare, you look for ways things are alike and ways they are different.

Machines That Turn

FIND OUT

- what fixed and movable pulleys are

- how a wheel and axle works

VOCABULARY

pulley

wheel and axle

Pulleys

You may have seen the wheels of pulleys on a sailboat or a flagpole. A **pulley** is made up of a rope or chain and a wheel around which the rope fits. When you pull down on one rope end, the wheel turns and the other rope end moves up. A pulley that stays in one place is called a *fixed pulley*. Fixed pulleys are often used to raise and lower something lightweight, such as a flag or a small sail, while you stay on the ground or the deck.

A fixed pulley is like a lever that has its fulcrum in the middle. Both the lever and the pulley change only the direction of the effort force. They do not change the size of the effort force.

A different kind of pulley can change the size of the effort force. This pulley is called a movable pulley because it is free to move up and down. One end of its rope is tied down. The load is hooked to the pulley. Pulling up on the rope makes both the pulley and the load rise.

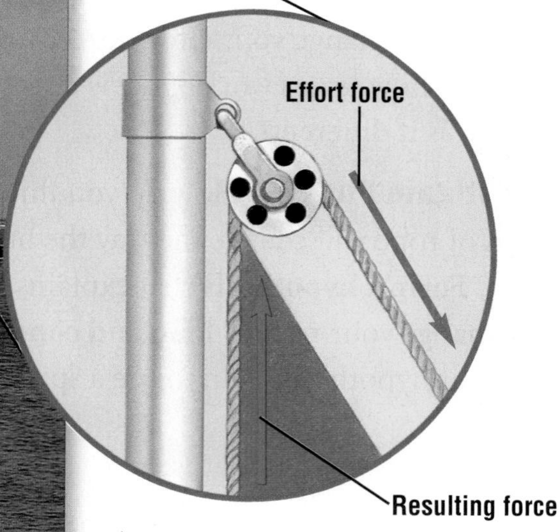

Effort force

Resulting force

▲ Using a fixed pulley, a sailor on a boat deck can lift a sail to the top of the mast.

130886

A movable pulley doesn't change the direction of the effort force. A pull up on the rope also pulls up on the load. But a movable pulley does increase the resulting force. To lift a load of 50 newtons, you need to pull up with only a 25-newton force.

As with a lever, you don't get more work out of a movable pulley than you put in. It doubles your lifting force, but you pull twice as far. To lift a load 2 meters, you must pull up 4 meters of rope.

Pulleys can be put together to make pulley systems, a form of compound machine. For example, you can use a fixed pulley with a movable pulley. The movable pulley increases your force. The fixed pulley changes the direction of your force.

Adding more movable pulleys to a system increases your force even more. Each movable pulley you add also increases the length of rope you must pull to lift a load.

✔ How does a movable pulley change your force?

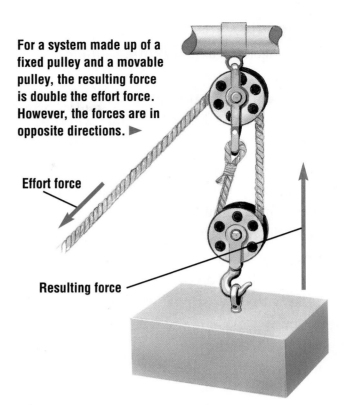

For a system made up of a fixed pulley and a movable pulley, the resulting force is double the effort force. However, the forces are in opposite directions. ▶

Effort force

Resulting force

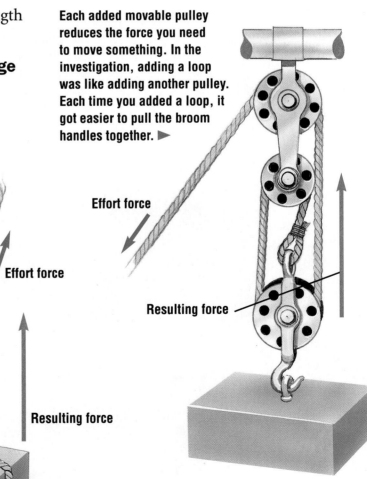

Each added movable pulley reduces the force you need to move something. In the investigation, adding a loop was like adding another pulley. Each time you added a loop, it got easier to pull the broom handles together. ▶

Effort force

Resulting force

For a single movable pulley, the resulting force is double the effort force. The resulting and effort forces are in the same direction. ▶

Effort force

Resulting force

Wheels and Axles

A wheel and axle is another simple machine that can make a job easier. A **wheel and axle** (AKS•uhl) is made up of a large wheel attached to a smaller wheel or rod. A doorknob is part of a wheel and axle. The large round knob turns a smaller axle. The axle is what pulls in the latch to open the door. Without the large knob, it would be difficult to turn the axle. The small effort force you use to turn the knob becomes a large resulting force put out by the axle.

As with other simple machines, you can't get more work out of a wheel and axle than you put in. Effort force is made larger. But the distance the outside of the knob turns is larger than the distance the axle moves.

✓ **How does a wheel and axle make a job easier?**

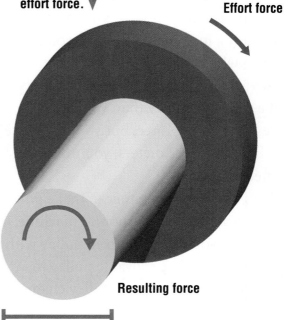

When it is turned, this wheel moves twice as far as the axle. This means that the resulting force is double the effort force. ▼

Effort force

Resulting force

The wheel on this water valve is much larger than the axle. A small effort force on the large wheel makes the axle put out a large resulting force. So the valve is closed tightly but can be opened quickly in an emergency. ▶

Wheel
Axle

•FIRE STATION # 4•

▼ The crank on this fishing reel is the wheel. The reel is the axle. Your effort force becomes a larger resulting force so you can pull in a heavy fish.

Summary

A pulley is a simple machine similar to a lever. A fixed pulley changes the direction of an effort force. A movable pulley makes the resulting force larger than the effort force. Fixed and movable pulleys can be put together to make pulley systems. A wheel and axle is a simple machine in which an effort force on a large wheel makes a larger resulting force on a smaller wheel, or axle.

Review

1. Which kind of pulley makes your effort force larger?

2. Which kind of pulley has the effort force in the opposite direction to the resulting force?

3. Does a wheel and axle change the direction of the effort force, the size of the force, or both? Explain.

4. **Critical Thinking** You want to lift a heavy box 20 meters off the ground. Describe a pulley system that could help you move the box.

5. **Test Prep** Which simple machine can **NOT** be used to increase force?

   A wheel and axle   C fixed pulley

   B lever   D movable pulley

LINKS

MATH LINK

Find a Rule Measure the effort force and resulting force arrows of the pulleys on pages F78–F79. Then look carefully at the pulleys and ropes. Can you find a rule you could use to predict how a pulley or pulley system multiplies your effort force?

WRITING LINK

Persuasive Writing—Opinion Brunel's Portsmouth Pulley Works opened in 1803. It made a pulley called a block and tackle. Suppose you write advertising for this business. Find out more about a block and tackle. Then write a flyer describing the benefits of using pulleys. Explain why the Brunel block and tackle is better than handmade pulleys.

PHYSICAL EDUCATION LINK

Complex Machine A bicycle is a complex machine—a machine made up of two or more compound machines. Observe a bicycle and list all the machines you can find. For each machine, explain how it connects to other machines, or how it makes riding easier or safer for the bicyclist. Make and label a drawing to show what you learned.

TECHNOLOGY LINK

Learn more about amazingly small machines by viewing *Micromachines* on the **Harcourt Science Newsroom Video.**

LESSON 3

How Do Some Other Simple Machines Help Us Do Work?

In this lesson, you can . . .

INVESTIGATE an Archimedes' screw.

LEARN ABOUT how inclined planes, screws, and wedges do work.

LINK to math, writing, technology, and other areas.

Make an Archimedes' Screw

Activity Purpose Archimedes (ar•kuh•MEE•deez) was one of the first known scientists. He lived and worked in Greece around 250 B.C. He used science that he learned to make many inventions. One of his inventions, called the Archimedes' screw, is still used all over the world. It is a machine for lifting water. An Archimedes' screw moves water from rivers into canals for irrigation. In this investigation you will **make a model** of an Archimedes' screw and demonstrate how it works.

Materials

- round wooden pole, such as a piece of a broom handle, 20 cm long with nail
- meterstick or metric ruler
- marker
- length of rubber or plastic hose, about 40–50 cm long
- 6 strong rubber bands
- large pan of water or sink that can be filled with water

Activity Procedure

1. Use the meterstick and marker to divide the pole into five equal sections.

2. Use a rubber band to hold the hose to one end of the pole. The band should not be so tight that it closes off the hose, but it should be tight enough to hold the hose in place.

◄ **This water-skier flies into the air off the end of a ramp, a common kind of inclined plane.**

3 Wind the hose around the pole in a spiral so that it passes over your marks. (Picture A) Use a rubber band to hold the top of the hose in place. Put two or three more bands around the hose and pole so that nothing slips. Wiggle the hose around so the ends open at right angles to the length of the pole. You have built an Archimedes' screw.

4 Put the nail end of the Archimedes' screw in the large pan or sink of water so the device rests on the head of the nail and makes a low angle with the bottom of the pan. Make sure both ends of the screw are over the pan. (Picture B) Turn the Archimedes' screw clockwise 12 times. Now turn the screw in the other direction 12 times. **Observe** what happens.

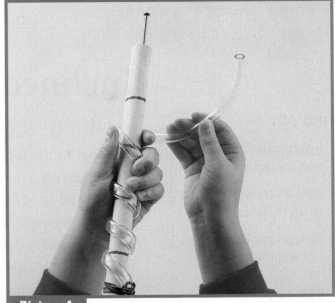

Picture A

Draw Conclusions

1. What happened when you turned the Archimedes' screw the first time? What happened the second time?

2. A screw is a type of inclined plane, a flat sloping surface. A ramp is an example of an inclined plane. Where was the inclined plane in the model you made?

Picture B

3. **Scientists at Work** The Archimedes' screw you built is not a completely useful tool. The screw is hard to turn, and there are easier ways to move water. But it is useful as a **model.** It shows how the machine works. Why might it help to make a small model before building a full-sized machine?

Investigate Further There are many inclined planes around you. Select one day to see how many ramps and screws you can find at school and at home. Make a list of those you find. Tell how each helps people do work.

Process Skill Tip

Scientists often find it helpful to make a small **model** to study an idea or device. Then they can use what they learn from the small model to build a larger device.

Inclined-Plane Machines

Inclined Planes

FIND OUT

- **how an inclined plane reduces effort**
- **how a screw is related to an inclined plane**
- **how to use inclined planes as a wedge**

VOCABULARY

inclined plane
efficiency
screw
wedge

To get to the top of a mountain, would you rather bicycle along a gentle slope or a steep path? You have to travel much farther on the gentle slope, but you have to use more force to pedal up the steep path. Both slopes are a kind of simple machine called an inclined plane. An **inclined plane** is a flat surface that has one end higher than the other.

An inclined plane changes an effort force into a larger resulting force. The direction of the effort force is along the plane. The resulting force pushes up on the object. When you slide a box up a ramp, you push along the ramp. The ramp pushes up on the box. The steeper the ramp, the less it changes the effort force, and the harder it is to slide the box.

As with other simple machines, you can't get more work from an inclined plane than you put into it. Remember, work is force times distance. An inclined plane is longer than it is high. The distance an object moves along the plane is more than the distance it moves up. So, even though it takes less force to move an object, you have to push it farther.

✔ **How does an inclined plane help you do work?**

◄ An inclined plane, or ramp, reduces the force needed to move the box to the height of the truck bed. Using a wheeled cart reduces friction, which makes the ramp more efficient.

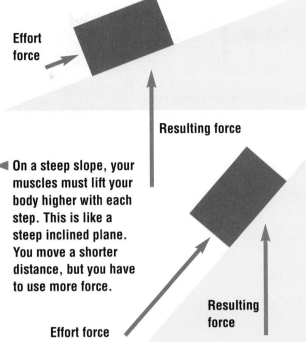

Hiking up a slope that does not rise much for the distance traveled is like going up a gentle inclined plane. You have to travel farther, but you use less force with each step.

Effort force

Resulting force

On a steep slope, your muscles must lift your body higher with each step. This is like a steep inclined plane. You move a shorter distance, but you have to use more force.

Effort force

Resulting force

Efficiency

You actually get less work you can use from an inclined plane than you put into it. When you slide a box up a ramp, some work must go to overcoming friction. That "extra" work does not go into lifting the box. So, an inclined plane is not perfectly efficient. **Efficiency** (eh•FISH•unh•see) is how well a machine changes effort into useful work.

Efficiencies are usually given as percents. An efficiency of 100 percent would be perfect. However, all machines have some friction. So, no machine ever has an efficiency of 100 percent. Most are much lower. For example, most car engines have an efficiency of about 30 percent.

✓ **How does friction affect use of an inclined plane?**

This ramp is an inclined plane. People in wheelchairs can use the ramp instead of stairs. Wheelchair ramps are usually very gentle slopes. This reduces the amount of force needed to move a wheelchair up the ramps. ▼

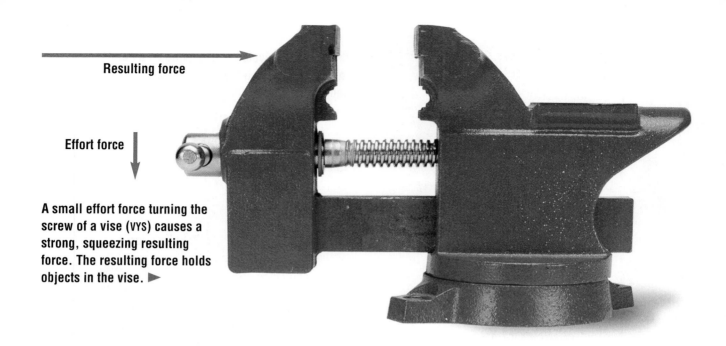

Resulting force

Effort force

A small effort force turning the screw of a vise (VYS) causes a strong, squeezing resulting force. The resulting force holds objects in the vise. ▶

Screws

Wrapping an inclined plane around a pole makes a **screw**. On a screw the long ramp of the inclined plane is wrapped into a space that is the same height as the inclined plane but has almost no width.

Turning a screw moves things up the spiral ramp. The Archimedes' screw you made in the investigation worked this way. Turning the Archimedes' screw pushed water to the top of its tube. The force needed to turn the screw was smaller than the force needed to lift the water straight up.

As other inclined planes do, a screw trades force for distance. The path of the water through the Archimedes' screw was longer than the height it moved up. Lifting the water with an Archimedes' screw used less force.

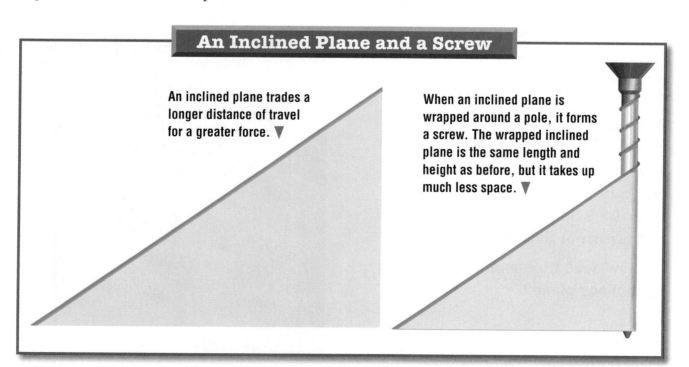

An Inclined Plane and a Screw

An inclined plane trades a longer distance of travel for a greater force. ▼

When an inclined plane is wrapped around a pole, it forms a screw. The wrapped inclined plane is the same length and height as before, but it takes up much less space. ▼

Resulting force

Effort force

▲ This picture shows wood cut away around a screw. A small effort force turning the screw makes a large resulting force holding the wood pieces together. Also, notice how the wood touches the screw over a large area.

You have probably seen screws holding together pieces of wood or metal. Using screws in this way actually takes several simple machines. The screwdriver used to turn the screw is a wheel and axle. If you start to use a screw by pushing it into the wood, the point of the screw is acting as a wedge.

Why is using a screw better than hammering a nail? A screw takes longer to move into wood. But putting a screw into wood takes less force than putting in a nail. A nail is held in just by friction against the wood. The ridges of a screw hook and hold the wood more tightly.

✔ **How is a screw like an inclined plane?**

Holes are often dug with a kind of screw called an auger (AW•ger). The screw turns to lift dirt up and out of the ground. ▶

◀ A spiral staircase is a form of screw that makes it easier to climb from one floor to another. One advantage of a spiral staircase is that it takes up less space than a regular staircase.

Wedges

Two inclined planes placed back-to-back form a **wedge**. The main difference between a wedge and an inclined plane is how they are used. An inclined plane lifts objects. A wedge pushes things apart. An effort force down on the wide end of a wedge is changed to a much larger resulting force out from the sides of the wedge. Most blades of cutting tools such as knives, chisels, and axes are wedges. Often wedges are combined with levers to make cutting even easier.

✔ How is a wedge related to an inclined plane?

▲ The sharp edge of a cooking knife is a wedge. To chop vegetables, a cook may rest the point end of the knife on the cutting board. This makes the knife a compound machine, a combination of a wedge and a lever.

Effort force

Resulting force

Resulting force

As the point of a wedge moves into a solid, the inclined planes of its sides push out. A small effort force on the wide end of the wedge is changed into a much larger resulting force out from its sides. ▶

The blade of an ax is one form of a wedge. The force of the ax down is changed into a resulting force out to the sides that splits the wood. Although chain saws are now used to cut down trees, people still use axes to split wood for fireplaces and stoves. ▶

Summary

An inclined plane is a simple machine used to move things to a different height. It takes more force to move an object up a steep inclined plane than a gently sloping one. When an inclined plane is wrapped around a pole, it becomes a screw. Two inclined planes put together form a wedge.

Review

1. How are screws and wedges related to inclined planes?

2. Name three ways screws are used.

3. Does a screw change the size of the effort force, the direction of the force, or both?

4. **Critical Thinking** How can an inclined plane help you safely lower a heavy object?

5. **Test Prep** Which simple machine is the part of scissors that pushes things apart?

   A screw

   B inclined plane

   C lever

   D wedge

LINKS

MATH LINK

Measure Length Measure and compare the effort and resulting force arrows on the top inclined plane on page F85. How many times does the inclined plane multiply your effort force?

WRITING LINK

Narrative Writing—Story Suppose you must move a piano into a second-floor apartment. Write a short story for your family, describing how you would use simple machines to meet your goal.

ART LINK

A Museum and a Machine There is a famous inclined plane in the Guggenheim Museum in New York City. Find out its location and its use.

PHYSICAL EDUCATION LINK

Playing on the Planes Many sports are based on moving up or down an inclined plane. Make a list of sports that use this idea. (HINT: Look at the picture on page F82 to get started.)

GO ONLINE TECHNOLOGY LINK

Visit the Harcourt Learning Site for related links, activities, and resources.
www.harcourtschool.com

Simple Machines and Water Transportation

Since ancient times, people have used boats to explore new areas, to ship goods from one place to another, and just to enjoy traveling. All of the early boats were moved by human muscle and a lever, either a paddle or an oar.

Floating Logs

The earliest boats were probably hollowed-out logs or rafts made of logs tied together with tree roots. Native American peoples made very fine canoes from wood, leather, and tree bark. Dugouts were another type of log boat. A large tree trunk was hollowed out by using fire, a pounding tool called a mallet, and an adz, a simple type of wedge.

Inuits use small hunting boats called kayaks (KY•aks). Kayakers use an unusual oar. It has a paddle blade at each end. This means that the fulcrum of the oar is first at one hand and then at the other as the kayaker puts one end of the oar and then the other in the water.

More Power

The Phoenicians (fuh•NEE•shuhnz) lived on the eastern coast of the Mediterranean Sea. They designed and built ships that were fast because the ships used large teams of rowers. Each side of a ship had one, two, or three long lines of rowers. Each rower had one long oar. The fulcrum of the oar was the point at which the oar went outside the ship.

Looking for ways to make boats faster, boat builders turned to the wind as a source of power. The Egyptians were among the

The History of Water Transportation

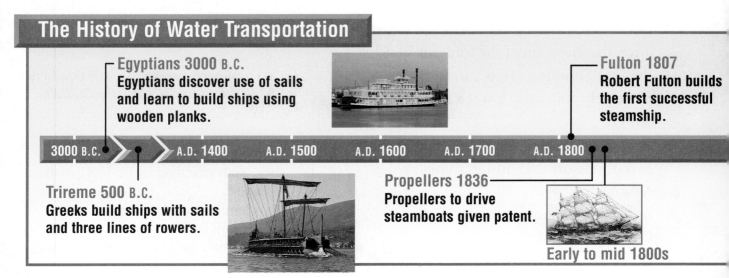

Egyptians 3000 B.C.
Egyptians discover use of sails and learn to build ships using wooden planks.

Fulton 1807
Robert Fulton builds the first successful steamship.

3000 B.C.   A.D. 1400   A.D. 1500   A.D. 1600   A.D. 1700   A.D. 1800

Trireme 500 B.C.
Greeks build ships with sails and three lines of rowers.

Propellers 1836
Propellers to drive steamboats given patent.

Early to mid 1800s

first to build boats that could use either sails or human rowers.

The largest and fastest sailing ships ever made were built in the mid-1800s. They were called clipper ships because they seemed to "clip off" the miles by going so fast. The large sails of a clipper ship were raised using human muscle and a pulley system called a block and tackle. Another simple machine used on clipper ships was a windlass, a type of wheel and axle. With it, a team of people could raise and lower the heavy anchor.

A Lot More Power

During the early 1800s, steam engines changed ship designs forever. Sails slowly disappeared. Newer ships were pushed by huge paddle wheels. Some had a wheel on each side, while others had a single wheel in the back.

In the late 1800s, ships slowly changed from using paddle wheels to using propellers. A propeller looks something like a fan blade. Because of their spiral shape, propellers are sometimes called screws. As a propeller turns, it pulls a boat through the water much as a screw pulls two pieces of wood together. But it takes very big screws

to move a ship. Each of the four propellers on the *Queen Mary*, a British ocean ship launched in 1934, was more than 5 meters (18 ft) across and weighed 38.5 tons!

Today 95 percent of business goods still travel from country to country on the ocean. The power source for large boats has changed from human muscles, to wind, to steam, and finally to other fuels. But simple machines are still on board as part of bigger, more complicated machines.

THINK ABOUT IT

1. Describe two ways simple machines helped to solve problems on a boat or ship.

2. How have more recent ship builders used what earlier people had learned about building boats and ships?

This kayaker's oar is a lever. As he paddles, the fulcrum changes from hand to hand with each stroke.

Today
Huge supercargo ships carry goods all over the world.

A.D. 1900   A.D. 2000

Queen Mary 1934

Wilbur and Orville Wright

INVENTORS

Even as boys, the Wright brothers were fascinated by machines. They sold homemade mechanical toys to earn money when they were young. Orville Wright built his own printing press, and they published a weekly newspaper in Dayton, Ohio. Wilbur Wright was the editor. Later, they began to sell and to rent bicycles. Then they made bicycles in a room above the shop.

The Wright brothers became interested in flying in the 1890s. They read everything they could about how things fly. In 1899 they built their first glider.

In 1903 the two brothers built a biplane, an airplane with two levels of wings. The wings were made by covering wooden frames with cloth and then varnishing the cloth. The two wooden propellers were turned by a 12-horsepower gasoline engine built by the Wrights.

The brothers also made a way to control the plane. A "cradle" was connected to the wings by wires and pulleys. By shifting weight from side to side, the pilot could twist a wing tip to keep the plane balanced.

Orville Wright made the first successful flight on December 17, 1903. He launched the plane from an 18-meter (60-ft) rail on a sand flat. The plane stayed in the air about 12 seconds and flew at about 48 km/hr (30 mi/hr) for just 37 meters (120 ft). The brothers made three more trials that day. Wilbur stayed up the longest—59 seconds—and traveled 260 meters (852 ft).

The brothers preferred to work with no outside help. They improved their airplanes over the next two years. In 1908, Wilbur Wright made the first official public flights in France. The brothers predicted planes would deliver mail and carry passengers. They also hoped that airplanes might prevent a war.

THINK ABOUT IT

1. How do you think the Wrights' work with toys and bicycles prepared them to build a glider?

2. The Wright brothers worked by themselves as a team. What are some benefits of doing that? What are some problems it can cause?

▼ Wilbur   Orville ▼

◄ Wright brothers' biplane at sand flat

MAKE A SCREW

How are screws and inclined planes related?

Materials

- ruler
- sheet of paper
- scissors
- unsharpened pencil
- tape

Procedure

❶ Draw a right triangle on the paper and cut it out. Imagine that this triangle is an inclined plane.

❷ Draw a dark line along the longest edge of the triangle.

❸ Tape the pencil to the back of the inclined plane.

❹ Wrap the triangle around the pencil. Observe the results.

Draw Conclusions

What simple machine have you modeled? How do you know that you could move up the machine and get to the top of the pencil, just as you could move up a straight inclined plane?

USING A WEDGE

How does a wedge work?

Materials

- wooden doorstop
- several books

Procedure

❶ Work with a partner. Use your hands as you would use bookends, and hold the books up on a table or desk.

❷ Have a partner put the narrow end of the doorstop between two of the books and gently push down.

❸ Observe what happens to the books. Record your observations, including how the books felt as your partner pushed down on the doorstop.

❹ Trade roles and repeat the activity.

Draw Conclusions

What did you feel as the doorstop was pushed down? What was the result of the action? What do you think will happen with a wider wedge? A narrower wedge? Try it and see.

Vocabulary Review

Use the terms below to complete the sentences. The page numbers in ( ) tell you where to look in the chapter if you need help.

simple machine (F70)   **wheel and axle** (F80)
lever (F70)   **inclined plane** (F84)
fulcrum (F70)   **efficiency** (F85)
effort force (F70)   **screw** (F86)
work (F74)   **wedge** (F88)
pulley (F78)

1. A basic device that can change the amount or the direction of force, or both at once, is a ____.

2. ____ results when a force produces a movement in the direction of the force.

3. Two inclined planes placed back-to-back form a ____.

4. A simple machine made up of a bar and a fulcrum is a ____.

5. A ____ is made up of an inclined plane wrapped around a pole.

6. To raise a heavy load, you could use a system made up of one fixed ____ and several movable ones.

7. The part of a lever around which the bar moves is the ____.

8. A large wheel connected to a smaller wheel is a ____.

9. ____ is the force that is put into a simple machine.

10. A flat surface that has one end higher than the other is an ____.

11. ____ is how well a machine changes effort into useful force.

Connect Concepts

Use the Venn diagram below to classify the listed machines as either levers or inclined planes.

lever   screw   pulley   scissors
inclined plane   wedge   wheel and axle   knife

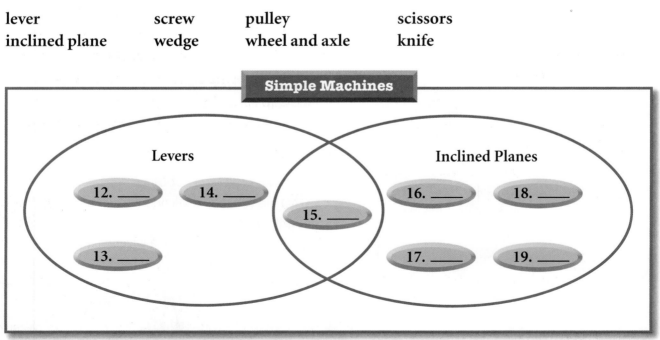

Simple Machines

Levers   Inclined Planes

12. ____   14. ____   16. ____   18. ____

15. ____

13. ____   17. ____   19. ____

Check Understanding

Write the letter of the best choice.

20. In a lever, the force that is used to move the bar is called the —

  A effort force

  B resulting force

  C fulcrum

  D machine

21. When the resulting end of a lever moves a shorter distance than the effort end, it moves with —

  F the same force

  G no force

  H a smaller force

  J a greater force

22. To use a pulley to change both force and direction, you need —

  A one fixed pulley

  B one movable pulley

  C one fixed and one movable pulley

  D two fixed pulleys

23. When you turn a doorknob, you are using —

  F a wheel and axle

  G a pulley

  H a fulcrum

  J an inclined plane

24. A wedge changes an effort force —

  A down to a resulting force up

  B around to a resulting force straight

  C down to a resulting force sideways

  D out to a resulting force in

Critical Thinking

For items 25 through 27, describe how you might use each of the following simple machines to remove a large rock from a garden plot. Tell the advantages and disadvantages of using each machine.

25. A lever

26. A pulley (or pulley system)

27. An inclined plane

Process Skills Review

28. You want to calculate the amount of work done as you move a box up a ramp. What do you need to **measure** in order to make your calculations? What tools would be useful in making these measurements?

29. You are digging and making an old-fashioned well. Decide whether to put a fixed pulley or a wheel and axle at the top of the well to raise the bucket. **Compare** these two machines. Explain which you would choose and why.

30. How could you be sure the choice you made in item 29 above is the best one without building the well?

Performance Assessment

Distance and Force

Investigate how the length of a ramp affects the force needed to move a load. Use three boards of different lengths, three books, a spring scale, and a rock. Make a table to record your data. When you have finished, make a bar graph of your data. Use it to explain what you found.

There are many places where you can learn about forces and motion. Visit the places below and learn how electricity is generated and how machines work. You'll also have fun while you learn.

Museum of Science

WHAT A museum featuring science and technology exhibits

WHERE Boston, Massachusetts

WHAT CAN YOU DO THERE? Tour the museum and learn about electricity at the Theater of Electricity exhibit.

The Tech Museum of Innovation

WHAT A hands-on technology museum that works to encourage new ideas

WHERE San Jose, California

WHAT CAN YOU DO THERE? Explore the museum, visit the exhibits, and learn about robots and other machines.

Self-reliant AUVs

Go solo to track sensory trails

GO ONLINE Plan Your Own Expeditions

If you can't visit the Museum of Science or The Tech Museum of Innovation, visit a museum or a science center near you. Or log on to The Learning Site at **www.harcourtschool.com** to visit these science sites and learn about electricity and machines.

References

Using Science Tools

Using a Hand Lens

A hand lens magnifies objects, or makes them look larger than they are.

1. Hold the hand lens about 12 centimeters (5 in.) from your eye.

2. Bring the object toward you until it comes into focus.

Using a Thermometer

A thermometer measures the temperature of air and most liquids.

1. Place the thermometer in the liquid. Don't touch the thermometer any more than you need to. Never stir the liquid with the thermometer. If you are measuring the temperature of the air, make sure that the thermometer is not in line with a direct light source.

2. Move so that your eyes are even with the liquid in the thermometer.

3. If you are measuring a material that is not being heated or cooled, wait about two minutes for the reading to become stable, or stay the same. Find the scale line that meets the top of the liquid in the thermometer, and read the temperature.

4. If the material you are measuring is being heated or cooled, you will not be able to wait before taking your measurements. Measure as quickly as you can.

Caring for and Using a Microscope

A microscope is another tool that magnifies objects. A microscope can increase the detail you see by increasing the number of times an object is magnified.

Caring for a Microscope

- Always use two hands when you carry a microscope.
- Never touch any of the lenses of a microscope with your fingers.

Using a Microscope

1. Raise the eyepiece as far as you can by using the coarse-adjustment knob. Place your slide on the stage.

2. Always start by using the lowest power. The lowest-power lens is usually the shortest. Start with the lens in the lowest position it can go without touching the slide.

3. Look through the eyepiece, and begin adjusting it upward with the coarse-adjustment knob. When the slide is close to being in focus, use the fine-adjustment knob.

4. When you want to use a higher-power lens, first focus the slide under low power. Then, watching carefully to make sure that the lens will not hit the slide, turn the higher-power lens into place. Use only the fine-adjustment knob when looking through the higher-power lens.

You may use a Brock microscope. This is a sturdy microscope that has only one lens.

1. Place the object to be viewed on the stage.

2. Look through the eyepiece, and begin raising the tube until the object comes into focus.

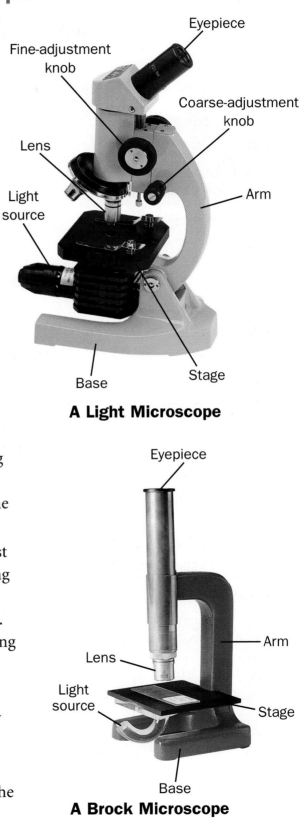

A Light Microscope

A Brock Microscope

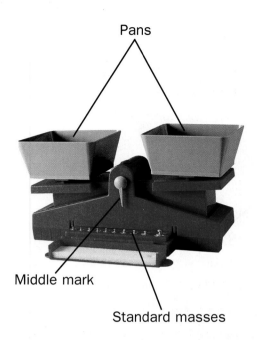

Pans

Middle mark

Standard masses

Using a Balance

Use a balance to measure an object's mass. Mass is the amount of matter an object has.

1. Look at the pointer on the base to make sure the empty pans are balanced.

2. Place the object you wish to measure in the left-hand pan.

3. Add the standard masses to the other pan. As you add masses, you should see the pointer move. When the pointer is at the middle mark, the pans are balanced.

4. Add the numbers on the masses you used. The total is the mass in grams of the object you measured.

Using a Spring Scale

Use a spring scale to measure forces such as the pull of gravity on objects. You measure weight and other forces in units called newtons (N).

Measuring the Weight of an Object

1. Hook the spring scale to the object.

2. Lift the scale and object with a smooth motion. Do not jerk them upward.

3. Wait until any motion of the spring comes to a stop. Then read the number of newtons from the scale.

Measuring the Force to Move an Object

1. With the object resting on a table, hook the spring scale to it.

2. Pull the object smoothly across the table. Do not jerk the object.

3. As you pull, read the number of newtons you are using to pull the object.

Measuring Liquids

Use a beaker, a measuring cup, or a graduate to measure liquids accurately.

1. Pour the liquid you want to measure into a measuring container. Put your measuring container on a flat surface, with the measuring scale facing you.

2. Look at the liquid through the container. Move so that your eyes are even with the surface of the liquid in the container.

3. To read the volume of the liquid, find the scale line that is even with the surface of the liquid.

4. If the surface of the liquid is not exactly even with a line, estimate the volume of the liquid. Decide which line the liquid is closer to, and use that number.

Beaker   **Graduate**

Using a Ruler or Meterstick

Use a ruler or meterstick to measure distances and to find lengths of objects.

1. Place the zero mark or end of the ruler or meterstick next to one end of the distance or object you want to measure.

2. On the ruler or meterstick, find the place next to the other end of the distance or object.

3. Look at the scale on the ruler or meterstick. This will show the distance you want or the length of the object.

Using a Timing Device

Use a timing device such as a stopwatch to measure time.

1. Reset the stopwatch to zero.

2. When you are ready to begin timing, press *Start*.

3. As soon as you are ready to stop timing, press *Stop*.

4. The numbers on the dial or display show how many minutes, seconds, and parts of seconds have passed.

Measurement Systems

SI Measures (Metric)

Temperature
Ice melts at 0 degrees Celsius (°C)
Water freezes at 0°C
Water boils at 100°C

Length and Distance
1000 meters (m) = 1 kilometer (km)
100 centimeters (cm) = 1 m
10 millimeters (mm) = 1 cm

Force
1 newton (N) = 1 kilogram ×
    1 meter/second/second (kg-m/s^2)

Volume
1 cubic meter (m^3) = 1m × 1m × 1m
1 cubic centimeter (cm^3) =
    1 cm × 1 cm × 1 cm
1 liter (L) = 1000 milliliters (mL)
1 cm^3 = 1 mL

Area
1 square kilometer (km^2) =
    1 km × 1 km
1 hectare = 10 000 m^2

Mass
1000 grams (g) = 1 kilogram (kg)
1000 milligrams (mg) = 1 g

Rates (Metric and Customary)
kmh = kilometers per hour
m/s = meters per second
mph = miles per hour

Customary Measures

Volume of Fluids
8 fluid ounces (fl oz) = 1 cup (c)
2 c = 1 pint (pt)
2 pt = 1 quart (qt)
4 qt = 1 gallon (gal)

Temperature
Ice melts at 32 degrees
    Fahrenheit (°F)
Water freezes at 32°F
Water boils at 212°F

Length and Distance
12 inches (in.) = 1 foot (ft)
3 ft = 1 yard (yd)
5,280 ft = 1 mile (mi)

Weight
16 ounces (oz) = 1 pound (lb)
2,000 pounds = 1 ton (T)

Health Handbook

Good Nutrition

The Food Guide Pyramid

No one food or food group supplies everything your body needs for good health. That's why it's important to eat foods from all the food groups. The Food Guide Pyramid can help you choose healthful foods in the right amounts. By choosing more foods from the groups at the bottom of the pyramid and fewer foods from the group at the top, you will eat the foods that provide your body with energy to grow and develop.

Fats, oils, and sweets
Eat sparingly.

Meat, poultry, fish, dry beans, eggs, and nuts 2–3 servings

Milk, yogurt, and cheese
2–3 servings

Fruits
2–4 servings

Vegetables
3–5 servings

Breads, cereals, rice, and pasta 6–11 servings

Estimating Serving Sizes

Choosing a variety of foods is only half the story. You also need to choose the right amounts. The table below can help you estimate the number of servings you are eating of your favorite foods.

Food Group	Amount of Food in One Serving	Some Easy Ways to Estimate Serving Size
Bread, Cereal, Rice, and Pasta Group	1 ounce ready-to-eat (dry) cereal	large handful of plain cereal or a small handful of cereal with raisins and nuts
	1 slice bread, $\frac{1}{2}$ bagel	
	$\frac{1}{2}$ cup cooked pasta, rice, or cereal	ice cream scoop
Vegetable Group	1 cup of raw, leafy vegetables	about the size of a fist
	$\frac{1}{2}$ cup other vegetables, cooked or raw, chopped	
	$\frac{3}{4}$ cup vegetable juice	
	$\frac{1}{2}$ cup tomato sauce	ice cream scoop
Fruit Group	medium apple, pear, or orange	a baseball
	$\frac{1}{2}$ large banana or one medium banana	
	$\frac{1}{2}$ cup chopped or cooked fruit	
	$\frac{3}{4}$ cup of fruit juice	
Milk, Yogurt, and Cheese Group	$1\frac{1}{2}$ ounces of natural cheese	two dominoes
	2 ounces of processed cheese	$1\frac{1}{2}$ slices of packaged cheese
	1 cup of milk or yogurt	
Meat, Poultry, Fish, Dry Beans, Eggs, and Nuts Group	3 ounces of lean meat, chicken, or fish	about the size of your palm
	2 tablespoons peanut butter	
	$\frac{1}{2}$ cup of cooked dry beans	
Fats, Oils, and Sweets Group	1 teaspoon of margarine or butter	about the size of the tip of your thumb

Preparing Foods Safely

Fight Bacteria

You probably already know to throw away food that smells bad or looks moldy. But food doesn't have to look or smell bad to make you ill. To keep your food safe and yourself from becoming ill, follow the steps outlined in the picture below. And remember—when in doubt, throw it out!

FIGHT BAC!

Keep Food Safe From Bacteria ™

CLEAN Wash hands and surfaces often.

SEPARATE Don't cross-contaminate.

CHILL Refrigerate promptly.

COOK Cook to proper temperatures.

Food Safety Tips

Tips for Preparing Food

- Wash hands in warm, soapy water before preparing food. It's also a good idea to wash hands after preparing each dish.

- Defrost meat in the microwave or the refrigerator.

- Keep raw meat, poultry, fish, and their juices away from other food.

- Wash cutting boards, knives, and countertops immediately after cutting up meat, poultry, or fish. Never use the same cutting board for meats and vegetables without washing the board first.

Tips for Cooking Food

- Cook all food completely, especially meat. Complete cooking kills the bacteria that can make you ill.

- Red meats should be cooked to a temperature of 160°F. Poultry should be cooked to 180°F. When done, fish flakes easily with a fork.

- Never eat food that contains raw eggs or raw egg yolks, including cookie dough.

Tips for Cleaning Up the Kitchen

- Wash all dishes, utensils, and countertops with hot, soapy water. Use a soap that kills bacteria, if possible.

- Store leftovers in small containers that will cool quickly in the refrigerator. Don't leave leftovers on the counter to cool.

Being Physically Active

Planning Your Weekly Activities

Being active every day is important for your overall health. Physical activity helps you manage stress, maintain a healthful weight, and strengthen your body systems. The Activity Pyramid, like the Food Guide Pyramid, can help you choose a variety of activities in the right amounts to keep your body strong and healthy.

The Activity Pyramid

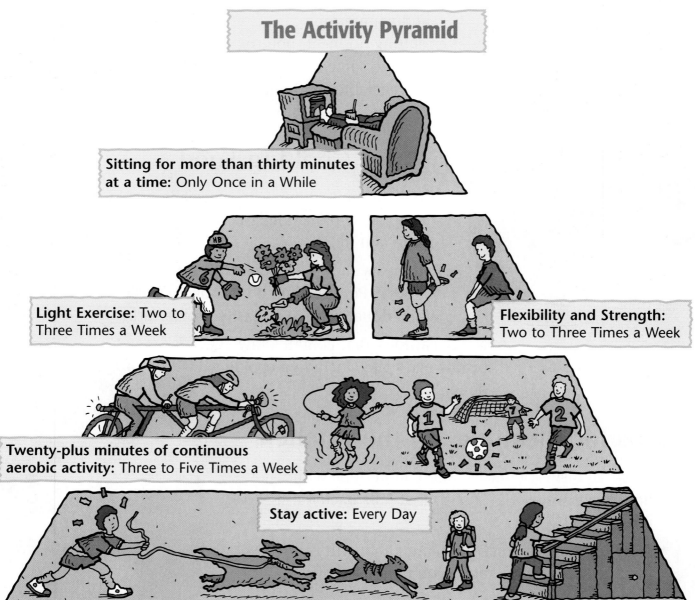

Sitting for more than thirty minutes at a time: Only Once in a While

Light Exercise: Two to Three Times a Week

Flexibility and Strength: Two to Three Times a Week

Twenty-plus minutes of continuous aerobic activity: Three to Five Times a Week

Stay active: Every Day

Guidelines for a Good Workout

There are three things you should do every time you are going to exercise—warm up, work out, and cool down.

Warm-Up When you warm up, your heart rate, breathing rate, and body temperature increase and more blood flows to your muscles. As your body warms up, you can move more easily. People who warm up are less stiff after exercising, and are less likely to have exercise-related injuries. Your warm-up should include five minutes of stretching, and five minutes of low-level exercise.

Workout The main part of your exercise routine should be an aerobic exercise that lasts 20 to 30 minutes. Aerobic exercises make your heart, lungs, and circulatory system stronger.

You may want to mix up the types of activities you do. This helps you work different muscles, and provides a better workout over time.

Cool-Down When you finish your aerobic exercise, you need to give your body time to cool down. Start your cool-down with three to five minutes of low-level activity. End with stretching exercises to prevent soreness and stiffness.

Using a Computer Safely

Good Posture at the Computer

Good posture is important when using the computer. To help prevent eyestrain, stress, and injuries, follow the posture tips shown below. Also remember to grasp the mouse lightly and take frequent breaks for stretching.

top of screen at or just below eye level

shoulders in line with ears and hips

neck and shoulders relaxed

arms at sides, bent as shown

wrists straight

feet flat on floor

Safety on the Internet

You can use the Internet for fun, education, research, and more. But like anything else, you should use the Internet with caution. Some people compare the Internet to a real city—not all the people there are people you want to meet and not all the places you can go are places you want to be. Just like in a real city, you have to use common sense and follow safety rules to protect yourself. Below are some easy rules to follow to help you stay safe on-line.

Rules for On-line Safety

- Talk with an adult family member to set up rules for going on-line. Decide what time of day you can go on-line, how long you can be on-line, and appropriate places you can visit. Do not access other areas or break the rules you establish.

- Don't give out information like your address, telephone number, your picture, or the name or location of your school.

- If you find any information on-line that makes you uncomfortable, or if you receive a message that is mean or makes you feel uncomfortable, tell an adult family member right away.

- Never agree to meet anyone in person. If you want to get together with someone you meet on-line, check with an adult family member first. If a meeting is approved, arrange to meet in a public place and take an adult with you.

Bicycle Safety

A Safe Bike

You probably know how to ride a bike, but do you know how to make your bike as safe as possible? A safe bike is the right size for you. When you sit on your bike with the pedal in the lowest position, you should be able to rest your heel on the pedal. Your body should be 2 inches (about 5 cm) above the support bar that goes from the handlebar stem to the seat support when you are standing astride your bike with both feet flat on the ground. After checking for the right size, check your bike for the safety equipment shown below. How safe is *your* bike?

headlight

horn

white front reflector

red rear reflector

clear reflector

pedal reflectors

clear reflector

Your Bike Helmet

About 400,000 children are involved in bike-related crashes every year. That's why it's important to *always* wear your bike helmet. Wear your helmet flat on your head. Be sure it is strapped snugly so that the helmet will stay in place if you fall. If you do fall and strike your helmet on the ground, replace it, even if it doesn't look damaged. The padding inside the helmet may be crushed, which reduces the ability of the helmet to protect your head in the event of another fall. Look for the features shown here when purchasing a helmet.

approval sticker

quick-release strap

padding

hard shell

air vent

Safety on the Road

Here are some tips for safe bicycle riding.

- Check your bike every time you ride it. Is it in safe working condition?

- Ride in single file in the same direction as traffic. Never weave in and out of parked cars.

- Before you enter a street, **STOP. Look** left, then right, then left again. **Listen** for any traffic. **Think** before you go.

- Walk your bike across an intersection. **Look** left, then right, then left again. Wait for traffic to pass.

- Obey all traffic signs and signals.

- Do not ride your bike at night without an adult. Be sure to wear light-colored clothing and use reflectors and front and rear lights for night riding.

Fire Safety

Fires cause more deaths than any other type of disaster. But a fire doesn't have to be deadly if you prepare your home and follow some basic safety rules.

- Install smoke detectors outside sleeping areas and on every other floor of your home. Test the detectors once a month and change the batteries twice a year.

- Keep a fire extinguisher on each floor of your home. Check them monthly to make sure they are properly charged.

- Make a fire escape plan. Ideally, there should be two routes out of each room. Sleeping areas are most important, as most fires happen at night. Plan to use stairs only, as elevators can be dangerous in a fire.

- Pick a place outside for everyone to meet. Choose one person to go to a neighbor's home to call 911 or the fire department.

- Practice crawling low to avoid smoke.

- If your clothes catch fire, follow the three steps shown here.

1. STOP

2. DROP

3. ROLL

Earthquake Safety

An earthquake is a strong shaking or sliding of the ground. The tips below can help you and your family stay safe in an earthquake.

Before an Earthquake	During an Earthquake	After an Earthquake
• Attach tall, heavy furniture, such as bookcases, to the wall. Store the heaviest items on the lowest shelves. • Check for fire risks. Bolt down gas appliances, and use flexible hosing and connections for both gas and water lines. • Strengthen and anchor overhead light fixtures to help keep them from falling.	• If you are outdoors, stay outdoors and move away from buildings and utility wires. • If you are indoors, take cover under a heavy desk or table, or in a doorway. Stay away from glass doors and windows and from heavy objects that might fall. • If you are in a car, drive to an open area away from buildings and overpasses.	• Keep watching for falling objects as aftershocks shake the area. • Check for hidden structural problems. • Check for broken gas, electric, and water lines. If you smell gas, shut off the gas main. Leave the area. Report the leak.

Storm Safety

• **In a Tornado** Take cover in a sheltered area away from doors and windows. An interior hallway or basement is best. Stay in the shelter until the danger has passed.

• **In a Hurricane** Prepare for high winds by securing objects outside or bringing them indoors. Cover windows and glass with plywood. Listen to weather bulletins for instructions. If asked to evacuate, proceed to emergency shelters.

• **In a Winter Storm or Blizzard** Stock up on food that does not have to be cooked. Dress in thin layers that help trap the body's heat. Pay special attention to the head and neck. If you are caught in a vehicle, turn on the dome light to make the vehicle visible to search crews.

First Aid

The tips on the next few pages can help you provide simple first aid to others and yourself. Always tell an adult about any injuries that occur.

For Choking . . .

If someone else is choking . . .

1. Recognize the Universal Choking Sign—grasping the throat with both hands. This sign means a person is choking and needs help.

2. Put your arms around his or her waist. Make a fist and put it above the person's navel. Grab your fist with your other hand.

3. Pull your hands toward yourself and give five quick, hard, upward thrusts on the choker's belly.

If you are choking when alone . . .

1. Make a fist and place it above your navel. Grab your fist with your other hand. Pull your hands up with a quick, hard thrust.

2. Or, keep your hands on your belly, lean your body over the back of a chair or over a counter, and shove your fist in and up.

For Bleeding . . .

If someone else is bleeding . . .

Wash your hands with soap, if possible.

Put on protective gloves, if available.

Wash small wounds with soap and water. Do *not* wash serious wounds.

Place a clean gauze pad or cloth over the wound. Press firmly for ten minutes. Don't lift the gauze during this time.

If you don't have gloves, have the injured person hold the cloth in place with his or her own hand.

If after ten minutes the bleeding has stopped, bandage the wound. If the bleeding has not stopped, continue pressing on the wound and get help.

If you are bleeding . . .

- Follow the steps shown above. You don't need gloves to touch your own blood.

- Be sure to tell an adult about your injury.

First Aid

For Nosebleeds . . .

- Sit down, and tilt your head forward. Pinch your nostrils together for at least ten minutes.

- You can also put an ice pack on the bridge of your nose.

- If your nose continues to bleed, get help from an adult.

For Burns . . .

Minor burns are called first degree burns and involve only the top layer of skin. The skin is red and dry and the burn is painful. More serious burns are called second or third degree burns. These burns involve the top and lower layers of skin. Second degree burns cause blisters, redness, swelling, and pain. Third degree burns are the most serious. The skin is gray or white and looks burned. All burns need immediate first aid.

Minor Burns

- Run cool water over the burn or soak it in cool water for at least five minutes.

- Cover the burn with a clean, dry bandage.

- Do *not* put lotion or ointment on the burn.

More Serious Burns

- Cover the burn with a cool, wet bandage or cloth. Do *not* break any blisters.

- Do *not* put lotion or ointment on the burn.

- Get help from an adult right away.

For Insect Bites and Stings . . .

- Always tell an adult about bites and stings.

- Scrape out the stinger with your fingernail.

- Wash the area with soap and water.

- Ice cubes will usually take away the pain from insect bites. A paste made from baking soda and water also helps.

▲ **deer tick**

- If the bite or sting is more serious and is on the arm or leg, keep the leg or arm dangling down. Apply a cold, wet cloth. Get help immediately!

- If you find a tick on your skin, remove it. Crush it between two rocks. Wash your hands right away.

- If a tick has already bitten you, do not pull it off. Cover it with oil and wait for it to let go, then remove it with tweezers. Wash the area and your hands.

For Skin Rashes from Plants . . .

Many poisonous plants have three leaves. Remember, "Leaves of three, let them be." If you touch a poisonous plant, wash the area. Put on clean clothes and throw the dirty ones in the washer. If a rash develops, follow these tips.

- Apply calamine lotion or a baking soda and water paste. Try not to scratch. Tell an adult.

- If you get blisters, do *not* pop them. If they burst, keep the area clean and dry. Cover with a bandage.

▲ **poison ivy**

- If your rash does not go away in two weeks or if the rash is on your face or in your eyes, see your doctor.

Sense Organs

Eyes

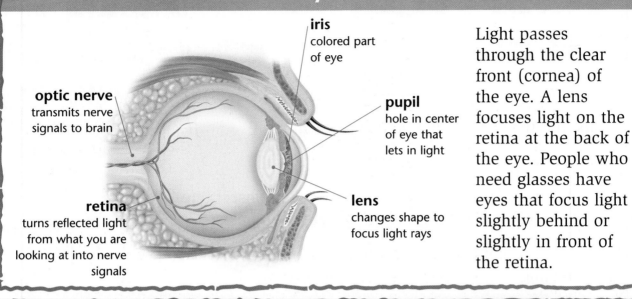

iris
colored part
of eye

optic nerve
transmits nerve
signals to brain

pupil
hole in center
of eye that
lets in light

retina
turns reflected light
from what you are
looking at into nerve
signals

lens
changes shape to
focus light rays

Light passes through the clear front (cornea) of the eye. A lens focuses light on the retina at the back of the eye. People who need glasses have eyes that focus light slightly behind or slightly in front of the retina.

Ears

Sounds make the eardrum move back and forth. The small bones in the middle ear send waves to the fluid in the inner ear. Hairs in the inner ear then move, passing signals to a nerve. Your brain reads the signals, and you hear the sound.

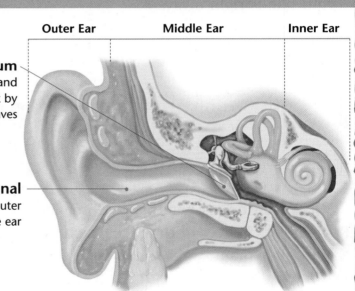

Outer Ear   Middle Ear   Inner Ear

eardrum
moves back and
forth when hit by
sound waves

ear canal
connects outer
ear to middle ear

Caring for Your Eyes and Ears

- Wear safety glasses when participating in activities where you can get hit or where a foreign object can hit an eye, such as sports and mowing grass.

- Avoid listening to very loud sounds for long periods of time. Loud sounds destroy the delicate hairs in the inner ear. You can lose your hearing little by little.

Nose

olfactory (sense of smell) bulb
a group of nerves that carry information to the olfactory tract

olfactory tract
carries information from the olfactory bulb to the brain

nasal cavity
main opening inside nose

nostrils
openings to nose

The inside of your nose is lined with moist surfaces that are coated with mucus. When these surfaces are irritated, they swell and make more mucus. This extra mucus causes a runny nose. Pollen or cold germs can cause this to happen.

Caring for Your Nose, Tongue, and Skin

- If you have a cold or allergies, don't blow your nose hard. Blowing your nose hard can force germs into your throat and ears.

- When you brush your teeth, brush your tongue too.

- Always wear sunscreen when you are in the sun.

Tongue

taste buds

Germs live on your tongue and in other parts of your mouth. Germs can harm your teeth and give you bad breath.

Skin

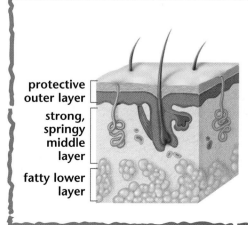

protective outer layer

strong, springy middle layer

fatty lower layer

Your skin protects your insides from the outside world. Your skin has many touch-sensitive nerves. Because your skin can feel temperature, pain, and pressure, you can avoid cuts, burns, and scrapes.

Skeletal System

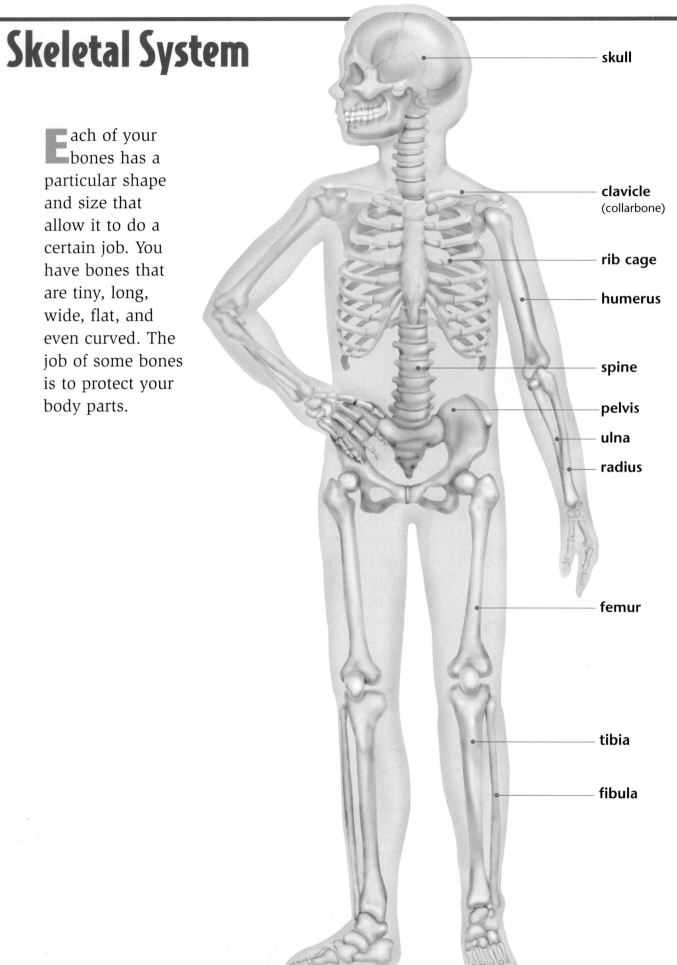

ach of your bones has a particular shape and size that allow it to do a certain job. You have bones that are tiny, long, wide, flat, and even curved. The job of some bones is to protect your body parts.

skull

clavicle
(collarbone)

rib cage

humerus

spine

pelvis

ulna

radius

femur

tibia

fibula

Spine, Skull, and Pelvis

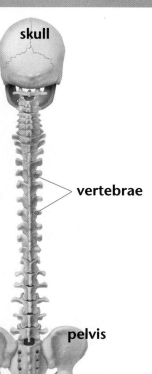

skull

vertebrae

pelvis

Spine Your spine, or back-bone, is made up of small bones called vertebrae that protect your spinal cord. Each vertebra has a hole in it, like a doughnut. These bones fit together, one on top of the other, and the holes line up to form a tunnel. Your spinal cord runs from your brain down your back inside this tunnel. Cartilage disks sit like cushions between the vertebrae.

Skull The bones in your head are called your skull. Some of the bones in your skull protect your brain. The bones in your face are part of your skull too.

Pelvis Your spine connects to your hipbone, or pelvis. Your pelvis connects to your thighs. Your flexible spine, pelvis, and legs are what let you stand up straight, twist, turn, bend, and walk.

Caring for Your Skeletal System

• Calcium helps bones grow and makes them strong. Dairy products like milk, cheese, and yogurt contain calcium. Have two to three servings of dairy products every day. If you can't eat dairy products, dark green, leafy vegetables such as broccoli and collard greens or canned salmon with bones are also sources of calcium.

• Sit up straight with good posture. Sitting slumped over all the time can hurt muscles around your spine.

Activities

1. **Make a stack of candy rings and run a string down through it. This is how your spinal cord runs through your spine.**

2. **Stand facing a wall. Without moving your feet, how far can you twist your body? How far can you see behind you?**

3. **Find the bony part of your hipbone that sticks out near your waist. Pick up one leg. Where does the thigh bone connect to your pelvis? How far is it from the bony part?**

Muscular System

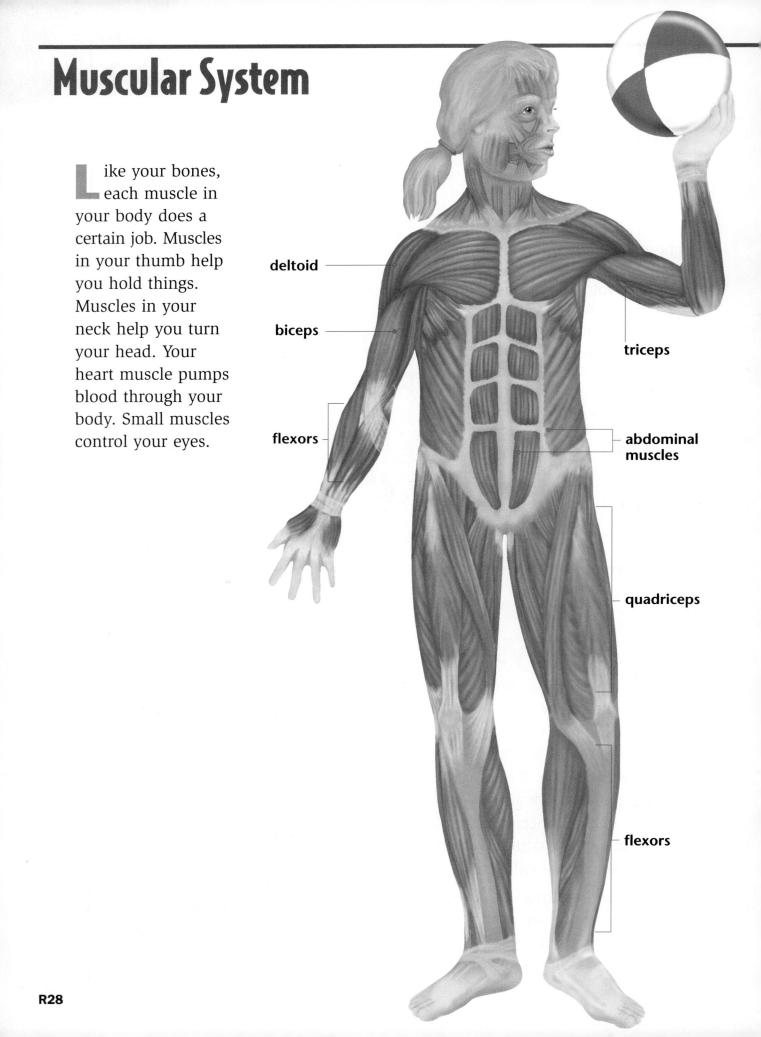

ike your bones, each muscle in your body does a certain job. Muscles in your thumb help you hold things. Muscles in your neck help you turn your head. Your heart muscle pumps blood through your body. Small muscles control your eyes.

deltoid

biceps

flexors

triceps

abdominal muscles

quadriceps

flexors

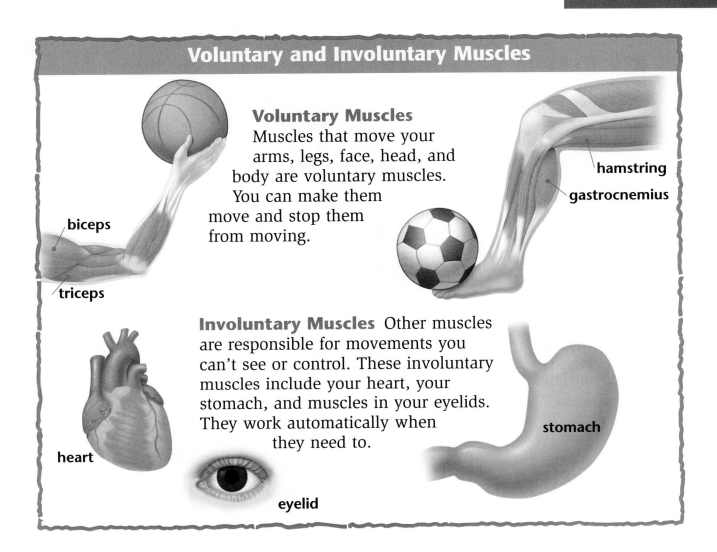

Voluntary and Involuntary Muscles

Voluntary Muscles
Muscles that move your arms, legs, face, head, and body are voluntary muscles. You can make them move and stop them from moving.

biceps

triceps

hamstring

gastrocnemius

Involuntary Muscles Other muscles are responsible for movements you can't see or control. These involuntary muscles include your heart, your stomach, and muscles in your eyelids. They work automatically when they need to.

heart

eyelid

stomach

Caring for Your Muscular System

- Exercise makes your muscles stronger and larger.
- Warming up by moving all your big muscles for five to ten minutes before you exercise helps prevent injury or pain.

Activities

1. **Look into a mirror and cover one eye. Watch the pupil in the other eye. How does it change? Did you change it?**

2. **Try not to blink for as long as you can. What happens?**

3. **Without taking off your shoes, try moving each of your toes one at a time. Can you move each of them separately?**

Digestive System

ood is broken down and pushed through your body by your digestive system. Your digestive system is a series of connected parts that starts with your mouth and ends with your large intestine. Each part helps your body get different nutrients from the food you eat.

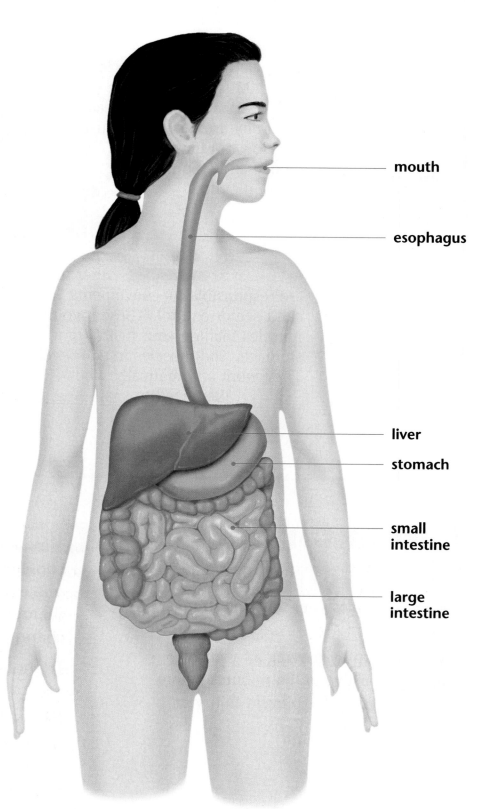

mouth

esophagus

liver

stomach

small intestine

large intestine

Small and Large Intestines

Small Intestine When food leaves your stomach and goes to your small intestine, it is a thick liquid. The walls of the small intestine are lined with many small, finger-shaped bumps. Tiny blood vessels in the bumps absorb nutrients from the liquid.

Large Intestine After nutrients are absorbed in your small intestine, the leftover liquid goes to your large intestine. Your large intestine absorbs water from the liquid. The solid waste leaves your large intestine when you go to the bathroom.

Caring for Your Digestive System

- Fiber helps your digestive system work better. Eat foods with fiber, such as fresh vegetables, beans, lentils, fruits, cereals, and breads, every day.

- Eat a balanced diet so that your body gets all the nutrients it needs.

Activities

1. Find the small and large intestines on the diagram of the digestive system. About how far is it from your belly button to where the small intestine starts?

2. On the diagram of the digestive system, trace the path that food takes through your body.

3. Draw a long line on a sheet of notebook paper. Fold the paper like an accordion. The line is like the path of food over the bumps in the small intestine.

Circulatory System

Food and oxygen are carried by your blood through your circulatory system to every cell in your body. Blood moves nutrients throughout your body, fights infection, and helps control your body temperature. Your blood is mostly made up of a watery liquid called plasma. It also contains three kinds of cells.

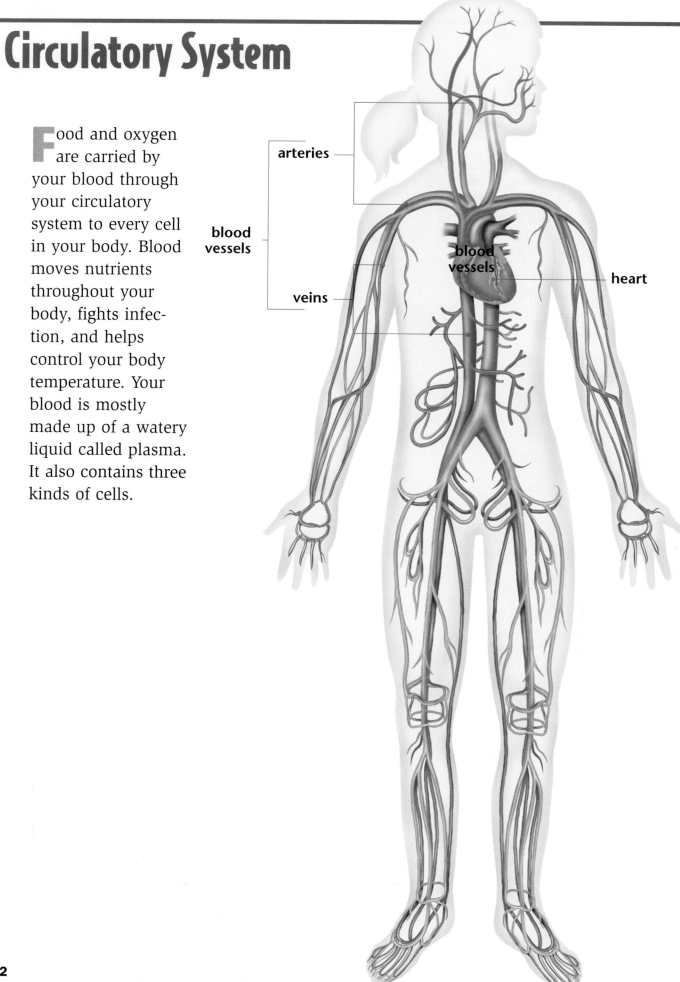

arteries

blood vessels

blood vessels

veins

heart

Blood Cells

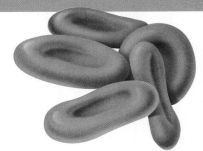

Red Blood Cells Red blood cells carry oxygen from your lungs to the rest of your body. They also carry carbon dioxide from your body back to your lungs, so you can breathe it out.

Platelets Platelets help clot your blood, which stops bleeding. Platelets clump together as soon as you get a cut. The sticky clump traps red blood cells and forms a blood clot. The blood clot hardens to make a scab and seals the cut.

White Blood Cells When you are ill, your white blood cells come to the rescue. Some types of white blood cells identify what is making you ill. Some organize an attack. Others kill the invading germs or infected cells.

Caring for Your Circulatory System

- Never touch another person's blood.
- Don't pick scabs. If you pick a scab, you might make it bleed and the clotting process must begin again.

Activities

1. **On the diagram of the circulatory system, trace the path of blood from the heart to the knee.**

2. **Red blood cells are medium-size and are the most common cells in your blood. White blood cells are larger and are the least common. Platelets are the smallest blood cells. Draw a picture of what a drop of blood might look like under a microscope.**

Respiratory System

Your body uses its respiratory system to get oxygen from the air. Your respiratory system is made up of your nose and mouth, your trachea, your two lungs, and your diaphragm.

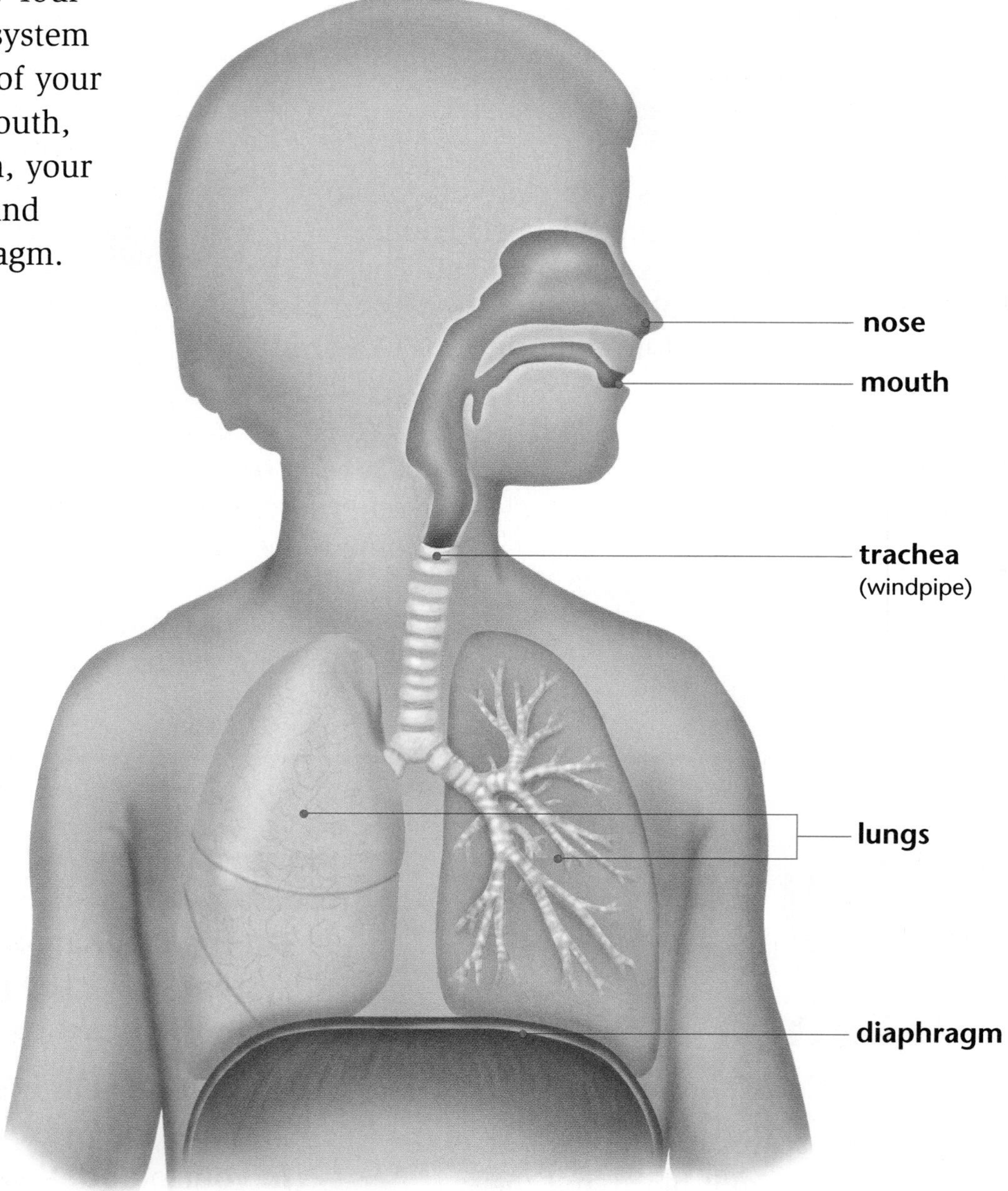

nose

mouth

trachea
(windpipe)

lungs

diaphragm

Functions of the Lungs

trachea

Breathing When you inhale, or breathe in, air enters your mouth and nose and goes into your trachea. Your nose helps warm the air and add moisture to it. Your trachea connects your nose and mouth to your lungs. Your trachea divides into two smaller tubes that go to your lungs.

bronchi

Filtering The two smaller tubes are called bronchi. Your trachea and bronchi are lined with many small hairs and coated with mucus. The mucus traps germs and small bits of dust and dirt. The small hairs constantly sweep the mucus up and out. This keeps dirt and germs out of your lungs.

Caring for Your Respiratory System

• Avoid smoke and other air pollution. They can paralyze the tiny hairs and cause you to become ill.

• Get plenty of exercise to keep your heart and lungs strong.

Activities

1. Take several breaths through your nose. Notice how the inside of your nose feels when you breathe in. Moisten a paper towel and take several breaths through the towel. Does your nose feel different?

2. Take a deep breath and hold it. Have someone measure your chest with a tape measure. Breathe the air out, and have someone measure your chest again. Is your chest bigger when you breathe in or when you breathe out?

Nervous System

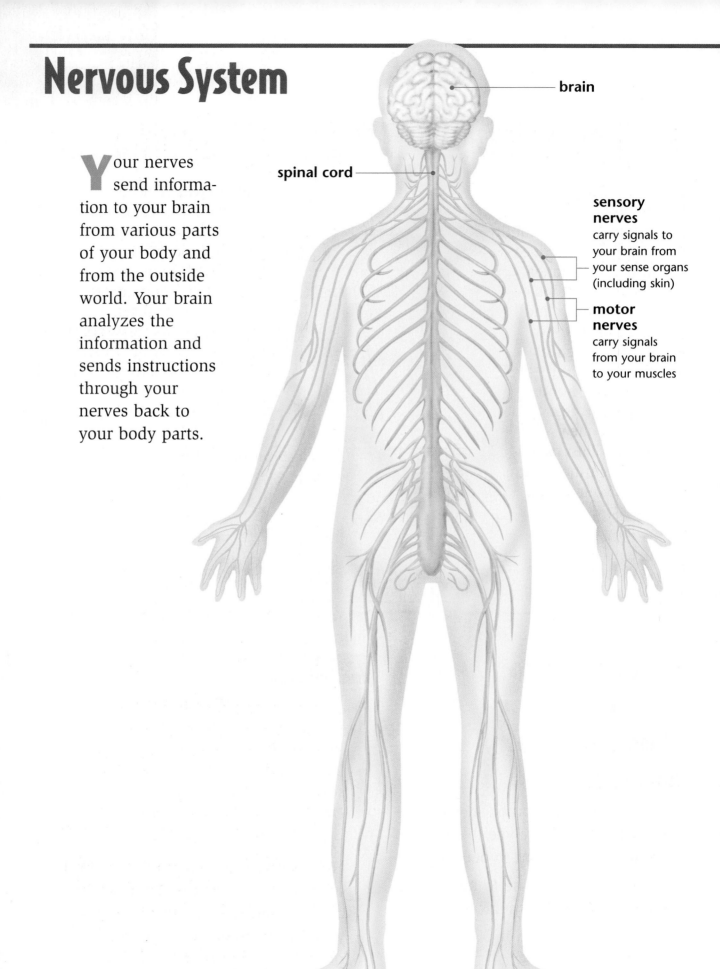

Your nerves send information to your brain from various parts of your body and from the outside world. Your brain analyzes the information and sends instructions through your nerves back to your body parts.

brain

spinal cord

sensory nerves
carry signals to your brain from your sense organs (including skin)

motor nerves
carry signals from your brain to your muscles

Messages to and from the Brain

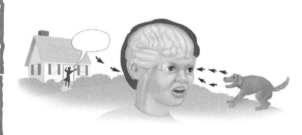

Incoming Messages Your sensory nerves send signals to your brain from your sense organs. Every minute your brain receives millions of these signals. Your brain has to decide how to deal with each piece of information. For example, your brain might decide to deal with a barking dog nearby before it deals with a person calling to you from a distance.

Outgoing Messages Every minute, millions of nerve signals also leave your brain. Your motor nerves carry these messages. Your motor nerves connect to your muscles and tell them what to do. When you ride your bike, your brain helps you maintain balance and sends instructions to all the muscles you use to ride a bike.

Caring for Your Nervous System

- Eat a healthful, balanced diet. Your brain needs energy and nutrients to work well.

- Always wear a helmet when you ride your bike, skate, or use a skateboard.

Activities

1. **Balance on one foot for as long as you can. Close your eyes and try again. Was it easier or harder the second time?**

2. **Pick up five pennies. Try it again wearing a glove. Why was it harder?**

3. **Hold a ruler at one end and dangle it just above a partner's open index finger and thumb. Drop the ruler through the gap. Where on the ruler does your partner grab? Try it several times, and then switch roles.**

Using Science Reading Strategies

Scientists use reading strategies in their work. They read to find out everything they can about a topic they are investigating. The following are some good strategies to use and how you might use them as you read Harcourt Science.

Gases

A **gas** is matter that has no definite shape and takes up no definite amount of space. Like particles in liquids, the particles in gases are not arranged in any pattern. Unlike particles in liquids, however, particles in gases don't stay close together. This is because particles in gases are moving much faster than particles in liquids.

The amount of space a gas takes up depends on the amount of space inside its container. A gas always fills the container it is in. If the container is open, the gas particles move out.

Most matter can change state from a solid to a liquid to a gas. You can see this when you leave an ice cube in a pan on a hot stove. In a few minutes, the cube changes from a solid to a liquid. Minutes later the liquid is gone—the water has become a gas called *water vapor*. The gas particles have moved off in all directions.

Heating matter makes particles move faster. When ice is heated, some particles begin to move fast enough to break away from their neighbors. As the regular arrangement of particles breaks down, the ice melts. Heated particles of liquid water move faster and faster. After a while they move fast enough to bounce away from each other. The liquid boils, or changes quickly into a gas.

✔ **How does heating matter change its state?**

◄ Water vapor is a gas that you can't see. Its particles fly out the whistling teakettle spout. Some particles cool and clump together to form tiny water drops. The drops are the white mist that you can see.

◄ A lot of air is squeezed into the tank carried by this diver. The tank valve is open. Particles of gases move out of the tank as the diver breathes in.

E8

When reading a text like this...

> Heating matter makes particles move faster. When ice is heated, some particles begin to move fast enough to break away from their neighbors. As the regular arrangement of particles breaks down, the ice melts. Heated particles of liquid water move faster and faster. After a while, they move fast enough to bounce away from each other. The liquid boils, or changes quickly into a gas.
>
> **page E8**

A good strategy to use is...

Use Prior Knowledge

Think about questions like these:

- What new information are you learning?
- How does the information fit in with what you already know about this scientific topic?

What you might say to yourself...

"I've seen water boiling. It certainly looks like the particles are moving faster as the water bubbles. But I never realized that as it boiled, the water was turning into a gas. Now that I think of it, there is steam rising above a pot of boiling water. And if you leave a pot boiling, all the water will disappear. That must be because the heated water was turned into a gas and spread out into the air."

When reading a text like this...

Temperature and Thermal Energy

Two pieces of matter can be at the same temperature but not have the same amount of thermal energy. Temperature measures the *average* amount of motion of the particles in a piece of matter. Thermal energy is the *total* energy of motion of the particles in a piece of matter. More matter equals more particles. More particles equals more energy of motion.

page E43

A good strategy to use is...

Use Text Structure and Format

Think about how the information is arranged in the section you are reading. What headings and captions are used? How did the author organize the paragraphs?

- Do the paragraphs tell about causes and effects?
- Do they show the sequence in a process?
- Do they compare two or more things?
- Do they classify concepts?

What you might say to yourself...

"The heading makes me think that this material is organized into a compare-and-contrast pattern.

"As I read this section, I see I'm right. Temperature and thermal energy are being compared. I need to think about how these two scientific concepts are alike and how they are different.

"As I read on, I have to remember that the author can switch patterns from section to section, even from paragraph to paragraph."

When reading a text like this...

Air Conditioning

You already know that when thermal energy moves from one place to another, the place it moves to gets hotter. The place it moves from gets colder. That's part of what makes air conditioners work.

page E60

A good strategy to use is...

Reread

If something you read doesn't make sense to you, go back and read it again. Maybe the passage involves a scientific concept from an earlier chapter. You may need to look back at that chapter to remind yourself of information you need to understand the passage.

What you might say to yourself...

"Now that I've reread this first paragraph, I see that it refers to information about thermal energy. I think I'd better look back at the section on thermal energy to remind myself. Then I'll reread this paragraph to see if I understand it....

"All right. I'm all set and ready to move on."

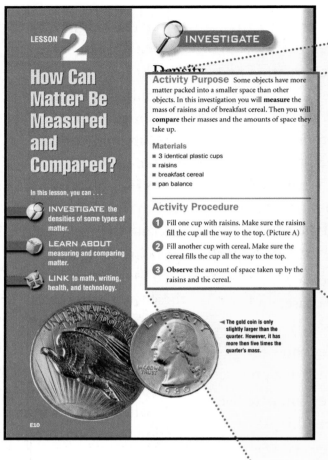

Activity Purpose
Some objects have more matter packed into a smaller space than other objects. In this investigation you will **measure** the mass of raisins and of breakfast cereal. Then you will **compare** their masses and the amounts of space they take up.

Materials
- 3 identical plastic cups
- raisins
- breakfast cereal
- pan balance

Activity Procedure

1 Fill one cup with raisins. Make sure the raisins fill the cup all the way to the top. (Picture A)

2 Fill another cup with cereal. Make sure the cereal fills the cup all the way to the top.

3 Observe the amount of space taken up by the raisins and the cereal....

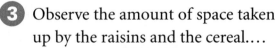
page E10

A good strategy to use is...
Adjust Reading Rate

Think about the kind of science text you are reading. You have to read some kinds of text more slowly and carefully than others.

What you might say to yourself...

"I see three kinds of text on this page: The first paragraph is **description,** telling me what the activity is about. The next kind of text is a **list,** telling me what I'll need for the investigation. The last kind of text is **directions,** telling me step by step what I need to do.

"I can probably read the description once and read it fairly quickly—just to get an idea of what the activity is about.

"I'll glance through the list quickly, although I may read it more than once—to make sure I have everything I need.

"I'll have to slow down and read the directions carefully. Then I'll have to reread them a few times to make sure I'm conducting the investigation properly."

When reading a text like this...

How Water Interacts with Other Matter

Water and Sugar

If you put a spoonful of solid sugar into a glass of liquid water and stir, what happens? The sugar seems to disappear. The glass still contains a clear liquid. Where did the sugar go?

The answer is that the sugar and the water formed a kind of mixture called a solution....

page E18

A good strategy to use is...

Self-Question

Think about questions you could ask yourself to be sure you understand what you're reading. As you read your science textbook, one way to check yourself is to turn heads into questions that you answer as you read.

What you might say to yourself...

"I can turn both of these heads into questions that I'll try to answer as I read. My first question would be, 'How does water interact with other matter?' I'll wait to answer that question until I finish the whole section.

"The question I'll answer first, after I read a few paragraphs, comes from the second heading. That question is, 'How do water and sugar interact?'"

When reading a text like this...

The much smaller particles in matter are always moving from one place to another at random. The particles in a solid jiggle back and forth like balls on a spring. The particles in a liquid slide past each other. The particles in a gas move quickly in many directions....

page E42

A good strategy to use is...

Create Mental Images

Think about the picture an artist might draw to illustrate the passage you're reading. If a passage is describing a process, try to picture in your mind what the text is describing. That way, you can tell if you're understanding what you're reading.

What you might say to yourself...

"First, I'm picturing a solid rubber ball. The particles jiggle back and forth as the ball bounces. Now I'm picturing a stream of water with the particles flowing past each other. Finally, I'm picturing steam rising from a pot of boiling water. I'm imagining the particles spreading out into the kitchen."

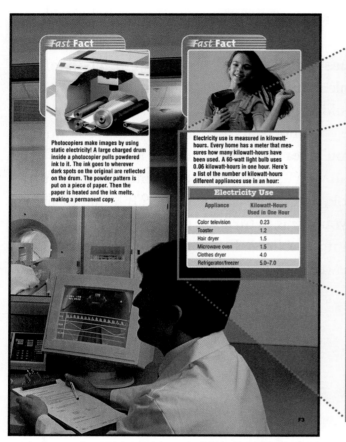

When reading a text like this...

Electricity use is measured in kilowatt-hours. Every home has a meter that measures how many kilowatt-hours have been used. A 60-watt light bulb uses 0.06 kilowatt-hours in one hour. Here's a list of the number of kilowatt-hours different appliances use in an hour:

Electricity Use

Appliance	Kilowatt-Hours Used in One Hour
Color television	0.23
Toaster	1.2
Hair dryer	1.5
Microwave oven	1.5
Clothes dryer	4.0
Refrigerator/freezer	5.0–7.0

page F3

A good strategy to use is...

Use Graphic Aids

Look at any pictures, graphs, charts, diagrams, or time lines that are included with the text. Think about why the author included these graphic aids.

- Are they there to help you organize the information you are learning? Then use them as you read.

- Are they there to add new information? Then take time to study them carefully, to learn the new information.

What you might say to yourself...

"After reading the paragraph, I see that the chart on this page is adding new information. I need to spend some time reading through it.

"To read the chart, I'm going to start by reading the information by columns to see what is listed. Then I'll read across the rows to see how the information is related.

"Now, I'm going to spend a bit of time comparing the entries in the chart. I want to see which appliance uses the least electricity and which one uses the most. I wonder if any appliances use the same amount. Yes, I see two that do."

When reading a text like this...

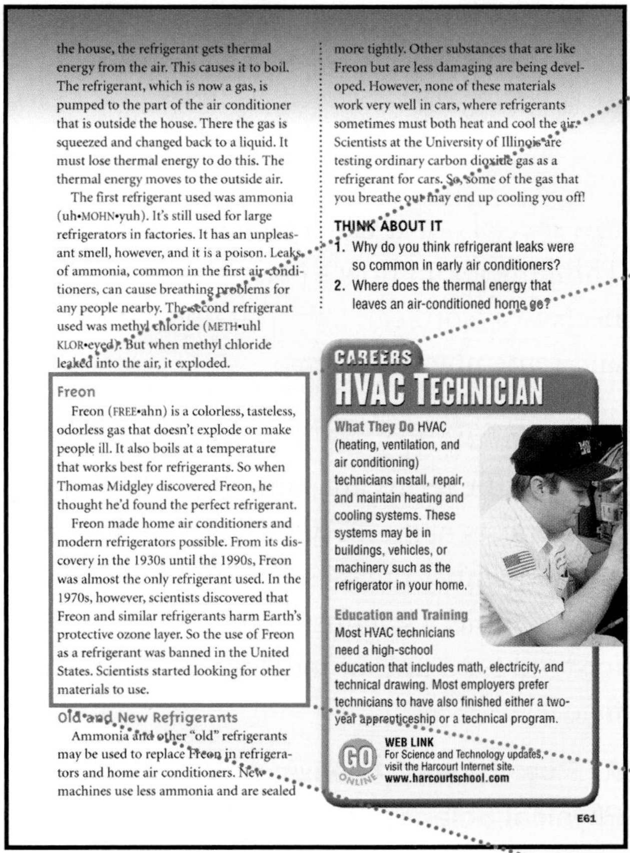
the house, the refrigerant gets thermal energy from the air. This causes it to boil. The refrigerant, which is now a gas, is pumped to the part of the air conditioner that is outside the house. There the gas is squeezed and changed back to a liquid. It must lose thermal energy to do this. The thermal energy moves to the outside air.

The first refrigerant used was ammonia (uh•MOHN•yuh). It's still used for large refrigerators in factories. It has an unpleasant smell, however, and it is a poison. Leaks of ammonia, common in the first air conditioners, can cause breathing problems for any people nearby. The second refrigerant used was methyl chloride (METH•uhl KLOR•eyed). But when methyl chloride leaked into the air, it exploded.

Freon

Freon (FREE•ahn) is a colorless, tasteless, odorless gas that doesn't explode or make people ill. It also boils at a temperature that works best for refrigerants. So when Thomas Midgley discovered Freon, he thought he'd found the perfect refrigerant.

Freon made home air conditioners and modern refrigerators possible. From its discovery in the 1930s until the 1990s, Freon was almost the only refrigerant used. In the 1970s, however, scientists discovered that Freon and similar refrigerants harm Earth's protective ozone layer. So the use of Freon as a refrigerant was banned in the United States. Scientists started looking for other materials to use.

Old and New Refrigerants

Ammonia and other "old" refrigerants may be used to replace Freon in refrigerators and home air conditioners. New machines use less ammonia and are sealed more tightly. Other substances that are like Freon but are less damaging are being developed. However, none of these materials work very well in cars, where refrigerants sometimes must both heat and cool the air. Scientists at the University of Illinois are testing ordinary carbon dioxide gas as a refrigerant for cars. So, some of the gas that you breathe out may end up cooling you off!

THINK ABOUT IT

1. Why do you think refrigerant leaks were so common in early air conditioners?
2. Where does the thermal energy that leaves an air-conditioned home go?

CAREERS

HVAC TECHNICIAN

What They Do HVAC (heating, ventilation, and air conditioning) technicians install, repair, and maintain heating and cooling systems. These systems may be in buildings, vehicles, or machinery such as the refrigerator in your home.

Education and Training Most HVAC technicians need a high-school education that includes math, electricity, and technical drawing. Most employers prefer technicians to have also finished either a two-year apprenticeship or a technical program.

GO ONLINE WEB LINK For Science and Technology updates, visit the Harcourt Internet site. www.harcourtschool.com

E61

Freon

Freon (FREE•ahn) is a colorless, tasteless, odorless gas that doesn't explode and does not make people ill. It also boils at a temperature that works best for refrigerants. So when Thomas Midgley discovered Freon, he thought he'd found the perfect refrigerant.

Freon made home air conditioners and modern refrigerators possible. From its discovery in the 1930s until the 1990s, Freon was almost the only refrigerant used. In the 1970s, however, scientists discovered that Freon and similar refrigerants harm Earth's protective ozone layer. So the use of Freon as a refrigerant was banned in the United States. Scientists started looking for other materials to use.

page E61

A good strategy to use is...

Summarize and Paraphrase

Think about how you could shorten a passage without omitting any key ideas. When you finish reading a section, sum up the main points in your own words before moving on. When you finish a chapter, look for a chapter summary to help you recall the main points. If there is no summary, come up with one of your own.

What you might say to yourself...

"When I summarize this section, I want to include all the important points as briefly as possible. Here is my summary:

For 60 years, Freon was the main refrigerant used in air conditioners and refrigerators because it was safe and had the right boiling point. But in the '70s, scientists found it harmed Earth's ozone layer, so it was banned in the '90s. Now scientists are looking for new refrigerants."

Building a Science Vocabulary

Reading and remembering science words can be hard. It's almost like learning a new language. That's why it's important to know how some science words came to be what they are. Knowing how the language of science works will not only help you to read and better understand science words. It will also help you enjoy learning them a lot more.

Eponyms: Words Named After People

Eponyms are words that come from people's names. The fourth Earl of Sandwich had a special food named for him—the sandwich. And the leotards that many dancers wear today are named after a tightrope walker, Jules Léotard, who wore this special outfit when he performed. Thinking about how a person's name connects to a word can help you understand and remember it better.

Real People Behind Scientific Words

Scientific terms are sometimes the same as scientists names. This is a way to honor and remember the scientists and their work. For example, a scientist's name may be used to stand for a unit of measure in his or her field.

A "Real-Person" Eponym from Physical Science

newton This is a unit of force. It is named for Sir Isaac Newton (1642–1727), an English scientist and mathematician who studied how forces change the way objects move. Do you see the connection between his work and the word named for him?

Other "Real-People" Eponyms

ampere	kelvin
Celsius	ohm
Fahrenheit	volt
hertz	watt

IV

Imaginary People Behind Scientific Words

Not all scientific eponyms come from real people. Some come from ancient gods, goddesses, and other imaginary beings. Thinking about the story of the imaginary creature and how he or she acts will help you learn new words.

An "Imaginary-Person" Eponym from Physical Science

echo You may have read a Greek myth about a maiden named Echo. In the myth Echo misbehaved and was punished by Zeus, king of the Greek gods. From that day on, Echo was not allowed to speak first. She could only repeat what someone else said. One day she saw a handsome young man named Narcissus. She fell in love with him, but he would have nothing to do with her. Poor Echo faded away until only her voice was left, repeating whatever is said to her.

You can probably see the link between the story of Echo and the word *echo*.

Other "Imaginary-People" Eponyms

Achilles tendon
arachnid
atlas
mercury
volcano and vulcanism
all planets in our solar system,
    except Earth

THINK ABOUT IT

In Roman myths, the god Vulcan was the god of fire. Why do you think Vulcan's name was used to help form the word *volcano*? Do you know other names from Greek or Roman myths? Can you find a connection between those names and any words in our language?

Greek and Latin Roots in Scientific Terms

Many words in English come from other languages. Two languages of long ago — Greek and Latin—have given us many of our words. People use Greek and Latin roots (also called word parts) to make new words. This is especially true of scientific terms. Think of all those science words like *biology* that share the ending *-logy*. (The Greek root *log* means "study of." *Biology* means "the study of life.") Knowing a word's root can help you figure out its meaning. You can find information about a word's root in many dictionaries.

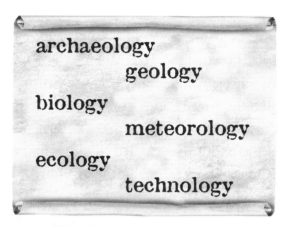

THINK ABOUT IT

Maybe some day you'll be a scientist who invents or discovers something new. Then you'll need to name it. What do you think inventions with names like these would do?

- soluble thermal conductor
- remote thermostat

Don't worry if you've never heard of either one. Neither has been invented yet. Maybe you'll be the scientist who does!

Some Roots in Science Vocabulary

Root	Meaning	Vocabulary Word(s)	Other Scientific Words
duc, duct	"to lead"	conductor, conduction	conduct, deduce, deduction, produce, production, induce, induction, reproduction
mob, mot	"to move"	motion	automobile, mobility, motor, remote
pos	"to put or place"	position	deposit, dispose, decomposition, positive (charge)
solu, solv	"to free"	dissolve, solubility, solution	solve, soluble, solute, solvent
sta, stit	"to stand or set"	static (electricity)	stable, status, institute, constitution
therm	"heat"	thermal energy	geothermal, thermo-dynamics, thermometer, thermostat

Other Common Roots in Scientific Words

Root	Meaning	Scientific Words
astro	"star"	asteroid, astronaut, astronomy, astrophysics
fac, fic, fect, fy	"to do or make"	factor, manufacture, efficient, beneficial, infection, disinfect, electrify, magnify
frag, fract	"to break"	fragile, fragment, diffraction, fraction, refract
ge, geo	"earth"	geography, geology, geomagnetism, geometry, geothermal
meter	"to measure"	magnetometer, metric, spectrometer, thermometer
photo	"light"	photochemical, photoconductor, photograph, photosphere, photosynthesis
volu, volv	"to turn or roll"	revolve, revolution, volume

A Word Family from Science

You will find the root *solu, solv* in three vocabulary words: *dissolve*, *solubility*, and *solution*. A word web of these and related words might look like this:

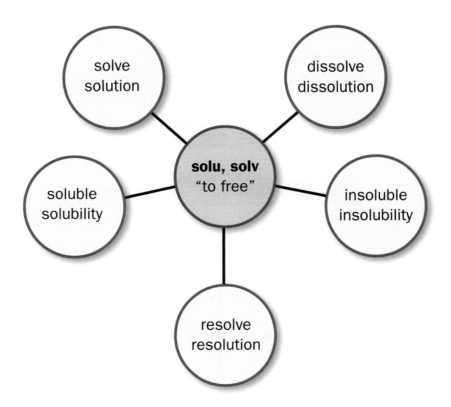

Phonics: Sounds and Spellings in Scientific Terms

You can use what you know about letters and sounds to help you read and pronounce new science words. Here are some things to keep in mind:

Some letters and letter combinations almost always sound the same.

In English, there are some letters and letter combinations that almost always stand for one sound.

- The letter combination *ph* almost always stands for the sound of the letter *f.* You can see this in the following vocabulary words:

    *am**ph**ibian, atmos**ph**ere, eso**ph**agus, **ph**otosynthesis, seismogra**ph***

- The letter combination *ew* almost always stands for the long *u* sound ($\overline{oo}$ or $y\overline{oo}$). You can see this in the following vocabulary words: *newton* and *screw.*

A letter can stand for different sounds, depending on the letter that follows it.

A letter may stand for more than one sound. The sound to use depends on a pattern.

- The letter *c* sounds like the *k* sound in *cat* when *c* is followed by the vowel *a, o,* or *u.* It also sounds like the *k* sound in *cat* when it is followed by most consonants. The letter *c* sounds like the *s* sound in *cider* when *c* is followed by *e, i,* or *y.* Which pattern does each of these vocabulary words fit?

    acceleration, cast, cell, core, epicenter, force, fulcrum, spinal cord, rock cycle, circuit

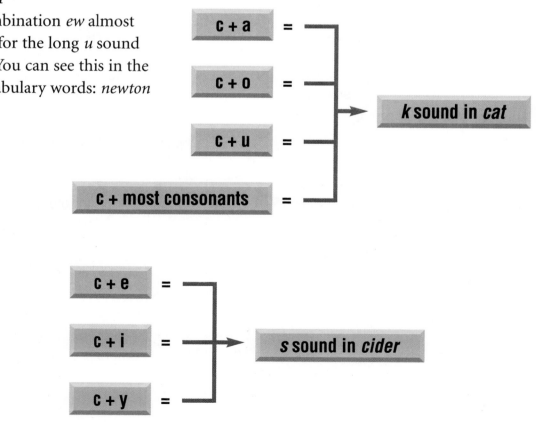

- The letter *g* usually sounds like the *g* in *game* when *g* is followed by the vowel *a*, *o*, or *u* or by other consonants. It often sounds like the *g* in *gym* when followed by *e*, *i*, or *y*. Which pattern does each of these vocabulary words fit?

  fungi, gas, genus, germination, gravity, magma, oxygen, wedge

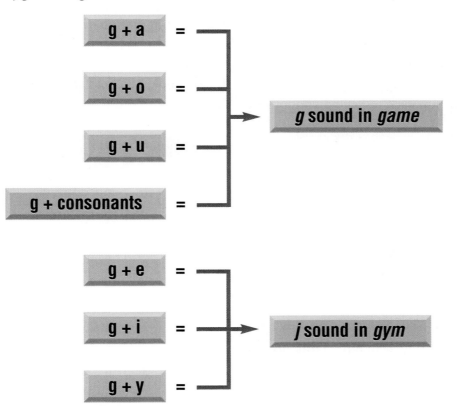

Some letters and letter combinations don't follow the rules.

A letter or letter combination may have several sounds that it can stand for. If you're not sure which sound is being used, you just have to keep trying, or check a dictionary.

- One example is the letter combination *ch*. The most common sound it stands for is the one you hear in *chair*. But almost as often, *ch* stands for the *k* sound you hear in *school*. Then there's the sound for *ch* that shows up in the word *parachute*—it's like the *sh* in *show*. Which sound for *ch* does each of these vocabulary words contain?

  charge, echo, niche, pitch, simple machine, stomach

THINK ABOUT IT

The study of speech sounds and letters is called *phonetics*. It comes from the Greek root *phon,* which means "sound." Which letter patterns help you know how to say *phonetics*?

Glossary

As you read your science book, you will see words that may be new to you. The words have phonetic respellings to help you quickly know how to say them. In this Glossary you will see a different kind of respelling. Here, diacritical marks are used, as they are used in dictionaries. *Diacritical respellings* can show more exactly how words should sound.

When you see the ′ mark after a syllable, say that syllable more strongly than the other syllables. The page number after the meaning tells where to find the word in your book. The boldfaced letters in the Pronunciation Key show how each respelling symbol sounds.

PRONUNCIATION KEY

a	add, map	m	move, seem	u	up, done
ā	ace, rate	n	nice, tin	û(r)	burn, term
â(r)	care, air	ng	ring, song	yōo	fuse, few
ä	palm, father	o	odd, hot	v	vain, eve
b	bat, rub	ō	open, so	w	win, away
ch	check, catch	ô	order, jaw	y	yet, yearn
d	dog, rod	oi	oil, boy	z	zest, muse
e	end, pet	ou	pout, now	zh	vision, pleasure
ē	equal, tree	ŏŏ	took, full	ə	the schwa, an
f	fit, half	ōō	pool, food		unstressed vowel
g	go, log	p	pit, stop		representing the sound
h	hope, hate	r	run, poor		spelled
i	it, give	s	see, pass		*a* in *above*
ī	ice, write	sh	sure, rush		*e* in *sicken*
j	joy, ledge	t	talk, sit		*i* in *possible*
k	cool, take	th	thin, both		*o* in *melon*
l	look, rule	th	this, bathe		*u* in *circus*

Other symbols:
- • separates words into syllables
- ′ indicates heavier stress on a syllable
- ′ indicates light stress on a syllable

absorption [ab•sôrp′shən] The stopping of light when it hits a wall or other opaque object **(E106)**

abyssal plains [ə•bis′əl plānz′] Huge flat areas of ocean floor that are covered with thick layers of sediment **(D50)**

acceleration [ak•sel′ər•ā′shən] A change in the speed or direction of an object's motion **(F48)**

adaptation [ad′əp•tā′shən] A body part or behavior that helps an organism meet its needs in its environment **(A48)**

air mass [âr′mas′] A huge body of air which all has similar temperature and moisture **(D13)**

air pressure [âr′presh′ər] Particles of air pressing down on the Earth's surface **(D7)**

amplitude [am′plə•tōōd′] A measure of the strength of a sound wave; shown by height on a wave diagram **(E72)**

anthracite [an′thrə•sīt′] A hard, black rock; fourth stage of coal formation **(C55)**

artery [är′tər•ē] A blood vessel that carries blood away from the heart **(A105)**

arthropod [är′thrə•pod] An invertebrate with legs that have several joints **(A16)**

asteroid [as′tə•roid] A small rocky object that moves around the sun **(D71)**

atmosphere [at′məs•fir] The layer of air that surrounds our planet **(D6)**

axis [ak′sis] An imaginary line which runs through both poles of a planet **(D65)**

barometer [bə•rom′ət•ər] An instrument that measures air pressure **(D20)**

bituminous coal [bi•tōō′mə•nəs kōl′] A fairly hard, dark brown or black rock; third stage of coal formation **(C55)**

brain [brān] The control center of your nervous system **(A110)**

buoyancy [boi′ən•sē] The ability of matter to float in a liquid or gas **(E20)**

camouflage [kam′ə•fläzh′] An animal's color or pattern that helps it blend in with its surroundings **(A52)**

capillary [kap′ə•ler′ē] A tiny blood vessel that allows gases and nutrients to pass from blood to cells **(A104)**

carbon dioxide [kär′bən dī•ok′sīd′] A gas breathed out by animals **(A72)**

cardiac muscle [kär′dē•ak mus′əl] A type of muscle that works the heart **(A99)**

cast [kast] A fossil formed when sediments or minerals fill a mold; it takes on the same outside shape as the living thing that shaped the mold **(C38)**

cell [sel] The basic building block of life **(A6)**

cell membrane [sel′ mem′brān] The thin layer that encloses and gives shape to a cell **(A7)**

cell wall [sel′ wôl′] A structure that keeps a cell rigid and provides support to an entire plant **(A8)**

charge [chärj] A measure of the extra positive or negative particles that an object has **(F6)**

chemical change [kem′i·kəl chānj′] A change that produces one or more new substances and may release energy **(E28)**

chemical reaction [kem′i·kəl rē·ak′shən] Another term for chemical change **(E28)**

chloroplast [klôr′ə·plast′] A part of a plant cell that contains chlorophyll, the green pigment plants need to make their food **(A8)**

circuit [sûr′kit] A path that is made for an electric current **(F12)**

cirrus [sir′əs] Wispy, high-altitude clouds that are made up of ice crystals **(D15)**

climate [kli′mit] The average temperature and rainfall of an area over many years **(A41, B28)**

comet [kom′it] A small mass of dust and ice that orbits the sun in a long, oval-shaped path **(D71)**

community [kə·myoo′nə·tē] All the populations that live in the same area **(B14)**

compression [kəm·presh′ən] The part of a sound wave in which air is pushed together **(E71)**

condensation [kon′dən·sā′shən] The process by which water vapor changes from a gas to liquid **(D34)**

conduction [kən·duk′shən] The transfer of thermal energy caused by particles of matter bumping into each other **(E49)**

conductor [kən·duk′tər] A material that electric current can pass through easily **(F13)**

conservation [kon′sər·vā′shən] The careful management and wise use of natural resources **(B68)**

consumer [kən·soo′mər] A living thing that eats other living things for energy **(B21)**

continental shelf [kon′tə·nen′təl shelf′] The ocean floor of the shore zone **(D49)**

convection [kən·vek′shən] The transfer of thermal energy by particles of a liquid or gas moving from one place to another **(E50)**

core [kôr] The dense center of Earth; a ball made mostly of two metals, iron and nickel **(C6)**

crater [krā′tər] A large basin formed at the top of a volcano when the top falls in on itself **(C22)**

crust [krust] Earth's outer layer; includes the rock of the ocean floor and large areas of land **(C6)**

cumulonimbus [kyoo′myoo·lō·nim′bəs] Towering, dark rain clouds with a nimbus, or halo, of gray-white **(D15)**

cumulus [kyoom′yə·ləs] Puffy cotton-ball clouds that begin to form when water droplets condense at middle altitudes **(D15)**

cytoplasm [sīt′ō·plaz′əm] A jellylike substance that fills most of the space in a cell **(A7)**

decomposer [dē′kəm·pōz′ər] A living thing that feeds on the wastes of plants and animals or on their remains after they die **(B21)**

deep ocean current [dēp′ ō′shən kûr′ənt] An

ocean current formed when cold water flows underneath warm water **(D44)**

density [den′sə•tē] The property of matter that compares the amount of matter to the space it takes up **(E14)**

dissolve [di•zolv′] To form a solution with another material **(E19)**

diversity [di•vûr′sə•tē] Variety **(B29)**

dormancy [dôr′mən•sē] State of much lower activity that some plants enter to survive colder weather **(A78)**

earthquake [ûrth′kwāk′] A vibration, or shaking, of Earth's crust **(C14)**

echo [ek′ō] A sound reflection **(E86)**

ecosystem [ek′ō•sis′təm] Groups of living things and the environment they live in **(B12)**

efficiency [i•fish′ən•sē] How well a machine changes effort into useful work **(F85)**

effort force [ef′ərt fôrs′] The force put on one part of a simple machine, for example, when you push or pull on a lever **(F70)**

electric cell [i•lek′trik sel′] A device that supplies energy to move charges through a circuit **(F12)**

electric current [i•lek′trik kûr′ənt] A flow of electric charges **(F12)**

electric field [i•lek′trik fēld′] The space around an object in which electric forces occur **(F8)**

electromagnet [i•lek′trō•mag′nit] An arrangement of wire wrapped around a core, producing a temporary magnet **(F25)**

embryo [em′brē•ō] A young plant **(A20)**

energy [en′ər•jē] The ability to cause a change **(E42)**

energy pyramid [en′ər•jē pir′ə•mid] A diagram that shows how much food energy is passed from one organism to another along a food chain **(B22)**

environment [in•vī′rən•mənt] Everything that surrounds and affects an animal, including living and nonliving things **(A40)**

epicenter [ep′i•sent′ər] The point on the surface of Earth that is right above the focus of an earthquake **(C15)**

esophagus [i•sof′ə•gəs] The tube that connects your mouth with your stomach **(A112)**

evaporation [ē•vap′ə•rā′shən] The process in which a liquid changes to a gas **(D34)**

fault [fôlt] A break in Earth's crust along which rocks move **(C14)**

fibrous roots [fī′brəs r$\overline{oo}$ts′] Long roots that grow near the surface **(A79)**

flowers [flou′ərz] Reproductive structures in flowering plants **(A22)**

focus [fō′kəs] The point underground where the movement of an earthquake first takes place **(C15)**

food web [f$\overline{oo}$d′ web′] A diagram that shows how food chains connect and overlap **(B23)**

force [fôrs] A push or pull **(F46)**

fossil [fos′əl] A preserved clue to life on Earth long ago **(C36)**

fossil fuel [fos′əl fyo͞o′əl] Fuel formed from the remains of organisms that lived long ago **(C52)**

frame of reference [frām′ uv ref′ər•əns] The things around you that you can sense and use to describe motion **(F41)**

friction [frik′shən] A force that keeps objects that are touching each other from sliding past each other easily **(F58)**

front [frunt] The border where two air masses meet **(D14)**

fruit [fro͞ot] The part of a flowering plant that surrounds and protects the seeds **(A22)**

fuel [fyo͞o′əl] A material that can burn **(E56)**

fulcrum [fo͝ol′krəm] The fixed point, or point that doesn't move, on a lever **(F70)**

fungi [fun′jī′] Living things that look like plants but cannot make their own food; for example, mushrooms **(A26)**

G

gas [gas] The state of matter that has no definite shape and takes up no definite amount of space **(E8)**

gas giants [gas′ jī′ənts] Planets which are large spheres made up mostly of gases—for example, Jupiter, Saturn, Uranus, and Neptune **(D78)**

germinate [jûr′mə•nāt′] To sprout; said of a seed **(A84)**

gravity [grav′ə•tē] A force that pulls all objects toward each other **(F56)**

greenhouse effect [grēn′hous′ i•fekt′] The warming of Earth caused by the atmosphere trapping thermal energy from the sun **(D12)**

H

habitat [hab′ə•tat′] An environment that meets the needs of an organism **(B20)**

heart [härt] The muscle that pumps blood through blood vessels to all parts of the body **(A105)**

heat [hēt] The transfer of thermal energy from one piece of matter to another **(E48)**

hibernation [hī′bər•nā′shən] A period when an animal goes into a long, deep "sleep" **(A59)**

humidity [hyo͞o•mid′ə•tē] The amount of water vapor in the air **(D21)**

hygrometer [hī•grom′ə•tər] A tool to measure moisture in the air **(D21)**

hyphae [hī′fē] Densely packed threadlike parts of a fungus **(A27)**

I

inclined plane [in′klīnd plān′] A flat surface with one end higher than the other **(F84)**

infrared radiation [in′frə•red′ rā′dē•ā′shən] The bundles of light energy that transfer heat **(E52)**

inner planets [in′ər plan′its] The planets closest to the sun; Mercury, Venus, Earth, and Mars **(D76)**

instinct [in′stingkt] A behavior that an animal begins life with **(A56)**

insulator [in′sə•lāt′ər] A material that current cannot pass through easily **(F13)**

intertidal zone [in′tər•tīd′əl zōn′] A narrow strip, along the shore, that is covered with water during high tide and exposed during low tide **(B36)**

invertebrate [in•vûr′tə•brit] An animal without a backbone **(A16)**

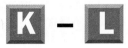

kinetic energy [ki•net′ik en′ər•jē] Energy of motion **(E42)**

large intestine [lärj′ in•tes′tən] The last part of the digestive system where water is removed from food **(A113)**

lava [lä′və] Melted rock that reaches Earth's surface **(C20)**

lever [lev′ər] A simple machine made up of a bar that turns on a fixed point **(F70)**

lignite [lig′nīt] A soft, brown rock; the second stage of coal formation **(C55)**

liquid [lik′wid] The state of matter that takes the shape of its container and takes up a definite amount of space **(E7)**

loudness [loud′nes] Your perception of the amount of sound energy reaching your ear **(E78)**

lungs [lungz] The main organs of the respiratory system **(A104)**

magma [mag′mə] Melted rock inside Earth **(C20)**

magma chamber [mag′mə chām′bər] An underground pool that holds magma, below a volcano **(C21)**

magnet [mag′nit] An object that attracts certain materials, such as iron or steel **(F18)**

magnetic field [mag•net′ik fēld′] The space all around a magnet where the force of the magnet can act **(F19)**

magnetic pole [mag•net′ik pōl′] The end of a magnet **(F18)**

mantle [man′təl] The thickest layer of Earth; found just below the crust **(C6)**

mass [mas] The amount of matter something contains **(E6)**

matter [mat′ər] Everything in the universe that has mass and takes up space **(E6)**

metamorphosis [met′ə•môr′fə•sis] The process of change; for example, from an egg to an adult butterfly **(A44)**

microorganisms [mī′krō•ôr′gən•iz′əmz] Organisms that are so small they can only be seen with a microscope; many have only one cell **(A9)**

mid-ocean ridge [mid′ō•shən rij′] A vast chain of mountains that runs along the centers of Earth's oceans **(D50)**

migration [mī•grā′shən] The movement of a group of one type of animal from one region to another and back again **(A57)**

mimicry [mim′ik•rē] An adaptation in which an animal looks very much like another animal or an object **(A52)**

mold [mōld] A common type of fungi that often look cottony or woolly **(A28)**

mold [mōld] A fossil imprint made by the outside of a dead plant or animal **(C38)**

motion [mō′shən] A change of position **(F40)**

natural gas [nach′ər•əl gas′] A gas, mostly methane, usually found with petroleum **(C53)**

near-shore zone [nir′shôr′ zōn′] Ocean zone that starts at the low-tide mark and goes out into the ocean **(B36)**

nerve [nûrv] A group of neurons that carries signals from the brain to the body and from the body to the brain **(A110)**

neuron [noŏr′on′] A nerve cell **(A110)**

newton [noō′tən] The metric, or Système International (SI), unit of force **(F51)**

niche [nich] The role or part played by an organism in its habitat **(B21)**

nucleus [noō′klē•əs] A cell's control center **(A7)**

nutrient [noō′trē•ənt] A substance, such as a mineral, which all living things need in order to grow **(A72)**

opaque [ō•pāk′] Reflecting or absorbing all light; no image can be seen **(E106)**

open-ocean zones [ō′pən•ō′shən zōnz′] The deep parts of the oceans, located far from shore **(B36)**

orbit [ôr′bit] The path that an object such as a planet makes as it revolves around a second object **(D64)**

organ [ôr′gən] A group of tissues of different kinds working together to perform a task **(A98)**

outer planets [ou′tər plan′its] The planets farthest from the sun; Jupiter, Saturn, Uranus, Neptune, and Pluto **(D78)**

oxygen [ok′si•jən] One of the many gases in air **(A41)**

parallel circuit [par′ə•lel sûr′kit] A circuit that has more than one path along which current can travel **(F14)**

peat [pēt] A soft, brown material made up of partly decayed plants; first stage of coal formation **(C55)**

petroleum [pə•trō′lē•əm] A thick brown or black liquid fossil fuel; crude oil **(C53)**

phase [fāz] One of the different shapes the moon seems to have as it orbits around Earth **(D64)**

photosynthesis [fōt′ō•sin′thə•sis] The process by which a plant makes its own food **(A73)**

physical change [fiz′i•kəl chānj′] Any change in the size, shape, or state of a substance **(E26)**

pistil [pis′təl] A flower part that collects pollen **(A85)**

pitch [pich] A measure of how high or low a sound is **(E79)**

planet [plan′it] A large object that moves around a star **(D71)**

plate [plāt] Continent-sized slab of Earth's crust and upper mantle **(C8)**

pollination [pol′ə•na′shən] Transfer of pollen from a stamen to a pistil by wind or animals **(A85)**

population [pop′yoō•lā′shən] A group of the same species living in the same place at the same time **(B13)**

position [pə•zish′ən] A certain place **(F40)**

precipitation [prē•sip′ə•tā′shən] Water that falls to Earth as rain, snow, sleet, or hail **(D35)**

preservation [prez′ər•vā′shən] The protection of an area **(B72)**

prism [priz′əm] A solid object that bends light; not a lens **(E110)**

producer [prə•doos′ər] A living thing, such as a plant, that makes its own food **(B21)**

pulley [pool′ē] A simple machine made up of a rope or chain and a wheel around which the rope or chain fits **(F78)**

radiation [rā′dē•ā′shən] The bundles of energy that move through matter and through empty space **(E52)**

reclamation [rek′lə•mā′shən] The repairing of some of the damage done to an ecosystem **(B63)**

redesign [rē′di•zīn′] Changing the design of packaging or products in order to use fewer resources **(B71)**

reflection [ri•flek′shən] The bouncing of light off an object **(E102)**

refraction [ri•frak′shən] The bending of the path of light when it moves from one kind of matter to another **(E104)**

relative motion [rel′ə•tiv mō′shən] A motion that is described based on a frame of reference **(F41)**

resistor [ri•zis′tər] A material that resists the flow of current but doesn't stop it **(F13)**

revolution [rev′ə•loo′shən] The movement of any object in an orbit, such as Earth moving around the sun **(D65)**

rotation [rō•tā′shən] The motion of a planet or other object as it turns on its axis **(D65)**

salinity [sə•lin′ə•tē] The amount of salt in water **(B30)**

satellite [sat′ə•līt′] An object that moves around another object in space; the moon is a satellite of Earth **(D64)**

screw [skroo] An inclined plane wrapped around a pole **(F86)**

seismograph [sīz′mə•graf′] An instrument that records earthquake waves **(C16)**

series circuit [sir′ēz sûr′kit] A circuit that has only one path for current **(F14)**

shelter [shel′tər] A place where an animal is protected from other animals or from the weather **(A43)**

shore zone [shôr′ zōn′] The place where land and ocean meet **(D49)**

simple machine [sim′pəl mə•shēn′] One of the basic machines that make up other machines **(F70)**

small intestine [smôl′ in•tes′tən] A long tube of muscle where most food is digested **(A112)**

smooth muscle [smooth′ mus′əl] A type of muscle found in the walls of some organs such as the stomach, intestines, blood vessels, and bladder **(A99)**

solar energy [sō′lər en′ər•jē] The energy given off by the sun **(E57)**

solar system [sō′lər sis′təm] A group of objects in space that move around a central star **(D70)**

solid [sol′id] The state of matter that has a definite shape and takes up a definite amount of space **(E6)**

solubility [sol′yo͞o•bil′ə•tē] A measure of the amount of a material that will dissolve in another material **(E19)**

solution [sə•lo͞o′shən] A mixture in which the particles of different kinds of matter are mixed evenly with each other and particles do not settle out **(E18)**

sonic boom [son′ik bo͞om′] A shock wave of compressed sound waves produced by an object moving faster than sound **(E88)**

sound [sound] A series of vibrations that you can hear **(E70)**

sound wave [sound′ wāv′] A moving pattern of high and low pressure that you can hear **(E71)**

space probe [spās′ prōb′] An uncrewed space vehicle that carries cameras, instruments, and other research tools **(D88)**

speed [spēd] A measure of an object's change in position during a unit of time; for example, 10 meters per second **(F42)**

speed of sound [spēd′ uv sound′] The speed at which a sound wave travels through a given material **(E84)**

spinal cord [spī′nəl kôrd′] The tube of nerves that runs through your spine, or backbone **(A110)**

spore [spôr] A tiny cell that ferns and fungi use to reproduce **(A27, A85)**

stability [stə•bil′ə•tē] The condition that exists when the changes in a system over time cancel each other out **(B8)**

stamen [stā′mən] A flower part that makes pollen **(A85)**

star [stär] A huge, burning sphere of gases; for example, the sun **(D70)**

static electricity [stat′ik ē′lek•tris′i•tē] An electric charge that stays on an object **(F6)**

stomach [stum′ək] A bag made up of smooth muscles that mixes food with digestive juices **(A112)**

storm surge [stôrm′ sûrj′] A very large series of waves caused by high winds over a large area of ocean **(D41)**

stratosphere [strat′ə•sfir′] The layer of atmosphere that contains ozone and is located above the troposphere **(D8)**

stratus [strā′təs] Dark gray clouds that form a low layer and sometimes bring light rain or snow showers **(D15)**

striated muscle [strī′āt•ed mus′əl] A muscle with light and dark stripes; a muscle you can control by thinking **(A100)**

succession [sək•sesh′ən] The process that gradually changes an existing ecosystem into another ecosystem **(B52)**

surface current [sûr′fis kûr′ənt] An ocean current formed when steady winds blow over the surface of the ocean **(D44)**

system [sis′təm] A group of parts that work together as a unit **(B6)**

taproot [tap′ro͞ot′] A plant's single main root that goes deep into the soil **(A79)**

telescope [tel′ə•skōp′] A device people use to observe distant objects with their eyes **(D84)**

temperature [tem′pər•ə•chər] A measure of the average energy of motion of the particles in matter **(E43)**

thermal energy [thûr′məl en′ər•jē] The energy of the random motion of particles in matter **(E42)**

tide [tīd] The daily changes in the local water level of the ocean **(D42)**

tissue [tish′o͞o] A group of cells of the same type **(A98)**

trace fossil [trās′ fos′əl] A fossil that shows changes that long-dead animals made in their surroundings **(C37)**

translucent [trans•lo͞o′sənt] Allowing some light to pass through; blurry image can be seen **(E106)**

transparent [trans•pâr′ənt] Allows most light to pass through; clear image can be seen **(E106)**

transpiration [tran′spə•rā′shən] The giving off of water vapor by plants **(A78)**

trenches [trench′əz] Valleys that form on the ocean floor where two plates come together; the deepest places in the oceans **(D50)**

troposphere [trō′pə•sfir′] The layer of atmosphere closest to Earth **(D8)**

tuber [to͞o′bər] A swollen underground stem **(A87)**

vein [vān] A large blood vessel that returns blood to the heart **(A105)**

vent [vent] In a volcano, the rocky opening through which magma rises toward the surface **(C20)**

vertebrate [vûr′tə•brit] An animal with a backbone **(A16)**

visible spectrum [viz′ə•bəl spek′trəm] The range of light energy that people can see **(E110)**

volcano [vol•kā′nō] A mountain that forms when red-hot melted rock flows through a crack onto Earth's surface **(C20)**

volume [vol′yo͞om] The amount of space that matter takes up **(E13)**

water cycle [wôt′ər sī′kəl] The constant recycling of water on Earth **(D34)**

wave [wāv] An up-and-down movement of water **(D40)**

wavelength [wāv′length] The distance from one compression to the next in a sound wave **(E72)**

wedge [wej] A machine made up of two inclined planes placed back-to-back **(F88)**

weight [wāt] A measure of the force of gravity upon an object **(F57)**

wheel and axle [hwēl′ and ak′səl] A simple machine made up of a large wheel attached to a smaller wheel or rod **(F80)**

work [wûrk] That which is done on an object when a force moves the object through a distance **(F74)**

A

Abdominal muscles, R28
Absorption, E106
Abyssal plains, D50
Acceleration, F48
  pushing and, F49
Activity pyramid, R12
Adams, John C., D91
Adaptations, A48
  animal, A48–53, A56–61
  plant, A74, A80
Agricola, Georgius, C58
Air
  in atmosphere, D6
  property of, D4–5
  sun and, D12
Air masses, D13
  meeting of, D14
  over water, D21
Airplane, inventors of, F92
Air pressure, D7, D18–20
Aldabra tortoises, A37
Aldrin, Edwin, D87
Algae
  in food chain, B21
  green, A4
  as one-celled organisms, A9
  polyps and, B30
Aluminum
  density of, E3
  recycling, B69
American bison, A51
American cockroach, A62
American holly, A22
Ammonoids, C33–34
Amoeba, A9
Ampere, F12
Amplitude, E72–73
Anaconda, B29
Anemometer, D21
Anemone, B31, D42
Animal adaptations
  behaviors, A56–61
  body parts, A48–53
Animal behaviorist, A64
Animal cells, A7
Animals
  body coverings, A50
  body supports, A16
  body types, A14–15

color and shape, A52
  fast, A36
  hibernation of, A59
  largest, A3
  learned behaviors of, A60–61
  migration of, A57
  needs of, A40–45
  tracks, C40
  and their young, A44
  in tropical rain forests, B32
Animal tracks, C40
Animatronic dinosaur, C45
Anthracite, C55
Antiquities Act, B74–75
Ants, A16, A68
  robot, A62–63
Apollo 11, D87
Appalachian Trail, B75
Archaeopteryx, C42
Archer, F46
Archimedes' screw, F82–83
Arctic fox, A43
Arms
  bones and muscles in, A99
  movement, A100
Armstrong, Neil, D87
Arteries, A105–106, R32
Arthropods, A16
Ascension Island, A57
Asteroids, D71
Astronauts, F62
  Apollo mission, D87
  space shuttle, D87
  using moon rover, D82
Atlantic green turtle, A57
Atlantic Ocean, D31
Atlas statue, E3
Atmosphere, D6
  greenhouse effect, D12
  layers of, D8
  mass of 1-m×1-m column, D7
  telescopes and, D85
Atmospheric scientist, D26
Auger, F87
Axis, D65
  Earth's, D72

B

Babbage, Charles, F67
Backbone, A99

Bacteria
  as decomposers, B21
  fighting, R10
  in soil, A2
Balance, using, R4
Barometer, D20
Barrel cactus, A75
Bathyscaph, D54
Bats
  echoes and, E66
  North American, A59
  skeleton of, A17
  sound and hearing of, E67
Bay of Fundy, D42
Beaker, R5
Bears
  brown, A42
  in food chain, B21
  polar, A50
Behaviors
  adaptive, A56–61
  instinctual, A56
  learned, A60–61
Berson, Dr. Solomon, A116
BetaSweet carrots, A88–89
Biceps, A99–100, R28–29
Bicycle
  friction and, F58–59
  helmet, R17
  safety, R16–17
  Ultimate Bike, F61
Bicycle mechanic, F61
Birds
  adaptations, A49
  beaks, A46–48
  carrying seeds, A84
  migration of, A58
Bituminous coal, C55
Black-footed ferrets, B48
Blizzard safety, R19
Blood, A105–107
Blood cells, R33
Blood vessels, R32
Blue jets, D25
Blue-ringed octopus, A12
Blue whale, A3
Boats, F90–91
Bobsled, accelerating, F49
Boiling points (chart), E38
Bones
  dinosaur, C44
  human, A98–99

with screw, F86
with wedges, F88
with wheel and axle, F80
Revolution, Earth's, D65
Rib cage, A99, R26
Richter scale, C16
Ride, Sally, F62
River turtle, B29
Roaches, robot, A62–63
Robins, sound and hearing of,
E67
Robot ants and roaches, A62–63
Robot volcano explorer, C26–27
Rocks, age of, C48
Roots, underwater mangrove,
B15
Rose hip, A22
Rotating-drum barometer, D20
Rotation, Earth's, D65, D72
Rotifers, A10
Ruler, using, R5
Rust, E29

S

Safety
bicycle, R16–17
earthquake, R19
fire, R18
Internet, R15
storm, R19
Saffir-Simpson Hurricane
Scale, D3
Saguaro cactus, A69
Salinity, B30
Salmon, B62
bear catching, A42
migration of, A58
Salt water
fresh water from, D32–33
ocean water as, D36–37
Saltwater crocodile, A3
San Andreas fault, C14
Sandstone, C36
Satellite, D64, F56
Satellite photograph, D22
Saturn
distance from sun, D69, D71
as outer planet, D78
rings around, D80
tilt of, D61

Titan, D80
weight on (chart), F57
Sayler, Gary, A32
Scale
dial spring, F52
electronic, F52
large, F53
spring, F51–52, R4
Science tools, using, R2–5
Screws, F86–87
Scuba support crew, D55
Sea Around Us, The (Carson),
D56
Sea fan, B31
Seahorse, A37
Seashore ecosystem, B43
Seasons, D66
Sea urchin, B30
Sedimentary rocks, C36, C44
Seedlings
growth of, A82–83
in mangrove swamp, B14
Seeds
plants with, A20–23, A84
watermelon, A18
Seesaw, F72
Seismograph, C16
Seismologist, C28
Sense organs, caring for, R24–25
Sensors, A63
Sensory nerves, R36
Series circuit, F14
Serving size, R9
Shadows, light and, E101
Shale, C36
Sharks, whale, A3
Shelter, animals' need for, A43
Shield volcanoes, C21
Shore zone, D49
Shoulder muscles, A99
Shrimp, B12
Silent Spring (Carson), D56
Silver, tarnishing of, E28
Simple machines, F70
inclined planes, F84–85
lever, F68–74
pulley, F76–79
screw, F86–87
water transportation and,
F90–91
wedges, F88

wheel and axle, F76, F80
Skeletal muscle, A96
Skeletal system, A98–99
bones in, R26
caring for, R27
Skeleton
bat, A17
coral polyp, B30–31
human. *See also* Skeletal system
Skin, caring for, R25
Skin adhesive, A114–115
Skull, R26–27
Small intestine, A111–112,
R30–31
Smooth muscle, A96, A100
Snails, A15, B21
Snowshoe hare, A52
Sodium chloride, D36
Soil
bacteria in, A2, B21
fungi in, A2
nutrients in, A72
Sojourner probe, D88
Solar energy, E57
Solar system, D70
asteroids, D71
comets, D71
planets, D71
sun, D70
Solid, E6
Solubility, E19
Solution, E18
Sonic boom, E88
Sound
ranges of (chart), E67
speed of, E84
wave, defined, E71
wave diagram, E73
waves, E72–73
Southern Hemisphere, D66
South Pole
Earth's axis and, D65
ocean water near, D37
Space exploration
crewed missions, D87
space probes, D88–89
space station, D87
telescopes and, D84–86
Species
competition among, B48
endangered, B48–49

J.F. Maxwell/Falls of the Ohio State Park; C64 (b) Sandy Felsenthal/Corbis.

Unit D

Unit D Opener (fg) Dorling Kindersley; (bg) FPG International; D2-D3 Warren Faidley/International Stock; D3 (t) Bob Abraham/The Stock Market; D3 (b) NRSC Ltd/Science Photo Library/Photo Researchers; D4 Keren Su/Stock, Boston; D6 Space Frontiers-TCL/Masterfile; D10 Bruce Watkins/Earth Scenes; D12 Peter Menzel/Stock, Boston; D14-D15 C. O'Rear/Corbis; D15 Warren Faidley/International Stock; D16 (b) Bill Binzen/The Stock Market; D18 J. Taposchaner/FPG International; D20 Sam Ogden/Science Photo Library/Photo Researchers; D21 (t) Breck P. Kent/Earth Scenes; D21 (b) B. Daemmrich/The Image Works; D22 (c) 1998 Accu Weather; D24 Geophysical Institute, University of Alaska, Fairbanks/NASA; D25 Pat Lanza/Bruce Coleman, Inc.; D26 (t) Clark Atlanta University; D26 (b) NASA/Science Photo Library/Photo Researchers; D30-D31 Warren Bolster/Stone; D31 (t) Warren Morgan/Corbis; D31 (b) Tom Van Sant, Geosphere Project/Planetary Visions/Science Photo Library/Photo Researchers; D32 Philip A. Savoie/Bruce Coleman, Inc.; D36 (tr) A. Ramey/Stock Boston; D36 (bl) Richard Gaul/FPG International; D38 John Lel/Stock, Boston; D40 E.R. Degginger/Photo Researchers; D41 (t) Fredrik Bodin/Stock, Boston; D41 (b) Peter Miller/Photo Researchers; D42 (t), D42 (c) Francois Gohier/Photo Researchers; D42 (b) Steinhart Aquarium/Tom McHugh/Photo Researchers; D46 Ralph White/Corbis; D49 (i) Dr. E.R. Degginger/Color-Pic; D49 (t) David R. Frazier; D50-D51 Marie Tharp/Oceanic Cartographer; D54-D55 Ben Margot/AP Photo/Wide World Photos; D55 Thomas Ives/The Stock Market; D56 (t) Erich Hartmann/Magnum Photos; D56 (b) Ron Sefton/Bruce Coleman, Inc.; D60-D61 Ton Kinsbergen/ESA/Science Photo Library/Photo Researchers; D61 NASA; D62 Dr. E. R. Degginger/Color-Pic; D68 Tom Till; D71 Frank Zullo/Photo Researchers; D72-D73 M. Agliolo/Photo Researchers; D74 NASA; D77 (t) U.S. Geological Survey/Science Photo Library/Photo Researchers; D77 (b) David Crisp and the WFPC2 Science Team (Jet Propulsion Laboratory/California Institute of Technology)/NASA; D77 (tc) NASA; D77 (bc) National Oceanic and Atmospheric Administration; D78 NASA; D78-D79 Erich Karkoschka (University of Arizona Lunar & Planetary Lab) and NASA; D79 (r) Dr. R. Albrecht, ESA/ESO Space Telescope European Coordinating Facility, NASA; D79 (l) Lawrence Sromovsky (University of Wisconsin - Madison), NASA; D80, D81, D82 NASA; D84 (r) Michael Freeman; D84 (tl) David Nunuk/Science Photo Library/Photo Researchers; D84 (bl) Omikron Collection/Photo Researchers; D85 (t) Simon Fraser/Science Photo Library/Photo Researchers; D85 (b) Robert Frerck/Stone; D85 (ti) Roger Ressmeyer/Corbis; D86 (bg) Shahn Kermani/Liaison International; D86, D87, D88, D89 NASA; D90 (r) Jean-Loup Charmet; D90 (l) NASA; D91 (t) The Granger Collection, New York; D91 (c) Sylvester Allred/Visuals Unlimited; D91 (b) Mark E. Gibson/Dembinsky Photo Associates; D92 J. Kelly Beatty; D92 (bg) Science VU/Visuals Unlimited; D96 (t) Mark E. Gibson; D96 (b) W. Metzen/H. Armstrong Roberts, Inc..

Unit E

Unit E Opener (fg); Dennis Yankus/Superstock; (bg); Pierre-Yves Goavec/Image Bank; E2-E3 Jon Riley/Stone; E3 Dr. E.R. Degginger/Color-Pic; E4 Superstock; E6 Michael Denora/Liaison International; E8 (b) Bob Abraham/The Stock Market; E10 (l) Lee F. Snyder/Photo Researchers; E14-E15 (b) Richard R. Hansen/Photo Researchers; E16 Stone; E20 (t) Kathy Ferguson/PhotoEdit; E20 (b) Doug Perrine/Innerspace Visions; E20 (bi) Felicia Martinez/PhotoEdit; E21 (b) Chip Clark; E22 (bg) Norbert Wu/Mo Yung Productions; E22-E23 Richard Pasley/Stock, Boston; E24 Stockman/International Stock; E29 (cl) Dr. E.R. Degginger/Color-Pic; E29 (br) Grace Davies; E29 (bl) Index Stock Imagery/PictureQuest; E30 (i) P. Degginger/H. Armstrong Roberts, Inc.; E30 (b) Jack McConnell/McConnell & McNamara; E30-E31 Paul A. Souders/Corbis; E32 Courtesy of J. G.'s Edible Plastic; E33 David R. Frazier; E34 (l) United States Nuclear Regulatory Commission; E34 (r) Tom Carroll/Phototake; E38-E39 Ray Ellis/Photo Researchers; E39 (t) Peter Steiner/The Stock Market; E39 (b) Murray & Assoc./The Stock Market; E40 Craig Tuttle/The Stock Market; E43 (t) Jim Zipp/Photo Researchers; E44 Ted Horowitz/The Stock Market; E48 D. Nabokov/Gamma Liaison; E50 (b) L. West/Bruce Coleman, Inc.; E50 (i) Jonathan Wright/Bruce Coleman, Inc.; E51 Gary Milburn/Tom Stack & Associates; E52 Jeff Foott/Bruce Coleman, Inc.; E56 (t) Craig Hammell/The Stock Market; E56 (b) Russell D. Curtis/Photo Researchers; E57 (tl) Stu Rosner/Stock, Boston; E57 (tr) John Mead/Science Photo Library/Photo Researchers; E57 (br) John Cancalosi/Stock, Boston; E58 (b) David Falconer& Associates; E58 (tr) Telegraph Colour Library/FPG International; E58 (cr) Charles D. Winters/Photo Researchers; E58 (bi) Montes De Oca & Associates; E59 Paul Shambroom/Science Source/Photo Researchers; E61 Danny Daniels/The Picture Cube; E62 Minnesota Historical Society; E62 (i) Peter Vadnai/The Stock Market; E66-E67 Stephen Dalton/Photo Researchers; E67 Carl R. Sams, II/Peter Arnold, Inc.; E68 A. Ramey/PhotoEdit; E71 (b) Summer Productions; E71 (li) Michelle Bridwell/PhotoEdit; E71 (tri) Peter Langone/International Stock; E72 (l) Ian O'Leary/Stone; E76 Randy Duchaine/The Stock Market; E78 (r) Jim Zipp/Photo Researchers; E78 Spencer Grant/PhotoEdit; E82 (t) Bose Corporation; E82 (b) Bose/Lisa Borman Associates; E84-E85 (b) NASA; E90-E91 Bruce Forster/Stone; E91 (i) Jon Riley/Folio; E96-E97 NASA; E97 (t) Chip Simons; E97 (b) David Madison/Bruce Coleman, Inc.; E100 (l) Mark E. Gibson; E100 (r) Bob Daemmrich/Stock, Boston; E103 Jan Butchofsky/Dave G. Houser; E105 (t), 105 (c) Richard Megna/Fundamental Photographs; E108 (b) Randy Duchaine/The Stock Market; E110 Tom Skrivan/The Stock Market; E111 (tr) David Woodfall/Stone; E113 Roy Morsh/The Stock Market; E114-F115 Paul Silverman/Fundamental Photographs; E115 (t) Ed Eckstein for the Franklin Institute Science Museum; E115 (b) Peter Angelo Simon/The Stock Market; E116 (t) Schomburg Collection; E116 (bl) Jim Davie; E120 (t) Sal Dimarco/Black Star; E120 (b) Jack Olson.

Unit F

Unit F Opener (fg) Steve Berman/Liaison International; (bg) Photone Disk #50 ; F2-F3 Pete Saloutos/The Stock Market; F4 Doug Martin/Photo Researchers; F9 Charles D. Winters/Photo Researchers; F10 Cosmo Condina/Stone; F15 Dr. E.R. Degginger/Color-Pic; F16 National Maritime Museum Picture Library; F19

Richard Megna/Fundamental Photographs; F20-F21 (t) Phil Degginger/Color-Pic; F22 Gamma Tokyo/Liaison International; F24-F25 Spencer Grant/PhotoEdit; F25 Tom Pantages; F27 (t), F27 (c) Phil Degginger/Color Pic; F27 (b) Bruno Joachin/Liaison International; F27 (bg) W. Cody/Corbis Westlight; F30 (t) PhotoDisc; F30 (b) Corbis-Bettmann; F31 Phil Degginger/Color-Pic; F32 (i) Fonar Corporation; F32 Jean Miele/The Stock Market; F36-F37 PictureQuest; F37 (t), F37 (ti) Dwight R. Kuhn; F37 (br) Tony Freeman/PhotoEdit; F38 (b) David R. Frazier; F40 (t) Mark E. Gibson; F42 (b) Bob Daemmrich/Stock, Boston; F44 (b) Miro Vintoniv/Stock, Boston; F46 (bl) Jean-Marc Barey/Agence Vandystadt/Photo Researchers; F47 (tr) Daniel MacDonald/The Stock Shop; F49 Bernard Asset/Agence Vandystadt/Photo Research; F50 (t) Kathi Lamm/Stone; F53 Terry Wild Studio; F54 (b) William R. Sallaz/Duomo Photography; F57 (c) Photo Library International/ESA/Photo Researchers; F57 (cr) Photo Researchers; F58 (bl) Michael Mauney/Stone; F60 (b) Brian Wilson; F60 (t) PA News; F61 (b) Michael Newman/PhotoEdit; F62 (t) UPI/Corbis-Bettmann; F62 NASA; F66-F67 (bg) Dan Porges/Bruce Coleman, Inc.; F67 (tr) R. Sheridan/Ancient Art and Architecture Collection; F67 (tl) The Granger Collection, New York; F68 (bl) William McCoy/Rainbow; F70 (bl) Yoav Levy/Phototake/PictureQuest; F73 (tr) Michael Newman/PhotoEdit; F74 (tr) David R. Frazier; F78 (bl) Mark E. Gibson; F80 (b) Jeff Dunn/Stock, Boston; F82 (bl) Tom King/Tom King, Inc.; F84 (b) Aaron Haupt/David R. Frazier; F85 (tl) Dan McCoy/Rainbow; F85 (br) Michael Newman/PhotoEdit; F85 (cl) David Falconer/Folio; F86 (t) Superstock; F87 (r) Churchill & Klehr; F87 (bl) Staircase & Millwork Corporation, Alpharetta, GA; F88 (br) Tony Freeman/PhotoEdit; F90 (bg) Corel; F90 (l) Archive Photos; F90 (c) Noble Stock/International Stock; F90 (bl) Alexandra Guest/John F. Coates; F91 (l) Eric Sanford/International Stock; F94 (l) Archive Photos; F92 (r) Library of Congress/FPG International; F92 (bl) Library of Congress; F96 (t) Christian Heeb/Gnass Photo Images; F96 (b) Maxine Cass.

Health Handbook: R23 Palm Beach Post; R27 (t) Andrew Spielman/Phototake; (c) Martha McBride/Unicorn Stock; (b) Larry West/FPG International; R28 (l) Ron Chapple/FPG; (c) Mark Scott/FPG; (b) David Lissy/Index Stock.

All other photographs by Harcourt photographers listed below, © Harcourt:
Weronica Ankarorn, Bartlett Digital, Victoria Bowen, Eric Camden, Digital Imaging Group, Charles Hodges, Ken Karp, Ken Kinzie, Ed McDonald, Sheri O'Neal, Terry Sinclair.

Art Credits

Mike Atkinson A85, B22, B23; Jean Calder A99, A100 - 101, A110, A111; Susan Carlson D22; Mike Dammer A33, A65, A91, A117, B45, B77, C29, C61, D27, D57, D93, E35, E63, E93, E117, F33, F63, F93; John Edwards E111; John Francis B14 - 15; Lisa Frasier E56-57; George Fryer C6 - 7, C20, C21, D20; Thomas Gagliano D48 - 49, E73, E78, E79, E80, F14; Patrick Gnan E60, F74; Terry Hadler E14, E19, E49, F78, F79; Tim Hayward C44, C48; Robert Hynes A16, A22, B28 - 29, B30 - 31; Joe LeMoniier A64, A90, E66; Mapquest A57, B40, C46; Janos Marffy D66; Michael Maydak B38 - 39; Sebastian Quigley D12 - 13, D44, D65, D76 - 77, D78 - 79, E6, E7, E8, E22, E72, F6, F7, F20, F24, F56; Eberhard Reinmann A98, A104 - 105, A106, A112, E74; Mike Saunders A7, A8, A20, A26, A27, A73, A84, B52 - 53, C7, C36, D8 - 9, D52 - 53, D70, D71, D72 - 73; Steve Seymour B7, B40 - 41, B62, B63, C8, C9, C10, C15, D14, D43, D86, E43, E44, E51, E52, E70, E85, E88 - 89, F8, F13, F49, F72; Shough E112; Bill Smith Studio D93; Walter Stuart A10 - 11, A14, A15; Steve Weston C14, C22, C23, D15, E72, E86 - 87, F18, F80, F86, F87, F88, F93

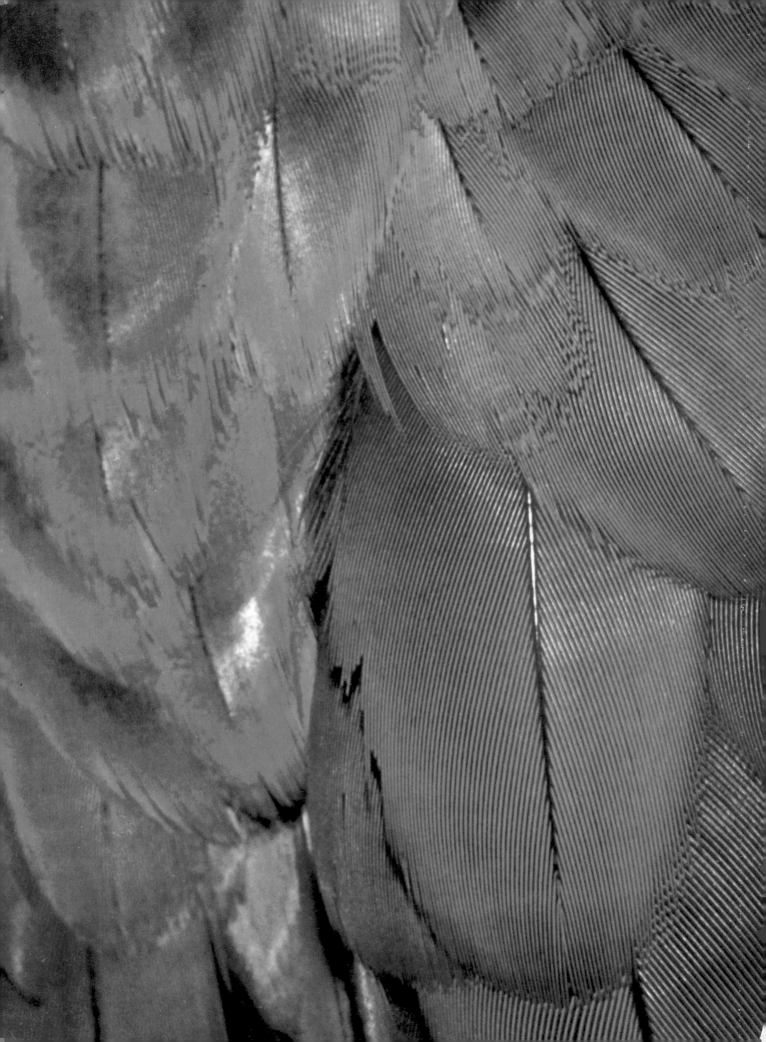